LAW AND PRACTICE OF INTERNATIONAL FINANCE

COMPARATIVE FINANCIAL LAW

AUSTRALIA
The Law Book Company
Brisbane * Sydney * Melbourne * Perth

CANADA
Carswell
Ottawa * Toronto * Calgary * Montreal * Vancouver

AGENTS:
Steimatzky's Agency Ltd., Tel Aviv;
N.M. Tripathi (Private) Ltd., Bombay;
Eastern Law House (Private) Ltd., Calcutta;
M.P.P. House, Bangalore;
Universal Book Traders, Delhi;
Aditya Books, Delhi;
MacMillan Shuppan KK, Tokyo;
Pakistan Law House, Karachi, Lahore.

COMPARATIVE FINANCIAL LAW

QUICK REFERENCE GUIDE

LAW AND PRACTICE OF INTERNATIONAL FINANCE

COMPARATIVE FINANCIAL LAW

By

Philip R Wood

BA (Cape Town), MA (Oxon)

Solicitor of the Supreme Court

Visiting Professor, Queen Mary
& Westfield College,
University of London

LONDON
SWEET & MAXWELL
1995

Published in 1995 by
Sweet and Maxwell Limited of
South Quay Plaza, 183 Marsh Wall,
London E14 9FT
Computerset by Interactive Sciences, Gloucester
Printed in Great Britain by
Butler & Tanner, Frome and London

No natural forests were destroyed to make this product:
only farmed timber was used and re-planted

**A CIP catalogue record for this book is
available from the British Library**

ISBN 0 421 54280 2

To my wife Marie-elisabeth, my twin sons
John Barnaby and Richard,
my daughter Sophie and my son Timothy

PREFACE

This book is the first of a series of six works on international financial law which, taken together, are the successor to my *Law and Practice of International Finance* which was published in 1980 and which has been reprinted eight times.

The works now cover a much broader range of subjects, with substantial additions in the fields of comparative law, insolvency, security, set-off, payments, and title finance, as well as specialist subjects like securitisations and swaps and derivatives. But the works have the same objectives as the original book. However great a gap there may be between the aim and the actuality, the objectives I have sought to achieve were and are to be practical as well as academic, to provide both a theoretical guide and legal source-book as well as a practitioner's manual, to be international, to provide serious comparative law information, to get to the point as quickly as possible, to provide answers as opposed to posing problems without solving them, to simplify the difficulties, to find the principles underlying the particularity, to inform, and, most of all, to be useful.

The six works are separate but they are nevertheless related. Together the books are intended to form a complete library for the international banking and financial lawyer, as well as for specialists in related areas such as insolvency, leasing, and ship and aircraft finance. The topics covered by each volume are summarised on the inside of the front cover.

These books advance a fundamentally new approach to comparative law in this area and, for the first time I think, provide the essential keys to understanding the world's jurisdictions, to unlock the dark cupboard of financial law so that the light may shine in. The core of this first book is a classification and snap-shot of all the jurisdictions in the world – more than 300 of them – according to various financial law criteria. These criteria are developed in subsequent chapters in this book and in succeeding books in the series. I believe that this is the first time that a classification of this type has been done in this detail. My hope is that this information will help those who need to know about international and comparative law, that it will help to mitigate legal surprises and legal risks and, in the wider context, that jurisdictions will be better equipped to make essential choices as to what their legal systems should achieve. This is particularly important in view of the fact that at least 30 per cent of the world's population live under legal systems which are still emerging and that the remainder live in jurisdictions divided into camps which often do not agree on legal fundamentals.

The books also contain lists of about 250 research topics in total which might be appropriate for further research and which I hope will be useful to prospective writers.

I am acutely conscious of the fact that, in writing about legal systems other than my own (which is England), I will often have committed some real howlers and I hope that my foreign colleagues will be tolerant of my ignorance. Obviously one must always confirm the position with competent local lawyers.

As regards style, I have endeavoured to be as economical as possible. The citation is selective: there are now millions of cases and it is hopeless to try and list even a proportion of them. I am easily terrorised by footnotes and therefore, if material is good enough to go in the footnotes, it is good enough to go in the text: as a result there are no footnotes in these works. At least one does not have to read the text in two places at once. Tables of cases and statutes seemed less sensible in a work endeavouring to cover hundreds of jurisdictions where there is an avalanche of names and numbers and dates and acts and statutes and decrees, and, in view of this, I decided to omit them.

I have endeavoured to reflect the law roundabout the middle of 1994 based on the international materials then available to me.

Philip R Wood   March 17, 1995
One New Change
London

Request for Information

Works on the law in the jurisdictions of the world must rely heavily on information from private sources. With a view to improving the information in any subsequent editions there may be, the author would be very pleased to receive papers of all kinds on subjects covered by this and other works in this series – seminar papers, essays, articles, client briefings by law firms, memoranda, notices of book publications, and the like. Material should be sent to me at the following address:

Philip R Wood
Allen & Overy
One New Change
London EC4 9QQ

Fax: 0171 330 9999

ACKNOWLEDGEMENTS

I owe to many a debt of gratitude in the help they gave me in preparing this work.

I am grateful to numerous partners and colleagues at Allen & Overy for their advice and assistance. In particular Paul Philips worked with me on some aspects and Bridget Harris and Lisa Mullen did background research on prejudgment attachments. Osamu Nomoto of Mitsui, Yasuda, Wani & Maeda, Tokyo, contributed much Japanese case law and comment while he was on secondment to my firm.

I owe a particular debt to the authors of the works listed in the bibliography and of a very large number of articles and books not listed without which it would not have been possible to write this book: if I have used their words, as I believe I often have, this is because they said it much better than I ever could.

There are many others – practitioners, students, academics, bankers and others – who have contributed to this work in one way or another: it would be impossible for me to thank them all individually.

None of the above is of course responsible for the defects in this work.

I am most grateful to my secretary Sue Wisbey and to the Allen & Overy word processing department who laboured so magnificently to type this work.

I am thankful to my publishers for their hard work and patience in bringing this work – and the other books in this series – to fruition and also for their support through all the years.

My brother John, my sister Melanie and my mother all encouraged me and were tolerant of my efforts.

Finally, I owe an enormous debt to my wife and children and can only express my affection for them by the token of dedicating this book to them.

CONTENTS

CONTENTS

PART II: GOVERNING LAW OF FINANCIAL CONTRACTS

PART IV: INTERNATIONAL PAYMENT SYSTEMS

PART V: MATERIALS

ABBREVIATIONS

ABGB	Austrian General Civil Code
Art	Article
BA	Bankruptcy Act
BC	Bankruptcy Code
BGB	German Civil Code
BL	Bankruptcy Law
c	chapter (of laws)
CC	Civil Code
CCP	Code of Civil Procedure
CO	Code of Obligations
ComC	Commercial Code
Conflicts Restatement	Restatement of the Law, Conflict of Laws 2d, by the American Law Institute
Dicey	Lawrence Collins (general editor), *Dicey and Morris on the Conflict of Laws* (12th ed 1993) Sweet & Maxwell
EISO	Philip Wood, *English and International Set-off* (1989) Sweet & Maxwell
IA	Insolvency Act
ICSID	International Centre for the Settlement of Investment Disputes
IR	Insolvency Rules (England)
Mann, Money	FA Mann, *The Legal Aspect of Money* (5th ed 1992) Clarendon Press, Oxford
Ord	Order
PILA	Private International Law Act 1987 (Switzerland)
Restatement	Restatement of the Law by the American Law Institute
RSC	Rules of the Supreme Court (England)
s	section
Sched	Schedule
UCC	Uniform Commercial Code (United States)
ZPO	Code of Civil Procedure (*Zivilprozessordnung*)
Zweigert/Kötz	K Zweigert and H Kötz, *An Introduction to Comparative Law* (2nd ed 1987)

PART I

COMPARATIVE FINANCIAL LAW

CHAPTER 1

INTRODUCTION TO INTERNATIONAL FINANCIAL LAW

General

Of course we in the world have come a long way in this area of the law. But   **1–1**
not nearly far enough.

Financial law is our servant, not our master. We tell it what to do and
how to do it. It is there for our convenience – to be useful and to satisfy our
sense of justice.

It is not for the law to chain us down. It is not for the law to put a spoke
in a wheel which is spinning freely and well. It is for the law only to provide
the oil and only such controls as are necessary to ensure the wheel can spin
without damage to itself or ourselves.

The world is a mosaic of jurisdictions – about 300 of them. But claims
know no boundaries.

There have only been two revolutions in commercial law. The first was
the Roman revolution in the first few centuries after Christ. The second took
place a millennium and a half later, on an island in the North Sea.

Claims as property

This book is the first of a series of works on international financial law   **1–2**
which are therefore concerned mainly with the law of debt claims.

There is a trilogy of property: land, goods and claims. Land is the most
venerable. The law has worked out how to record its ownership, how to
sell, mortgage, lease or attach it, and whose law governs dealings in land.
This flows naturally from its permanence, stability, immovability, undeni-
able specificity.

With goods, the confusion starts. It is true that on the whole the nations
of the world have reached a broad consensus on the most primitive and
basic rules of the responsibility of sellers and buyers. But there the consensus
ends. Anything more complicated, such as how to transfer part of a fungible

---

bulk, or whether one may pledge the goods without handing over possession, or the impact on a lease of the goods if the owner or his mortgagee sells the goods, meets with furious disagreement and a cacophony of voices, each urging some different solution. This is so, even though the world's most adroit legal minds have been devoting their entire adult existence to the problems for at least twenty centuries and more. One would have hoped that this was enough time to ascertain the natural law, the best and most convenient solution.

Hence when one comes to claims, one must not expect too much. Yet the wealth stored up in these claims is immense. The amount of business transacted on just one summer's day in the world's payment transmission systems and in securities markets exceeds the annual gross national product of the entire world, save only a handful of the largest economies, and annually far exceeds the gross national product of all countries by a huge multiple. It is pointless not to organise ourselves better in our globe so as to ensure that this class of property serves us well.

To do so, the policies must be clear.

Claims are intangible, invisible and have no smell. But they can be manufactured quite easily: the method of production is embodied mainly in the law of contract. They have their own secret shape, form and taffeta personality. They can masquerade as visible property if they are wrapped up in the form of negotiable instruments, debenture certificates and other writings. Indeed, some states insist on this wrapping for nearly all claims – a sweet but antiquarian view.

The advantage of claims is that they do not have to be fed or watered. They do not have to be weeded. Compared to goods, sale and transportation costs are small – especially if they are in a form which can be suitably immobilised and dematerialised and owed by central keepers, like banks and securities custodians. In terms of amount, most claims are located with keepers.

1–3   But the real distinguishing characteristic of claims is that they cannot be used by humans for any mortal purpose until converted into other property – food or flowers or a field. The result is an instinctual prejudice against this apparently non-usable, non-productive property, a prejudice which is of ancient heritage, which has been ritualised at various periods by the traditional religions the world over, and which is expressed in usury laws, consumer credit laws, anti-mortgage laws, insolvency laws and, more recently, in the more excessive versions of securities regulation. The fear of this dark unknown property is enormously potent in all societies and is tied to a fear of power and wealth.

But these childhood dreads must be put aside. The notion that the property is inherently wicked and that those who deal in it are bound to be wicked is quite naive. Claims are morally neutral and those who deal in them no doubt are equally as good or evil as those who deal in any other kind of asset, according to one's view of the propensities of human nature.

Naturally some assets are riskier than others. Poisons and gunpowder are more dangerous than apples and lawbooks. Diamonds are more vulnerable to theft than pebbles. By a similar process of comparison, a share in a single collective investment scheme investing in speculative securities in a single speculative sector of industry in a single mercurial country needs more care and attention, and greater solicitude for investor protection, than a US Treasury. A multi-trillion dollar payments system is more interesting to the larcenous interloper, armed with a computer firing its electronic frauds, than a finance lease of a lorry. It goes without saying that the law and the practice must recognise these points.

A second distinguishing characteristic of claims as property is that they require two persons to give them existence – typically a debtor and creditor. A debtor must hand over something or other before the creditor is satisfied. Usually this handing over is merely the creation of another claim in favour of the creditor against a substitute debtor – as where a borrower repays a loan by arranging for the creditor's account at the creditor's bank to be credited. The asset transmutes itself, but still there are two persons – the creditor and his new debtor, the bank. If the creditor wishes to use the asset, he has to exchange it for land or a factory or whatever other real thing he requires.

The impact of this duality on the law leads to acute perplexity about where the property is. Does the debtor have it or the creditor? This has been universally resolved in the case of bank accounts – the depositor has the property, even though the bank has the notes and coins. That is, the creditor has it, not the bank as debtor. The depositor is the owner of the asset – the benefit of the deposit – and he can transfer it, cancel it, give it away in his will. But nevertheless when one is identifying the location of the property to decide which country's law is to apply in determining how one transfers the asset or whether the property is situate in the territory of an expropriating state so that it can lawfully take what is in its domain, one reaches different results. The duality also gives rise to bewilderment on arcane matters, such as whether the creditor can assign his debt back to the debtor by way of security without causing the debt to self-destruct.

That the property is an invisible fiction is not an objection that need detain us. The law creates many figments of the imagination for our advantage and benefit. The company is another illustration of this inventiveness. A company is a mere mark in a registrar's book, a non-existent person, a creature of legal fancy. But there is no question that this chimera and shadow is of immense utility and convenience, and there is no question that

1–4

the abstract conception sustains us and has just as much reality as the life of ideas and the spirit.

Outline of international finance

International credits

1–5 As mentioned, this series of works is primarily concerned with credit. It is proposed by way of background to summarise the scope of the subject so as to put the discussion of financial law into context, but to leave the detail to subsequent volumes where each topic can be reviewed comprehensively.

What is credit? Credit is derived from the use of money as a medium of exchange.

I am a shoemaker. I desire a loaf of bread. But the bakery may not want my shoes in exchange for a loaf that day. So I sell my shoes to a person who is desirous of shodding his feet. He pays me money – coins or fiat paper money (which my country has decreed will be money) or "bank money" by transferring money from his bank to my bank account. With that money I buy the loaf. In the meantime I deposit my spare money in the bank. I give the bank credit – I lend the bank my money. The bank in turn lends out this money – together with that of others – to a new company which has no money but which wishes to build an electricity power station. The electricity company borrows now and pays back later out of the profits from selling electricity. That borrowing is also credit – the most important credit in our context. In return for that credit, the electricity company pays a charge to the bank – interest – which the bank uses to pay its staff, its rent and its other business expenses and to pay interest on my deposit account. If my money, plus that of other people like me, is insufficient for this power station loan, the bank borrows the extra from other banks who have a surplus. If enough banks lend to each other, we have a money market. A bank borrows from another bank at, say, 10 per cent p.a. and re-lends at 11 per cent p.a. making a gross profit of one per cent.

The result of this credit is that the electricity company can build its power station immediately. The world has a power station now to light its way instead of having to wait in the darkness. Unless the electricity company had a magic wand or was conveniently located at the end of the rainbow, there are few other ways we could have this power station. Therefore credit is absolutely fundamental to industrial development. So am I with my shoes, so is the bank, so is the money market.

The electricity company could have raised the necessary money by issuing share capital to those willing to subscribe. Unlike a loan, share capital may not usually be repaid until the company is wound up. It may not be secured by a mortgage. Dividends are payable on the shares only if the company has profits and the directors so decide, but interest on a loan is mandatory. So loans are much simpler and safer than shares. But both are capital.

The loans may be made by banks under the terms of a loan agreement or 1–6 raised from other institutions (such as pension funds, large corporations, insurance companies or government agencies) which have funds to invest and which will normally expect to receive a certificate or bond recording the terms of their loan which they can transfer. In the case of these other institutions, the funds come from pension moneys or insurance premiums or other surplus moneys arising from their operations. They could deposit these moneys with banks but the interest rate on debt securities may be higher.

The borrowers are governments, state entities, international organisations (like the World Bank), provinces, municipalities, large industrial corporations, single-purpose project companies (like our electricity power station) and the like. They are not individuals or small enterprises. We are not concerned with consumer credit or small business finance.

The credits may be unsecured or protected by security, such as a mortgage of land and buildings or a pledge of investment securities. They may be guaranteed as where a parent company guarantees a loan by a subsidiary. Asset protection may take other forms, of which financial leasing is a notable example.

Private international law

The focus is on international transactions, not domestic finance. An inter- 1–7 national transaction is one which has contacts with more than one legal jurisdiction. That international element may arise from the fact that a lending bank is located in one jurisdiction and the borrower in another, or that the bank lends in a foreign currency and not the domestic currency of the borrower, or that bonds are sold to foreign investors by an international syndicate of managers.

A jurisdiction is a territory which has different laws from another. A country may have a single system of law – like France and Japan – or it may have several systems of law, as in federal nations like the United States and Canada. There are at least seven different legal systems in the British Isles. With legal jurisdictions, there are many gradations of difference, just as one may have linguistic gradations ranging from the same language with different accents, to dialects of the same language, to different languages in the same group, through to completely different languages. Often language groups harmonise their language in specific areas when it is essential that they understand each other – Latin for botanists, English for airline pilots. So it is with legal jurisdictions.

Since the credits have an international element, it is necessary to study how the differences between legal systems are resolved.

For example, if a corporation is prevented from repaying an international loan by reason of an exchange control introduced by its home state, will foreign courts recognise that the borrower is relieved of its obligation, and will those foreign courts have jurisdiction over the borrower to order it to pay or allow it not to pay? Would foreign creditors be able to bankrupt the corporation in their own countries? If the corporation is a central bank owned by the state, will it be entitled to claim it is immune from the courts of another state because it is a sovereign creature?

This is the province of private international law and sometimes public international law. Hence a review must be made of the conflicts of law rules as to contracts and insolvency, as well as the jurisdiction of the courts to hear disputes and to enforce claims and the question of sovereign immunity.

In the matter of contracts, a reasonable degree of international consensus has been reached on private international law when compared to other areas of law. States have accepted their differences and amicably decided how the conflicts will be resolved: their courts apply their own rules for deciding which law is to be applied and there is much convergence on the rules of priority. The principle of liberality in freedom of choice of law for contracts has won through in the industrialised states. This relative orderliness is not however true of insolvency conflicts.

Term loans and syndicated loans

1–8   Bank credits are bank lending financed by deposits, primarily from other banks in money markets or from issues of negotiable certificates of deposit or from customer deposits. Borrowers require medium or long-term loans (e.g. three to 15 years) to finance capital investments and the like. But depositors are only prepared to lend to their banks by way of deposit short-term, e.g. six months or on demand. Banks therefore act as intermediaries and borrow short to lend long. Their gross profit is the spread or margin between the interest they pay to their depositors on the short-term deposits and interest they earn on the long-term loan, e.g. one per cent, not much in any event. Hence the floating rate term loan agreement – a contract which has been so frequently polished that it is now overlaid with an impressive, but nevertheless impenetrable, patina of tradition. The rate of interest which the borrower pays the bank changes periodically when the rate at which the bank borrows changes – it floats.

Because these loans last for a period of years before the borrower must repay in full, the lender expects protections in case something should go wrong in the meantime and prejudice final repayment. For example, the borrower must provide continuing information as to its financial condition, not dispose of all its assets or go into some other business. Hence, apart from the financial terms, loan agreements contain covenants regarding the management of the borrower's business in very limited areas crucial to the lender. If the borrower defaults in paying a principal or interest instalment or becomes insolvent or fails to comply with a term of the agreement, the lender can call in the loan immediately before its full term has expired and before it is too late, but not otherwise. These are the events of default.

Huge loans involve spreading the risk amongst a group or syndicate of banks who lend separate portions of the loan under the terms of a single agreement organised and administered by an agent bank. Hence the syndicated credit agreement. The amounts are usually in the region of $10 million to $200 million but can be much larger, e.g. $7 billion. Like bilateral term loan agreements, these multilateral contracts have also sacramentalised their own rites and in particular have produced much liturgy, by no means brief, as to the duties of the members of this little communion to each other and as to the role of their chief priest, the agent bank.

The syndicated loan was probably originally an American idea. In the nineteenth and early twentieth centuries British and Continental European banks tended to finance their industrial customers by single-bank credits. In England, enterprises would typically borrow from one bank which would provide a demand loan and take a fixed and floating charge over all the assets. Although the loan was on demand and therefore technically was unpredictable, banks of course did not call it in unless the position was hopeless and often long after the position was hopeless. The system worked well. But in the United States, the approach was different. The pattern there was for a group of banks to make the loan under a common agreement, to agree to lend for a fixed period determinable only on an event of default, and to lend unsecured but on terms that the borrower was prohibited from granting security to anybody else – the negative pledge.

These agreements are remarkable for their egalitarian emphasis on equality between creditors. They have a cross-default, which is an event of default sparking off on non-payment by the borrower of another loan, so that no creditor can steal a march on the others. They have the negative pledge, just mentioned, which enforces the equality principle that all creditors must be unsecured so that on insolvency the assets are equally divided. They have a pro rata sharing clause whereby the syndicate banks agree to share equally any individual receipts recovered by one bank in excess of those paid to the others – a romantic idea which has, however, been more honoured in the breach than the observance.

London eurocurrency market

1–9   The American style was imported to London in the 1960s with the growth of the London eurocurrency market, initially promoted by American banks, quickly joined by Canadian, Japanese, British and European banks, those from other nations and, after the oil price increases in the 1970s, by Arab banks.

The London eurocurrency market was, and is, a deposit market between banks. Banks borrow short-term deposits from each other – for one, three, six, nine or twelve months, but usually three or six months – to finance bilateral or syndicated medium term loans to foreign states, state enterprises and large industrial undertakings. The market was and remains primarily a US dollar market and other currencies were less commonly used for various reasons, including the importance of the US dollar as a reserve currency and the desire of central banks in Japan and Europe to maintain sovereignty over their own currencies, a desire expressed in exchange controls, statutory borrowing controls (Britain) and administrative guidelines (especially in Germany, Japan and Switzerland).

The term "eurocurrency market" was coined to describe this deposit market. Eurocurrency is not a special currency issued by banks in the form of notes and coins embossed with the head of Charlemagne. Eurocurrency is financial vernacular for a deposit payable at a branch of a bank outside the country of the currency. Thus a eurodollar is a US dollar deposit payable by a bank outside the United States – even if the bank is in Singapore. The term is apt because of course most money is now bank money, i.e. payable by a bank, as opposed to notes and coins.

1–10   The London eurocurrency market originated from a variety of economic, political, legal and other factors.

The US dollar supplanted sterling as the prime reserve currency after World War II. US dollars were deposited by central banks, governments and others with banks abroad, partly as result of the US balance of payments deficit, partly because of the absence of US capital and exchange controls. Regulation D of the US Federal Reserve imposed reserve requirements on deposits taken by US banks, reducing the interest payable on US deposits so that depositors earned more in Europe. A reserve requirement is a requirement that a bank deposit moneys interest free with the central bank so that the depositing bank has sufficient liquidity to pay its own depositors if they should demand repayment in greater amounts than expected – a run on the bank.

Regulation Q of the Federal Reserve put a ceiling on interest payable by US banks on time deposits, so foreign banks in Europe could pay higher interest, thereby attracting US dollar deposits.

The growth was fed by the desire of major banks to expand their business internationally away from the limited market for domestic lending.

Sovereign depositors favoured UK political stability and non-interference. This was probably supported by the fear by communist governments of US seizures, such as the attempt in 1948 by the US Treasury to block the withdrawal of $20 million of Czech gold from the Federal Reserve. London was also favoured because it had a developed financial and legal infrastructure and because of the language. An enormous fillip was given to the market by the petrodollar explosion after the 1973 oil cartel, followed by a doubling of the oil price in 1979–1980. Oil producers deposited oil profits in safe Western banks short-term. These banks lent medium-term largely to lesser developed countries to help them pay for oil and to develop their economies – a process sometimes referred to as "recycling" or "intermediation".

State insolvencies and beyond

The result was catastrophic. The banks assumed that repayment by the less   **1–11** rich countries could always be made out of new loans. This was falsified by the inability of many lesser developed countries even to pay interest, leading to multiple state insolvencies in the 1980s, commencing with Poland and Turkey and ultimately gathering up in its dark chariot most countries in Latin America, Africa, communist central Europe and elsewhere, but not the leading industrial states.

A state is insolvent when it cannot repay its foreign currency debts – states can always pay debts in their own currency simply by printing more money (although this itself can have serious domestic economic consequences, notably inflation). To repay foreign currency, the state must be able to earn sufficient foreign currency, e.g. from exports. Many of these lesser developed states simply did not earn enough – an unfortunate circumstance with a history going back for centuries. Banks, together with governmental creditors through their informal committee known as the Paris Club, spent most of the 1980s rescheduling these massive defaulted loans: it took many years to restore bank balance sheets, aided by accounting manoeuvres which were as imaginative as they were necessary. It was only in 1988 that the leading central banks were able to require that banks maintain capital of eight per cent to their weighted portfolios in the Basle Agreement of that year, a remarkable illustration of international cooperation.

In the meantime the market did not stay still. Eurocurrency markets sprang up elsewhere – Paris, Singapore, Hong Kong. The lending reverted to large corporate loans, some of them exploiting every imaginable type of facility that the financial mind could engender – short-term revolving notes, competitive tender panels whereby banks bid to lend on a revolving basis, acceptances (which are effectively guarantees by the banks of trade bills of exchange issued by the borrower so that the borrower could sell them). Hence the arrival of the multi-option facility – popularly referred to as an "all-singing all-dancing" facility – whose life was as short as its documentation long. A revolving loan is a short-term loan which is repaid out of the proceeds of a new loan – the loans turn over or revolve. In the same period, substantial loans were made to finance takeovers of companies, including takeovers by the existing management (management buy-outs). That cycle ended with yet more spectacular insolvencies in the late 1980s and early 1990s, this time of large industrial and property corporations, caught in a deep economic recession and high interest rates.

Project finance

1–12 Of particular persistence throughout this period, and growing in the 1990s, were bank credits to finance projects – the development of an oil or gas field, a mine, a toll bridge or tunnel, a refinery, a pipeline or an ordinary office or shop development. Many are stupendous industrial projects, like giant electricity power stations. The essence of project finance is that banks lend to a project company, owned by the project sponsors, to finance the development. The project company carries on solely the business of building and operating the project so that, if the project fails, the banks have no other source of repayment, except for whatever guarantees and the like they have been able to negotiate. As a result, project finance can be risky and requires close attention to structure, to the security available, to the commercial contracts and to any government concession.

Following the wave of privatisations in the 1980s and beyond, whereby governments sold state enterprises to the public or to private companies, and the dismantling of the ideology of state corporatism, many countries now seek to finance their infrastructure and industrial expansion by granting a lease or other property right to private sponsors who build the project, operate it and then transfer it back to the public sector after repaying the capital and reaping a profit for their efforts and expertise which are usually prodigious. By these "build-operate-transfer" projects, states harness private industrial enterprise and capital but without burdening the state budget. The foreign capital is often backed by finance or guarantees from export credit agencies supporting their national exporters of equipment for the project. Whether this project capital will enjoy better fortune than its forbears remains to be seen.

Bond issues

Bond issues are lending in the form of negotiable debt securities subscribed   **1–13**
by investors and payable to whoever physically has them – the bearer.
Investment banks organise the issue and underwrite the initial sale but
otherwise banks do not act as intermediaries. The investor carries the
default risk, whereas in bank loans the bank carries the default risk.

The transaction is a loan, but the terms of the loan are set out in securities, each of which is in a relatively small amount, e.g. $10,000, so as to faci-
litate transfers by the investors. The main differences with bank loans are
that the securities must be freely and easily marketable (banks do not
usually trade loans), that the investors may be multitudinous and anony-
mous, that the terms of bonds tend towards greater standardisation and
simplicity, and that the issue of the bonds attracts the adversities of securities regulation. Bond issues are generally listed on a stock exchange, such as
London or Luxembourg, not to provide a market but to enlarge the number
of potential investors: many institutions cannot, by choice or regulation,
invest in unlisted securities because they are usually riskier. The market is
known as the international capital market or the primary market – "primary" to connote new issues as opposed to the secondary market for trades in
securities already issued.

Although this is disputed, the first real eurobond issue was an issue by the
Italian Autostrade in 1965. The essence of the transaction was that the US
dollar bonds were listed in London, and that the issue was managed by
European banks and sold to European investors. This was no more than a
revival of the numerous eighteenth and nineteenth century issues in Europe
and latterly in the United States.

The market developed in London for a variety of reasons. First, securities   **1–14**
regulation in Europe for issues to sophisticated investors was very liberal
and avoided the cumbersome US requirements which insisted on the prep-
aration and registration of a massive and time-consuming prospectus.
Secondly, a US interest equalisation tax in 1963 imposed a tax penalty on
US investors buying foreign bonds. Thirdly, US restrictions on direct overseas investment by US corporations in the late 1960s forced US foreign sub-
sidiaries to borrow abroad. Other factors were that European fees were
cheaper than in the US and that there was a substantial European demand,
e.g. in Switzerland, for private portfolio investment.

The bonds may be foreign bonds, which are bonds issued by a foreign
issuer and subscribed by investors in a single country, e.g. bonds issued by a
Swedish company and purchased by Japanese investors. But more usually
bonds are purchased by investors internationally in which event they are

referred to as eurobonds, reflecting their birthplace, or as international bonds.

The investors are invariably sophisticated investors, not the general public. Typically they are governments, insurance companies, pension funds, investment companies or trusts, banks and large corporations. Although the Belgian dentist is famed as the archetypal eurobond investor, purchases of bonds by individuals are small, although individuals may invest in funds which hold bonds and of course individuals are the ultimate beneficiaries, however remote they may be from the actual holder. Hence the market is wholesale, not retail, and rules of law designed to protect innocent individuals from others and from themselves play, or should play, no leading role.

1–15   The bonds may be ordinary bonds evidencing a simple debt or they may be convertible into shares of the issuer or its parent or have attached to them warrants to subscribe for shares: these are equity-linked bonds. The bondholder will convert if equity shares will be worth more, or produce more income, than the bonds.

Bonds typically have maturities of between seven to twelve years, sometimes shorter, sometimes longer. But there are various other types of instrument of shorter maturities, such as medium-term notes and short-term revolving issues of commercial paper having maturities of less than a year and rolled over into a fresh issue on maturity.

Although the bonds are negotiable bearer securities, the investors do not put them under their mattresses. Instead they deposit them with a custodian to look after them in safe-keeping. When they desire to transfer them, all that happens is that the custodian debits the account of the seller and credits the account of the buyer. The bonds lie sleepily where they are, in a vault somewhere, often thousands of miles from the office of the custodian. Because of the vast amounts of these investment securities – more than $1,400 billion with one single custodian in Brussels – the system is convenient and safe. Indeed, if it were not for custodians, a mountain of paperwork would utterly crush the market and everybody in it. These custodians are therefore granaries or silos for intangibles. They are keepers.

Yet despite the splendid simplicity of this arrangement, more than half the world's legal systems circle the custodian proposition with suspicion, clucking their tongues and shaking their heads.

Secured finance

1–16   At one time most international finance was unsecured – apart from guarantees. But security is of increasing importance and hence it is necessary to review the scope of security internationally, including specialist secured loans, such as ship and aircraft finance.

Security is needed for all manner of dealings – whether project finance or trade finance or ordinary loans or margin collateral for dealings on organised exchanges. The asset can be land and buildings or goods or contracts or receivables or intellectual property rights or investment securities – anything – but each attracting its own little rules which are all different. States totally disagree on the scope and utility of security and even states which share the same history and heritage have diametrically opposed views on the subject.

Ship and aircraft mortgage loans are of particular interest because the chattel roams the world's jurisdictions. Accordingly the accumulated law which has grown up to deal with the international legal collisions is particularly profuse, and a fruitful indicator of the attitudes taken by legal systems. Some of this law is like barnacles on the hull of a ship which should really now be scraped off.

It is also necessary to review guarantees and their main variants – the curious comfort letter, the standby letter of credit, the first demand bond and the like. Guarantors have been the darlings of the courts in all jurisdictions since they did not expect to have to repay what they did not receive. As a consequence, the guarantee contract is encrusted with law.

Title finance

An alternative to security is title finance. In title finance the financier has title 1–17 or ownership of the asset, as opposed to a mortgage or security interest. A favoured form is the financial lease, widely used for aircraft and other large pieces of equipment. The financier buys the equipment from the manufacturer and then leases it to the operator for its full useful life. Instead of repaying a loan plus interest, the lessee-operator pays rentals which together amount to the original capital cost plus interest. Effectively the lessor is secured since, if the lessee defaults, the financier can cancel the lease and sell the equipment, accounting to the lessee for any surplus, in the same way that a mortgagee sells the mortgaged asset and, after repayment of the loan, pays any excess back to the mortgagor. Indeed, the operator could instead have borrowed the money to buy the asset, e.g. an aircraft, and mortgaged the aircraft to the lender to service the loan. The substantive business effect would be very similar to a finance lease.

Other forms of title finance are widely used, for example in relation to trade finance. These forms include retention of title, and the discounting or factoring of commercial receivables.

Other classic forms include sale and leaseback and sale and repurchase ("repos"). Repos are commonly used for bullion and securities. A similar concept is harnessed for stock borrowings.

Then there are securitisations which are a sophisticated form of factoring receivables, pioneered by American investment banks and their lawyers. These receivables may be home mortgage loans or bonds or trade receivables or consumer receivables or even defaulted sovereign loans, placed in "vulture funds". They are sold by the original creditor or originator to a single-purpose company which raises finance by a bond issue or bank loan to fund the purchase and creates security over the receivables in favour of the lender to secure the finance. In that way the originator raises money on the strength of its assets by a sale, instead of by borrowing the money and mortgaging the assets. There are innumerable variations, including trusts of receivables.

The rationale of these asset-based transactions varies. But in essence they have the commercial effect of security and indeed many of them are designed to avoid what are seen as the archaic obstacles of mortgage law. The attitude of courts and legislators to quasi-security has ranged from enthusiasm to hostility – a diversity of view which is often inconsistent with the attitude of the jurisdiction concerned to security generally. Some countries are glad to find an escape from the cage of mortgages and hence by subterfuge support form over substance. Others are displeased that the birds are flying out and seek to re-bolt the gate.

Financial trading

1–18   Apart from loans and other credits, financial institutions engage in trading financial products. The original product is foreign currency which businesses require to finance their trade and other dealings. They buy one currency with another, like buying peas with beans. A company in England which has to pay for a Japanese machine must buy yen with sterling to pay for it. It buys the yen from its bank, so that banks end up with currencies of many nations to re-sell or lend out. Hence the establishment of a foreign exchange market peopled by banks. The foreign exchange market is immense and is dominated by the US dollar, commonly paired with Deutschmarks or Japanese yen. On a single April day in the early 1990s the volume of foreign exchange transactions was estimated by the Bank for International Settlements to be $880 billion which, if multiplied out for a year, discloses a not inconsiderable sum. The largest market is in London.

Other financial products are of more recent origin. They commenced in the 1980s with interest swaps. These are contracts whereby, for example, an issuer of fixed rate bonds agrees to pay amounts equal to floating rate interest to a borrower of a floating rate loan, and the floating rate borrower agrees to pay the fixed rate issuer amounts equal to his fixed rate. In other words, they each agree to pay amounts equal to each other's interest. In the late 1980s there was a rapid development of other derivative products – futures and options – whereby one party agrees to pay the other (or grants the other an option to call for the payment of) the difference between the market value of an asset, such as gold or grain or a security or a basket of securities or a currency, on the day of the contract and its value on the agreed future date. These transactions are called derivatives because they are derived from another asset. They are air on air and tend to mystify the practitioner and the regulator more than the normal.

Financial trading is swift and informal – deals are commonly struck by dealers on the telephone, and then subsequently matched and confirmed, i.e. evidenced by an exchange of written notes of the transaction which are then checked against each other to see that they agree. Because of this speed and informality, the markets have developed standard forms of master agreement which govern all deals struck between the contractors and which save the time and expense of documenting each transaction separately – and avoid the risk that the dealers will not get round to the paperwork in good time.

International payments

In order to complete these transactions, the money has to be moved from debtor to creditor. This is not achieved by handing over a sackful of notes or by a Wells Fargo coach and horses protected by Colt 45s. It is achieved, less excitingly perhaps, but more efficiently, by credit transfers from the debtor's bank to the creditor's bank. A credit transfer is not assignment of bank deposits, but rather a simple reduction of the debtor's balance at his bank and an increase of the creditor's balance at his bank. The process may involve a chain of four banks or more. A great deal can go wrong in the process – not just fraud or mistakes, but also the insolvency of a participant. Commonly the payments in a particular currency are funnelled through a handful of major banks operating a clearing system in the country of the currency and having accounts at the central bank. Because, again, the amounts are so large, particularly at the spout of the funnel in the central clearing system, the risks are commensurably of staggering proportions.

1-19

Set-off and netting

It is obvious that reciprocal transactions will produce reciprocal claims criss-crossing each other between the participants in international finance. Set-off is the process of setting one off against the other so that only a net balance is payable by one to the other. Netting is a more developed form of set-off but the concept is the same.

1-20

The effect of set-off is to reduce the exposure of a party to his counter-party's insolvency. The reduction of risk can be dramatic – as much as 90 per cent in the foreign exchange markets. The result is a massive lowering of the risk of cascade or domino insolvencies which could threaten a large number of institutions all at once and hence threaten the financial system, to the ultimate loss of the tax-payer and of the individuals whose bank collapses. The cascade risk is known as systemic risk – the risk of the destruction of the financial system.

One would expect the world's jurisdictions enthusiastically to embrace set-off and netting since it would seem obviously to be to our advantage. But though the majority of industrialised states do adopt this policy, it is by no means universal and a large bloc of important states opposes it.

Regulation of international finance

1–21 Then there is the question of regulation. The main objectives of regulation are to protect the public from incompetence and deceit, from their own imprudence or lack of sophistication, and from the insolvency of regulated institutions and debtors. The original regulation of money took the form of usury and gaming laws, primarily designed to protect over-optimistic individuals against debt and speculation and the miseries they can bring. Usury and gaming laws have been overtaken in importance over the last 60 years or so by securities regulation and bank regulation. Both have regimes requiring securities dealers and banks to be officially licensed and to show competence and honesty, both have elaborate regimes for official supervision and monitoring of the financial health of dealers and banks, and securities regulation has disclosure rules whereby investors are to be informed of the quality of the investments that are offered.

Of course there is also consumer credit legislation, which is of minimal importance in our context, and also the various national restrictive practices in the form of exchange controls and borrowing controls. The latter two have been more or less dismantled in the main industrialised states, but exchange controls remain of significance.

There are marked differences between securities regulation and bank regulation. Securities regulation surprises the bystanding observer – a jumble of bizarre and gothic statutes bristling with such ferocious detail, often born of a deep moral anxiety about cheating, as almost entirely to bury the plain objectives which all sensible people subscribe to. Many states effectively erect a paper wall against access by foreign enterprises to local savings. By contrast, bank regulation on the whole is comparatively harmonious and sensible at the international level.

The reason for this disparity is probably that bank insolvencies could potentially be so damaging to the public, to world order and to prosperity that concerted action was essential. Other reasons are that the banking population is much less than the population of those involved in the securities business and so is more manageable, that there is less public involvement in securities than in banking and so a diminished public interest, that banks are supervised by a few regulators dominated by the central banks of a handful of leading industrialised countries, and that central bankers are less disposed to allow unsophisticated emotions about money to interfere with their judgment of what is necessary.

Insolvency law

In credit transactions, the main risk for the creditor is that he will not be paid because the borrower is insolvent. Hence much of the law and practice in this area is concerned with the insolvency risk.   1–22

Examples taken at random are: (1) the importance of guarantees, security, title finance and set-off in order to mitigate the insolvency risk; (2) covenants in term loan agreements and bonds, such as the negative pledge, pari passu clause, anti-disposal clause and financial ratios variously designed to protect the credit; (3) events of default in term loan agreements and bonds, such as a cross-default, intended to provide early warning of financial difficulties; (4) the appointment of bond trustees and bondholder representation of bondholders, in order to facilitate a debt restructuring where the issuer is in financial difficulties; (5) the potential liability of lead managers of syndicated loans and managers of bond issues for inaccuracies in offering circulars if the borrower is insolvent and therefore unable to pay; (6) capital adequacy rules for banks and investment businesses whereby their solvency is subject to official supervision; and (7) disclosure rules imposed by securities regulation and stock exchanges in relation to prospectuses and the issuer's continuing financial condition so that credit risks are disclosed so far as practicable.

Insolvency is fundamental to credit. This subject is therefore a central topic and includes the private restructuring of debt of enterprises in financial difficulties and the risks of lender liability.

It is not easy for creditors to escape future insolvencies. One has only to take each 10-year slice of history since 1900 and examine what transpired in each decade. Those who woke, entranced by optimistic dreams, on the first day of each decade could hardly imagine the political and economic disaster, the upheavals, the catastrophes, that would strike down their hopes at some time during that decade – with only a few decades offering tolerable calm and peace. It is not therefore altogether a matter for reprimand nor is it   1–23 perplexing that financiers who advance loans, which may have a term approaching that length of period, should find that prophecy is more difficult than history.

Of course most loans are repaid. If that were not so, banks would go out of business and their depositors could not safely deposit their money with them. Yet the risks are great.

The loss of a loan of $10 million earning a net profit of one per cent requires a portfolio of $1 billion to replace it. Banking is not for amateurs. But we must have banks as keepers of people's means of exchange. And the solvency of these keepers must be safeguarded.

Jurisdictions differ fundamentally on their insolvency policies. The laws of one group assist creditors, usually the keepers, to escape insolvency, while others seek to enlarge the debtor's estate as much as possible. These opposing views, which are fiercely contested, are without doubt the key to unlock the comparative law of commerce and finance.

State loans

1–24 Historically a substantial part of international borrowing for centuries has been by states or their more recent creatures, a central bank or a state entity. States are special creatures of law, primarily because, although they can and do become insolvent, they cannot be subjected to bankruptcy proceedings. One cannot sell a state to pay its creditors, or, rather, one could (e.g. the sale of Louisiana by Napoleon), but politically it is usually out of the question. For long, states were protected by sovereign immunity whereby they could not be sued in foreign courts, but that has now been reduced and is invariably waived by contract in formal bonds or credit agreements. Hence they are technically unprotected by the freeze on creditor enforcement actions which is the main feature of muncipal bankruptcy laws, but they are still protected by a range of defences, largely based on creditor consensus and mature conduct. This situation shows how bankruptcy can be resolved without a bankruptcy law. It also shows the usefulness of agreed rescheduling agreements as a tool in coping with insolvency.

Other extraordinary features of states include the anomalous situation which arises if they break up or there are other territorial changes. Who is responsible for the debt? Then there is the question of the breakaway territory who everybody refuses to acknowledge or speak to, but which is nevertheless undeniably there. These questions are the province of state succession and state recognition.

Finally, under this head are international organisations which are companies owned by states and which are not formed under the municipal law of any state, but are created by a treaty. Astonishingly, it took some time for their very existence to be recognised, but now that they have passed from ghosthood to some less spectral condition, it remains to be determined what their powers are and in particular whether the natural law of bankruptcy can apply to them.

Subordinated loans

Subordinated loans are credits which are junior to all other creditors or to a   1–25
single creditor. Sometimes they are a substitute for equity, sometimes they are merely a way of increasing the finance available. Vast numbers of junior capital bonds are issued, mainly by banks as substitute capital. Project sponsors commonly invest their capital in the project company by way of subordinated loans ranking after the bank finance, instead of equity shares. Institutions may be prepared to lend money to finance an acquisition of a company on a junior basis – "mezzanine finance". The legal technology, despite some initial faltering, is now firmly established in the leading states.

Legal opinions

Finally, there is the role of lawyers. Apart from drafting and negotiating   1–26
documentation, they must plan and structure the transaction and hopefully facilitate it. Their task may range from the purely technical to strategic commercial advice and commonly includes the management of the transaction's documentation. Like the medieval notaries, they must advise on its legal effect and draw attention to legal difficulties which would not be obvious or which would defeat legitimate expectations. But they are also expected to give a formal legal opinion at the closing of a financial transaction. These opinions often do not say much, but they are part of the ritual which cannot be avoided.

CHAPTER 2

CRITERIA FOR COMPARATIVE LAW

Importance of comparative law

2–1   Comparative law is of unquestionable importance. International transactions span borders and, in view of the amounts at stake, it is essential to
plot the laws of the world's jurisdictions, or at least to know more or less
what to expect.

An issue of eurobonds can involve 30 jurisdictions or more. Borrowers of
syndicated loans may be located anywhere. A bank which acts as custodian
for securities may deposit them with sub-custodians in several dozen countries. An international options and futures exchange may be taking collateral which ultimately emanates from participants all over the world even
if the exchange deals only with its own local members who in turn deal with
the international customers. A payments system could in principle involve
institutions in every country which has a banking system. Projects are
financed in a great range of states, from the most industrialised to the poorest on the globe: those financing them need to know if the law allows them
to do what they hope to do.

2–2   Of course comparative law is useful to enrich one's understanding of
one's own laws, to enhance awareness of the range of possible solutions, to
help frame new laws with the benefit of the thinking and experience of
others and without having to re-invent the basics, to promote international
harmony, to correct prejudices, to discover the similarities which underlie
the differences, so often veiled by different legal idioms and argot but meaning the same thing, or even merely to satisfy curiosity as an end in itself. But
these laudable and admirable objectives pale before the sheer urgency of
being able to transact business in an atmosphere of knowledge rather than
ignorance, so that transactions are not set aside or liabilities incurred by
legal ambush, legal surprise, legal incomprehension.

Voltaire's comment is as true now as it was in pre-revolutionary France:

"Is it not an absurd and terrible thing that that which is true in one village is false in
another? What kind of barbarism is it that citizens must live under different

laws? When you travel in this kingdom you change legal systems as often as you change horses" (*Oevres de Voltaire VIII* (1838) Dialogues p 5).

Harmonisation

Although there are many examples of harmonisation – by uniform model 2–3 laws or international conventions or the adoption of common ideas – no one can wait for legal harmonisation to be brought to fruition. There is too much disagreement. This disagreement applies even in relation to basic policies, never mind the refinements. Except in relation to the most elementary and primitive concepts which one can truly say are natural law because generally accepted by civilised nations, the universal lex mercatoria is a long way off.

Legal uniformity is needed to reduce the expense of investigation, to avoid wasteful conflicts, to enhance useful transactions, to reduce dangers, perils and losses from nullified transactions, to put businesses on an even competitive legal field, to avoid unfairness and injustice and to promote international legal safety.

Variety is favoured in life, in nature, in art. But variety is not suitable for international financial law. Individual personalities do not lose their interest merely because they all speak the same language: on the contrary, social intercourse is improved and its benefits more widely enjoyed.

Of course the depth and range of legal institutions appropriate for a country may vary. But the concept that one country should have a less civilised or less consistent commercial law than another is unquestionably wrong since it implies that the peoples of one country are not as morally entitled as another.

The question of how much international uniformity is needed and where 2–4 it is needed most urgently are matters for debate. The ultimate ideal is complete uniformity in essential mainstream areas, but it takes jurists of knowledge, wisdom and vision, with a genuine sense of the need for human co-operation, to achieve it. It also requires a determination not to sink to the lowest common denominator and not to allow purely temporal political policies or chauvinism or outworn dogmas to interfere.

Apart from some attainments by uniform laws in federal states and treaties between states or model laws, the international legal community has often opted for the less ambitious programme of determining common rules of recognition as opposed to common rules of substantive law. An example is the principle in the Geneva Aircraft Convention of 1948 that contracting states will recognise each others aircraft mortgages if properly constituted in accordance with the laws of the flag state and publicly recorded there, but without requiring each state to allow aircraft mortgages or requiring uniform rules as to their creation. Many other examples will be found in this series of works.

Legal criteria generally

2–5 In light of the current disharmony, a guide is needed to impose a pattern which will make some sense of the mosaic. Of course it will always be necessary to investigate the detail specifically and individually for any particular transaction and no amount of classification can avoid that burden, particularly as jurisdictions formerly in the same family have often gone off on their own on this or that issue, given their legislative supremacy. This is especially true of the advanced jurisdictions.

The grouping of legal systems into families according to various criteria is not new and much invaluable work has been done by the leading comparativists. Sometimes their canvas is very large in seeking to encompass all fields of law – family law, inheritance, criminal law, constitutional law, administrative law, commercial contracts, torts, property. A canvas which seeks to paint the entire firmament is ambitious and the result can be mere generality. Fortunately, the canvas in this series of works is only one small part of the complete picture and this makes it more realistic, one hopes, to achieve the degree of detail sufficient to be useful at the level of actual practice.

Classification must proceed on the basis of criteria. First one may mention criteria which have more intellectual interest than utility and for various reasons are limited in their fruitfulness in the fields covered by this work. These are:

- the degree of codification;
- differences in basic contract law;
- a miscellany of cultural criteria.

Codified and non-codified states

2–6 A basic division between legal systems is that between those which have codified their law and those which have not. For example, the Franco-Latin and Germanic countries as a rule have codes covering the whole field of law, from family relations to insolvency. This is not true to quite the same extent in common law countries or in the Scandinavian countries, plus a few others.

A classification based on degree of codification is of limited utility. How the law is written down is unimportant compared to its substantive content. The oft-repeated assertions that contracts in code countries can be shorter because it is all in the code, or that code countries do not follow case law precedent, or that code law is simpler, or that if it is not allowed by the code it is not allowed at all, are largely popular misconceptions. In the industrialised states, there are differences in emphasis, but that is all. Further, most important commercial law is now written down in all developed states – statutes or acts or codes on companies, insolvency, securities regulation, financial statements, property, insurance, negotiable instruments. That leaves mainly the basic and routine rules of contract, agency, tort and the like. Those opposed to universal codification argue that the basic rules are too general, even when codified, or are easily discoverable from the works of the great authors who themselves often set out the law in the form of summary rules. They say that no codification of the law of torts or delict has ever done more than produce a few broad generalisations and that codification petrifies the law. Those in favour of codification maintain that it is sensible and useful to distil and simplify the legal infrastructure in this way and that this distillation is appropriate when the legal system has settled down.

In any event some common law states have codes of basic law, such as the Indian Contracts Act 1882 and the codes drafted by the New Yorker David Dudley Field, still in force in California, North and South Dakota, Idaho and Montana, though much amended. The United States has systematised large areas of basic law in numerous uniform acts and in the unofficial Restatements of the Law of the American Law Institute which do not have the force of law but are habitually referred to by American courts. That effort was motivated by despair at the huge mass of case law and a desire to simplify and to make the law more accessible.

Although lawyers dispute how much codification is needed, a knowledge   2–7
of which of the main codes is adopted by a state is usually very accurate in determining the legal bias of that state. For example, the French, German, Austrian and Swiss Codes each have enjoyed wide acceptance elsewhere, particularly the French and German codes, and each has its own colouring and tint.

The French codes of the turn of the nineteenth century have been the foundation for the codes of probably around 80 jurisdictions all over the world – in Europe, Africa, the Middle East, Latin America, Indochina – so that France was a major central supplier of law. Sometimes the codes were imposed by conquest or colonisation, sometimes they were freely adopted. The German codes of the turn of the twentieth century have been influential in about twenty states, including Japan, China and Russia, although in China and Russia the original Germanic codes were obliterated. The Swiss codes of around 1912, for all their splendid virtues and popular style as drafted by Eugen Huber, did not achieve such international sway – they came too late – but they were influential on international thinking and Turkey, for example, took them over almost word for word under Kemel

Attaturk in the mid–1920s. The Austrian codes of around 1811 were mainly dominant in central Europe and the former Yugoslavia, although Hungary for long remained the only non-codified country in Europe, outside Scandinavia. That leaves the Dutch code of 1992 – the biblical forty years in the making and the newest code of any industrialised state.

The English exported their legal system mainly by colonisation over three centuries so that it too covered more than 80 jurisdictions, plus about 50 in the United States. But their legal imperialism did not extend to the Middle East, where they were the dominant power for decades, and was not intrusive in countries like South Africa.

Basic law of contract

2–8 One could investigate the differences between jurisdictions in their basic contractual doctrines, e.g. the idea of consideration or contractual cause or contractual intent, the impact of mistake, whether a contract is complete when the acceptance is posted or when it reaches the other side, whether offers can be revoked before acceptance, whether contracts have to be in writing, the extent to which the courts reform contracts when the parties have not thought of a particular situation, the availability of third party beneficiary contracts, whether or not the courts award specific performance or only damages, and the impact of force majeure or other frustrating events. These studies are absorbing but they do tend to show that, while there are often significant differences in terminology, most developed states seem to arrive at similar conclusions in the areas which really matter, at least so far as international financial transactions are concerned.

> Some examples may be given. The English have an archaic notion that consideration is necessary for a contract but in practice consideration is unimportant in financial law except perhaps in relation to guarantees and other discrete areas, such as debt subordinations. Common law states allow an offer to be withdrawn before acceptance whereas many other countries do not. This too is unimportant in the financial arena. When the situation arises, if one party wishes the offer to be kept open, he can be given an option for consideration that it will be kept open, whereas if a party wishes to be able to withdraw before acceptance, but the law is otherwise, he can so provide in his offer. Differences in the doctrine of specific performance of contracts do not appear to give rise to major objections in international finance or any major collision because it is on insolvency when the doctrine really matters and there completely different ideas supervene. Doctrines of force majeure have limited relevance to debt contracts. The result is that, for ordinary unsecured loan or deposit contracts, for documentary letters of credit, and for "first demand" guarantees, the legal treatment in most commercially developed states will tend to be similar. Of course, this is not to say that in special cases divergences on

the primitive rules of contract are not crucial, but only that they assume much greater importance in trade contracts, as opposed to financial contracts – sale of goods, transportation, construction and the like.

Miscellaneous cultural criteria

One could classify according to the education system for lawyers and the   2–9
training of judges or according to legal techniques in conducting litigation, or according to the institutions of the law and how the courts are organised, or one could make judgments about the fairness and sophistication of a nation's tribunals. One could attempt to discern degrees of legal nationalism or chauvinism or narcissistic narrow-mindedness in the rules themselves. But these criteria tend to be subjective and fragmentary – or else obvious and elementary – and do not deal with the substantive law in sufficient detail to cope with the daily transaction of business. Nevertheless they still remain suitable areas for fruitful research which enhance an understanding of international law.

General style as criteria

Then one may consider aspects of the general style of a jurisdiction. Possible   2–10
candidates relevant to our study – by no means an exclusive list – include:

- the emphasis on predictability;
- the degree of legal liberalism in commercial law;
- the degree of criminalisation of commercial law;
- the attitude to big pocket liability;
- attitudes to dispute resolution;
- policies on hard and soft law.

The weakness of these as criteria is that they also are too general and that it is possible to find episodic examples of each in all the leading jurisdictions. But they contain important values and anecdotal evidence suggests substantial international disparities. It is therefore worth reviewing them briefly.

Predictability

The predictability and certainty of the law are key policies in international   2–11
finance since such huge amounts are involved. Throughout legal history, jurists, going back to Aristotle and Cicero, have debated the conflict between detailed rule and wide discretion, imperative law and judicial empiricism, law and equity, between statutory literalism and the intent and spirit of the statute, the rule of the legislator (with the judiciary as mere

mechanical interpreters) and the rule of the judge invested with full creative powers, the law of the codifier and the law of Louis IX under his oak at Vincennes.

In some states, creditors are somewhere. In other states, they are nowhere. One might say that this is not wholly unsatisfactory because one simply adjusts to one's location. What is problematic, however, is if the creditor is maybe somewhere, maybe nowhere, but it is not possible to tell in advance.

The first aspect of predictability is whether the jurisdiction has a sophisticated body of law which covers the questions which arise most frequently in sufficient detail so that reasonably safe predictions can be made as to how the court would decide the question.

All that can be said is that the major industrialised countries do have a very substantial body of case law interpreting their codes and statutes and general principles. Much has already been decided and, if it has not been decided, the solution can usually be reasoned from what has been decided. In some instances, there is far too much law to cope with.

But it must be recognised that absolute legal predictability is not attainable. There are too many factual situations for that and no statute or rule of law can cover all possible situations. Indeed the attempt to be too precise can lead to statutory over-particularisation and rigidity can conceal the law beneath a bristling forest of detail, can hide the principles and render the law inaccessible and incomprehensible. A misrepresentation may range from a puff, a fib, a careless mistake to a deliberate and knowing fraud on a grand scale and the law must reflect these possibilities. Some capriciousness remains and necessarily so, to achieve justice. Hence predictability is relative.

2–12   When it comes to statutes, states have very different ideas on the degree of detail which is needed. A few examples will suffice.

> In a Quebec statute regulating securities, the regulated investments were simply defined as "securities", but Britain determined that a definition of investments required four pages. In the United States, a prohibition on conflicts of interest by trustees as bondholder representatives elaborated itself expansively into a prescriptive list full of busy detail, but Luxembourg, Japan and Britain merely outlaw "conflicts of interest" and leave it to reasoning and decided case law to fill this out. In the United States, the criminal offence of insider dealing was developed by case-law from a ten-line general anti-fraud section, whereas by contrast the European Union decided that the matter should properly be dealt with in a Directive approximately 1000 per cent longer. Given this range of response on the same point, generalisations about national characteristics are unsafe. The proper course for the law-maker is to decide the degree of particularity that each individual issue requires, having regard to importance,

comprehensibility, risk, fairness and the rest – a process which is highly judgmental – and then to distil the rule down to its most laconic minimum, its purest essence, to the extent consistent with the policies. The proper course for the jurist and researcher is to decide whether the law-maker has succeeded or whether improvements are in order.

A second aspect of predictability is whether the courts follow their own precedents and are bound by the decisions of higher courts. It is often remarked that in code states the doctrine of *stare decisis* does not apply to the degree found in common law courts: Napoleon was deeply suspicious of judicial discretion. His view was that it was all in the code and the job of the courts was to apply it, but not to amplify it. He was by no means alone in this view amongst nineteenth century European jurists or thinkers – Jeremy Bentham (1748–1832) was only one of the champions of codified certainty as opposed to judicial pragmatism and Voltaire remarked that to interpret the law is to corrupt it.

This seems to be a fading division on all sides. As mentioned, there are no doubt differences in emphasis, but courts in the industrialised states, whether codified or common law, tend to follow decided cases because of the need for certainty, consistency and the security of transactions.

A third aspect of predictability is whether the courts adhere to established rules, unless clearly wrong, or whether they judge each case according to the particular merits and according to overriding ideas of equity and fairness. In this area there do appear to be differences between the highly developed states, but they are difficult to pin down and require a detailed comparison of cases decided on the same facts.

A very elementary example is the ability of a creditor to accelerate a loan   2–13 immediately if an event of default has occurred, however technical, and the loan agreement expressly allows the creditor to do so. We are of course dealing here only with major corporate debtors and the like – not individuals. If the loan is secured and there are vague concepts of good faith or of abuse of legal rights or grace periods of uncertain duration, then a creditor may be liable in damages for a substantial amount for an unlawful foreclosure on the debtor's property. In England the rule is that, if a loan is payable on demand or is payable on the occurrence of a certain specified event of default, however technical, then, outside the consumer context and apart from gross unconscionability (which would be remote in international finance), the contract is effective and the debtor has but a few hours to find the money before the creditor can enforce, e.g. by appointing a receiver in respect of a floating charge. It is up to the debtor to negotiate grace periods in the original contract. By contrast Ontario case law imposed a good faith grace period which at once provoked a flood of litigation by disappointed debtors. This tendency is said to be apparent in other jurisdictions which have specific "good faith" overrides in the code, e.g. the Greek CC Art 281 and the German BGB s 242.

But if there is to be a grace period, how long is to be? Is it to be a day, a week, a month? How is the creditor to know and how is the court to impose its own views subsequent to the event and the negotiation of the credit documentation as to what is fair? Is the court to make a judgment as to whether the debtor ought to be given another chance or as to the likelihood of an upturn in the debtor's economic fortunes? The ordinary depositor would be very surprised if, on presenting his order to his bank for repayment of his deposit, his bank responded that it would perhaps consider implementing the order in a couple of weeks or so. The depositor would be even more nonplussed if it was obvious that his bank was about to go bankrupt.

Still, there are sometimes cases of obvious unconscionability and sometimes there is a real conflict between what is seen as fair and the needs of predictability. The comparative lawyer can merely note that predictability is a higher value in some jurisdictions than others, but that most developed jurisdictions espouse predictability in commercial and financial law to a considerable extent.

Liberalism

2–14   Another very general test is the commercial liberality of the jurisdiction. The question here is whether parties are given a wide freedom to contract as they wish or whether they are restricted by various prescriptive and mandatory rules. One may ignore contracts which are obviously unconscionable or immoral or which conflict with some fundamental policy. One may ignore consumer restrictions, which are adhered to by all the developed jurisdictions and which protect consumers against unfair contract terms which they had no opportunity to negotiate and against surprise clauses, e.g. the laundry and bus ticket cases. Plainly there was no freedom of contract in those cases. In the business arena those consumerist considerations do not apply.

Freedom of contract in our context affects such matters as restrictions on the freedom of the parties to select the governing law of a contract even if totally unconnected to the contract, limitations on freedom of choice of forum to hear disputes, refusal to allow the free marketability of debts, prescriptive rules about the qualities of negotiability, restrictions on the availability of security, limitations on the matters on which bondholders may vote and thereby bind a dissentient minority, the degree of documentary ceremony, and the degree to which bankruptcy law disturbs bargains in the interests of social engineering. This freedom impacts on the flexibility to develop new legal techniques – subordinations, dematerialisation of securities, pledges of fungible securities and the myriad possibilities that financial transactions explore.

There are many examples of paternalism in the law, benevolent or other- 2–15
wise, ranging from documentary formalities designed to prevent fraud but
which become an instrument of fraud, to regulatory regimes which
unreasonably fetter a market. No doubt one could hunt down many illustrations of where the schoolmaster legislator has given way to the urge to
shackle, straitjacket, regulate, prescribe, control and, if possible, shut down
altogether, in a case which does not merit this treatment. Probably few jurisprudential concepts have given rise to more discussion than the impact of
law on liberty and when the imposition of legal constraint on individual
self-assertion is justifiable, the extent to which liberty must be pooled, the
control of individual freedom for the collective good. The role of contractual dirigism by the state, which insists on obligatory clauses and which
nullifies others, is only one very small part of this debate. Illustrations of the
wider debate concern state absolutism, the role of the criminal law in
enforcing morals, free speech, freedom to use one's property as one likes –
all the way down to such matters as how fast one may drive one's car on the
motorway.

But it is not particularly fruitful to characterise the financial law of jurisdictions on the basis of this criterion. It is true that the overall colouring of
some legal systems seems more regimented or prescriptive, or even despotic,
while others leave parties to work out their own happiness or misery as they
wish. But the feature is too vague a signpost.

Criminalisation of commercial law

Related to the commercial liberality or otherwise of a jurisdiction is its 2–16
attitude to abuse. Some jurisdictions appear better able than others to tolerate abuse in the interests of some higher objective. They do not forthwith set
out to prohibit some particular commercial transaction or some particular
financial group merely because of an atrocious scandal. They do not assume
that, because there is one rotten apple, the whole lot is rotten.

All civilised states agree broadly that the province of the criminal law is
crime not sin, that, as Grotius observed, some matters are punishable by
God not man (since otherwise all frail humanity would be oppressed by
prosecution), that there is no point in punishing wrongs which would put
most of the population in jail (e.g. for failure to pay a debt on time), that the
criminal law aims at deterrence, reform and perhaps retribution in varying
degrees, that the law should be the same for everybody, that punishment
must be proportionate to the offence, that the criminal law must be clear,
comprehensive and publicised, that it must not be retroactive, and that liability should normally depend on intent and should not be strict (as in the

case of the unfortunate Oedipus). But these are truisms, generally accepted principles of criminal policy.

2–17   When one comes to the all-important detailed implementation, jurisdictions divide on where the line should be drawn. One may discover a complete range of jurisdictional attitudes on particular issues from benign tolerance of human fallibility, accompanied by some knuckle-rapping or a reprimand, to vindictiveness and despatch of the heretic to the stake for burning. This is especially so in the field of insolvency where emotions run high. For example, the attitude of the jurisdiction affects such matters as the imposition of disqualification penalties on directors who are thought to have caused the insolvency. It may lead to inquisitorial proceedings to investigate suspected financial wrongdoing, but dispensing with proper protections for the accused. It may lead to evangelical enthusiasm in regulatory statutes and compliance with securities regulation.

Nobody objects to administrative penalties which do not carry serious criminal taint, e.g. a fine for failing to file accounts on time at the commercial registry. These are the parking offences of commercial law. Nobody dissents from the proposition that deliberate frauds, e.g. a knowing lie in a prospectus that the company has struck oil when it has not, merit the full wrath of the criminal law. Where the problems arise, however, is where the law determines that a breach is criminal when the threshold of moral conduct is too high or is impracticable (the centuries-old dispute about the degree of positive full disclosure required for commercial transactions is a case in point) or when the conduct is so remote from immoral behaviour as ordinarily understood by a reasonably sophisticated person that the slur of criminal misconduct is unjust. An example is the debate about whether it should be a serious crime for a company to guarantee a bank loan to buy its own shares or otherwise to give financial assistance to a purchaser of its own shares.

Apart from direct criminal sanctions, a rule of law may in effect have a penal consequence if it results in unreasonable nullification of the transaction or in exorbitant or treble damages. The punishment may exceed the crime. A mortgagee who loses his security because he has not complied with some technical filing requirement of little real import is in effect penalised. The difference with crime proper is that the penalty is not accompanied by criminal taint and the loss of reputation. But a penalty it remains.

Big pocket liability

2–18   Another policy question is the appropriate degree of big pocket liability, i.e. the imposition of liability on a bystander who happens to be involved in some way but who is not really responsible. Examples are lender liability, environmental liability, the liability of managers and underwriters of an issue of debt securities for mistakes in the prospectus, the liability of regulatory authorities for the failure of a firm they regulate, the liability of auditors, lawyers or other professionals and the liability of banks which transfer money when it is alleged that they should have known that wrongdoing was afoot.

Big pocket liability results from merely having a big pocket, not fault. It stems sometimes from a primitive desire to exact revenge, no matter from whom, sometimes from the expectation that somebody must pay for life's losses. There are, it is true, some situations where big pocket liability is generally considered justifiable. One example is the vicarious liability of an employer for the wrongdoings of his employee if committed in the course of his employment. Another is the responsibility of a bank for honouring a cheque with a forged signature on it, even though the bank could not realistically have detected the fraud. Nobody would trust their money to banks if the rule were otherwise. Tax liability must inevitably be graded according to wealth. Strict liability, i.e. liability without fault, is sometimes found in the law of tort – product liability, liability for inherently dangerous things on one's land, liability for a traffic accident – but these are not true instances of big pocket liability.

In any event, apart from these cases which are widely acknowledged, big pocket liability which is sought to be justified on the basis of spreading the cost or imposing the burden on those best able to bear it or as a system of social welfare is an unappealing ethical concept and has to be applied sparingly. It offends the basic principle that all are equal before the law, whether they are bad or good, rich or poor. Robin Hood has always been an attractive character, but on the other hand it is possible to view him as a mugger.

Attitudes to dispute resolution

Another broad and vague typology would classify the style of jurisdictions   2–19
according to their attitude to litigation as a means of dispute resolution.

It needs first to be recognised that in international financial contracts, there is usually little dispute about the facts and judicial enforcement is primarily a sanction for non-payment of a debt which is clearly owing. Arbitration is quite unsuitable for reasons which are given later. And judicial enforcement is rare in major financial arrangements: either the lender reschedules or insolvency proceedings are commenced. The court sanction is there primarily because a contract without sanctions is futile.

Apart from litigation springing from embargoes, exchange controls, expropriations and similar events, litigation tends to arise in relation to such matters as non-disclosure in securities transactions, responsibilities in relation to financial trading contracts, such as the sale of loans or the entry into of speculative derivatives transactions, errors in bank payments, alleged knowledge by banks of frauds of their customers, the conduct of banks in dealing with insolvent companies under the general rubric of lender liability, and the personal liability of the management of failed financial institutions.

Many commentators have pointed to differences between societies on the matter of litigation. Popular mythology has it that Japan is the least litigious of all the industrial societies in the world and this is said to be attributable to the oriental view that it is crude and boorish to cause a government court publicly to declare a person in the wrong. It is better to conciliate and to achieve a face-saving and courteous compromise where each side gives up something. This may be a traditional view, reflected in Confucianism. One wonders, however, whether these traditional attitudes have much force in the commercial arena.

2–20   The United States by contrast is highly litigious. A survey cited that 18 million new civil lawsuits were filed in the US in 1989 – one for every 10 adults. The reasons are well documented. These include: (1) the availability of juries in civil damages cases (stemming from the Seventh Amendment to the Bill of Rights) so that they are chancellors, (2) the contingent fee system whereby the lawyer takes a cut of the damages if the case is won, but otherwise nothing, (3) the rule that a losing litigant does not have to pay the other side's costs so he has nothing to lose in having a go, (4) liberal rules allowing class actions, (5) liberal long-arm jurisdiction statutes allowing actions to be brought in a home court based on minimal contacts, and (6) the enforcement of regulatory statutes by encouraging the private citizen to pursue an action by awarding him the bounty of treble damages so that the citizen becomes a policeman, a public watchman, the attorney-general himself. This is accompanied by a freedom to make extravagant allegations of fraud in court pleadings which are reported in the press so that the victim is publicly vilified before the case comes to court. It is accompanied by expansive rights of discovery which some allege are necessary to prevent judicial ambush but which others say are intrusive and can amount to a mere fishing expedition.

> In one case in 1993, where the defendant corporation acted in shockingly bad faith, a jury in West Virginia recorded their disapproval by an award of damages of $10 million when the actual damages suffered were $19,000. This was 527 times the actual loss. The Supreme Court declined to interfere. In a 1994 case in New Mexico, an 81-year-old lady burnt herself when removing the cap from a cup of hot coffee (bought from the fast-food chain McDonald's) which she held between her legs while driving. The jury awarded damages of $2·9 million. This was 290 times the medical expenses. A juror is reported to have said that the jury was delivering a message to the fast food industry: "The

coffee's too hot out there." Lest it be thought that these are just silly cases from the backwoods, a Texan jury in the 1980s awarded damages of $7.53 billion against Texaco Inc in favour of another oil company Pennzoil for alleged tortious interference in a contract and added punitive damages of $3 billion for good measure.

The concept of the little ordinary citizen being able to bring the big face-less far-off corporation to book in his own courthouse, before his own townsman on the jury, and not to have to pay if he loses, has an enormous emotional hold which is not easy to change. Many US commentators argue that the effect of this unique combination of plaintiff-protection policies is a fear of the depredations of the law, an atmosphere of legal insecurity, the criminalisation of commercial law, unpredictability, illiberality and big pocket liability and that the harassment effect of litigation and the uncertainty of the outcome leads to cash settlements when the attack had little intrinsic merit. Those of the opposing view advance various propositions to the effect that on balance the policies serve other more compelling interests, particularly in relation to personal injury claims and helping those who otherwise would not have access to a legal remedy. 2–21

Regardless of which side one thinks has the most merit, it is clear that, even on matters like administrative judicial procedures, choices have to be made which can have a very considerable – and unexpected – impact on justice.

Hard and soft law

An interesting cultural factor is the attitude to hard and soft law. Hard law is black-letter law which lays down precise, prescriptive and mandatory rules. An example of soft law is that administered by regulatory authorities and others by way of guideline, official or club pressure and administrative indications which do not have legal force. However they do have a compelling force if the society concerned is disposed to abide by them or if the guidance emanates from an authority which has the sanction of revocation of a licence or other unpleasant consequences. Soft law may be a legal vacuum which is filled only by unwritten rules, conventions, traditional mores, expected standards, but no external compulsion. The participants may choose to comply by reason of a culture of sociability, mutual forbearance, a recognition that the individual advantage requires common restraint, and a desire not to incur the disapproval of one's peers – a form of social contract, without legal sanctions imposed by judicial authorities. 2–22

For example, it is said that in Japan the grey law of ministerial guidance is much more important than what the statutes actually say, while in the United States bank regulation is typically black-letter law. The exclusion of commercial banks from insurance business is achieved in the United States by black-letter statute and in Britain by the express disapproval of the Bank of England which has no legal force but which commercial banks abide by. A classic and much quoted example is the UK Panel on Take-overs and Mergers whose rules are not legally binding but which the market adheres to on pain of expulsion from the club: the rules are to be intepreted according to the spirit, not the letter. The London Approach, published by the Bank of England as a banking code of conduct for the rescue of troubled business, is another example. Soft law of this type is particularly noticeable in Germany which until recently did not have any securities regulation in the normal sense. German banks nevertheless policed the market with admirable efficiency and good sense. The self-regulation of markets, of trades, callings and professions are other cases in point.

It would certainly be an intriguing line of enquiry to ascertain the extent to which commercial societies do govern themselves by soft law and why. Relevant policies include, on the one hand, the need for flexibility, the degree of responsibility and integrity of participants, the number of firms in the regulated sector, the expense of state involvement, and a desire not to overdo the avalanche of prescriptive law. On the other side, there would be the desire to ensure that the law is clear to all and that the authorities do not assume arbitrary autocratic controls. It is difficult to generalise. For our purposes one may only note the distinction, while recognising that its utility as a test of comparative differences is limited.

Insolvency law as an indicator

2–23 All of the above criteria have some interest, but most of them are either too subjective or too narrow or too susceptible to prejudice or unquantifiable or for some other reason unsatisfactory. Their main objection is that they do not go to the real substance of the law.

However there is a general test which does appear to have some usefulness in our context and which also appears to be reasonably accurate in providing a functional grouping of the families of law in the world so far as financial and commercial law is concerned. This is the attitude to insolvency.

The reason that insolvency law is an indicator is that on insolvency the law has to make a particularly hard choice between one side or the other. There is not enough money to go round and there is no possibility of avoiding the choice.

It is usually the case that the law has to decide the winner and the loser, the victor and the victim. This is why the law is ultimately so ruthless. It is particularly ruthless on insolvency because of the profound effect that insolvency has upon people's lives, upon business dealings and upon the economy of the state itself. Unquestionably bankruptcy is fundamental to commercial and financial law and numerous major doctrines in commercial law which really matter (beyond the most basic and primitive rules of contract) are in some way or another traceable back to what happens on insolvency.

Insolvency law is, for example, one of the foundations of when title   2–24
passes in a contract of sale, and it is the foundation of security and guarantees. There is no point in allowing retention of title if it fails on insolvency because the whole object of retention of title is that it should succeed on insolvency. There is no point in having a law of pledge if the pledge is set aside on the bankruptcy of the debtor since the only reason for taking the pledge is to protect the creditor against that bankruptcy. There is no point in having ease of set-off between parties if it does not function on insolvency because that is precisely when one party wishes to be protected against the default of the other. The efficacy of corporate law is much reduced if it is ineffective to protect the owners or managers when the corporation becomes insolvent – one of the basic objectives of corporate law is not merely to achieve administrative or mechanistic convenience but to protect those who capitalise and manage the enterprise against the failure of the venture. The strength of a law of unjust enrichment or recovery of wrongful takings is weakened if it does not operate to give a proprietary recovery on insolvency since that is usually when it is really needed.

A subsequent work in this series sets out a scale of jurisdictions according   2–25
to whether they are pro-debtor or pro-creditor in their legal rules. A pro-creditor jurisdiction seeks to help a creditor to escape the debacle, e.g. by recognising a wide security or a set-off, while a pro-debtor jurisdiction seeks to aggrandise the debtor's estate, e.g. by restricting security, refusing insolvency set-off, setting aside title finance, such as hire purchase (so that the leased asset is treated as belonging to the lessee on his bankruptcy), by refusing divided ownership and the trust (so that trust assets go to the trustee's creditors), by clawing back all payments and transfers by the insolvent member in long suspect periods with a minimum of defences available to creditors (so that transactions are unsafe and the formal insolvency is retroactive), by promoting corporate rehabilitation procedures (thereby making the consensual rescue more difficult), and by allowing the insolvent estate to insist on the performance of profitable contracts by the counter-party but allowing it to repudiate the unprofitable contracts ("cherry-picking"). These labels are of course very simplistic and the scaling itself is unreliable and subjective – it is not possible to be scientifically accurate.
Suffice it to say here that the scaling overrides the civil code/common law

classification and certainly overrides any classification based upon whether a state is developed or undeveloped. It is surprising to note that, on the basis of the criteria used, most traditional English jurisdictions are on the extreme pro-creditor end of the scale (although Australia, England and Ireland are not as extreme) and that France is on the extreme pro-debtor end, even though England and France are both neighbouring industrialised countries sharing a common outlook. The United States and Canada fall about the middle of the scale, while Germanic and Scandinavian countries appear more pro-creditor and Franco-Latin countries more pro-debtor. Japan and Korea tend to the pro-creditor end of the scale.

2–26   The scaling is based upon a variety of criteria, notably the scope and efficiency on bankruptcy of security and of title finance, such as retention of title and financial leasing; the availability of insolvency set-off; the aggressiveness of corporate rehabilitation statutes; the recognition of the trust and the ownership of assets in the possession of the debtor as opposed to reputed ownership; the armoury of the veil of incorporation; the attitude to preferential transfers; and the attitude to contract and lease rescission on insolvency. All of these topics are analysed on a comparative basis in subsequent volumes in this series of works on financial law.

The criteria are based on legal rules, not on current cultural attitudes. Thus, it is not necessarily true to say that one culture is populist pro-debtor *in practice* while another is mercantilist pro-creditor. But it is true that the legal rules of jurisdictions do show diversity so that there is often a gap between culture and law. If the gap is too great, people lose confidence in their legal system.

Something may be said about some of these criteria here, but first it is worth alluding to a doctrine which seems to have acquired an imperial sway in the jurisdictions of the world of extraordinary potency. This is the doctrine of false wealth.

False wealth

2–27   False wealth is the principle that a debtor's apparent assets are treated as his real assets so that creditors are not induced into giving false credit. Therefore if a debtor actually possesses securities belonging to another or is the legal and registered holder of land which belongs to another, then he is treated as the beneficial owner on his insolvency and the securities and the land go to his creditors unless it was quite clear to the creditors that he did not have beneficial ownership. In other words, the real owner is expropriated, because he was a secret owner.

This curious doctrine, sometimes known as reputed ownership, invades entire legal systems like the roots of a plant spreading its spores everywhere through the soil. For example, it leads to the non-acceptance of the trust (or divided ownership) in all of the civil code systems, subject only to limited exceptions. Hence if a custodian or nominee holder of securities becomes insolvent without having marked the negotiable securities and packaged them separately or without having registered the real owner in the register kept by the issuer of these securities, then those securities, which may belong to pension funds or insurance companies, go to pay the creditors of the custodian. Vast numbers of securities are in fact deposited with custodians.

If the owner of a debt assigns it to a third party, then in a great many   2–28
countries – mainly but not wholly in the Franco-Latin group – the assignment is ineffective on the seller's insolvency if he has not given notice to the debtor because he has not been dispossessed of the debt. This is so even though it is not plausible that creditors are induced into giving false credit by apparent ownership. A large part of the assets of modern corporations are in fact held in the form of invisible property and creditors cannot possibly tell whether or not notice of assignment has been given to the corporation's creditors or whether corporations have or have not registered their investments in their own name. In jurisdictions which adopt this rule, the factoring of trade receivables is permitted only under very restrictive conditions and securitisations are impossible without a special statute.

The doctrine results in an insistence upon possessory pledges, especially in relation to chattels, securities and receivables. Unless the creditor actually takes possession of the chattel – which is impracticable in most cases – or is registered as the holder of the security, then he does not have sufficient possession to destroy reputed ownership and loses his security on the debtor's insolvency.

The adoption of false wealth results in the inability of parties to recover   2–29
mistaken payments or delinquent takings on the insolvency of the recipient. If a director misappropriates money of the company and puts it in his bank account, then in a false wealth country, on the director's bankruptcy, the money goes to pay the director's creditors even though it is clearly the company's money and there is no reason why the miscreant's creditors should get this windfall. This trust – quaintly called the "constructive trust" in common law countries – is rarely adopted by civil countries, which shows how powerful the false wealth ideology is. Common law countries incline to the view that it is a matter of anguish if a person's property is wrongfully taken from him; it is a matter of double anguish if the property is still obviously in the miscreant's bankrupt estate but the law will not return it; it is a matter of triple anguish if the property is used to pay someone else. The contrary view is that the victim is not entitled to special protection disturbing the equality principle.

The doctrine finds an expression in notions of abusive credit whereby a bank which continues to provide credit to an impecunious debtor may be liable to other creditors for giving an appearance of wealth.

Although the doctrine is primarily a continuing feature of the Germanic and Franco-Latin systems, it lives on in elaborate public filing requirements for security over moveables and intangibles so favoured by the common law systems.

One could go on citing examples which go to the heart of financial law.

2–30　　The objection to secret ownership by third parties probably also derived its power from another source which was not primarily insolvency-related. This was that the fear that the presence of secret ownership might destabilise transactions, especially commercial transactions, by giving rise to unpredictable priority disputes. How could a buyer or mortgagee be sure of getting good title or a safe mortgage if some third party might suddenly appear and claim the property as his and upset the sale or mortgage? The common law answer to this, which is not a complete answer by any means, is to protect purchasers, mortgagees and the like from the true owner if they gave value, acted in good faith and had no notice of the true owner. There is no doubt that the presence of these potential secret owners makes the common law much more complicated as regards priorities and it is this feature more than any other which makes the common law in its commercial aspects so much more labyrinthine – not, as is often thought, the absence of basic codification.

There were no doubt other reasons for the false wealth doctrine. Unquestionably it was endorsed by the tax authorities to prevent evasion (also unsuccessfully attempted by the English in their Statute of Uses 1535) and may also have been supported by the fear of fraud, particularly the secreting of assets to evade creditors.

2–31　　It became dressed up in all sorts of other justifications – transparency, truth, absolute enjoyment of an asset, the abolition of deception, the abolition of feudalism, the protection of the individual, the protection of capital and commerce, the protection of liberty, to have and to hold.

It is extraordinary how apparently technical rules of law can become politicised as grand themes of public order and fundamental morality. It is now impossible to disentangle the motives which fed false wealth. They supported each other and became inextricably entwined. One can no longer distinguish the original rule from its chameleon rationalisations, one can hardly find the humble little idea crushed beneath this huge superstructure of idealism and concept.

Honest minds may legitimately differ about the pros and cons of false wealth in its application to a particular question and about whether it should stay or be replaced by some improved transparency rule or be discarded altogether.

As shown, there are innumerable applications and each would have to be examined individually and objectively. In any event the degree to which a jurisdiction has abandoned this single doctrine or firmly adheres to it is a fertile indicator of where that jurisdiction now stands in this area of law.

Doctrine of specificity

The false wealth principle is closely related to the doctrine of specificity. 2–32 This holds that, in order to transfer an asset, the asset must be in existence and must be specifically identified. If this particularisation is insisted upon, transfers and pledges of future property are impossible, substitutions of collateral (such as revolving portfolios of investment securities) are difficult, and it is not possible to transfer or pledge part of a fungible mass. The rule is fatal to floating charges over all present and future property and inconvenient for the transfer of dematerialised securities and for custodianship. In light of the importance and volume of large value transfers and pledges of invisible property, the presence of the doctrine in its extreme form is a major hindrance. One cannot possibly transfer or pledge each piece by number of its certificate or produce itemised lists of commercial receivables or nuts and bolts. The doctrine has been largely abandoned by the common law jurisdictions, except in isolated or well-established pockets (such as the sale of goods) which can be avoided by the trust. It has been legislated away in a number of civilian countries in relation to securities kept by central depositories.

One reason that specificity flows from false wealth is that publicity requires identification and segregation. This cannot be achieved unless the asset is individualised. Hence the accent on individuation, notably in the Franco-Latin systems.

The origin of the doctrine of specificity may perhaps have been nothing more sophisticated than the mortal predilection for things which one can see and feel – a natural inclination which subsequently becomes devotionalised into some abstract dogma, a tendency which is not unusual in the law.

Litmus tests

With this background in mind one may briefly explore some litmus tests of 2–33 jurisdictional attitudes which are particularly critical in this field, in that they tend to be indicative of the overall approach of a jurisdiction. Their usefulness is that the questions which elicit the answers are short and simple and that the results are quite accurate about the general legal orientation. It is, after all, convenient to know if a legal system is acidic or alkaline or neutral – pink or blue or white – even if one must nevertheless at some point examine the chemical composition in greater detail. Some of the tests are:

- the attitude to security;
- insolvency set-off;
- the trust;
- assignments of debts.

It will be seen that in all of them false wealth plays a role, sometimes submerged, sometimes dominant. One can leave other important tests, such as the veil of incorporation or the attitude to corporate rehabilitation statutes, for analysis in subsequent books in this series.

Security

2–34   Security is employed in every conceivable context in international finance – universal security to secure finance for a project, security over goods to finance trade, margin collateral to secure dealings on futures and options exchanges, security over investments to support bank finance for the transfer of investments in clearing-houses for investment securities, mortgages of ships and aircraft to finance the purchase money, even the humble lien, which everybody recognises, to protect the supplier who has not been paid – the vendor, the repairer, the warehouseman, the custodian, the crew, the airport.

The rationale of security is to protect the creditor against the insolvency of the debtor. The proponents of security put forward other rationales – for example, that security is desirable to mitigate the risk of cascade or domino insolvencies, to encourage capital to finance ventures, to facilitate a debt restructuring if a project gets into difficulties and to reduce the cost of credit. They maintain that the ethical basis is that he who pays for the asset should have the right to the asset and that the conditional security right is a fair exchange for the credit. They say that the desire to protect the impecunious and unsophisticated debtor from himself and from the money lender is at odds with the realities of modern wholesale finance provided by responsible institutions and that the small debtor is adequately covered by consumer protection laws.

The opposing polices are that security violates the equality principle on bankruptcy and defeats small creditors. Those subscribing to this view maintain that we should be aiming at more creditor equality, not a complex ladder of priorities.

When one surveys the international reception of security, one is staggered   2–35
by the disparities. There is not the remotest consensus. One group of states allows a universal monopolistic security over all the assets of the debtor, allows it to reach future assets, including assets coming into existence after the bankruptcy of the debtor, imposes no ceremonial formalities to warn the debtor, holds the debtor to any agreement that he may not prepay and hence shake off the security, imposes no limits on who may take the security, permits the security to cover all future debt without stating a maximum amount, allows the secured creditor to sell the collateral without court intervention, and permits the secured creditor privately to appoint a possessory manager to run the business without selling and on terms that the creditor is not responsible for the conduct of the manager. This group comprises about 80 English-based states and is joined, with qualifications, by the United States, Sweden, Finland and Russia, amongst others.

The English argument has been that this pro-creditor system in fact also protects debtors because a well-secured bank is likely to stay with the situation longer, because the business can be sold as a whole without the devastation of value caused by piecemeal sale, and because possessory management on a default via a receiver enables the business to be continued pending sale so that, again, its value is not lost by an abrupt stoppage while the secured creditor goes through a time-consuming and expensive public auction procedure. They aver that enforcement is in any event a last resort and that banks in practice are disinclined to pounce unless all is lost, so that judicial protectionism of corporate debtors is not necessary.

Yet another group of states rejects this approach. They allow security   2–36
over land, as practically everybody does, but make it difficult to take security over goods, receivables, contracts and investments. They do so either by prohibiting the security altogether or else by imposing onerous initial formalities, levying unrealistic documentary taxes, excluding security for future debt or revolving credits, insisting on a maximum amount, downgrading the security below priority creditors (taxes, bankruptcy costs, employees) so that one never knows what it is worth, and by placing obstacles in the way of enforcement, such as the cumbersome and expensive judicial public auction, compulsory grace periods and freezes on enforcement. These countries include the more traditional members of the Franco-Latin group (subject to wide exceptions). Countries like Austria do not appear to favour a wide grant of security.

The international position is reviewed in another volume in this series, with some comment on the policy implications of the various approaches.

However, whatever side one cleaves to as the most consonant with convenience and fairness, it is evident that mutual international agreement on policy is nowhere to be seen.

Insolvency set-off

2–37   A second litmus test is insolvency set-off. Insolvency set-off allows a creditor who is owed a debt by an insolvent which has not yet matured to set it off against a debt which he owes to the insolvent which also has not yet matured. If the creditor can set off, it is plain that the creditor escapes the insolvency and is paid in full to the extent of the set-off. If he cannot, then the creditor must pay in what he owes and merely prove on the debt owed to him on which he will receive some tiny dividend, if anything at all.

The view espoused by most of the Franco-Latin jurisdictions is that insolvency set-off is a violation of the pari passu principle and that the set-off is like an unpublished security interest causing assets to disappear on bankruptcy and depleting the debtor's estate. In particular it depletes the debtor's estate without creditors knowing it is there. Hence it offends false wealth.

But the common law, Germanic and Scandinavian countries take a different view. They say that it is unjust that a defaulter should insist on payment but not pay himself. They say that insolvency set-off helps creditors escape the debacle and hence mitigates the knock-on or cascade effect of bankruptcy and that set-off reduces exposures and hence the cost of credit. They hold that set-off prevents the debtor from being bankrupted on a debt he does not owe if the overall position is taken into account. This group is joined by China, Korea, Japan, Panama and Thailand.

2–38   The remedy is not without economic significance. For example, the exposures in financial markets can be substantially reduced by the availability of set-off so that the reduction in risk is significantly mitigated.

Although these are generalisations which are subject to exceptions, a country which does not have insolvency set-off is also usually hostile to security and makes it difficult to take non-land security if it can be taken at all, has expansive attitudes to the preferential reach of preferential transfers made in the suspect period, has a low opinion of the veil of incorporation as a protection against insolvency, disapproves of attempts by suppliers to protect themselves against insolvency by retention of title and the like and requires that assignment of debts be notified to the debtor if those assignments are to be effective on the insolvency of the seller. The test is therefore quite useful in terms of litmus paper.

Again, ideas of fairness, economic advantage and ideology are intertwined. And again, one finds no convergence which enables one to say that a particular policy is adhered to by the overwhelming majority of states.

Recognition of the trust

The trust finds its way into many departments of financial law and is prob- 2–39
ably the source of more mystification than any other legal institution.

The essence of the trust is that ownership is divided between the nominal, representative, legal or titular holder of the asset – the trustee – and
the real beneficial owner. If the trustee becomes insolvent, then the beneficial owner can claim the property ahead of the creditors of the insolvent
trustee and is not expropriated. The essence of the trust is its validity on
the bankruptcy of the trustee – a trust invalid on bankruptcy is pointless
and dangerous.

There is nothing conceptually strange about the idea of split ownership.
A warehouse which holds furniture for depositors is a trustee in this sense,
although everyone, including the common law states, flinch from applying
the trust language and prefer instead something safe, like "bailment".
Hence, the idea itself is quite routine. The real question is whether this secret
ownership ought to be publicised.

Examples of the use of the trust in international finance are: 2–40

– trustees of bonds for the benefit of bondholders;

– syndicate agents which hold the security for the benefit of the syndicate
banks;

– collective investment schemes, such as investment funds and unit trusts;

– trusts of specific securities or of fungible securities held by custodians
for the collective benefit of depositors of those securities in clearing-
houses, e.g. Euroclear, Cedel, the US Depository Trust Corporation and
many others; the amounts involved are stupendous;

– subordination trusts of the proceeds of the junior debt and trusts of the
proceeds of letters of credit;

– third party beneficiary contracts, e.g. exculpation clauses in syndicate
loan agreements protecting employees of the agent bank;

– trusts of the benefit of contracts held by market agents for outside
clients as principal, protecting the principal if the agent should become
insolvent;

– securitisations and equipment trusts in asset-based finance.

The trust was rejected by the civilian countries on account mainly of false
wealth plus an assembly of other rationalisations, despite the fact that it was
an institution developed by the classical Romans and was much in evidence
in Europe prior to Napoleon's time, e.g. in family law (the usufruct of the
husband or the parent). The Napoleonic rejection seems to have been

motivated partly by a desire to simplify property, to grant the citizen the absolute right of enjoyment and disposition of property freed from feudal burdens, and to promote capitalism. When the German jurists settled the BGB, the view which predominated was that *in rem* proprietary rights must be registered publicly and that there could be no proprietary *in rem* right effective on insolvency without this publicity. This was against the spirited advice of the Germanist professor at Berlin, Otto von Gierke (1841–1921) who described it as a "horrible legal blunder".

2–41   But it is not true to say that civil countries do not have the trust at all and that it is purely a common law institution. Of course a different word is used in civilian countries – in rem remedy or vindication or revindication or fiduciary ownership. Firstly, a number of civilian countries have directly absorbed the Anglo-American trust, either by statute or case law – usually by statute. Examples are South Africa, Japan, Liechtenstein and Panama. Secondly, many civilian countries have installed the trust where it was felt to be useful. Examples are: (1) the holding in trust of fungible investment securities by central depositories in Austria, Germany and the Netherlands; (2) an exemption in favour of banks allowing them to act as custodian trustees in some Latin American countries; (3) the acceptance of fiduciary ownership in the Chilean Civil Code drafted by the Venezuelan Andrés Bello and subsequently adopted by Ecuador (1860), Colombia (1873) and a number of central American states; (4) the trust by a bankrupt agent of his claim for the sale price against the third party buyer for the benefit of his principal (most countries have this); (5) various other direct actions; and (6) the French third party beneficiary contract, the *stipulation pour autrui*.

Interesting examples of the acceptance of the trust by Napoleonic countries include the adoption of the trust by Quebec in 1879 to sanction gifts for McGill University and the Fraser Institute in Montreal, its adoption by Louisiana in 1882 to allow Paul Tulane's gifts to Tulane University (followed by bank trusteeship in 1902, bondholder trustees in 1914 and trusts of land in 1938), and the remarkable French case of *De Renesse v Robineau*, D 1928, 2, 121 where the court validated a legacy for the creation of a foundation to provide for the poor widows and orphans of the Banque de France and, in case of a shortage in this class of beneficiaries, to the poor orphans and widows of the Credit Lyonnais: see Vera Bolgár, "Why No Trusts in the Civil Law?" 2 *American Journal of Comparative Law* 204 (1953).

2–42   Nevertheless, these are all exceptions to the general rule, enacted to meet special situations and limited to the scope of the statutory dispensation. Thus the statutory *Sammelverwahrung* (collective ownership) is restricted to certain classes of securities (not all securities) under the *Depotgesetz* (Custody Act) in Austria and Germany. Almost uniformly in the civil countries, for example, a syndicate agent cannot hold the security as trustee for the banks with the result that it is not possible to novate bank debt on a change of participants without discharging the security.

In any event, it seems to be true that, outside the common law states, the constructive trust and tracing, e.g. of moneys wrongfully taken away from the real owner or of mistaken payments, is uniformly rejected so that this is an important test of a legal system's orientation.

Notification of assignments of debts

Another test is whether a sale of a debt is effective on the bankruptcy of the seller if the sale is not notified to the debtor. This is different from whether the notice is desirable for priority against competing assignees, for directing the debtor to pay the assignee and the like. The test is relevant because of the economic importance of ease of transfers of claims, either by sale or by security assignment. A rule which requires notification to the debtor is based on false wealth – the seller is not dispossessed, even though other creditors cannot possibly know whether their debtor's debtors have been notified and how. The rule is also influenced by other policies, notably a desire to protect debtors from a change of creditors, a desire for certainty, a wish to control trafficking in lawsuits, a wish to prevent the impecunious from assigning away their income – a medley of diffuse resentments against dealings in intangible property. 2–43

This criterion is useful as a refinement because many countries which do not recognise secret beneficial ownership, e.g. the trust, do facilitate sales of debts in the interests of commerce. The common law countries allow debts to be sold over the telephone and without notification and are joined by the Germanic group. But Japan and Korea remain outside this group: notification to the debtor or other formality is required for validity. Most of the Franco-Latin group require notification although there has been some erosion of this, notably the Dailly Act of 1981 in France and the abolition of the rule in Belgium in 1994. 2–44

But as so often happens when a state is unwilling to surrender an age-old policy, the carve-outs in the refusing states tend initially to be grudging and hedged about with limits. This was evidenced by the tight rules allowing negotiability in the Geneva Conventions of 1930–31 on negotiable instruments, a formalism which led to the rejection of the Conventions by common law states. There are many other examples tending to show how difficult it is to change a legal policy which has become entrenched and how the initial breach in the wall is often a discriminatory statute in favour of some institutions, but not the entire citizeny, or a statute restricted by qualifications – giving an inch, but not a mile.

CHAPTER 3

SUMMARY OF GROUPS OF JURISDICTIONS

Classification in summary

3–1   One may attempt a broad classification of financial law of jurisdictions into families of the law on the basis of the tests discussed in the previous chapter and on the basis of other criteria which are noted in more detail in the summary categorisations in subsequent chapters.

    This grouping is not a grading between good and bad. There are no moral implications whatsoever: the classification is neutral on ethics. The differences do not arise out of moral differences between peoples. Further, the current legal culture of a jurisdiction can be, and often is, quite different from the bare legal rules. Nor is the classification a guide as to which states have a stable legal and judicial system with high standards and those which do not. Efficient commercial law systems are very expensive to run and many countries are more preoccupied with survival than legal refinement. Some legal systems in a group are stagnant, while others in that group are on the move.

    The classification is tentative. It has not been possible to check the position on all issues in all states and the research required to do so would be stupendous. Hence, some jurisdictions may be wrongly categorised.

3–2   Subject to these qualifications, the suggested classification is as follows:

GROUP	CLASS	JURISDICTIONS	POPULATION MILLIONS	
Group 1A	Traditional English	146*	1797 m	(33.4%)
Group 1B	American common law			
Group 2	Mixed Roman/common law	15	243 m	(4.5%)
Group 3	Germanic and Scandinavian	13	360 m	(6.7%)
Group 4	Mixed Franco-Latin/Germanic	13	279 m	(5.2%)
Group 5	Traditional Franco-Latin	76	982 m	(18.3%)
Group 6	Emerging jurisdictions	18	1488 m	(27.7%)
Group 7	Islamic jurisdictions	14	108 m	(2%)
Group 8	Unallocated jurisdictions	13	116 m	(2.2%)
	Totals	308	5373 m	(100%)

* About 79, if Australia and common law Canada and US are each treated as one.

It is worth remarking that this financial classification, based on criteria relevant to international finance, is more or less consistent with the general classifications developed by the leading comparative lawyers. The main group which is not now mentioned is socialist law: this represented an attempt to localise commercial law somewhere between the Dark Ages and feudalism and had little to offer the civilised jurist. It is now defunct.

It would be possible to sub-divide the groups by applying more detailed criteria, or, more usefully, to produce several classifications by reference to different criteria on the lines of the classifications elsewhere in this series of works.

Group 1: Traditional English and American common law

Group 1 countries comprise Group 1A and Group 1B jurisdictions. Group   3—3
1A countries are the English-influenced group, including England itself, Australia, Canada (except Quebec), India, New Zealand, Hong Kong, Malaysia, Singapore and a great many other territories, some of them small island states – about 84 jurisdictions in all. Their main characteristics include (amongst others) an exceptionally wide grant of security, acceptance of the "form over substance" test for title finance so that it is not recharacterised as security, mandatory insolvency set-off, mild corporate insolvency rehabilitations if there are any at all (subject to exceptions, notably in Canada and New Zealand), rejection of false wealth in all its branches (except publication of security in a public register), a reasonably firm veil of incorporation, dislike of retroactive insolvencies requiring a disgorge of preferential transfers (but with Australia taking a different view), and liberal conflicts of law rules, both as to contracts and insolvency.

The United States of America and its related states and territories – about   3—4
62 jurisdictions in all – are classified in Group 1B because of significant differences in emphasis from Group 1A. This group is comprised mainly of the US common law states – which is all the states, except Louisiana – plus a few affiliated island territories, plus, surprisingly, Liberia. Liberia is the oldest African independent state, where the US dollar is legal tender and whose importance springs from its having the largest shipping register in the world, based on US maritime law and administered from New York. The building at 80 Broad Street, Monrovia, is the traditional registered office for one-ship companies, and may well be one of the most densely populated residences for non-people in the world.

The US group shares both similarities and differences with the traditional English group. The main substantive similarities are the enthusiastic adoption of the trust, and in particular the constructive trust, and a broadly pro-creditor attitude, evidenced, e.g. by the availability of universal security and insolvency set-off. But the US retreats from this resolute stance in a number of respects. False wealth has surfaced in an exceptionally wide publicity system for security in Art 9 of the Uniform Commercial Code and in the recharacterisation of title finance . The corporate rehabilitation proceeding in BC 1978 Chapter 11 is pro-debtor by international standards, though surpassed by France and Italy, and perhaps reflects an egalitarian pro-debtor view which is deeply rooted in American history and which was crystallised in the 1978 bankruptcy legislation by the consumerism of the 1970s. The preference rules are amongst the toughest in the world. Contract and lease rescissions under *ipso facto* clauses are curtailed on bankruptcy. But the underlying pro-creditor view is evidenced by the fact that directors are not caught by wrongful trading rules, and successful liability attacks on directors for insolvency do not seem excessive, comparatively speaking, for such a large country. However the doctrine of equitable subordination is not generally found in English-based countries.

3–5   The intense resentment or fear of fraud appears to influence American law and practice in a more pronounced manner than in traditional English jurisdictions. This is evidenced by tough black-letter securities and banking regulation, by a fraud statute directed at racketeering but widely used in ordinary civil actions, by the retention of the need for writing for contracts in the form of the old Statute of Frauds, stemming from the English Act of 1677 and now largely abandoned in traditional English jurisdictions, perhaps by the emphasis on formal transactional legal opinions, by the pre-occupation with priorities in the filing system for security interests over personal property in Art 9 of the UCC (by reason of a fear that the debtor will use the same property to raise money twice), and by a greater incidence of treble or punitive damages in civil claims.

It is important to remember that the US is an extremely large jurisdiction – the third most populated country in the world with a highly industrialised economy – and that there are bound to be much internal diversity and conflicting pressures in financial law. Although it is not a homogenous jurisdiction with a single legal culture in the sense that England and Japan have a single legal culture, it is notable how much homogeneity and harmony has in fact been achieved, especially if one compares the US legal system to those of that other great industrial bloc, the European Union.

This American homogeneity was no doubt assisted by the common reception of English common law and by a common language. The problems associated with achieving a similar homogeneity in Europe, or indeed the rest of the world, is evidenced by the legal separateness of Louisiana in the US and Quebec in Canada: both are French-based jurisdictions which have tended to maintain their traditions in areas where federal law does not compel uniformity.

Group 2: Mixed Roman/common law

These jurisdictions do not have much in common, except a perceptible 3-6
departure from the mainstream Germanic or Roman view in the general
direction of Group 1 – the common law group.
  The group has about 15 members and comprises mainly:

- Japan and Korea
- The Southern African group, e.g. South Africa, Botswana, Zimbabwe
- The Channel Islands group, e.g. Jersey
- Scotland, Quebec and Sri Lanka
- The ingenious principality of Liechtenstein

Group 3: Germanic and Scandinavian

This group comprises mainly the Germanic and Scandinavian group num- 3-7
bering about 13 jurisdictions, including the following:

- Germany
- Netherlands and its related states (e.g. Aruba and Indonesia)
- Poland
- Finland, Norway and Sweden
- Switzerland
- Taiwan

  Some of the chief characteristics include a move towards universal security taking them 50 to 75 per cent of the way, enthusiasm for title finance
without recharacterisation, insolvency set-off, general lack of sympathy for
tough corporate rehabilitation proceedings, a dislike of noisy regulatory
statutes and a preference for soft law. It is possible that numerous members
of emerging jurisdictions in Group 6 might join this group and that the
underlying legal approach is much more widespread than the number of jurisdictions might suggest. Japan and Korea are only just out of this group and
arguably still within it.

Group 4: Mixed Franco-Latin/Germanic

This group comprises about thirteen jurisdictions which straddle the classic 3-8
Franco-Latin group and the more mercantilist Germanic or common law
group. The chief members include:

- Austria
- Czech and Slovak Republics

- Denmark
- Hungary
- Italy
- Thailand
- Turkey

The group might be joined in due course by former members of Yugoslavia – for the moment placed in the emerging jurisdictions in Group 6.

Group 5: Traditional Franco-Latin

3–9　These are the Franco-Latin group and comprise about 76 jurisdictions, including the following:

- Belgium
- Egypt
- France
- Greece
- Luxembourg
- Portugal
- Spain
- Most Latin American countries
- Most former French, Belgian and Portuguese possessions in Africa, the Caribbean and Indochina.

Although there are numerous exceptions, the main characteristics include a traditional adhesion to the false wealth doctrine and to the doctrine of specificity, a hostility to security, a patchy acceptance of title finance without recharacterisation, no insolvency set-off, a historical objection to the free marketability of claims, perhaps a greater suspicion of the veil of incorporation (although this may be historical and on the way out in most members of this group), and an expansive notion of the retroactive effect of preferential transfers.

This group probably includes French-orientated jurisdictions like Kuwait and the United Arab Emirates which are for the moment located in the Islamic jurisdictions in Group 7 and whose codes are based on Egyptian models which in turn came from France.

Group 6: Emerging jurisdictions

3–10　These are emerging jurisdictions – about 18 of them – which are rapidly modernising their laws and which may join any of the above groups. It remains to be seen.

They include:

- China
- Russia
- Vietnam
- the former Yugoslav states
- the three Baltic republics
- some of the Eastern European members of the former USSR

The fact that this group includes China and Russia shows how fundamentally important the choices are for the future of commercial law in the world.

Group 7: Islamic jurisdictions

These are Islamic jurisdictions which have not historically had a commercial   3–11
culture, largely by reason of Shariah objections to interest, indemnities and
insurance. Some have developed a distinction between the law applicable to
private individuals and commercial law, reminiscent of the old European
distinction between private canonical law and the law merchant. Hence
commercial law is in some of these jurisdictions in the spirit of one or other
of the main industrialised states, usually France by reason of the supremacy
of Egyptian law and lawyers in the region (Egyptian law is French-based).
As noted, this is particularly true of Kuwait and the United Arab Emirates,
but Qatar seems undecided.

There are about 14 of these jurisdictions, including:

- most western Arabian Gulf states
- Afghanistan
- Asian members of the former USSR, e.g. Kazakhstan, Tajikistan and Uzbekistan.

Group 8: Unallocated

Finally there is a small group of 13 jurisdictions which are not allocated.   3–12
They are:

- Antarctica jurisdictions
- Bhutan
- Cambodia
- Eritrea
- Ethiopia
- Korea (North)

- Laos
- Maldives
- Nepal
- San Marino
- Somalia
- Vatican City
- Western Sahara

CHAPTER 4

DEVELOPMENT OF LEGAL SYSTEMS

Timing of codification

A question of extraordinary fascination is how it is that legal systems which   4–1
share a common cultural tradition and heritage should diverge so utterly on
questions which affect how their citizens transact business. For example,
France and England are at opposite poles on many legal doctrinal issues in
financial law, although at various times in their history each owned the
other and, even though they may themselves vehemently deny it, they enjoy
a mutual civilisation and a common attitude to life, regardless of the diversity of their legal systems.

The reason for the international divergence is probably nothing to do
with grand cultural movements or anything more complicated than acci-
dents of history. One must not of course discount *Volksgeist* or economic
development or cultural conventions or the forceful role of thinkers. But
timing is very important.

Legal cultures change very slowly. It has been said that with one stroke of
the legislator's pen, whole libraries have to be pulped. That is not true of the
substance of the law. The underlying legal bias changes only over centuries.
Only bus-timetable law is ephemeral and volatile – fiscal law and securities
regulation and similar ephemera.

Law is similar to religion in that the moral attitudes are very deep and
become articles of faith which, once declaimed with simplicity by a prophet
possessed of convincing moral authority, are difficult to change or question.

It is true that some legal systems do undergo great creative shifts and then
settle down to stability, minor adjustments, occasional tinkerings, the filling
out of the detail. But these legal earthquakes transforming the landscape are
less frequent than is commonly supposed and legal changes appear more
often as a slow steady creep of continental plates. Stable change has its
advantages: the law is a known quantity and is predictable, it does not over-
react to an episode or to a transient political philosophy or to some fad or
fashion of the day. There is time for reflection, for a historical consensus to
be reached.

French developments

4–2   When the French codes were written down, they were a masterpiece of legal style. They were economical, musical, elegiac. The civil code was initially prepared by the Duc de Cambacérès who, on the instructions of the National Assembly in 1793, produced his first draft in six weeks with huge verve (the Assembly, with typical client unreality, wanted it in a month). Understandably it was many years before it was settled: Portalis was probably the leading influence, but Napoleon himself attended many drafting meetings. The Civil Code came into force in 1804 and the Commercial Code was completed in 1807.

The codes took an enormous hold on the imagination. They voiced a heroic liberalism generated by a marvellously prestigious European power, celebrating its might with convincing charisma. Stendhal is said to have read part of the civil code every day to refine his feeling for the language. Even now the French lapidary and poignant style of drafting is exemplary and consistently better than anybody else's. But notwithstanding the revolutionary intent of Napoleon, and notwithstanding the radicalism of the changes in family law and the abolition of feudalism, when it came to commercial law the codes largely codified Roman law, as transmuted by mediaeval and subsequent ideas which were pro-debtor and anti-money in their bias. The codes were written before the industrial revolution really got under way in France and before mercantilist ideas began to prevail. The commercial law was the received law of the time, as developed by French jurists, notably the learned Domat (1625–1696) and the indefatigable Pothier (1699–1772) and was not revolutionary. It was perfectly right and proper and sensible that the law should have been rooted in tradition. Because they were such splendid legal codes, they were extremely attractive to other countries which rapidly imported them as the most civilised model which one of the most civilised nations in the world could provide. It is not therefore surprising that they should have taken such a strong root which remains more or less unchanged to this day.

Napoleon could truly say in exile on St Helena: "It is not in winning 40 battles that my real glory lies, for all those victories will be eclipsed by Waterloo. But my Code civil will not be forgotten, it will live forever."

German developments

4–3   The German civil code, the impressive BGB (*Bürgerliches Gesetzbuch*) was put together after the industrial revolution, as a result of thirteen years work ending in the mid–1890s, and came into force on January 1, 1900. The German commercial code (the HGB) stemmed from 1861 and the final version came into force also in 1900. The German Bankruptcy Act, the *Konkursordnung*, was enacted in 1877, also after industrialisation and after laissez-faire mercantilism, and after Herbert Spencer's *Social Statics* of 1850. Hence the German ideas had advanced a long way beyond the Napoleonic view. The codes were strongly influenced by jurists who were seeped in Roman law. The Pandectists still ruled the roost. Insolvency set-off found its way into the bankruptcy act, but, when it came to the great concepts of the civil law, the draftsmen were less concerned with bankruptcy and they adhered resolutely to the notion of false wealth. But the subsequent case law shows a benign disregard for false wealth where it could. For example the Germanic countries have never been impressed by the Anglo-American elaborate publicity systems for personal property security and certainly did not allow false wealth to stultify title finance. And the codes acknowledged the free assignability of claims. In retrospect it seems that the great German lawyer Friedrich Carl von Savigny (1779–1861) was right to stop the codification of German law when it was proposed by Anton Thibault in 1814 and to counsel delay until the necessary research had been carried out.

German writers sometimes bemoan the abstractness of their codes, their 4–4 lack of poetry and their glaciality compared to the French. They should not be so modest. They are codes of stunning mastery of principle and of detail and provide more solutions to more questions than any other. This was because, unlike the French before them, with their grand maxims and large principles, and the Swiss after them, with their famous and realistic acknowledgement in Article 1 of the Civil Code admitting to gaps in the law which must be filled in the spirit of the legislator (an acknowledgement expressed in terms almost exactly echoing Aristotle and St Thomas Aquinas), the Germans set out to cover the field and to be as complete and comprehensive as possible. That they did so in a terse manner, without falling into the trap of the Prussian General Law of the Land of 1794 with its 17,000 paragraphs, was a brilliant achievement.

The English revolution

It has been mentioned that there have been two revolutions in commercial 4–5 and financial law. The first was the Roman revolution in the classical period. The second was the English revolution which was fully in train by 1750 and which was substantially completed by 1900. Perhaps there have been others which careful legal archaeology will uncover.

The Romans were ultimately successful in recording their legal system. This was completed by Justinian (527–565) and his lawyers in the sixth century AD, although this compilation was more a disorganised collection of legal pieces and was not wholly an accurate reflection of what the classical Romans had in mind. It was lost during the Dark Ages, rediscovered by the medieval jurists, commencing mainly in the University of Bologna in the eleventh century, cleansed by the anti-money bias of the ecclesiastical theoreticians, turned inside out, dogmatised, glossified, post-glossified, abstractified and finally politicised by Napoleon.

4–6   The English, despite their prolific literary enthusiasm as publishers of more books than any other country in the world, never got round to writing down their revolution in comprehensive legal codes. Their great legal inventions were developed mainly by case law and not by legal ideologists. This casuistic mode of proceeding was similar to that of the classical Romans and the English contribution often almost seems like an independent rediscovery of Roman commercial thought. Apart from the *Commentaries on the Laws of England* by Sir William Blackstone (1723–80), the closest they get to recording their legal system is in *Halsbury's Laws of England* – a compilation stating the entire legal regime and not greatly different in effect from Justinian's efforts, first published in 1907 and now in its fourth edition with 56 volumes plus supplements. But on the other hand they did codify much of their commercial law, such as sale of goods, bills of exchange, company law and insolvency law.

Some of their inventions were the dropping of the dogma of false wealth (in case law by 1820, although it dribbled on in individual bankruptcies – as opposed to corporate liquidations – until consigned to oblivion in 1986) and the wholehearted adoption of divided ownership via the trust. They allowed the free assignability of debts so that they could be sold without formality and without notice to the debtor. They reduced the doctrine of specificity to its essential minimum and they got rid of the concept that one could not sell or mortgage a future asset which was not yet in existence: it was enough that one could tell whether an asset was caught if it fitted the description when it materialised. They espoused the idea of granting a proprietary interest in fungible assets (by the trust) which is now essential to the operation of custodianship systems for fungible securities. They developed the universal floating charge and possessory management through a receiver to keep the business going. They insisted on set-off and netting: the first recorded insolvency set-off case was 1612 sanctioned by statute in 1705.

4–7   If the old law was out of keeping, but unimportant economically, they just left it as it was, as an unsightly but irrelevant pre-Cambrian excrescence. An example is nineteenth century bills of sale legislation preventing non-possessory chattel mortgages by individuals, but not applying to companies and side-stepped by the title finance device of hire purchase so as to allow secured consumer credit. Another example is the doctrine of contractual consideration. In their drive forward, they left a lot of legal litter behind which, if they were tidier, they ought to put in the dustbin.

They realised the importance of choice on insolvency and made that choice with conviction, leaving it to the integrity of their banks and to debtor-creditor mutuality of interest to restrain harsh conduct. They prioritised the consensual rescue culture for insolvent businesses. They abolished usury laws in 1854 and sharply reduced the formalities for contracts in the interests of commerce. They developed a system of conflict of laws which was highly liberal, e.g. they were one of the first countries to permit a free choice of law, largely because of the importance of maritime law, especially ship charterparties. Because the system was so flexible, with priority being given to freedom of contract and divided ownership, it was less inclined to become out-of-date. They and the Americans exploited this flexibility by transactional techniques of refined sophistication.

They built up a great goodwill for their judicial standards which led to   4–8
the availability of the London commercial court as an international tribunal – more than half the cases there do not involve British parties. This goodwill, accompanied by a variety of historical factors, also led to English law being used as the governing law of a large proportion of international financial transactions. Their bench was free of dogma and they developed commercial law from the time of Lord Mansfield onwards with a huge fertility and a sense of sweetness and light and courtesy.

To the Englishman, his legal system is Shakespearean. But any objective writer must renounce tribalism and must acknowledge that there is also Dante, Goethe, Molière and Tolstoy.

Of course the English have their counter-revolutionaries, their circumlocutionaries, their obscurantists, their anti-clockwisers. No doubt all legal communities have these persons. One must not deprecate them: at least they are interested. Their only fault is that they cannot see the whole landscape: history will soon put us all in that category – if we are not in it already. All flat-earthers cease to be such if they are taken up to view the earth from the heavens.

American developments

The American common law jurisdictions took over the English revolution   4–9
with enormous energy and vigour. They took the trouble of synthesising the revolution, mainly the result of the efforts of American academic scholarship of prodigious diligence – Beale, Scott, Williston, Llewellyn and many others of equal stature. This systematic ordering was achieved not only in the semi-official Restatements of contract, trust, tort, conflicts of law and

the like of the American Law Institute, but in a series of Uniform Acts and in the magnificent Uniform Commercial Code. Because the country is so rich and diverse in its cultures, they explored every possibility, tried everything, went down every path, founded philosophical jurisprudential schools of every conceivable inclination. They refused to be waylaid by the puritanical theocrats and populists who kept snapping at their system of commercial law from inside and often wounding it.

Conclusion

4–10   About 33 per cent of the world's population live under a common law system. About 20 per cent live under a Franco-Latin system. About 17 per cent live under a Germanic or other midway system. The remaining 30 per cent of the world's population are still in the process of formulating their commercial law. They may divide themselves between these other groups or join one of them or strike out on their own.

One cannot value a legal system by the number of worshippers at its temple. But as each cult of law, by sermons of winning cogency and conviction, presses its prayer-book as being the source of all salvation, the detached onlooker is bewildered by the doctrines and the dogmas and the creeds and the metaphysics, and must enquire whether, now that the information is available, now that the evidence has been produced and the witnesses heard, now that the trial has lasted so long, we may not perhaps proceed to judgement.

4–11   So there the matter rests for the present.

There are those who will say that the revolutionaries are wrong. They will say that there ought to be a counter-revolution and that the ancient regime should be restored.

Others will say that both revolutionaries and counter-revolutionaries are wrong and what is now needed is yet another revolution which will produce something better.

CHAPTER 5

GROUP 1A: TRADITIONAL ENGLISH JURISDICTIONS

This and subsequent chapters contain a more detailed classification of the   5–1
world's jurisdictions. The objective of these chapters is only to group the
world's legal systems, not to provide a comprehensive description of their
laws. The details of most of the legal concepts mentioned below are extensively discussed, on an international and comparative basis, in other books
in this series and it is not realistic here to do more than summarise in the
briefest of terms. But the governing law of financial contracts and judicial
jurisdiction in respect of financial contracts, as well as the recognition of
foreign money judgments, are described later in this book. An index of jurisdictions and their groups is located in a table at the end of this book.

Population and religious details are based on the *Encyclopaedia Britan-
nica Annual* 1992 where the data may be based on an estimate several years
prior to 1992. Much of the statutory citation is drawn from, or checked
against, the three volume work *Foreign law: Current Sources of Codes and
Basic Legislation in Jurisdictions of the World*, edited by Thomas H Reynolds (University of California, Berkeley) and Arturo A Flores (Golden Gate
University, San Francisco), American Association of Law Librarians Service
No 33, which is an indispensable work for any comparative lawyer. Other
citation is drawn from various digests, works on comparative law in specific
areas, and private sources. Special mention must be made of K Zweigert and
H Kötz, *An Introduction to Comparative Law*, translated from the German
by Tony Weir (2nd ed 1987) Oxford.

Members of the European Union are subject to EU directives on securities   5–2
regulation, insider dealing, company law and other matters. Some of these
are voluminous, but often not particularly dramatic in terms of really fundamental changes, at least so far as English commercial law is concerned. The
European Judgments Conventions and the Rome Convention on Applicable
Law of 1980 are important. Some EFTA states have orientated their relevant statutory law with EU directives in mind.

Main comparative characteristics of Group 1A (traditional English jurisdictions)

General

5–3   The jurisdictions in Group 1A are called the Traditional English jurisdictions since they all have a common heritage in English law. The financial law of the jurisdictions is largely pro-creditor.

The overall colouring is liberal with much flexibility permitted by virtue of (a) comparative contractual freedom, (b) the free availability of divided ownership (bailment or trust), (c) a tendency not to disrupt expectations on insolvency, and (d) dislike of formalities and judicial protectionism, e.g. in relation to the creation and enforcement of security. On the whole these jurisdictions object to big pocket liability, expansive notions of tort liability and the over-criminalisation of commercial law. The predictability of commercial bargains is a major legal policy, outside the consumer context. The doctrine of specificity, requiring specific identification of assets sold or charged, is retained for sale of goods and leases, but has been dropped for security and custodianship where generic descriptions suffice. Specific identification can be overcome in other cases by the trust, e.g. a seller can effectively sell a share of fungible assets by declaring a trust in favour of the buyer. This is essential for dealings in securities. Naturally there will be differences of emphasis between the jurisdictions on most of these points.

Security

5–4   The jurisdictions have a universal corporate floating charge; informal corporate security over receivables without notification to the debtors; informal security over investment securities without registration of the pledgee in the books of the issuer; corporate non-possessory chattel mortgages; compulsory publication of some corporate charges by registration at a companies registry (which, unlike the American system, is not an explicit priority system) within 21 or 30 days of the creation of the charge; self-help enforcement by possessory management through a receiver and private sale as opposed to a judicially-ordered public auction; usually no compulsory grace periods on enforcement; free availability of charges over future property without particular specification which can reach post-insolvency property, and free availability of security for all future debts without stating a maximum amount. Taxes and wages do not rank ahead of security, but usually do rank ahead of the floating charge. Rights of substitution, e.g. for collateralised investment securities, do not destroy the charge, but may demote it to a floating charge, whereas in Franco-Latin countries, this dominion by the pledgor may destroy the security interest altogether. Most of the above features and the general informality are not accepted by the Franco-Latin jurisdictions or, to a lesser extent, by some Germanic or mixed jurisdictions although this is very much a generalisation. Usual registered security for land, ships, aircraft.

Title finance

These transactions include retention of title, factoring of receivables, sale   5–5
and repurchase, financial leasing, hire purchase, sale and lease-back. The tendency is to uphold form over substance and not to recharacterise them as a mortgage requiring public registration for validity on the bankruptcy of the lessee/buyer. There is some hostility to retention of title clauses which catch proceeds of the sub-sale.

Insolvency set-off

There is a wide set-off of all mutual claims on insolvency. The set-off is   5–6
usually mandatory. Hence netting of contracts is freely allowed without special conditions, i.e. the regime is non-discriminatory, except in Canada.

Corporate rehabilitation proceedings

Generally, there is no form of corporate composition proceeding, other than a court-approved scheme of arrangement under the Companies Act. The application for a scheme does not impose stays on creditor proceedings and is laborious. Some countries have adopted specific judicial corporate rehabilitations, with wider freezes, notably Australia, Britain, Canada, Ireland, New Zealand (for special cases) and Singapore, but (subject to qualifications) these usually do not stay set-offs or contract rescissions or allow management to remain in possession and so are much milder than the versions found in France, Italy and the United States. In Britain, Singapore and Australia, the holder of universal security including a floating charge can veto the rehabilitation procedure, but in Britain floating charges over part of the assets (e.g. securities or inventory or receivables) are weak as a result of the corporate administration introduced in 1986.

False wealth and reputed ownership

Secret beneficial ownership and trusts are recognised, including trusts of   5–7
fungibles or pooled assets without individual identification, e.g. custodianship of fungible securities. Reputed ownership in very diluted form may still

apply to bankruptcies of individuals, although abolished in England since 1986 and weakened by case law from 1840, if not before. The law gives insolvency super-priority to the recovery of certain mistaken payments and moneys improperly obtained (constructive trusts) and also allows tracing. Undisclosed principals can intervene (important for markets) and (unlike many jurisdictions outside the common law groups) can also be sued by the counterparty of the agent.

Veil of incorporation

5–8   Directors are liable for fraudulent trading, which is the deliberate or reckless incurring of debts which the directors know are unlikely to be paid. The liability is rare. This is replaced in a few countries by tougher standards of wrongful trading, which impose an objective reasonableness standard: for example, Britain, Australia, Ireland, but not Canada. A firm separation of shareholders and the company, even in the case of groups, is the rule. A compulsory duty to petition if the company is actually insolvent or loses half its capital is rare, if it exists at all, thereby facilitating private consensual rescues.

The ultra vires rule for companies is virtually non-existent in Britain, partly as a result of EU directives, but may retain importance in some other countries, notably for guarantees. Normally a company may not give financial assistance for the purchase of its own shares but this is eroded in Britain for private companies.

Subordinated debt is recognised.

Two-tier boards and compulsory annual reserves out of profits are unusual.

The first English Companies Act of 1856 was consolidated in 1862. The most important Companies Acts after that were in 1929 and 1948. The changes thereafter were mainly trivial in import, although massive in volume, mainly as a result of European directives, and were consolidated in the Companies Act 1985.

Negligible disclosure standards in the numerous competing tax haven jurisdictions – mainly islands in the Caribbean and Pacific.

Preferential transfers

5–9   The jurisdictions have the traditional intentionally fraudulent transfer under the *actio pauliana* codified in the 1571 Statute of Elizabeth I. Long suspect periods for gifts and transactions at an undervalue in older statutes are usual, but there is substantial protection for other transactions by virtue of the doctrine that the debtor must have preferential intent (thereby enabling the courts to uphold transactions) and a general dislike for the retroactive effect of preference law with consequent unpredictability for commercial transactions (but with Australia taking a tougher view). Suspect periods are usually of six months, but note the avoidance of floating charges for pre-existing debt and the longer suspect period for floating charges, e.g. one year. Security for pre-existing debt may be upheld for fixed security if it is granted under pressure, e.g. to ensure survival, thereby again assisting consensual rescues. Security for pre-existing debt granted in the suspect period is almost always voidable in non-common law jurisdictions, subject to a few exceptions, e.g. the Netherlands.

Contract and lease rescission

Ipso facto clauses entitling a party to cancel an existing contract, licence or   5–10
equipment lease on the bankruptcy of the other party are generally upheld, except for grossly penal forfeitures or where statute has intervened and except in the case of Canada (since 1992). One result of this, coupled with insolvency set-off, is that market contracts can be freely netted on insolvency to reduce exposures. There are usually special provisions limiting landlord repossessions of commercial land leases.

Priority creditors

The usual corporate priority creditors are insolvency costs, certain wages,   5–11
employee benefits and taxes (up to specified limits for wages and taxes). Britain is amongst the countries which has limited the tax priority.

Conflict of laws

Freedom of express choice of law is honoured for contracts, if the choice is   5–12
bona fide, with no fixed presumptions if no express choice. There are highly developed rules for contract conflicts. Britain and Ireland are now governed by the 1980 EC Rome Convention on the Law Applicable to Contractual Obligations.

Exorbitant jurisdictions include fleeting presence of individuals, contracts made, broken or to be performed within the jurisdiction, and contracts governed by local law, but subject in each case to forum non conveniens principles.

There is a ready enforcement of foreign judgments on usual principles, without reopening the merits and without any need for reciprocity. An elaborate treaty network exists.

Sovereign immunity follows the restrictive doctrine by statute in some states (Australia, Canada, Pakistan, Singapore, UK) and probably on the basis of English case law in others.

As to bankruptcy conflicts, foreign insolvency administrators appointed at the place of incorporation are recognised, without local recognition proceedings. The tendency is to give effect to freezes on creditor executions by a home forum liquidation order. There is no discrimination against foreign creditors, but the courts apply the home bankruptcy law in the main, e.g. set-off. Formal treaties are unusual but there are special reciprocal provisions in the UK insolvency legislation. There has been a high degree of insolvency comity since the nineteenth century, probably attributable to a common insolvency culture.

Securities regulation

5–13   Often securities regulation is based on the English scheme of Companies Act controls requiring a registered prospectus for issues to the public and prescribed contents, plus prevention of fraud legislation in relation to investments. A "sophisticated investors" exemption for offers of securities is usual. There is tight regulation of collective investment schemes. Some states have substantially amplified the basic scheme, e.g. Australia, Britain and Canada. In Britain, attempts by the anti-fraud authorities to widen the scope of securities frauds in celebrated court cases in the 1980s did not succeed in the main, thereby confirming the English judicial tendency not to over-criminalise commercial law.

Contracts

5–14   Doctrine of consideration is retained, but is not important except for guarantees. Contracts are made where the acceptance is posted, if by letter, or when received, if by electronic means. Offers are revocable prior to acceptance. Usually there is no third party beneficiary contract, but a trust of the benefit of the contract fills the void so that effectively third party beneficiary contracts can be achieved. This is useful for "deed poll" guarantees of issues of notes and other debt securities. Oral contracts are widely allowed, except for guarantees and land contracts. There are the usual judicial manoeuvres to limit exculpation clauses, e.g. by stringent interpretation against the party relying on them. Statutory control of unfair contract terms applies in England, substantially neutered in the commercial context by judicial interpretation.

Usury

Usury laws were abolished in England in 1854, subject to extortionate   5–15
transactions. Usury controls are unusual in this group and have been
replaced in developed states by better targeted consumer credit laws which
do not impinge on international corporate finance, e.g. the British Consumer Credit Act 1974.

Gaming

Gaming laws are still prevalent in many states, but are substantially cur-   5–16
tailed by case law and (in England) by statute for market transactions.
Speculative contracts for differences may be suspect in some states.

Stamp duties

This is a typically British method of raising revenue, rightly rejected by the   5–17
Americans. On the way out in the UK but important in Australia (because it
is a source of revenue for individual states).

Codification of laws

Comprehensive codification is unusual for basic agency, contracts and torts.   5–18
But there are special acts for the most important commercial areas, e.g. sale
of goods, bills of exchange, insurance, companies, bankruptcy, etc.

Bills of exchange

Bills of exchange are of dwindling importance in international finance,   5–19
though they are still used in trade finance and in issues of commercial paper.
The three main international regimes are:

(1) countries based on the English Bills of Exchange Act 1882;
(2) the Geneva regime; and
(3) the American Uniform Commercial Code Art 3.

The Geneva regime is the most restrictive mainly because of Franco-Latin
objections to the free marketability of claims. The UCC regime is the most
liberal, with the English regime midway between.
In all three regimes the instrument must be unconditional and for a sum

certain. It is not necessary in England/United States to state in the note that it is a promissory note as required by the Geneva regime. But *avals* are problematic in the English regime because the Statute of Frauds 1667 s 4 requires guarantees to be in writing: the guarantor must specifically state that the note is guaranteed and a simple signature on the note by the guarantor is not enough. "Payment guaranteed" is sufficient in the US. English and American instalment notes are possible, but not under the Geneva regime (use separate notes for each instalment). Prepayment clauses, tax grossing-up clauses (unless possibly "free of taxes") and events of default (other than non-payment of an instalment) probably destroy negotiability under the English and Geneva regimes, but the US is more liberal. Fixed (but not floating rate) interest is allowed under the English regime, but under the Geneva regime interest is allowed only on bills payable at sight or at a fixed period after sight. The rules relating to conflicts of laws are different under all three regimes.

5–20   The Geneva regime comprises six Conventions of 1930 and 1931 setting out uniform laws on bills of exchange, conflicts of law, and on stamp duties, in relation to bills of exchange and promissory notes (1930) and cheques (1931). Countries following the Geneva regime (either by ratification of the Conventions or adoption of the rules in domestic law) include Austria, Belgium, Brazil, Czechoslovakia (now two republics), Denmark, Ecuador, Finland, France, Germany, Greece, Hungary, Italy, Japan, Luxembourg, Monaco, Netherlands, Norway, Poland, Portugal, Romania, Spain, the former USSR, Sweden and Switzerland, Turkey and the former Yugoslavia. In other words, probably most countries outside the common law group are based on the Geneva regime or something like it.

The US UCC Art 3, originally based on the Negotiable Instruments Law of 1896 (in turn based on the English 1882 Act) is much more liberal. Colombia and Panama based their law on the US 1896 version. The US flexibility may be traceable to the developed US commercial paper market and the wide use of notes to evidence loans under loan agreements.

UNCITRAL has produced a harmonising Convention on International Bills of Exchange and International Promissory Notes of 1988, a worthy, but little recognised, effort.

Bankruptcy procedure

5–21   Corporate liquidations are divided into voluntary winding-up (which may be a solvent members winding-up or an insolvent creditors winding-up, decided in both cases by a 75 per cent vote of shareholders), compulsory winding-up commenced by petition and ordered by the court, or a winding-up under the supervision of the court which is similar to a compulsory winding-up. A liquidator is appointed (a provisional liquidator may be appointed on petition). He is usually an accountant.

History of bankruptcy legislation

Typically the corporate law is contained in the Companies Act which covers 5-22 winding-up of companies and in the Bankruptcy Act which applies only to individual bankruptcies. The Companies Act applies certain provisions of the Bankruptcy Act by cross-reference, notably preferences, set-off, and proof of debts, but not reputed ownership (false wealth) which has never applied to corporate insolvencies. Insolvency law was consolidated in Britain in the Insolvency Act 1986 for both individuals and companies.

The first proper English bankruptcy act was in 1542 introduced by Henry VIII. This was superseded by an Act in 1571, which survived with amendment, to BA 1723. This was followed by rapid development in the nineteenth century in Bankruptcy Acts of 1824, 1844, 1849, 1861, 1869 and 1883 followed by BA 1914, which remained in force, with amendments, until 1985 and was replaced by the Insolvency Act 1986 which combined both corporate and individual insolvencies. Hence BA 1914 and the Companies Acts related provisions are common in former colonies. Note that the United States for most of the nineteenth century had only episodic federal bankruptcy legislation: continuous bankruptcy acts commenced there with the Bankruptcy Act of 1898 amended in the 1930s and extended in a well-drafted, but tough, codification in 1978 (in turn amended subsequently in detailed respects – mainly in the pro-creditor direction).

List of jurisdictions (84)

(65 jurisdictions if Australia and Canada are treated as one)

Anguilla	Population 7,600. British Caribbean colony. English law since 1623/4. BA c 9, CA c 335, on English lines.	5-23
Antigua and Barbuda	Population 81,600. Former English Caribbean colony since 1632, independent 1981. CA c 358 based on UK CA of early 1990s; BA c 19.	

Australia	Population 17,200,000. Intellectual jursidiction which has made an outstanding contribution to the common law. Eight common law jurisdictions. States: New South Wales, Queensland, South Australia, Tasmania, Victoria, Western Australia. Territories: Australian Capital Territory, Northern Territory. English law officially received from 1828 onwards. No appeal to UK Privy Council from 1986. Consolidating CA 1989 and BA 1966, amended by Corporate Law Reform Act 1992 to introduce a corporate rehabilitation. Much tougher preference laws than England. Bills of Exchange Act 1909. Amending securities legislation 1990–1992.
Bahamas	Population 261,000. CA c 279, BA c 59. 700 islands and 2,000 rocks spanning 500 miles. British since 1729, self-governing from 1973 and subsequently independent. Special acts for foreign companies. Securities Act 1971.
5–24 **Bangladesh**	Population 109,000,000, 87 per cent Muslim. Coastal state adjoining northeast India. Formally part of British India. Part of Pakistan on independence in 1947, independent Bengali state in 1971. Legal system probably similar to Pakistan before 1971.
Barbados	Population 260,000. English settlement 1623, independent 1966. CA 1982, believed to be based on Canadian legislation. BA c 303. Securities Exchange Act 1982, c 318A.
Belize	Population 192,000. British settlement since 1631, as British Honduras, self-governing 1964 and subsequently independent. BA c 201. CA c 206.

Bermuda	Population 59,800. British colony since at least 1612 (first English settlers were Virginia-bound shipwrecks 1609). Now self-governing. Important banking centre and tax haven. CA 1981 based on British CA 1948, but amended. BA modelled on English BA 1869, but much amended.
British Indian Ocean Territory	Population 200. British colony in middle of Indian Ocean, including Diego Garcia. Military and telecommunications islands.
Brunei Darussalam	Population 264,000, 66 per cent Muslim. British influence since 1847, independent 1983. CA 1956 c 39. BA c 67.
Burma	Population 42,560,000. Very poor. Province of India under British rule from late nineteenth century, independent 1948. Socialism may have obliterated English legal system, but perhaps it is still there.
Canada (excluding Quebec)	Population (excluding Quebec), 19,850,000; and total population with Quebec, 26,620,000. Exemplary and intelligent statutory draftsmanship in the finest tradition. Eleven common law jurisdictions. Provinces: Alberta, British Columbia, Manitoba, New Brunswick, Newfoundland, Nova Scotia, Ontario, Prince Edward Island, Saskatchewan. Territories: Northwest Territories, Yukon Territory. Canada Business Corporations Act for federal companies, with provincial equivalents. BA 1949, substantially amended by BIA 1992 to introduce commercial rehabilitation. Companies Creditors Arrangement Act dating from 1930s. Winding-up Act mainly intended for banks, insurance companies, loan companies and trust companies, but available generally. Major differences in Quebec which is French-based (French colony in

5–25

1663, civil law guaranteed by British in 1774). Some common law provinces have Personal Property Security Acts based on the American UCC Art 9. Provisions for bank security under Bank Act s 178, so as to give Quebec a floating charge in favour of banks. Bills of Exchange Act is federal. Securities legislation is provincial, though much cooperation especially between Ontario and provinces to the west of Ontario.

5–26   **Cayman Islands**

Population about 19,000. British Caribbean colony since 1670. Leading banking and tax haven jurisdiction. CL 1961.

Christmas Island

Population 1000. Island in the Indian Ocean, south of Java. External territory of Australia, originally annexed by Britain in 1888.

Cocos (Keeling Islands)

Population about 600. Pacific islands (west of Australia) consisting of two coral atolls, 14 sq km, external territory of Australia. Has adopted a (former) Bankruptcy Ordinance of Singapore.

5–27   **Cook Islands**

Population 18,000. Tiny self-governing island territory of New Zealand, 3000 km NE of New Zealand in the Pacific. NZ CA 1955 and Cook Islands International Companies Act (the latter is mainly for tax haven companies).

Cyprus

Population about 750,000 (but more if Turkish military and settlers included), mainly Greek Orthodox. Northern part occupied by Turkish settlers. British protectorate from 1878, independent 1960, English law officially received 1914 on annexation. Turkish invasion 1974 and Turkish Republic of Northern Cyprus declared in 1983 of northern one-third of island, but not recognised by international community. BA c 5. CA 1976 based on British CA 1948. Contracts Act 1980 codification based on Indian Contracts Act 1872. One of world's largest shipping registers based on British merchant shipping acts, as amended by local acts in 1963 and 1982.

Dominica

Population 83,400. Former British colony from 1756–1763. Independent 1978. Bankruptcy Ordinance, amended 1986. Companies Ordinance, amended 1986.

England

Population 46,200,000 (total UK 57,600,000). Leader of a radical commercial law revolution from the late 1700s and one of the world's greatest jurisdictions with substantial international influence. Triple A. Insolvency Act 1985. Companies Act 1985. Consolidating property and trust legislation of 1925. Maritime legislation is being up-graded and codified. Unfair Contract Terms Act 1977. Bills of Exchange Act 1882. Financial Services Act 1986.

5–28

Falkland Islands

Population 2,000. UK self-governing colony in S. Atlantic.

Fiji

Population 740,000. Pacific islands. CA 1983, based on British CA 1948.

Gambia

Population 880,000, 95 per cent Muslim. Former British colony, independent 1970. Officially received English law 1888. Insolvency Act 2 of 1967. CA 1955 c 29.

Ghana

Population 15,500,000. Former British West African colony of the Gold Coast, independent 1957. Strong legal tradition. Insolvency Act 153 of 1962. Companies Code 1963 based on British CA 1948.

Contracts Act 25 of 1960 incorporating English contracts law.

5–29 **Gibraltar**

Population about 30,000. British self-governing colony.

Grenada

Population 96,100. Former British Caribbean colony from 1763 (except for short French period). Independent 1973. Bankruptcy Ordinance c 29. Companies Ordinance 1927.

Guyana

Population 760,000. Former British colony from 1814 as British Guyana (previously Dutch but Roman-Dutch influence eradicated by reception of English law in 1816), independent 1966. Insolvency Act c 12.21, Companies Ordinance c 89.01.

Hong Kong

Population 5,900,000. British self-governing colony. Full reception of English law since at least 1843. New Territories lease expires 1997. Basic Law of 1990 of China will govern from 1997. This seeks to preserve original law of Hong Kong Special Administrative Region for 50 years. Bankruptcy Ordinance. Companies Ordinance of 1950 as amended, based on British CA 1929 but subsequently amended especially in 1984 and 1991. Securities Ordinance 1985. Protection of Investors Ordinance 1974. Securities and Futures Commission. Securities (Insider Dealing) Ordinance 1991. Trustee Ordinance c 29.

India

Population 871,200,000, 83 per cent Hindu. Exceptionally civilised legal tradition, sometimes more English than the English. Huge legal literature. CA 1956. Independent from Britain 1947. Twenty-five states and six territories, but largely integrated legal and court system. Personal bankruptcy governed by Presidency-Towns Insolvency Act 1909 and Provincial Insolvency Act 1920. Liquidations in Companies Act 1956. Banking Regulation Act 1949. Codified Indian Contracts Act 1872, reformed 1958. Securities Contracts (Regulation) Act 1956.

Ireland (N)

Population 1,570,000. English statutes usually applied locally.   5–30

Ireland (Republic)

Population 3,500,000. Independent 1922. Very sound and liberal jurisdiction. CA 1963, substantially amended in 1990 to introduce a corporate rehabilitation proceeding; bankruptcy legislation reformed and consolidated in BA 1988.

Isle of Man

Population about 65,000, self-governing UK Crown possession in the Irish Sea, home of the tailless Manx cat. Companies Consolidation Act 1931; BC 1892; Preferential Payments Acts of 1908 and 1973.

Israel

Population 4,800,000. British mandate 1922–1948. Commercial and financial law based on English law. Bankruptcy Ordinance 5740–1980. Companies Ordinance 5743–1983. Law on Recognition and Enforcement of Foreign Judgments 5718–1958 as amended in 1977. Bills of Exchange Ordinance, consolidated 1967. Securities Law 5728–1968, as amended. Joint Investment Trusts Law 5721–1961. Trust Law 1979 codifying the common law trust. Constructive trust and tracing are available.

Jamaica

Population 2,400,000. Former British colony from 1655, independent 1962. English law received from 1661. BA 1880, last amended 1982. CA 1965, last amended 1984.

Kenya

Population 25,900,000, 73 per cent Christian. Former British East African colony, independent 1963. BA c 53. Companies Ordinance 1962 c 486. English contract law received from 1961. Stock Traders Licensing Act c 498. Unit Trusts Act c 521.

Kiribati

Population 73,300. Pacific islands, formerly British colony of the Gilbert Islands.

5–31 Malawi

Population 9,200,000, 64 per cent Christian. Former British central African colony in Rift Valley, independent 1964. BA c 11.01. CA c 46.03, revised 1984. Capital Market Development Act 1990 and regulations 1992.

Malaysia

Population 18,240,000, 53 per cent Muslim, 17 per cent Buddhist. Thirteen states. Commercial law received from England. Self-governing from 1957, Malaysia formed 1963, Singapore withdrew 1965. BA 1967, revised 1988. CA 1965 revised 1973. Offshore Companies Act 1990. Contracts Act 1950. Islamic law generally restricted to personal matters. Bills of Exchange Act 1949, revised 1978. Securities Industry Act 1983, as amended. Trustee Act 1949.

Montserrat

Population 12,000. British Caribbean colony. BA 1843, last amended in 1985. CA 1885, as amended.

New Zealand

Population 3,400,000. Exceptionally sound commercial case law with no wobble. CA 1955, substantially amended or replaced in 1994; IA 1967 for individuals, last amended 1991. Draconian insolvency procedure initiated by the government for special cases under Corporations (Investigation & Management) Act 1989 dating back to 1934. Bank insolvencies covered by Reserve Bank of NZ Act 1989, similar to statutory management. Detailed contracts legislation. Securities Act 1978, as amended. Unit Trusts Act 1960, as amended.

Nigeria

Population 123,800,000, 50 per cent Christian, 45 per cent Muslim. Fecund legal literature. British colony, independent 1960. Federation of upwards of 20 states. Received English law from at least 1900. BA c 30. Company and Allied Matters Act 1990 c 59. Securities and Exchange Commission Act c 406.

Niue

Population 3000. South Pacific island to north-east of New Zealand. Self-governing territory under the protection of the British Crown in right of New Zealand. New tax haven jurisdiction with liberal companies regime inaugurated by the International Business Companies Act 1994.

Norfolk Island

Population about 2,000. External territory of Australia in south western Pacific, 35 sq kms. Relies on tourism. No formal bankruptcy law, apparently. 5-32

Pakistan

Population 126,400,000, 97 per cent Muslim. Independent from Britain 1947. Companies Ordinance 1984. Insolvency Act 1909 for Karachi, Provincial Insolvency Act 1920. Codified Contract Act 1872. Securities & Exchange Ordinance 1969, Rules 1971. Some Islamisation by special acts 1988–91.

Papua New Guinea

Population 3,750,000, 90 per cent Christian. Annexed to UK 1888, independent 1975. CA 1964 c 146, based on older

Australian uniform companies legislation. Official management which may be based on 1961 Australian version, in turn based on South African judicial management. Marketable Securities Act 1966.

Pitcairn Island

Population 52, said to be mainly descended from mutineers on HMS "Bounty" in 1790 and their Polynesian consorts. British Pacific island colony, under New Zealand protection.

5–33   **St Helena**

Population about 5,500. British colony in South Atlantic Ocean. Islands of Ascension and Tristan de Cunha are dependencies. Napoleon's home 1815 – 1821, although not by choice.

St Kitts and Nevis

Population 43,000. Settled by British 1623, independent 1983.

St Lucia

Population 154,000, 86 per cent Roman Catholic. ComC c 244 contains the bankruptcy rules, Title IV (for companies), Title IX for individuals. Companies legislation based on early British CA 1900s. Seems to be a hybrid French and English jurisdiction and the jurisdiction may be Group 2 rather than Group 1A. The civil code of 1879 came from Quebec CC 1868.

St Vincent and the Grenadines

Population 118,000. Former British Caribbean colony, independent 1979. BA 1928, last amended 1986. CA c 219, last amended 1988. International Companies Act 1982, revised 1983.

Seychelles

Population 67,800, 90 per cent Roman Catholic. 115 islands in Indian Ocean, former British colony, independent 1976. Hybrid French-English system. Codes based on French law drafted by A G

Chloros, CC 1976, ComC 1977. But commercial, bankruptcy and maritime law are said to be English-based. Possibly this jurisdiction should be Group 2, not Group 1A, like St Lucia. Bankruptcy and Insolvency Ordinance 1853. Companies Ordinance 1972. Conflict of laws based on French model. Fiduciaries in CC s 818.

Sierra Leone

Population 4,300,000, 40 per cent Sunni Muslim. Former West African British colony, independent 1961. English law received from 1890. CA 1942.

Singapore

Population 2,720,000, 28 per cent Buddhist, 19 per cent Christian, 16 per cent Muslim. Former British colony, became self-governing in 1959, seceded from Malaysia 1965. CA c 1950 based on Australian laws via Malaysia, revised 1990. Judicial management (based on corporate administration in British IA 1986) introduced by Companies (Amendment) Act 1987. BA c 20 amended 1988. Commodities Futures Act 1992. Futures Trading Act c 116. Securities Industry Act c 289. Application of English Law Act 1993 clarifies extent to which English law applies.

Solomon Islands

Population 330,000. British protectorate until 1978. CA c 66 based on British CA 1948. BA 1914 in same terms as British BA 1914.

Sudan

Population 29,200,000, 73 per cent Sunni Muslim. Like Egypt, a leading supplier of lawyers to the Middle East. Legal system Islamised since 1990 and commercial law may be in abeyance. Civil Transactions Act 1984 copied Jordanian CC, based on (French) Egyptian Code, so English law may be under threat. BA 1929 and CA 1925 based on English models, but may be superseded. Hence it is possible that the Sudan is not Group 1A any longer, but Group 7: however this may not be true of its underlying commercial and financial law.

5–34 **Tanzania**

Population 25,100,000, 34 per cent Christian, 33 per cent Muslim. Home to Kilimanjaro – highest mountain in Africa. Combines the former British colonies of Tanganyika and the island of Zanzibar, independent 1963–64. One of the poorest countries in the world. Tanganyika received English law in 1920. Bankruptcy Ordinance c 25. Companies Ordinance 1959, as amended.

Tokelau

Population 2000. About 3.9 square miles of atolls in South Pacific, a self-governing territory of New Zealand.

Tonga

Population 97,000, mainly Christian. Pacific island kingdom.

5–35 **Trinidad and Tobago**

Population 1,250,000. Former British Caribbean colonies, independent 1962. BA c 9.70 last amended 1981. Remedies and Creditors Act c 8.09. Companies Ordinance c 31.01. Securities Industry Act 1981.

Turks and Caicos Islands

Population about 8,000. British colony in the Bahamas group. UK Insolvency Act 1986 applies. Companies Ordinance 1981, as amended.

Tuvalu

Population 9,300. Formerly part of British colony Gilbert and Ellice Islands in Western Pacific. Independent 1978. Ten square miles spread out over an island chain of 370 miles.

Uganda

Population 17,700,000, 80 per cent Christian. Former British East African colony on shores of Lake Victoria, independent 1962. BA c 71. CA 1961 as amended.

Vanuatu

Population 150,000, 81 per cent Christian. Independent in 1980, formerly New Hebrides, jointly ruled by France and England. CA 1986. Commercial and insolvency law is said to be English-based, but this should be checked, e.g. availability of floating charge and insolvency set-off. Prevention of Frauds (Investments) Act 1990.

5–36

Virgin Islands (British)

Population about 13,000. British dependency in Antilles chain. English-style CA, but there are differences in the case of companies incorporated under the International Business Companies Ordinance.

Western Samoa

Population 166,000. Pacific islands, formerly New Zealand trust territory, independent 1962.

Zambia

Population 8,800,000. Shares Victoria Falls with Zimbabwe. Former British central African colony of N Rhodesia, independent 1964. CA c 686, based on British CA 1908. BA c 190. Received English law 1911. Stock Exchange Act 1991. US-style SEC, since 1994.

CHAPTER 6

GROUP 1B: AMERICAN COMMON LAW JURISDICTIONS

Main comparative characteristics

Group 1B comprises the American common law jurisdictions, which are sufficiently different from the Traditional English jurisdictions to form a separate group, though closely related.

Security

6–1 Universal business security is available, but possessory management through a receiver cannot displace management. And, unlike the English floating charge, preferential creditors (bankruptcy costs, taxes, employees) do not rank ahead. Elaborate publicity systems for security interests over personal property exist under the Uniform Commercial Code Art 9, which not only establishes publicity but also (unlike English-based company charge registration) is an explicit priority system. The strong false wealth doctrine in relation to security is hence satisfied by an efficient registration system. Enforcement of security is stayed on Chapter 11 rehabilitation proceedings under BC 1978, subject to adequate protection. The UCC rules, when coupled with the stays in the bankruptcy legislation, appear more protective of the debtor than in traditional English systems, e.g. grace periods of enforcement and bankruptcy stays. The ship mortgage laws are relatively cumbersome, though the formalities were relaxed in the 1990s.

Title finance

6–2 Unlike English-based systems, substance prevails over form, e.g. for the purposes of publicity under UCC Art 9. In other words, title finance transactions (e.g. retention of title, repos, financial leasing, factoring, securitisations) are more readily recharacterised as security interests and therefore may have to be publicised by filing (false wealth). This can, for example, lead to some complex structures for securitisations.

Insolvency set-off

Insolvency set-off is permitted, but in contrast to English-based systems, it is not mandatory and there is a control on build-ups of set-offs in the suspect period in BC 1978 which is more favourable to the debtor.

Corporate rehabilitation

The tough insolvency rehabilitation procedure of 1978, known as Chapter 11 and building on more limited provisions in the 1930s, is much more draconian than its counterparts in Australia, England and Singapore, by reason of the low entry requirements, wide freezes and the ability of the debtor's management to stay in possession. This was perhaps a product of the cultural trends of the 1970s and is not reflected at all in other English-based countries on the old English model. But Chapter 11 is not as pro-debtor as the French *redressement judiciare* of 1985 or the Italian extraordinary administration of 1979.

6–3

False wealth and the trust

There is a complete mastery of the trust (divided ownership) and acceptance of the constructive trust and tracing. These permit super-priority bankruptcy claims for return of wrongful takings and mistaken payments.

Veil of incorporation

This is reasonably firm. Unlike English-based systems, the personal liability of directors for wrongful or fraudulent trading is slight but directors appear to be more exposed for misrepresentation in connection with the issue of securities and under continuing disclosure obligations and for general mismanagement claims fomented by plaintiff-orientated litigation policies (see below). Personal liability of officers of failed banks for mismanagement appears not infrequent, but this trend may be magnified disproportionately by reason of the large numbers of bankruptcies of small local banks, possibly attributable to the ban on inter-state banking (on the way out). The liability of group companies does not appear excessive. The equitable subordination of creditor claims for unconscionable conduct is a peculiarly US development.

6–4

Corporate law appears flexible (especially in the much-favoured Delaware), but auditing disclosure standards are tougher than elsewhere. The ultra vires rule is sharply curtailed, usually on the basis of a model law. The giving by a company of financial assistance for the purchase of its own shares is usually controlled by bankruptcy preference doctrines, as opposed to English-based specific statutory prohibitions. The law of subordinated debt is highly developed.

Preferential transfers

6–5 The combination of federal and state rules on preferential transfers by an insolvent debtor in the suspect period make the rules amongst the most pro-debtor in the world because the defences are very limited. Hence insolvencies tend to be somewhat more retroactive than elsewhere in the world.

Contract rescission

Ipso facto clauses entitling a counterparty to cancel a contract on the insolvency of the other party are restricted by federal bankruptcy law. This is not reflected in most other jurisdictions in all groups except in a few having special statutes to similar effect, e.g. Canada, France, New Zealand (in special cases). As a result, the United States has introduced netting statutes of some complexity for certain markets which override the bankruptcy freeze on *ipso facto* clauses and the stay on set-off.

Conflict of laws

6–6 There are highly developed and complex conflict of laws rules and a general acceptance of freedom of choice of law in international contracts, subject to some pockets of resistance. Governmental interest analysis seems in theory to be more unpredictable than the somewhat cut-and-dried English rules reflected in the 1980 Rome Convention, but it is questionable whether this theory really does produce more uncertainty in important international contract cases.

There are broad similarities in English and US long-arm jurisdiction in contract cases, but significant differences of detail.

The attitude to foreign money judgments is liberal with a high degree of comity. There are no international treaties.

Comity in international insolvency conflicts was extended by the 1978 bankruptcy legislation, altering the previous position which was protective of US creditors.

Sovereign deimmunisation under 1976 legislation is relatively cautious compared to Italy, the Netherlands, Germany and England, and in this regard is similar in some respects to France and Switzerland.

Securities regulation

This is extremely tough, initially perhaps as a reaction to the Great Crash of 6–7 1929. There are elaborate disclosure requirements for prospectuses required to be registered which has tended to discourage foreign issuers and certainly restricted the primary distribution of Eurobond issues in the US. The previous unusually restrictive exemption for offers to sophisticated investors has been liberalised.

Contracts

There is a highly developed basic contract law, including third party beneficiary contracts. But many states retain writing requirements (Statute of Frauds), in contrast to the dismantling of these inconveniences in the leading English-based and Germanic states.

Usury

Usury laws are still widely prevalent, but are not usually problematic in international finance for various reasons.

Stamp duties

Documentary taxes are not levied – as a revolutionary reaction to Britain.

Negotiable instruments

The US has the most liberal system: see para 5–19.

Codification of commercial law

The Uniform Commercial Code covers sales, leases, commercial paper 6–8 (negotiable instruments), bank deposits and collections, funds transfers, letters of credit, bulk transfers, documents of title for goods, investment securities and personal property secured transactions. The approach to large value funds transfers outside the consumer context is sensible.

There are numerous uniform laws, enjoying varying degrees of state acceptance. Bankruptcy, securities and maritime law are federal. Some states have more extensive codification, e.g. California.

Dispute resolution

Plaintiff-protection and related policies are much more pronounced than elsewhere in the world, notably the contingent fee system, non-liability of the losing plaintiff for legal costs of the successful defendant, the jury system, class actions and treble or punitive damages.

There is some acceptance of big pocket theory of liability (lender liability, environment, securities misrepresentations, tort generally), but this may be on the wane.

List of United States common law jurisdictions

(excluding Louisiana) (62)

US States

6–9　Total population, excluding Louisiana, 247,925,000; with Louisiana, 252,177,000. States with population of about 5 million or more are noted in bold and rounded to the nearest million.

Alabama	Iowa
Alaska	Kansas
Arizona	Kentucky
Arkansas	Maine
California (30 million)	**Maryland** (5 million)
Colorado	**Massachusetts** (6 million)
Connecticut	**Michigan** (9 million)
Delaware	Minnesota
Florida (13 million)	Mississippi
Georgia (7 million)	**Missouri** (5 million)
Hawaii	Montana
Idaho	Nebraska
Illinois (12 million)	Nevada
Indiana (6 million)	New Hampshire

New Jersey (8 million)   South Dakota
New Mexico   Tennessee (5 million)
New York (18 million). Tri-   Texas (17 million)
ple A jurisdiction   Utah
North Carolina (7 million)   Vermont
North Dakota   Virginia (6 million)
Ohio (11 million)   Washington (5 million)
Oklahoma   West Virginia
Oregon   Wisconsin (5 million)
Pennsylvania (12 million)   Wyoming
Rhode Island   District of Columbia
South Carolina

US-influenced states

American Samoa	Population 38,000. Unincorporated US territory 6–10 in South Pacific.
Guam	Population 137,000. Self-governing Pacific island administered by the US. UCC applies.
Johnston and Sand Islands	Population 300. 320 acres of coral atoll. Unincorporated US territory in central Pacific.
Liberia	Population 2,700,000. West African independent republic. No bankruptcy law. Corporate law is Delaware-based. Has the world's largest shipping register, based on US law and administered in New York. UCC does not apply.
Marshall Islands	Population 49,000. Former US trust territory in Pacific. Independent 1979. Set up a Liberian-style shipping register during Liberian troubles in 1980s as an alternative.
Micronesia	Population 111,000. Pacific islands forming Federated States of Micronesia. Former US trust territory.
Midway Islands	Population 300. Two square miles of unincorporated US territory in central Pacific.
Nauru	Pacific island. Smallest republic in the world. Former US trust territory.

Northern Marianas   Pacific islands, commonwealth status with US from 1978. UCC applies.

Palau (Belau)   Tiny Pacific island state. Former US trust territory. Independent 1981.

Virgin Islands (US)   Population 102,000. Caribbean islands. UCC applies.

Wake Island   Population 250. Atoll of 2.5 square miles in central Pacific. Unincorporated US territory, administered by US Air Force.

CHAPTER 7

GROUP 2: MIXED ROMAN/COMMON LAW JURISDICTIONS

Main comparative characteristics

The jurisdictions listed in this chapter were originally Germanic or Roman,   7–1
but have been influenced by the common law approach, either in its English
or American form, in varying degrees or in specific areas. The group does
not have common characteristics, other than acceptance of the trust (but in
most cases not the constructive trust or tracing). Some have a common law
style. A case could be made for locating some of these jurisdictions in
Groups 3 or 4.

Japan and Korea may be taken together. They may be more appropriately
classified as Group 3. Japan took over parts of the German civil code of
1900 but in an earlier draft and under French advice, so that, in accordance
with Franco-Latin tradition, assignments of debts must be notified to the
debtor to be effective on the seller's bankruptcy – a typically Franco-Latin
rule. The Japanese bankruptcy law is based on the German nineteenth century *Konkursordnung*. After World War II, the American occupation authorities requested Japan to adopt certain US statutes as a condition of reopening their markets: these were a corporate reorganisation based on the
amendments to the US BA 1898 introduced by the Chandler Act of 1938
(the precursor to BC 1978 Chapter 11), the US securities legislation of the
1930s (substantially amended in the early 1990s) and a codified law of
trusts.

Apart from those overlaps, Japan has a typically Germanic system,
including insolvency set-off and the fiduciary transfer for security (not much
used). Title finance is widely accepted without recharacterisation. ⬆

Korea appears to be similar to Japan in many respects, but there are significant differences.

The **Southern African group** comprises South Africa itself, Botswana,   7–2
Lesotho, Namibia, Swaziland and Zimbabwe and is Roman-Dutch at the
foundation, overlaid by English common law. This is because South Africa
was originally colonised by the Dutch who laid down a proper legal infra-

structure which the English chose not to disturb, except superficially. They
were sufficiently satisfied with the system to carry it through into former
S Rhodesia (now Zimbabwe), colonised by Cecil Rhodes, but not to
N Rhodesia (Zambia since 1964): Zambia is Traditional English in Group
1A. The South African system is Roman in that it does not have insolvency
set-off, but it does have an inchoate and rather weak floating charge – the
notarial bond (up-graded in South Africa in 1993) – and there was a reception of the English consensual trust, but not the constructive trust. Company law is English-based. The position with regard to the notification of
assignments to the debtor should be checked. South Africa did not have an
aircraft mortgage until the early 1990s.

7–3   In the **Channel Islands group,** the background system of law is pre-
Napoleonic French but the borrowings from English have been considerable
– trust, insolvency set-off (in Guernsey by contract) and company law. The
scope of security is quite conservative. Jersey in particular has a large banking community.

    Quebec and **Scotland** have been receptive to mercantilist ideas, e.g. the
universal floating charge and insolvency set-off. But both retain a distinctive
Roman bias.

    Liechtenstein is Swiss-Austrian but has fully received the trust, but pre-
sumably not the constructive trust or tracing of trust property. The principality has insolvency set-off.

    Sri Lanka was a Roman-Dutch system like South Africa but much more
anglicised, e.g. insolvency set-off and the floating charge.

    That Swaziland and Japan should find themselves rubbing shoulders in
the same group is part of the humour of history. But there is no reason why
little Swaziland, a country of extraordinary beauty, should not produce one
of the world's greatest lawyers. As Pliny observed, *"Ex Africa semper ali-
quid novi"*.

List of Jurisdictions (15)

7–4 **Alderney and Sark**   See "Jersey" in this list.

    Botswana   Population 1,300,000, 50 per cent Christian.
South West Africa. Former British colony, the
Bechuanaland Protectorate, independent 1965.
David Livingstone's first mission. South African-
based legal system. Roman-Dutch law imported

from Colony of Cape of Good Hope in 1891, but criminal law is English-based. ICSID 1970.

Guernsey   See "Jersey" in this list.

Japan   Population 124,000,000, 40 per cent Shinto, 38 per cent Buddhist. CC 1898, as much French as German. ComC 1899 based more on German commercial code (HGB). CCP 1948 closely modelled on German ZPO of 1877. All extensively amended. Bankruptcy Law of 1922, modelled on German Bankruptcy Act 1877. Corporate Reorganisation Law 1952, modelled on US Chandler Act amendments of 1938 to US BA 1898. Company law in ComC. Negotiable instruments in Law 20 of 1932. Enterprise Hypothecation Law 1958, as amended. Securities and Exchange Law of 1948, as amended, modelled on US securities legislation of the 1930s but administered broadly by ministerial officials. Financial System Reform Act of 1992. Securities Investment Trust Law 1951. Code of Trusts. Germanic fiduciary transfer for personal property security, though not much favoured by banks. Assignments of debts must be notified.

Jersey   Jersey, Guernsey and Alderney and Sark are tax   7–5 haven banking centres, mainly for private banking. Self-governing possessions of British Crown off the coast of France from time of William the Conqueror who brought the bailiwicks of Guernsey and Jersey with him in 1066. Originally customary law of Normandy. Control of their own tax laws. Guernsey (consisting of eight islands, only three of which are populated) has two island dependencies – Alderney and Sark – which is a tiny but independent jurisdiction and is governed by a feudal Seigneur. Guernsey lawyers must be qualified English lawyers and have a certificate in Norman law from the University of Caen in France. Guernsey bankruptcy based on English BA 1914. Jersey insolvency laws are Norman based (mainly the désastre) originating from

1802 and codified in Bankruptcy (Désastre) Jersey Law 1990. See also Preferred Debts (Guernsey) Law 1983. Guernsey Company Law 1908, as amended in 1973. Companies (Jersey) Law 1991. Bills of Exchange (Guernsey) Law 1958, amended 1973. Trusts (Guernsey) Law 1989. Trusts (Jersey) Law 1984, as amended. Security Interests (Guernsey) Law 1993 liberalises security over personal property, but notification to debtor of assignments is required. Jersey and Guernsey have special relationship with the EU via the UK: they are free of EU customs and tax laws. Insider dealing law in Jersey.

7–6 Korea (South)
Population 43,300,000, 42 per cent Christian, 18 per cent Buddhist. Annexed by Japan 1910 till 1945 so that Japanese codes, in turn based mainly on the German codes, were introduced. CC 1958, CCP 1960, ComC 1962, all as amended. Conflict of Laws Act 1962. Company law in ComC. Securities and Exchange Act based on US securities legislation of 1930s but since substantially amended, especially in 1977. Securities Investment Trust Business Act 1969. Germanic fiduciary transfer for personal property security. Assignments of debts must be notified.

Lesotho
Population 1,800,000. Landlocked mountain state in South Africa. Former British Colony of Basutoland, independent 1966. The legal system is South-African based.

Liechtenstein
Population 29,000. Principality since 1332, situated between Switzerland and Austria. Close relationship with Switzerland since 1923, but basic legal foundations are Austrian. Major tax haven, particularly for individuals. CC 1812 – the Austrian AG BGB of 1811, as amended. ComC 1865 – the German HGB of 1965 via Austria, as amended. CCP of 1912, as amended – the Austrian ZPO. Companies law contained in Persons and Companies Law of 1926, reformed in 1980. Has every known form of legal entity devised by man and famed for the foundation.

Conflicts of laws is Austrian-based. BA 1973 (*Konkursordnung*). Fully received the common law trust (but probably not the constructive trust) – see Arts 897–932 of Persons and Company Law of 1926, reformed in 1980 legislation. Trust Enterprises Law 1928.

Mauritius   Population 1,100,000. Former British colony (formerly French) off east coast of Africa 1810, independent 1968. CC, CCP and ComC French-based, but much revised. IA 1956, CA 1984, English-based perhaps. Conflicts of law is traditional French. ICSID 1969. English Bills of Exchange Act c 393. Stock Exchange Act 1987. Trusts Act 1989. This state may be wrongly classified and might be group 4.

Namibia   Population 1,300,000, 80 per cent Christian. 7–7
German colony, then South African mandate (1922–1967), independent 1990. Article 140 of Constitution retains pre-independence (South African) laws till amended.

Quebec   Population 6,800,000. French-based codes, originally guaranteed by British in mid-1700s. New CC 1994. Thoughtful jurisdiction. New hypotheque can be created on all types of property, present and future, moveable or immovable, tangible or intangible, and may be possessory or non-possessory. Consolidation of enforcement provisions. Canadian bankruptcy law is federal so insolvency set-off is permitted. Bills of exchange legislation is federal (based on British 1882 Act). Securities Act 1983, as amended. Contains insider trading prohibitions. Quebec Securities Commission.

Scotland   Population 5,000,000. Floating charge by statute. Insolvency set-off developed by case law. Otherwise greater hostility to security (false wealth). Trusts (Scotland) Act 1921 as amended. British IA 1986 applies with modifications.

South Africa   Population 31,400,000, 80 per cent Christian. 7–8
Authentic legal scholarship, with uninterrupted

view back to Rome. Major supplier of first-class judges to the English judiciary. Roman-Dutch system originally based on mediaeval Roman law, as highly developed in pre-Napoleonic Holland. Dutch East India Company established a post at the Cape of Good Hope in 1652, subsequently settled by Dutch, German and French Huguenot colonisers. Occupied by the British in 1795. Britain annexed Natal in 1844, Transvaal in 1877, Orange Free State in 1900. Union of South Africa constituted in 1909, left the British Commonwealth 1960. No general codification. Insolvency Act 24 of 1936, last amended in 1991. English-based Companies Act 61 of 1973, as amended, contains typical English prohibition on financial assistance. Conflict of laws is English-influenced. Notarial bond conferring universal security upgraded in 1993, but this may not be so in other South African-based states. Bills of Exchange Act 34 of 1964, as amended. Stock Exchange Control Act 1 of 1985. Financial Markets Control Act 55 of 1989. Trust Property Control Act 57 of 1988. Common law trust originally introduced by case law, but not the constructive trust and no tracing by beneficiaries.

7–9　Sri Lanka

Population 17,200,000. Island state off southern tip of India. Former British colony of Ceylon, formerly Dutch, independent 1948. Legal anglicisation of Roman-Dutch legal system much more advanced than South African group (unlike South Africa, the population did not speak Dutch). No general codification. Insolvents Ordinance c 97. Settlement of Debts Law, Law 27/1975. Companies Act c 145, reformed by Law 17/1982. English approach to conflict of laws. Common law trust introduced and codified by statute.

Swaziland

Population 800,000, 77 per cent Christian. Small landlocked state between South Africa and Mozambique. Legal system is South African-based.

Zimbabwe   Population 9,600,000. Landlocked central African republic. Victoria Falls shared with Zambia. Former British colony of S Rhodesia. Unilateral declaration of independence 1965, finally independent 1980. South African-based legal system.

CHAPTER 8

GROUP 3: GERMANIC AND SCANDINAVIAN JURISDICTIONS

Main comparative characteristics

8–1   The jurisdictions listed in this chapter are largely pro-creditor, but are less radical than the traditional English jurisdictions.

Security

Unlike the Franco-Latin group, but like the Anglo-American group, the old insistence on possessory pledges for non-land security is side-stepped by various devices, notably the fiduciary transfer for goods, receivables and other non-land assets in Germany, Netherlands, Switzerland and others, and the statutory introduction of the enterprise floating charge in Scandinavian countries. The reception of the fiduciary transfer in Poland and the Czech and Slovak Republics appears likely, but remains to be seen. The fiduciary transfer is not as extensive as the English-based universal floating charge, largely by reason of the inability to charge assets generically (a degree of specific identification is required) and hostility to over-security (because of the absence of a public registration system).

Unlike the Franco-Latin group, but like the Anglo-American group, assignments of receivables do not usually have to be notified to the debtor to be effective on the assignor's bankruptcy but the Netherlands position is more complicated following CC 1992 and notification may be required in the Scandinavian countries (according to the author's sources, it is required in Sweden). This should be checked.

In contrast to Anglo-American jurisdictions, a registration system requiring the filing of security interests over personal property in a public bureau is unusual, and the general enterprise charge (in the form of the fiduciary transfer) is about 50 per cent as comprehensive as the English version, except in both cases for the wide Scandinavian floating charge. Security over future assets is possible, but cumbersome. Security for future debt is not usually problematic, but maximum amounts must be stated.

Usually there is no extra-judicial private sale as opposed to a judicially-mandated private or public sale, and possessory management through a receiver is rare, even for the Scandinavian floating charge. Bankruptcy costs, taxes and wages do not rank ahead of security.

Overall, security is more favoured than in Franco-Latin jurisdictions but is not as liberal as the Anglo-American jurisdictions so that legal protectionism of debtors is more pronounced than in common law countries.

Title finance

Like traditional English jurisdictions, but unlike Franco-Latin jurisdictions, there is a wide acceptance of retention of title, factoring of receivables, sale and repurchase, hire purchase, financial leasing, and sale and lease-back without recharacterisation as a mortgage on bankruptcy. In other words, the limitations of the Napoleonic security are avoided by transactions having the same commercial effect. This is the basis of the Germanic fiduciary transfer, although the transfer is fully recharacterised as a mortgage.   8–2

Insolvency set-off

Like the common law jurisdictions, but unlike the Franco-Latin jurisdictions, insolvency set-off is allowed in all this group (but Taiwan has not been checked). Netting is usually freely allowed without discrimination, and there are also special netting provisions in the bankruptcy laws of Germany and the Netherlands.

Corporate rehabilitation proceedings

Usually there is a conventional composition with high entry requirements, which is therefore little used. There are some modern corporate rehabilitation statutes although these are normally mild when compared to the French and American versions. The private consensual work-out seems to enjoy more favour than the public judicial version found in France, Canada and the United States.

False wealth and reputed ownership

In contrast to Anglo-American law, but in keeping with the Franco-Latin approach, secret beneficial ownership and trusts are not normally recognised on account of the false wealth doctrine. But there are some inroads on   8–3

this, e.g. for fungible securities held by central custodians (especially in
Austria, Germany and the Netherlands). Undisclosed principals are sometimes allowed to intervene on contracts undertaken by agents. There is
usually no bankruptcy super-priority for the recovery of mistaken payments
or money wrongfully obtained by the debtor, i.e. the Anglo-American
constructive trust or tracing is not accepted.

Veil of incorporation

The veil of incorporation is usually strong, both as regards directors and
shareholders. The special regime for corporate groups in Germany is not
found elsewhere.

Preferential transfers

8–4   There is the usual *actio pauliana* for intentionally fraudulent transfers. The
fixed suspect periods are usually much shorter than in the Franco-Latin
group. The creditor is usually safeguarded if he was unaware of the debtor's
insolvency, which is more protective than the Franco-Latin approach, but
the more creditor-protective English "intent" doctrine (which requires
debtor intent to prefer) is unusual. Netherlands preference law is markedly
pro-creditor and is hence similar to that in the Traditional English group.

Contract and lease rescission

Ipso facto clauses entitling a party to cancel an executory contract licence or
equipment lease on the bankruptcy of the other party are generally upheld.
There may be special provisions limiting landlord repossessions of commercial leases.

Conflicts of law

8–5   The attitude to freedom of choice of law is liberal. There are highly developed conflicts rules, especially in the Netherlands in view of its colonial history and its entrepot status as one of the leading maritime highways into
Continental Europe.
    Long-arm judicial jurisdiction is based on the presence of assets – the
toothbrush jurisdiction – in Germany and Scandinavian countries (also
Japan and South Africa, in Group 2), though this is usually tempered by a
requirement for other contacts.

Initially there was some hostility to the enforcement of foreign money judgments – reciprocity in Germany, a treaty required in the Netherlands and Scandinavia. But those attitudes have been largely overridden by liberal case law.

Sovereign immunity adopts the restrictive doctrine by case law, although the position in the Czech and Slovak Republics and Poland remains to be seen. Local nexus of the sovereign activity is required in Switzerland.

There are differing attitudes to the recognition of foreign insolvency administrations. Scandinavian countries and the Netherlands formally require a treaty, but case law leads to the opposite conclusion. There is patchy acceptance of the bankruptcy freeze of the foreign forum on local creditor executions.

Securities regulation

These jurisdictions have an aversion to noisy regulatory statutes, as opposed   8–6
to clubs run by universal banks who are traditionally in charge of securities issues. Until recently Germany had no securities regulation in the American sense. But soft law – which was highly effective – has been or is being replaced in Continental European and Scandinavian countries by new statutes driven by EU Directives and by the widening of eligibility to deal in securities ("deregulation") and, in Poland and the Czech and Slovak Republics, by statutes driven by post-communist privatisation.

Usury

There are still some vestiges of the old anti-moneylender view, shown, for   8–7
example, by objections to interest on interest, though these are easily circumvented by contractual devices.

Gaming

Gaming laws are still prevalent in many states, though now modified by legislation for some markets, e.g. in the Netherlands (1986) and Germany (1989).

Codification

Most of the countries, except in Scandinavia, have substantially codified their basic laws of contract, agency and the like.

Bills of exchange

The restrictive Geneva regime applies in the main: see para 5–19.

List of Jurisdictions (13)

8–8   Note: Some of the members of Group 6 – emerging jurisdictions – may be candidates for membership of this group.

Aruba   Population 66,000, self-governing part of Netherlands situated in the Southern Caribbean. Based on Dutch law, as with the Netherlands Antilles.

Finland   Population 5,000,000. Russian influence until independence in 1917. Widespread use of Swedish models, reflecting Swedish influence in eighteenth and nineteenth centuries. BA 1868, amended 1985 and (it is believed) in the early 1990s. CA 1978 conforming to Nordic corporate legislation. Sales and Contract law 1987. Standardised Options and Futures Trading Act 1988. Securities Trading Act 1989.

8–9   **Germany**   Population 79,100,000. One of the world's most brilliant legal jurisdictions and highly influential globally. Triple A. BGB (*Burgerliches Gesetzbuch* – civil code) 1896 (in force 1900). CCP (*Zivilprozessordnung*) 1877. HGB (*Handelsgesetzbuch* – commercial code) 1897 (in force 1900). New bankruptcy law in the offing to replace BA 1877.

Iceland   Population 260,000. Situated between Scotland and Greenland. Legal system is Nordic-based and legislation conforming with other Scandinavian countries is to be expected.

Indonesia   Population 181,500,000. Covers 13,667 islands stretched across 3200 miles. Fifth most populous country in the world. Dutch colony from end of seventeenth century, independent 1949. Dutch-based legal system, not absorbing the new Dutch CC 1992.

Netherlands	Population 15,000,000. Extraordinarily rich juris- 8–10 diction, especially private international law. In the tradition of Grotius, one of the world's greatest lawyers. New but cautious Dutch CC 1992, which took nearly 40 years to draft and which ranks as the newest comprehensive industrialised civil code in the world. But the code seems to place the Netherlands back into the false wealth tradition, notwithstanding more liberal case law and a gener- ally non-dogmatic approach to commercial law.
Netherlands Antilles	Population 191,000. Based on pre-1992 Dutch law. Bankruptcy law contained in Act of March 13, 1935 and Bankruptcy Decree 1931.
Norway	Population 4,300,000. No general codification. Bankruptcy governed by BA 1984. Company Law 1976. Important maritime law. Stock Exchange Law 1988. Securities Trading Law 1985.
Poland	Population 38,300,000. Independent 1918 but a 8–11 mature legal culture for centuries. Shook off communism in late 1980s. ComC 1934, German- influenced, contains provisions regulating com- panies, significantly amended after return to market economics. CC 1964 substantially amended 1990. Bankruptcy Act of 1934 and Composition Proceedings Act of 1934 based on German models and since revised. Conflict of laws governed by Law of November 12, 1965. Act on Public Trading in Securities and Trust Funds 1991.
Surinam	Population 420,000. Based on pre-1975 Dutch law. Former Dutch colony (Dutch Guiana), inde- pendent 1975.
Sweden	Population 8,610,000. Very advanced and inven- tive jurisdiction. Bankruptcy in BA 1988. Com- panies Act 1975, as amended. Prohibition on financial assistance by company to purchase its own shares. Conflict of laws is mainly case law. Contracts Act 1915. Contract Terms Act 1971.

Switzerland

Population 6,800,000. Superb jurisdiction which never puts a foot wrong. Code of Obligations of 1881, re-enacted as CC BK V in 1911, much revised. Influential CC 1912 prepared by Huber. No ComC since commercial law is contained in CC or CO. Companies Code is in CO Arts 772–887. Assignments do not have to be notified to the debtor to be valid. First-class Private International Law Act of 1987. Bankruptcy in Federal Law on Debt Collection Proceedings and Bankruptcy 1889, as amended.

8–12 Taiwan

Population 20,500,000. Home of exiled Chinese Kuomintang from 1949, previously Formosa. Background Swiss-German codes promulgated in mainland China around 1930, carried to Taiwan. CC 1929, amended 1982. CCP 1935, amended 1984. BA 1935 amended 1980. Company Law 1929, as amended. Law governing the Application of laws to Civil Matters involving Foreign Elements, 1953. Maritime Law 1929. Negotiable Instruments Law of October 30, 1929, as amended. Numerous laws regulating the sale of securities in Taiwan, e.g. Securities and Exchange Law 1968 as amended, backed by 1971 Rules regarding public prospectuses. Offshore Futures Trading Act 1992. Draft Trust Law not yet enacted as at mid-1994.

CHAPTER 9

GROUP 4: MIXED FRANCO-LATIN/ GERMANIC JURISDICTIONS

Main comparative characteristics

These jurisdictions are a mixture of the Franco-Latin approach and the Ger-   9–1
manic approach, though sometimes with a common law influence.

They are Franco-Latin in their attitude to security, which is usually very
limited. The tendency to recharacterise title finance as security is probably
more pronounced in some members of this group than in the Germanic
group, but more research is needed on this point. The jurisdictions are Germanic in that they usually allow insolvency set-off, although the position in
Hungary and Turkey has not been investigated. A few have cautious Germanic bankruptcy compositions and corporate rehabilitation statutes, e.g.
Austria. But Italy has a dramatic insolvency rehabilitation procedure for
large corporates. Both Franco-Latin jurisdictions and Germanic jurisdictions object to reputed ownership and the trust, and this attitude is reflected
in this group. In Italy, assignments must be notified to the debtor to be effective on the seller's bankruptcy, but this is not so in Austria. The position in
Denmark, Hungary and Thailand on assignment notification has not been
investigated. The law of preferences varies, with Italy adopting the Germanic approach (more protective of creditors) and Denmark the Franco-Latin
approach (it seems).

The group includes **Louisiana, Panama,** and the **Philippines.** The overall   9–2
colouring of these three states is Franco-Latin and so the attitudes to security are largely Franco-Latin and they may still preserve the rule that assignments of debts must be notified. But they have received some common law
influence, in the form either of the trust, or insolvency set-off or wider security. Panama has received insolvency set-off and, in light of the importance of
Panama as a shipping register (probably second in the world after Liberia),
English ideas about shipping mortgages, notably the possibility of covering
future debt and revolving credits, and possessory management through a
receiver on default, instead of the usual civilian judicial public auction. In

this respect Greece is similar, owing also to the significance attached to financing its merchant fleet. Quebec is considered to be Group 2.

The Philippines absorbed bankruptcy ideas from the US Bankruptcy Act of 1898 and is said to have received the trust. Whether they adopted the American insolvency set-off should be checked.

List of Jurisdictions (13)

9–3 **Austria**

Population 7,820,000. CC – the AGBG (*Allgemeines Bürgerliches Gesetzbuch*) of 1811, much amended. CCP (*Zivilprozessordnung*) of 1895, as amended, especially in 1983. ComC (*Handelsgesetzbuch*) of 1938. This was the German code of 1897 and has been much amended. BA 1914 (*Konkursordnung*), Composition Code 1914 (*Ausgleichsordnung*), both amended in 1982 to introduce an observation period. Company Law 1965 (*Aktiengesetz*), amended 1982. Stock and Commodity Exchange Act 1989, amending legislation, originally 1903. Fiduciaries in ABGB Arts 604–646.

Czech Republic

Population roughly 10,000,000. Flurry of new legislation overriding Russian-style enactments from the Communist era mixed with previous Austro-Germanic codes. New ComC 1991 contains provisions on companies. CC 1964 revised 1991, totally changing it. Law on Bankruptcy and Settlement of 1991 is on Austrian lines, containing a three-month observation period. Corporations Law 1990. Code of International Civil Procedure and Law of 1963 allows parties to choose governing law and applies fixed presumptions if they do not do so. Security over investments must generally be registered in books of issuer. Non-possessory security over chattels is difficult. Assignments of receivables must be notified to the debtor to be valid on bankruptcy of assignor.

9–4 **Denmark**

Population 5,200,000. No official general codification of basic law of contract, agency and the like. BA Law 298 of 1977, last amended in 1989. Law on Public Companies of 1973, as amended (*aktieselskab*). Law of Private Limited Companies of 1973 as amended (*anpartsselskab*).

Faeroe Islands   Population 45,000. Island territory of Denmark between Iceland and Scotland, self-governing since 1948. Legal system is Danish-based. Not part of the EU and EU directives do not apply.

Greenland   Population 53,000. The world's largest island, Danish territory in the Arctic Circle, self-governing since 1979. Not part of the EU and EU directives do not apply.

Hungary   Population 10,300,000. No codification until the arrival of the communists so that Hungary was the only major European non-codified state operating on common law principles. Subsequent CC 1959, CCP 1977, now extensively revised. Code of private international law 1979. Insolvency Act 1992. Compulsory petition on insolvency. Tough preference rules. Company law in Law on Economic Associations, Act VI of 1988, revised 1990. No express prohibition on financial assistance by company to purchase its own shares, as yet. Security over personal property very restricted. Assignments of debts must be notified to the debtor to be valid. Mortgages over real property allowed. Law on Securities and Stock Exchanges, Act VI of 1990.

Italy   Population 57,600,000. Leading jurisdiction for more   9–5
than 2000 years, an extraordinary achievement. Triple A. Prolific case law. CC 1942, CCP 1940, commercial law in CC BkV. BA 1942, based on German 1877 Bankruptcy Act. Company law in CC. Securities originally in Decree-Law 95 of April 8, 1974 (investment funds in Law 77 of March 23, 1983), all much amended and amplified by regulations. EC Directives on securities implemented in 1989. Ratified Hague Trusts Convention of 1986. Insolvency set-off. Protective Germanic preference laws. Assignments of debts must be notified to the debtor. Very limited security over personal property – the Germanic fiduciary transfer was rejected. But a limited form of enterprise charge was introduced in 1994, applying mainly to inventory. Ambiguous attitude to title finance.

Louisiana   Population 4,300,000. Fideicommissa or trusts prohibited in 1808 code, but subsequently relaxed in numerous enactments, e.g. allowing Paul Tulane's gifts to Tulane University (1882), bank trusteeship (1902), bondholder trustees (1914) and trusts of land (1938). UCC applies, except Art 9 on security interests. US bankruptcy law is mainly federal.

9–6 Panama

Population 2,500,000. Former Spanish colony, rebelled 1811, finally broke with Colombia 1903 on establishment of the Canal Zone. Banking centre for Latin America, and one of the largest shipping registers in the world. CC 1916, CCP 1984, ComC 1916, as amended, all in Napoleonic tradition. Maritime Code 1982, amended 1986. Bankruptcy in the Codes. Insolvency set-off in ComC Art 1578. Has ratified Bustamente Code. Companies governed by Law 32 of February 26, 1927, as amended. National Securities Commission created by law of 1970. Trusts Law of 1941 introducing the Anglo-American trust (but presumably not the constructive trust), replaced by Law 7 of January 5, 1984, and subsequent regulations.

Philippines

Population 62,400,000. Originally the islands were a Spanish colony, ceded to the US after the Spanish-American War of 1898, independent 1946. Reception of US law in some respects. CC 1950, ComC 1888 based on Spanish ComC 1886. Insolvency Law (Act No 1956) modelled on Spanish ComC for its suspension of payments and IA 1895 of California and US BA 1898 for its other provisions, but check if US insolvency set-off was adopted. Bulk sales law: Act 3952. Registered non-possessory chattel mortgages available: Act 1508. Publicity required for assignments of receivables in Franco-Latin tradition. Corporation Code, evidencing US ideas. Insurance Code taken verbatim from California. Uniform Negotiable Instruments Act modelled on US 1896 Act. Securities legislation is US-influenced with Securities and Exchange Commission (including registration of broker-dealers and margin regulations): see Batas Pambanso 178, Presidential Decree 1758.

9–7 Slovak Republic

Population roughly 5,000,000. Similar to Czech Republic.

Thailand

Population 55,900,000. Civil and Commercial Code. Assignments of debts must be notified to the debtor to be valid: CCC Art 306. Insolvency set-off in BA 1940 s 102. Very limited security over personal property. Seems to be conservative on recognition of foreign security and foreign judgments.

Turkey

Population 57,300,000. CC 1926, basically an 80 per cent translation of the Swiss CC and Code of Obligations introduced by Kemal Ataturk. Bankruptcy Law, Law 2004 of June 9, 1932, reformed by Law 538 of February 18, 1965. Company law contained in the French-based ComC. Conflict of laws in Law 2675 of May 20, 1982.

CHAPTER 10

GROUP 5: TRADITIONAL FRANCO-LATIN JURISDICTIONS

Main comparative characteristics

10–1   The Franco-Latin group comprises a substantial number of jurisdictions, all more or less influenced by the Napoleonic codes. These jurisdictions are largely pro-debtor. But there are episodic shifts in favour of pro-creditor protections and greater liberality in numerous cases. In some jurisdictions, e.g. Belgium, the shift is proceeding at a gathering pace and therefore one must be careful of the generalisations in this chapter.

Security

10–2   Security over non-land assets (goods, receivables, securities) must be a possessory pledge, but this position is eroded in many of the countries, e.g. France, Belgium, Luxembourg and Spain. Unlike the Anglo-American or Germanic groups, assignments of receivables must usually be notified to the debtor to be valid on the assignor's bankruptcy. Publication of corporate non-possessory security in a mercantile register is occasionally possible, usually for non-possessory chattel mortgages of specific assets like industrial machinery. The universal enterprise charge is rare, but allowed in some South American countries for corporate debenture issues. France, Belgium, Luxembourg and Spain (amongst others) have enterprise charges between 25 and 50 per cent as extensive as the common law universal floating charge. There is resistance to security over future assets and security for future debt – these are primarily inspired by debtor-protection policies. Specific identification of secured assets is the rule (doctrine of specificity), thereby limiting generic charges and charges over future assets. As also in the Germanic group, maximum amounts must usually be stated. Usually there is no private sale and almost invariably no possessory management through a receiver. Trustees of security are generally not recognised. Formalities prevail for land, ship and aircraft mortgages, and often in other cases as well, e.g. notarisation. Unlike the common law, Germanic and Scandinavian jurisdictions, bankruptcy costs, taxes and wages sometimes rank ahead of security, thereby diminishing its worth and rendering its value unpredictable.

Title finance

These transactions include retention of title, factoring of receivables, sale   10–3
and repurchase, financial leasing, hire purchase, and sale and lease-back. The overall traditional bias is against title finance which is therefore re-characterised as security (as a result of which it is usually void on bankruptcy because non-possessory), but generalisation is unsafe. One tendency is to escape the conservatism of mortgage law and to allow financial leasing without recharacterisation as a mortgage, but to recharacterise hire purchase (lease with an option to purchase). Thus, goods on hire purchase may be deemed to belong to the lessee on his bankruptcy. Another tendency is sympathy for the small trade creditor, so that seizures of goods unpaid for and still in the possession of the debtor are allowed, together with occasional statutory recognition of reservation of title, e.g. France. Factoring of receivables is usually prevented by a requirement that validity depends on notice to the debtor, but is allowed for negotiable instruments and (in a few cases) for securitisations complying with highly prescriptive statutes; as in France and Spain.

Insolvency set-off

There is generally no insolvency set-off except for single current accounts or   10–4
connected transactions (codified in France in 1994). There are netting statutes for certain markets in Belgium (very limited) and France (wider) but not Luxembourg (as at end 1994).

Corporate rehabilitation proceedings

Most countries have a conventional composition available pre- and post-bankruptcy. There is some variation in the entry requirements and the voting majorities, but on the whole these compositions are not much used. A few countries have adopted specific corporate rehabilitation statutes, notably an extremely draconian version in France enacted in 1985 which developed policies inaugurated in 1967. In the early 1990s, it appeared that France was modifying the extreme pro-debtor tendency of its bankruptcy law, which may have been influenced by the employee-protection policies of earlier years.

Reputed ownership

10–5   Secret beneficial ownership and trusts are not usually recognised on account
of the false wealth doctrine, but undisclosed principals are sometimes
allowed to intervene. There is usually no bankruptcy super-priority for the
recovery of mistaken payments or money wrongfully obtained by the
debtor, i.e. no Anglo-American constructive trust or tracing. Bank trusts are
statutorily allowed in many Latin American jurisdictions (taking the lead
from Chile), as are trusts for corporate debenture issues (influenced by
British nineteenth century investments).

Veil of incorporation

10–6   There is some suspicion of the corporate form in the more traditional jurisdictions. Directors are often easily liable for negligence, especially in France,
and (probably) Spain, but there is much variation. Management is usually
personally liable for failure to apply for bankruptcy or for failure to call a
shareholders meeting if more than one-half (usually) of the capital is lost.
Often there is a duty to apply for bankruptcy which inhibits private work-
outs. But the veil between shareholders and the company is usually firm,
even for groups.

Preferential transfers

10–7   There is the usual *actio pauliana* for intentionally fraudulent transfers. The
general effect is more pro-debtor than the English-based and Germanic jurisdictions, but perhaps not as pro-debtor as the US. Some transactions in the
suspect period are automatically void: gifts and transactions at an undervalue; prepayments of unmatured debts; abnormal payments of matured
debts; and security for pre-existing debt. The validity of security for pre-
existing debt is an acid test – often the security is granted to allow the debtor
to survive and is hence often allowed in Traditional English jurisdictions
and the Netherlands. The suspect period is fixed by the judge to the date of
actual insolvency, plus 10 days, so that it is theoretically unlimited but
sometimes there is a fixed period, e.g. Belgium (six months), France (18
months). Other transfers are voidable, regardless of debtor intent, but
usually the transferee must know of the insolvency.

Contract and lease rescission

Ipso facto clauses entitling a party to cancel an existing contract, licence or
equipment lease on the bankruptcy of the other party are generally upheld,

except where statute has intervened, as in France. There are sometimes special provisions limiting landlord repossessions of commercial lenders.

Conflict of laws

Free contractual choice of law was not favoured in the academic doctrine,   10–8
but this has been largely ignored by case law in the industrialised states. Rigid presumptions apply in the case of no express or implied choice by the parties, as opposed to the English centre of gravity approach. The applicable jurisdictions in Continental Europe are now governed by the 1980 Rome Convention.

Long-arm judicial jurisdiction includes nationality of plaintiff in French-based jurisdictions (but this should be checked). This rule led to retaliatory statutes in the Netherlands and Italy.

Initially there was some hostility to foreign money judgements and a tendency to re-open them on the merits (i.e. non-recognition), but this suspicious approach has been substantially mitigated by case law, e.g. in Belgium and France. The European Judgements Conventions apply to EU and EFTA states (but the date of ratification and any local modifications should be checked).

The recognition of foreign insolvency administrators appointed in the country of corporate domicile usually requires an *exequatur* or equivalent. This usually also implies recognition of the home forum bankruptcy freeze on local creditor attachments. In a few countries the *exequatur* is retroactive to the date of the home forum order (France), but normally dates from the *exequatur* in other countries. There are various bankruptcy treaties in Europe and Latin America. Some Latin American states operate discriminatory regimes against foreign creditors, especially Argentina.

Sovereign deimmunisation is mixed and the attitude is often influenced by political status. Thus Belgium was one of the earliest countries in the world to leap off the starting-blocks of deimmunisation for commercial transactions, but France was cautious, reflecting a traditional diplomatic leadership and sensitivity.

Securities regulation

The attitude to securities regulation is very mixed, but on the whole the Ger-   10–9
manic club culture is not accepted and is replaced by specific statutes of varying potency, e.g. in France. The regulatory authority is often a governmental agency on the lines of the US SEC, as in France and some Latin American countries.

Codification of laws

These jurisdictions have universal codification based on French models: civil code, commercial code, code of civil procedure, criminal code, code of criminal procedure.

Bills of exchange

The restrictive Geneva regime applies in the main: see para 5–19.

List of Jurisdictions (76)

10–10   Note: several members of Group 7 may properly be members of this group

        Algeria

Population 25,900,000, 99 per cent Sunni Muslim. French colony since mid-nineteenth century, independent 1962. CC 1975, CCP 1966, ComC 1975, all on old French lines. Development of commercial law stunted by post-independence socialist governments.

        Andorra

Population 55,400. Tiny state in the Pyrenees between France and Spain. Legal system probably based on pre-Revolution French and Spanish law. Very basic legal system and no general codification. There is a bankruptcy law of 1969, a suspension of payments and a company law. Special relationship with EU via France.

        Angola

Population 10,300,000. Former Portuguese colony in South West Africa, independent 1975. CC 1966; CCP 1961; very basic laws.

10–11   **Argentina**

Population 32,470,000. Independent from Spain 1816. Federal state with 22 provinces, separate Federal Capital and a national territory on US constitutional lines. Legal system influenced by French and Italian scholarship. CC 1869 as amended. ComC 1889, much amended. Bankruptcy Law of 1972, as amended in 1983, 1984. Commercial Companies Acts 1971–72, as amended. Conflict of laws in the Codes. No ratification of Bustamente Code.

Belgium

Population 10,000,000. Rapidly shifting legal system with excellent case law and legal literature. French-based codes. Bankruptcy law 1851 in ComC Bk III Arts 437–614.

Benin

Population 4,800,000. Former French West African colony independent 1960. French-based codes.

Bolivia

Population 7,500,000. Landlocked South American republic, independent 1825 (Simon Bolivar). New Italian-based codes in 1970s. Bankruptcy in CC, ComC, CCP.   **10–12**

Brazil

Population 153,300,000. Huge federal country. Portuguese ancestry, but eclectic ComC dating from 1850, after 17 years of work. CC 1917. Case law important. Bankruptcy Law of 1945, as amended. Corporation Law of 1976, as amended. Securities and Exchange Commission Law of 1976. Insider Trading Law of 1989. This country may be wrongly classified and is possibly Group 3.

Burkino Faso

Population 9,300,000, 43 per cent Muslim. Landlocked West African sub-Saharan state. French colony, independent 1960 as Upper Volta. French-based codes.

Burundi

Population 5,600,000, 85 per cent Christian. Central equatorial Africa. Belgian colony from 1919 (from Germany). Independent 1962. Belgian codes.   **10–13**

Cameroon

Population 12,240,000, 53 per cent Christian, 22 per cent Muslim. West equatorial

Africa. Republic formed in 1972 from French and British territories. The dominant Eastern Cameroon is French-based (80 per cent of population and 90 per cent of territory). Western Cameroon is English-based (similar to Nigeria) and received English law from 1900.

Cape Verde Island republic, off coast of West Africa. Population about 340,000, 100 per cent Christian. Former Portuguese colony, independent 1975.

10–14 Central African Republic Population 2,940,000, 83 per cent Christian. Landlocked state in sub-Saharan central Africa. Former French colony, independent 1960. French-based codes.

Chad Population 5,800,000, 44 per cent Muslim, 33 per cent Christian. Landlocked Saharan state. French colony, independent 1960. French-based codes.

Chile Population 13,390,000. Independent from Spain 1810. Eclectic codes (drafted by Venezuelan Andrés Bello), but in the Napoleonic tradition, widely copied in Latin America. Bankruptcy Law of 1931 substantially amended, especially in 1987. Securities Law of 1987. Civil Code Arts 732–763 and 1164–1166 recognise the trust. Laws of 1925 and 1930 allow banks to be trustees.

10–15 Colombia Population 33,600,000. Independent from Spain 1810. Codes in the Napoleonic tradition. Bankruptcy law in ComC Arts 1910–2010.

Comoros Population 480,000. French nineteenth-century colony in north Mozambique Channel off SE Africa, independent 1975.

Congo	Population 2,420,000. West equatorial Africa. French colony, independent 1960. French-based codes.
Costa Rica	Population 3,100,000. Central American state. Napoleonic-style codes. CC and ComC contemplate the trust, see ComC 633–662.
Cuba	Population 10,700,000. Independent from Spain 1898. Spanish codes in the Napoleonic style were overtaken by Castro revolution of 1959, and whittled away. Commercial law would have to be rebuilt.
Djibouti	Population probably about 325,000. Horn of Africa. Former nineteenth century French colony, independent 1977. Legal system may be in abeyance. Very poor, but not the poorest.
Dominican Republic	Population 7,320,000. Originally a Spanish Caribbean colony (Hispaniola), but legal system is French-based. CC, CCP, and ComC, all 1884. Bankruptcy law of 1962 in CC Arts 437–614. Stock exchange law of 1953.
Ecuador	Population 11,100,000. South American state on north-west coast. Codes in the Napoleonic tradition.
Egypt	Population 54,610,000. First-class legal culture with great influence in the Middle East. French-based codes CC 1948, CCP 1968, ComC 1883, all revised. Apart from bankruptcy provisions in ComC, there is a Composition Law No 56 of 1945. Capital Markets Law 1992.
El Salvador	Population 5,400,000. Central American state. Napoleonic-style codes.

Equatorial Guinea

Population 360,000. Spanish colony in equatorial West Africa, independent 1968.

France

Population 57,000,000. One of the world's greatest jurisdictions with enormous international legal influence. Triple A. Home to the Napoleonic codes. Dramatic bankruptcy legislation in 1985. Party to Hague Recognition of Trusts Convention 1985.

10–18 French Guiana

Population 120,000. Overseas department of France on north-eastern South American coast.

French Polynesia

Population 203,000. Pacific overseas territory of France.

Gabon

Population 1,220,000. West equatorial Africa. French colony, independent 1959. French-based codes.

Greece

Population 10,300,000. Independent from Turkey in 1820s. Some Swiss-Germanic influence in codes, but French-inspired on the crucial criteria. CC 1940 (in force 1946), CCP 1967, ComC 1910, all amended. Bankruptcy Law 1978, amended in 1910 and 1937. Reorganisations in Act 1386 of August 8, 1983. Corporation Law of 1963 as amended. Major maritime law which allows possessory management of ship by the mortgagee on default.

Guadeloupe

Population 395,000. Overseas French territory in Caribbean.

Guatemala

Population 9,200,000. Central American state. Napoleonic-style codes. Trusts in ComC 766–793.

10–19 Guinea

Population 7,100,000. West African coastal state. French colony since at least 1886. Independent 1958. CC 1983, CCP 1983, based on French models. ComC 1892–1985. Companies Law 1985. Conflicts Law 1962.

Guinea-Bissau Population 1,000,000. West African coastal state. Portuguese colony since 1839. Independent 1974. Portuguese law, but very basic.

Haiti Population 6,620,000. Caribbean. Independent 1804. French legal system of early 1800s.

Honduras Population 4,710,000. Central American **10–20** state. French-style codes.

Iran Population 57,000,000, almost all Muslim (91 per cent Shiite). Codes based on Ottoman codes of mid-nineteenth century, in turn based on French codes. CC 1928–35; CCP 1939; ComC 1932 (containing bankruptcy legislation). Overtaken since 1979 by Islamic revolution. Status of old codes is unclear.

Iraq Population 18,320,000, 96 per cent Muslim divided between Sunni and Shiite. Old French-based codes. CC 1953, CCP 1969. Companies Law 1983 ComC 1984. ComC 1970 Pt I containing bankruptcy law has been retained. Commercial law currently on hold.

Ivory Coast Population 12,500,000, 20 per cent Muslim, 20 per cent Christian. West African coastal state. Independent 1960. French-based codes.

Jordan Population 3,300,000, 93 per cent Sunni **10–21** Muslim. CC 1976; CCP 1988; ComC 1966. French-based codes via Syria, in turn based on Egypt. But may be some British influence in company law dating from the British Mandate period: Companies Law 1989. Bankruptcy is in ComC 1966 Bk 4.

Lebanon	Population 2,750,000. Mainly French-based codes. Code of Obligations and Contracts 1932, CCP 1985 (which may not be in force), ComC 1942, all as amended.
Libya	Population 4,300,000, 97 per cent Sunni Muslim. North African Italian colony 1912–1943, but legal system in force in 1969 was based on Egypt (French). Subsequent revolution renders the status of codes unclear.

10–22 **Luxembourg**

Population 380,000. French-based codes. Important banking centre. Stock exchange listing for many eurobonds. Germanic fiduciary transfer.

Macao

Population 400,000, 45 per cent Buddhist. Chinese south coast. Based on Portuguese law.

Madagascar

Population 12,400,000, 51 per cent Christian. Large island off south east African coast. French colony, independent 1958. French-based codes.

Mali

Population 8,300,000, 90 per cent Muslim. West Saharan state. French colony, independent 1959. French-based codes.

Malta

Population 360,000. Mediterranean island. British colony 1814–1964. CC 1870, CCP 1855, ComC 1857–88, all substantially amended. Based on French models. Bankruptcy in ComC Arts 477–540. Company and maritime law based on English law. This state may be wrongly classified.

10–23 **Martinique**

Population 365,000. French Caribbean overseas territory, 88 per cent Catholic.

Mauritania

Population 2,100,000, 99 per cent Muslim. Coastal French West African colony, independent 1960. Old French codes up to 1961, but now Islamicised, e.g. Code of Obligations and Contracts 1989.

Mayotte   Tiny French island dependency in Mozambique channel off SE Africa.

Mexico   Population 83,200,000. Federal republic with 29 states, Federal District and three territories. Commercial law is Federal. Napoleonic-style codes. Bankruptcy and Suspension of Payments Law of 1942, codified in ComC Bk 5.5.

Monaco   Population 28,000. Enclave principality on **10–24** French Riviera. French-based law. Foreign residents can establish trusts if national law so allows: Law 214 of February 27, 1936. Bankruptcy law in ComC Arts 408–582.

Morocco   Population 25,720,000, mainly Sunni Muslim. North African state. French protectorate, independent 1956. French-based codified commercial law in the main.

Mozambique   Population 14,600,000. Portuguese colony on south east African coast, independent 1975. Portuguese-based legal system.

New Caledonia   Population 172,000, 95 per cent Christian. SW Pacific islands, French overseas territory.

Nicaragua   Population 4,000,000. Central American state. Napoleonic-style codes.

Niger   Population 8,000,000. Landlocked Saharan **10–25** state. French colony, independent 1960. French-based codes.

Paraguay   Population 4,400,000. Landlocked South American state. Codes in Napoleonic-style.

Peru	Population 22,900,000. West coast of South America. Codes in Napoleonic tradition. Bankruptcy provisions in ComC, revised 1932, 1961, 1962, 1966.
Portugal	Population 10,500,000. Napoleonic-style codes, CC 1966, CCP 1961, ComC 1888, all amended. Decree-Law 177/86 of July 2, 1986 covers commercial insolvencies. Corporations Code of 1986, as amended.

10–26 **Puerto Rico** — Population 3,400,000. Former Spanish Caribbean colony. Ceded to US after Spanish-American War of 1898. Independent commonwealth established in 1953, associated with the US. CC and ComC based on Spanish models. No adoption of the American UCC.

Reunion — Population 610,000. French overseas island territory in south-western Indian Ocean.

Romania — Population 23,250,000, mainly Orthodox Christian. Black Sea coastal state. Old mid-nineteenth century French codes, installed in revised form in 1930s, overlaid in communist era ending in 1989, and now overtaken by new legislative programme.

10–27 **Rwanda** — Population 7,500,000. Central equatorial Africa. Former German colony, Belgian from 1916, independent 1959/62. Law is Belgian-based. BA 1934. Company Law 1988.

St Pierre & Miquelon — Population 7,000. Archipelago about 15 miles off the coast of Newfoundland. Overseas department of France.

Saõ Tomé e Principe — Population 123,000. West African island state, formerly Portuguese colony, independent 1975. Area 964 sq km.

Senegal	Population 7,520,000. Former West African French colony, independent 1960. All the French codes have been replaced, but replacements are still French-inspired. Company Law and bankruptcy in Code of Obligations 1963–1985 ss 927–1069. Company liquidations in Laws of 1984.
Spain	Population 40,000,000. Codes are in the mainstream Napoleonic tradition. CC 1889, CCP 1881, ComC 1885, all extensively revised. Securities Market Law 1988 establishing National Securities Market Commission (CNMV).
Syria	Population 12,500,000, 90 per cent Muslim (mainly Sunni). French mandate till 1946. Codes drafted by Abd Al-Sanhury, promulgated around 1950s based on Egyptian codes, in turn based on French codes.
Togo	Population 3,600,000. West African German colony of Togoland in nineteenth century. French mandate from 1922, independent 1960. French-based codes. Bankruptcy covered by Decree of June 25, 1942.
Tunisia	Population 8,300,000, 99 per cent Sunni Muslim. North Africa French protectorate from 1883, independent 1956. Commercial law is French-based.
Uruguay	Population 3,100,000. South American coastal state. Codes in the Napoleonic tradition as regards commercial law. Bankruptcy in ComC Arts 1524–1781.
Venezuela	Population 19,700,000. Much redrafting of codes, but still traditionally Napoleonic. Bankruptcy in ComC Arts 914–1089. Capital Market Law of 1975. Trustee Law of 1956. Banks may act as trustees (trust

The margin references **10–28** (Spain) and **10–29** (Tunisia) appear in the right margin.

documents must be notarised and publicly registered at a mercantile registry).

Wallis and Futuna Islands   Population 18,000. Self-governing French overseas territory in south Pacific.

Zaire   Population 35,000,000. Central African Belgian colony, independent 1960. French-based Belgian codes.

CHAPTER 11

GROUP 6: EMERGING JURISDICTIONS

Main comparative characteristics

Group 6 comprises emerging jurisdictions. For most of these jurisdictions, it **11–1** is perhaps too early to say which of the groups they will join. Some show pro-creditor leanings: thus China has imported insolvency set-off in its bankruptcy legislation and Russia has taken over the universal business pledge. Their attitude to the trust, to the constructive trust and to the doctrine of specificity remains to be seen.

One suspects that the Baltic states, China, Belarus and the Ukraine may join the Germanic group – insolvency set-off, cautious attitude to security, wide title finance, cautious insolvency rehabilitation, no trust and certainly no constructive trust. The Yugoslav states (total population 24,000,000) may veer to the Franco-Latin group but their former codes were Austrian-based. But this is pure surmise and it is open to them to join whichever group they think best.

List of Jurisdictions (18)

Albania	Population 3,300,000, 20 per cent Muslim. Republic located **11–2** to north-west of Greece on the Adriatic Sea. CC 1981, CCP 1981, amended 1987, ComC, communist-based but probably influenced by Italian models from CC 1928. Code of private international law 1964.
Armenia	Population roughly 3,400,000. Former USSR republic, to east of Turkey. Foreign Trade Law 1992.
Belarus	Population roughly 10,300,000. Law of Economic Insolvency and Bankruptcy 1991, a framework Act with 46 Articles. Enterprises Law 1990. Foreign Investment Law 1991. Investment Activity Law 1992.

Bosnia	Formerly part of Yugoslavia.
Bulgaria	Population 9,000,000. West shores of Black Sea. European-style codes were abrogated during communist period. Original style was probably a mix of Franco-Latin with strong Germanic influence in commercial and corporate law. Old CC, CCP 1952. Law on Companies 1991. Commercial and bankruptcy laws in draft in mid-1994.

11–3   China   Population 1,150,000,000. Vast body of new laws and regulations, impossible to keep up with. Commercial law utterly destroyed during the Cultural Revolution of the 1960s and now being rebuilt. General principles of Civil Law of 1986. Code of Civil Procedure 1991. Enterprise Bankruptcy Act 1986 applying to state enterprises and chapter 19 of Civil Procedural Law to other bankruptcies. Appears to be a six-month suspect period for voidable preferences. Special insolvency regulations for Shenzhen Special Economic Zone. Law on mortgages and security interests inchoate. National company law 1994. Some contract conflict of laws rules in Law of Foreign Economic Contracts 1986 s 5. Huge body of regulations on foreign investment. Various regulations governing issues of securities, notably for Guandong, Shanghai, Shenzhen.

Croatia	Formerly part of Yugoslavia.
Estonia	Population 1,600,000. Baltic republic. Bankruptcy Act 1992. Companies Act 1989. Licensing of the Fields of Activities of Companies Decree 1991.

11–4   Georgia   Population roughly 5,500,000. Former USSR republic, to east of Turkey.

Latvia	Population 2,700,000. Baltic republic. Laws of around 1990 include Companies Acts.
Lithuania	Population 3,800,000. Baltic republic. Post-communist programme of legal reform.

11–5   Moldava   Population 4,400,000. To the north of Romania. Formerly part of the USSR.

Mongolia   Population 2,140,000. Gobi desert. Bankruptcy Law 1991. Banking Law 1991. Foreign Investment Law 1993.

Russia   Population roughly 148,500,000. Pre-Revolution codes may   **11–6**
                 have been German-influenced. New Civil Code 1995. Law on
                 the Bankruptcy of Enterprises 1992. Advanced Pledge Act
                 1992 establishing (inter alia) a universal business charge,
                 amended by new Civil Code 1995. Special provisions on con-
                 tracts of adhesion. Law on Mortgage for real property. Law
                 on State Registration of Immovable Property and Trans-
                 actions.

Serbia   Formerly part of Yugoslavia.

Slovenia   Formerly part of Yugoslavia.

Ukraine   Population roughly 52,000,000. Bankruptcy Law 1992.   **11–7**
                 Foreign Economic Activity Law 1992. Protection of Foreign
                 Investment Law 1991. Law on Pledge of early 1990s. Securi-
                 ties and Stock Exchange Law 1992.

Vietnam   Population 67,600,000. French-based till 1945. Unified com-
                 munist country in 1975. Status of old French codes unclear.
                 New legislative programme in 1990s. Companies Law 1990.
                 Decree Law on Civil Contracts 1991. Ordinance on Econ-
                 omic Contracts 1989. Substantial foreign investment legis-
                 lation from 1988. BA 1994.

CHAPTER 12

GROUP 7: ISLAMIC JURISDICTIONS

Main comparative characteristics

12–1   The Islamic jurisdictions have historically not had a settled system of bankruptcy laws or a commercial culture. Some have adopted corporate, commercial and insolvency legislation. Sometimes the overall bias can be difficult to perceive, usually because of the absence of a developed case law. A few of the countries have a reasonably developed system of commercial law, often based on Egyptian codes, in turn based on the French. Hence it may be that several of these states should be in Group 5. There was substantial British influence in the Gulf region in the nineteenth and twentieth centuries, but English law was not usually imposed.

List of Jurisdictions (14)

12–2 **Afghanistan**

Population 17,000,000, Muslim, Sunni 74 per cent, Shiite 25 per cent. Very poor. CC 1976; ComC 1955 based on Ottoman ComC of 1850; CCP 1958. Companies in CC Arts 403–439. Conflict of laws in CC Arts 1–35; contracts in CC Arts 505–757. ICSID 1968. Legal system currently in abeyance.

Azerbaijan

Population roughly 7,200,000. Former USSR Asian republic, located on west shore of Caspian Sea.

Bahrain

Population 516,000, 85 per cent Muslim (60 per cent Shiite, 40 per cent Sunni). Archipelago of 33 islands in Arabian Gulf. British influence from 1820, independent 1971. More English legal influence than most of the other Gulf states. Bankruptcy governed by Legislative Decree 11 of 1987. Law of Commercial Companies, Decree 28 of 1975, as amended.

Kazakhstan Population roughly 16,800,000. Former USSR Asian republic, located on east shore of Caspian Sea. Mainly Sunni Muslim, but 38 per cent Russian. Bankruptcy Law of 1992, a framework act with 24 articles. Foreign Investment Law 1992.

Kirghistan Population roughly 4,500,000. Mainly Muslims, about 20 per cent Russian. Former USSR republic bordering China.

Kuwait Population roughly 400,000, 90 per cent Muslim (63 per cent Sunni, 27 per cent Shiite). British mandate from 1899 to 1961. But legal system was not anglicised and is mainly in the Napoleonic tradition, drawn from Egyptian sources. CC, CCP, ComC, all 1980 and based on Egyptian codes, in turn based on the French. Bankruptcy in ComC Arts 555–800, but rather basic. Company Law 15 of 1960, as amended. Various laws dealing with securities. 12–3

Oman Population perhaps 1,500,000, 85 per cent Muslim. Within British sphere of influence from 1862. Commercial law in ComC: Decree 55 of July 11, 1990, based on Kuwait model and therefore probably French, via Egypt. Commercial bankruptcy contained in Book V. Companies law in Bk II. Decree 53 of 1988 deals with Muscat Securities Market.

Qatar Population 450,000, 92 per cent Muslim (mainly Sunni). British influence until 1971, so the legal system may have an English colouring. Basic civil and commercial code based on Kuwait code of 1971 which is Napoleonic, via Egypt. Bankruptcy Code, Law 2/1961, but status of this seems unclear. Commercial Companies Law 11 of 1981 and Law 3 of 1961.

12–4 Saudi Arabia

Population 14,700,000, 99 per cent Muslim (mainly Sunni). Birthplace of Mahomet. Kingdom of Saudi Arabia formally established in 1932. Fairly slim commercial code in Decree 32 of 1931, as amended. Bankruptcy in ComC ss 103–137 dating from 1930s and contemplating personal bankruptcies only, although it is applied by analogy to corporate insolvencies. Detailed Saudi Regulations for Companies of 1965, as amended. Negotiable Instruments Regulations of 1964, as amended. Interest provisions in bill are void. Objection to interest renders mortgages difficult, including registration of land mortgages.

Tajikistan

Population roughly 5,400,000, mainly Sunni Muslims. Former USSR Asian republic bordering China.

Turkmenistan

Population roughly 3,700,000, mainly Sunni Muslims. Former USSR Asian republic on south-east shore of Caspian Sea.

12–5 United Arab Emirates

Population 1,950,000, 95 per cent Muslim (80 per cent Sunni), mostly in Abu Dhabi and Dubai. Seven principalities: Abu Dhabi, Dubai, Sharjah, Ajman, Umm al Quwain, Fuijeira, Ras-Al-Khaimah. British colonial influence from 1820 to 1971, but not legally intrusive. Energetic programme of universal codification. Commercial Companies Law. Civil Code in 1980s. New ComC in 1990s: this has a chapter on bankruptcy. Federal CPC. Codes are Napoleonic-based via Egypt.

Uzbekistan

Population roughly 21,400,000, mainly Sunni Muslims. Former USSR Asian republic to south of Aral Sea and to north of Afghanistan. Foreign Economic Activities Law 1991. Entrepreneurship Law 1991, amended 1993. Economic Associations, Partnerships and Companies Law 1992.

Yemen
Population 11,800,000, nearly 100 per cent Muslim, split almost equally between Sunni and Shiite.

CHAPTER 13

GROUP 8: UNALLOCATED JURISDICTIONS

List of Jurisdictions (12)

Finally, in Group 8 is a miscellany of jurisdictions which for various reasons are not allocated.

13–1 **Antarctica**   About 12 nations claim sovereignty over portions of this continent.

Bhutan   Population 1,500,000. Himalayan kingdom under British guidance 1865–1949. Said to have a codified law, but lawyers are apparently rare.

Cambodia   Population roughly 8,800,000. Situated in Indochinese peninsula. Catastrophic recent history. One of the poorest countries in the world. French protectorate 1864 to 1953, so basic legal system may be French-inspired. Revolutionary communism in 1970s and 1980s.

Eritrea   Population 2,900,000. Incorporated into Ethiopia in 1952. Independent 1993. Formerly subject to Italian and British colonial rule.

Ethiopia   Population 51,620,000. Civil and commercial codes from 1960, but no settled legal system. Legal system was probably originally English-based.

Korea (North)   Population 21,800,000. No commercial legal system.

Laos   Population 4,300,000. Situated in Indochinese peninsula. Landlocked and very poor. French protectorate from late nineteenth century until final independence in 1954, so basic legal system may be French-inspired. Revolutionary communism in 1970s and 1980s.

Maldives	Population about 220,000. Indian archipelago of about 1800 islands and sandbanks. Extremely poor. British protectorate from about 1796 till final independence in 1965, so legal system may be English, but perhaps like Sri Lanka and South Africa with perceptible Roman-Dutch influence.
Nepal	Population 19,400,000. Himalayan kingdom, home to Mt. Everest and Katmandu. Extremely poor. Not colonised by the British.
San Marino	Population 23,300. Tiny independent republic of 61 sq km on Adriatic side of central Italy. Napoleon respected its independence, confirmed by Congress of Vienna 1815.
Somalia	Population is perhaps 7,600,000. No settled legal system. Part Italian colony till 1946, and part British colony from 1900. British protectorate till independence in 1960. But post-independence CC 1933 based on 1948 Egyptian code.
Vatican City	Enclave in Rome. The Pope has absolute executive, legislative and judicial powers within the City. Population about 750. Banking operations are clothed in secrecy, which does not seem unreasonable.
Western Sahara	Shifting population of about 75,000 perhaps. Former Spanish territory, sought to be administered by Morocco.

13-2

PART II

GOVERNING LAW OF FINANCIAL CONTRACTS

CHAPTER 14

CHOICE OF LAW AND
THE ROME CONVENTION OF 1980

Factors governing choice of law

Introduction

Every legal issue under a financial contract must be determined in accord-   **14–1**
ance with a system of law. An aspect of a contract cannot exist in a legal
vacuum.

In England and in most developed countries the parties to a contract may
normally choose the governing or proper law of the contract which will govern many of its aspects. This law may, for example, be the law of the borrower's country, the law of the creditor's country, the law of the market,
such as the London Eurocurrency Market or the market in which the bonds
are issued, or a neutral system of law.

Strictly the law chosen is that of a judicial district: there are seven legal
systems in the British Isles of varying degrees of distinctiveness: England,
Scotland (anglicised Roman Law), Northern Ireland, Isle of Man, Jersey,
Guernsey, and Alderney/Sark. The last three have an anglicised pre-Napoleonic French legal system.

Private international law and international finance

This section reviews the conflict of laws rules primarily in relation to finan-   **14–2**
cial contracts – notably credit agreements and bonds. This is the simplest,
most highly developed and most predictable area of private international
law, exhibiting a large measure of international consensus amongst legally
developed states.

However, apart from the contract rules, there are a number of other areas
which are of considerable significance in this context and which are
reviewed in other works in this series on international finance.

14–3   1.   Probably the most important are the conflict of law rules relating to insolvency. These are the least developed and there appears to be little international consensus. This is probably because of the shock of collision of attitudes to insolvency amongst the world's leading jurisdictions, coupled with the intense dislocation and emotions generated by bankruptcy.

2.   The second area of prime importance are the conflict of laws rules relating to security and title finance. Both of these are central to insolvency since asset protection is intended as a defence against insolvency; hence they are dragged into the battle of bankruptcy laws.

3.   The conflict of laws relating to express trusts are relevant especially to mortgage trusts and trusts of bond issues. They are also of importance in relation to custodian trusts of securities. Again, the rejection of the trust in a large number of countries outside the Anglo-American group is primarily based on bankruptcy considerations – the false wealth or reputed ownership doctrine.

4.   Then there are the conflict of laws rules relating to torts or delicts. The most important tort in this context is misrepresentation, especially in relation to syndicated loans and to issues of debt securities.

5.   The conflict rules relating to securities regulation are in a field of their own, e.g. the need for the authorisation of dealers transacting business from abroad, the dispatch of unregistered prospectuses into a regulating state, fiduciary duties of brokers, and the impact of insider trading and other securities crimes. A reasonable degree of legal predictability can only come from a co-operation between regulatory authorities. The present regime is unsatisfactory.

6.   Finally, there are the rules relating to forcible expropriations which are reviewed later in this book.

14–4   In reviewing the subject, one is struck by how much is being done and also by how far there is still to go before a satisfactory international legal regime can be devised to confer a measure of security and predictability on international financial transactions. The ultimate solution is for jurisdictions to harmonise the law so that there are no longer any conflicts, but of course this is a very long way off and is probably impracticable. States have very different views on fundamentals. While there is much convergence on basic contractual doctrines, these are primitive when compared to insolvency, which is the foundation of commercial and financial law.

Factors influencing choice of law

Factors which influence the choice of law for a financial contract include: **14-5**
(1) non-legal preferences, such as patriotism, tradition, familiarity and convenience; (2) avoidance by the lender of a detailed investigation into an
unfamiliar system of law; (3) commercial orientation, stability and predictability of the chosen legal system; (4) the desire to coincide the governing law
with the law of the enforcing forum (which may be external) – legal unpredictability may result if the court is called upon to apply a foreign law with
which it is not familiar; (5) the ability to use lawyers who have special
experience in the type of financial contract concerned; (6) language; and (7)
insulation. Some of the factors are merely fear of the unknown and are not
justifiable in the case of the major civilised systems. But insulation is important and requires further examination.

Insulation

Insulation of the loan contract from legal changes in the borrower's country   **14-6**
is perhaps the most important reason for the choice of an external system of
law – it does not matter which law, so long as it is external. Historically the
most common changes protecting national debtors have been (a) legislation
imposing a moratorium on foreign obligations, (b) reduction of the interest
rate by legislation, (c) requirements that repayment must be made in local
currency to a local custodian, and (d) exchange controls. The risk may be
increased where the borrower is a state or is state-related or is nationally
important. These interferences often arise either because of political upheavals or because the state is insolvent – both of which are events against
which the private contractor seeks some defence.

   If the borrower's system of law is chosen a lender may be subject to
changes in the local law. This conclusion flows from the rule that the proper
law applying to the agreement is the law as it exists from time to time: *Re
Helbert Wagg & Co Ltd* [1956] Ch 323. As the House of Lords stated in
Kahler v Midland Bank [1950] AC 24, [1949] 2 All ER 621 "the proper
law, because it sustains, may also modify or dissolve the contractual bond".

The point is illustrated by two contrasting English cases.   **14-7**

> In *Re Helbert Wagg & Co Ltd* [1956] Ch 323, a subsequent German morator-
> ium law required a German borrower to make loan payments under a loan con-
> tract governed by German law to a government agency in Berlin in German
> marks instead of in pounds sterling. *Held*: the German law was effective to dis-

charge the borrower. The German moratorium law arose under a German contract.

On the other hand in *National Bank of Greece and Athens S A v Metliss* [1958]
AC 509, HL, a Greek decree reduced the interest rate on bonds issued by a
Greek bank and subject to English law. *Held*: the Greek law was disregarded
and the borrower was liable to pay arrears of interest. The English proper law
insulated the contract from changes in Greek law.

The result is that in England the lender can, by choice of external law,
have complete certainty in knowing that the borrower's country cannot
unilaterally alter the obligations by a change of local law. The piece of
paper, at least, is inviolate and retains its bargaining power: that piece of
paper, whether a credit agreement or bond or whatever, is all the creditor
has to represent the money and plainly his position is somewhat unhappy if
that, too, is destroyed.

It is not possible by contract to stabilise the law, e.g. that the governing
law is that at the time of the contract. The fluctuating governing law must
still be ascertained and will apply to this term of the contract. A change in
the governing law will override. But a contract can provide that an invali-
dating change of law will constitute an event of default (although the change
of law might override the ability to recover or the event of default itself).

Limits on insulation

14–8   Amongst the limits on the insulating effect of the choice of external law are:

1.   There may be **no external assets** capable of attachment to satisfy a judgment against the borrower. If the action were brought locally, the local
courts might ignore the foreign proper law to the extent it conflicted
with local overriding law, including perhaps the very laws (such as an
exchange control) against which the lender sought to be insulated. But,
as mentioned, it is preferable for a creditor to have a legal claim, even if
futile, than no claim at all.

2.   A subsequent exchange control in the borrower's country, e.g. ration-
ing payments, may, if that country is an IMF member, in certain circumstances achieve recognition in a few IMF states under **Art VIII 2(b)
of the Bretton Woods Agreement**: para 15–26 *et seq.*

3.   Local **insolvency proceedings** are in the main governed by local insolvency law. The comparative private international law of insolvency is
reviewed in another book in this series on financial law.

Differences in contract law

It has been remarked that some of the factors which influence choice of law   **14–9**
are based more on fear of the unknown than objective reality. Apart from
the desirability of an external system of law, the differences in financial contract law between the major legal systems (as opposed to insolvency law) are
perhaps not as great as may be imagined – at any rate in the areas which
really matter. But since states will presumably continue to impose embargoes, moratoriums, exchange controls and other interferences in contracts,
it is crucial that jurisdictions should uphold an express choice of law, even
though there is no connection between the transaction and the chosen system, so as to permit creditors to insulate the obligations against these
attacks.

Aside from this, however, in fully negotiated contracts, such as loan   **14–10**
agreements, bonds and finance leases, the principal differences in ordinary
contract law which apply in the leading commercial states and which may
affect a creditor materially include:

1. There are different attitudes to capitalised (rolled-up) interest and to
   penalty interest on default e.g. an extra one per cent. English law does
   not object to these but they meet with varying disapproval elsewhere.
   However in default situations, doubts about the recoverability of capitalised penalty interest are not usually regarded as fatal in the normal
   case since a creditor is often more concerned about recovering his
   scheduled interest plus capital, not any surplus. Penalty interest is really
   a discipline point.

2. There are differences between the attitude to loan accelerations for a
   minor breach or delay in payment, even though this is an express event
   of default. Outside consumerism, the English courts enforce the bar-
   gain of the parties strictly and, if the parties have agreed that a loan is
   accelerable on non-payment in full on the due date, it is accelerable
   even if payment is only a day late or $10 short. While it is up to the
   business parties to negotiate their own grace periods if they will, the
   courts will not substitute their own views of what they think is fair or
   reasonable. This is not true in all jurisdictions: courts in some countries
   apply concepts of good faith or reasonableness, examined elsewhere in
   this series of works under the general rubric of lender liability. In practice the point is often not particularly crucial since sudden accelerations
   like a bolt out of the blue are unusual, and accelerations of bank loans
   or bond issues on account of a triviality are virtually unheard of in the
   author's experience. Nevertheless there are cases where the ability to
   accelerate quickly could matter, e.g. where a debtor seeks to withdraw

a deposit from the lender, and the lender, fearing that the debtor is unable or unwilling to pay, seeks to accrue a set-off by accelerating the loan and has to hunt for a technical default. This situation may also arise where a creditor of the borrower attaches the deposit. Immediate acceleration could also be important in relation to secured credits and title finance where the value of the asset is volatile (investment securities) or the asset is liable to flee, e.g. an aircraft subject to a finance lease. And any lack of legal predictability and certainty tends to introduce a sense of unease.

3.   But there are significant differences to the attitude to the free assignability of claims and the need for notice to the debtor to validate the assignment as against creditors of the assignor. Banks generally desire that their loans should be freely marketable but in some countries there can be obstacles, e.g. formal notice to the debtor in the prescribed form.

4.   There may be differences in the attitude to guarantees if events happen which prejudice the validity of the guarantee: more research on this question is needed.

5.   There are different approaches to exculpation clauses, e.g. excluding the liability of a manager of a bond issue or a syndicated loan from misrepresentation, or a syndicate bank agent or bond trustee from duties of due diligence.

14–11   However in the case of financial trading contracts, such as foreign exchange contracts, options, swaps and futures, the impact of legal disparities in ordinary contractual matters is greater in significance. Examples are the attitude to the need for writing and the attitude to mistakes – misunderstandings are common in relation to deals struck over the telephone, although this has been mitigated by telephone recording of transactions – and the attitude to gaming (relevant to options and futures). The law of mistakes is also relevant to international credit transfers.

Rome Convention of 1980

Introduction

14–12   In member states of the European Union most conflicts rules in contract are governed by the 1980 EC Rome Convention on the Law Applicable to Contractual Obligations, implemented in the UK by the Contracts (Applicable

Law) Act 1990. The Convention makes few major changes of substance to previous English case law on the subject and hence is largely a codification – at least so far as our subject is concerned. A Brussels Protocol of 1988 to the Rome Convention enables national courts to refer issues to the European Court. The Convention has been ratified by most EU states.

The Convention represents a crystallisation of the views of a large number of highly sophisticated states with widely divergent legal traditions and therefore represents advanced thinking – at least in its main lines. Unlike many international conventions, it is not the lowest common denominator, although it is not free of the mood of the late 1970s in its consumer and insurance provisions.

This review will use the terms "applicable" law, "proper" law and "governing" law inter-changeably.

Other conflicts codes

Other major statements are: **14–13**

– The US Restatement on Conflicts of Laws (1971) produced by the American Law Institute.

– The Swiss Act on Private International Law of 1987 ("Swiss PILA 1987"). See *Switzerland's Private International Law Statute* 1987, annotated translation by Karrer and Arnold (Kluwer 1989). See also the unannotated translation, Symeonides "The New Swiss Conflicts Codification: An Introduction" 37 *Am J Comp Law* 187 (1989).

– Dicey & Morris, *The Conflict of Laws* (11th ed 1987), whose rules are effectively an elaborate code of English law prior to the Rome Convention and which may continue to be persuasive authority for English-influenced jurisdictions. The 12th edition reflects the Rome Convention.

The literature on the subject is huge. Amongst the leading comparative works are Ernst Rabel, *The Conflict of Laws: A Comparative Study* (1958–1964) and Ole Lando "Private International Law: Contracts" (1977) in *International Encyclopaedia of Comparative Law*, vol III, chapter 24. But there are many others.

There are conflicts codifications in a number of states, e.g. Turkey (1982), Austria (1979) and Hungary (1979), as well as the Bustamente Code applying in a number of Latin American states. Codes in codified countries usually contain basic rules.

Illustrations from countries outside the Rome Convention will be given in the course of this section.

Interpretation of the Convention

14–14 The Convention is to be interpreted in accordance with the principles laid down by, and any relevant decision of, the European Court. A report produced by Professors Giuliano and Lagarde on the Convention (the "Giuliano-Lagarde Report") may be consulted in ascertaining the meaning and effect of any provision of the Convention.

Scope of the Convention

14–15 The Convention applies to *contractual* obligations, not, for example, property transfers.

In England, the Convention applies in any situation involving a choice between the laws of different countries (Art 1 (1)), even if they are not EU states. Thus the English courts will apply the Convention to a contract governed by New York law between non-EU parties. This was to obviate a dual regime.

Exclusions

14–16 The following matters are excluded from the Convention (Art 1(2)):

(a) The status or **legal capacity of natural persons**, without prejudice to Art 11 (which relates to incapacity).

(b) Contractual obligations relating to wills and succession and **family** matters.

(c) Obligations arising under bills of exchange, cheques and promissory notes and other negotiable instruments (e.g. bearer bonds) to the extent that the obligations under such other **negotiable instruments** arise out of their negotiable character. This seems to apply to the characteristics of negotiability, e.g. the circumstances under which the transferee takes an instrument free from any defect in title of his predecessor and set-offs. But the exclusion should not extend to the contract pursuant to which the instrument was issued (e.g. a subscription agreement for a bond issue), nor to a contract for the purchase and sale of the instrument. Whether a document is characterised as a negotiable instrument remains a matter for the law of the forum. For the English conflicts rules on negotiable instruments, see Dicey pp 1419 *et seq*.

(d) Arbitration agreements and agreements on the **choice of court** (dealt with partly in the European Judgments Conventions: see chapter 19).

(e) Questions governed by the **law of companies** and other bodies corporate or unincorporate, such as the creation, by registration or otherwise, legal capacity, internal organisation or **winding up** of companies and other bodies corporate or unincorporate and the personal liability of officers and members as such for the obligations of the company or body. Note the exclusion of corporate bankruptcy.

(f) The question whether an **agent** is able to bind a principal (but not the principal-agent or agent-third party relationship), or an organ to bind a company or body corporate or unincorporate, to a third party. This excludes the ultra vires doctrine.

(g) The constitution of **trusts** and the relationship between settlors, trustees and beneficiaries, e.g. trustees of bond issues. Under the Hague Convention on the Law Applicable to Trusts of 1986, the validity, construction, effects and administration of a trust are governed by the law chosen by the settlor or, in the absence of any such choice, by the law with which the trust is most closely connected.

(h) **Evidence and procedure**, without prejudice to Art 14 (which deals with the burden of proof and mode of evidence).

(i) Contracts of **insurance** (but not reinsurance) which cover risks situated in the territories of EU member states.

The most important exclusion in practice is **corporate bankruptcy**. Most of the others are relatively unimportant in our context.

Choice of law

Article 3(1) allows the parties expressly to choose the applicable law. If no choice is made, the contract is governed by the laws of the country with which it is most closely connected: Art 4(1). See para 14–47 *et seq* for more detail.   **14–17**

Mandatory rules and public policy

Nothing in the Convention restricts the application of the rules of the law of the forum in a situation where they are mandatory: Art 7(2). An applicable rule of law may only be refused if such application is "manifestly   **14–18** incompatible" with the public policy of the forum: Art 16. The US Conflicts Restatement s 187 (2)(b) is to the same effect.

These Articles provide a gateway through which the English courts can apply English domestic and private international rules to foreign contracts, e.g. the rule that courts will not enforce contracts illegal at their place of performance: see below. Art 7(1) allows the court to defer to the rules of another country with which the situation has a close connection, but does not apply in the UK since it was considered to introduce too much unpredictability and to defer too subserviently to the ability of other states to interfere in the contract.

Summary of scope of applicable law

14–19 The applicable law primarily governs:

- the existence and validity of the contract;
- formal validity, subject to exceptions;
- interpretation;
- performance, but not the detail of performance;
- the consequences of breaches;
- the extinguishing of obligations, including prescription and limitation.

These are examined in more detail below.

Existence and validity

14–20 Existence and validity of the contract are governed by the applicable law: Art 8. Existence includes such matters as offer and acceptance, consideration, and presumably such matters as whether consent was initiated by duress, undue influence, mistake or misrepresentation. But a party may rely on the law of the country of his habitual residence to establish that he did not consent (e.g. acceptance by silence) if it would not be reasonable to determine the effect of his conduct by the protective applicable law: Art 8(2). Section 200 of the US Conflicts Restatement also refers existence and validity to the governing law, which also governs misrepresentation, duress, undue influence and mistake: s 201.

In practice the divergent attitudes in the world's legal systems as to whether or not an offer can be withdrawn before acceptance and as to the various indicia of seriousness (consideration, sealing, *cause* and other ritualistic pomp distinguishing commercial contracts from contracts to take a girl to a ball) are not of great significance in the context of international finance. Gifts are rare. The technical doctrine of consideration and sealed deeds are empty formalities in Anglo-American countries and it is only here and there that they retain their potency, e.g. in relation to guarantees. The French need for *cause* in CC Art 1131 has little bite left. The law relating to mistakes is of continuing significance in relation to credit transfers and to financial trading contracts, e.g. foreign exchange, where misunderstandings are very frequent, albeit mitigated by taped trading.

The English rule (not reflected in some civilian codes) is that an offer can be withdrawn before acceptance. Accordingly, a party which requires the offer to remain open can contract for a nominal consideration that the other party will keep it open so as to confer an option. If a party wishes to be able to withdraw before acceptance in a state which forbids this, the offer should so provide.

For an international survey of the indicia of seriousness and of attitudes to a mistake, see Zweigert/Kötz, vol 2, chapters 6 and 8 respectively.

Formal validity

Formal validity, e.g. whether writing, notarisation, sealing etc. is necessary for the contract to be valid and the manner of acceptance, is usually governed by the applicable law *or* the law of place of conclusion of the contract, i.e. the rule is permissive: Art 9(1). Previously the English courts treated such matters as procedural if they merely rendered the contract unenforceable by action, as opposed to invalid: *Leroux v Brown* (1852) 12 CB 808. It is considered that this is still the position, so that this is procedure excluded from the Convention by Art 1(2) and governed by the lex fori. As a result, the English courts should ignore a foreign formality if it merely renders the contract unenforceable abroad, but not invalid. But this remains to be decided. **14–21**

There are special rules for the formal validity of:

— certain consumer contracts (consumer's habitual residence): Art 9(5);

— contracts the subject-matter of which is immovable property (mandatory requirements of the country where the property is): Art 9(6).

The consensus in the US appears to be slightly different on formalities and possibly more restrictive. Section 141 of the US Conflicts Restatement states that whether a contract must be in writing or evidenced by writing in order to be enforceable is determined by the governing law of the contract and the comment seeks to argue that this should not be a procedural matter **14–22** which can be ignored if it arises under the law of a foreign state. But s 199 adopts the permissive rule that formalities are decided either by the governing law or the place where the parties execute the contract.

14–23   The Swiss PILA 1987 also appears somewhat more restrictive on form. Article 124 provides that a contract is valid as to its form if it conforms to the law governing the contract or to the law at the place where it is concluded. If, at the time of conclusion of the contract, the parties are in different countries, it is sufficient for it to conform to the law of one of those countries. But, if, for the protection of a party, the law governing the contract prescribes the fulfilment of a form, the form is governed by that law unless it permits the application of a different law.

14–24   Outside consumer contracts, formalities applying to commercial contracts bring the law into disrepute and it is right that the conflicts regime is permissive in validating the contract either by the applicable law or the law of the place of contracting (on the theory that the parties would not think of this until they signed and so would contact local lawyers). It is right that courts treat some formalities as procedural so that they can ignore tiresome foreign rules. In days of difficulty of proof and fears of widespread perjury and false witness, the avoidance of fraud by the requirement for writing may have been sound policy, but now, when courts are well equipped to decide questions of fact, the prevention of fraud has become an instrument of fraud and enables a party to evade a transaction, which he had quite clearly entered into, on a technicality.

In practice, loan agreements, guarantees, finance leases and bonds are invariably documented in writing with massive attention to detail, so that the rules as to formalities tend to be relevant only to financial trading contracts e.g. interbank deposits, foreign exchange, swaps, options and futures, and sales of securities – where deals are struck between traders orally and subsequently confirmed by an exchange of confirmations which are then matched by the parties. These transactions are usually recorded. Hence there tends to be a risk in the period between striking the deal and matching the confirmations if indeed the deal must be in writing.

14–25   The other main areas relevant in our context where formalities take their toll include:

– Contracts relating to land, which in England, Germany (BGB Art 313) and Switzerland (CO Art 216) must be in writing, but not in Austria (ABGB Art 432).

– Mortgages of land, ships and aircraft, and, sometimes, other security interests. The American UCC is conservative in requiring most non-possessory security interests in personal property to be in writing: Art 9 s 203(1)(a).

— Guarantees: These must be in writing in most US states, in England (Statute of Frauds 1677 s 4), apparently in France (CC Art 1236), but not Germany (HGB Art 350) or Austria.

— Consumer transactions which are outside our scope but may occasionally be relevant to bond issues to the public, particularly if there are exculpation clauses or provisions restricting the rights of bondholders or subjecting bondholders to majority votes.

— A consumerist, but watered down, provision in Art 17 of the European Judgement Conventions requiring derogations from the compulsory jurisdiction under forum selection clauses to comply with certain rules: see chapter 19.

— Assignments of claims. These must be in writing in Switzerland (CO Art 165), but not Germany (unless secured on land) or England. In England, writing is required for dispositions of equitable interests, which include interests under trusts and, possibly, second assignments of initially informal assignments: s 53(1)(c) of the Law of Property Act 1925.

According to a survey in Zweigert/Kötz, vol 2 chapter 4, in the French-   **14–26**
based systems, the accent is on informality in commercial transactions and the lack of formality generally affects only proof, not validity, and so can be ignored by a foreign court, since this is considered lex fori. Proof and evidence is for the court itself. The formalities required by CC Art 1341 (see also the Italian CC Art 2721) have been whittled down almost to vanishing point in most commercial contracts. The sanction of unenforceability as opposed to invalidity is the position in English-based systems and the US and, although the unenforceability is fatal in the local courts, the formality can properly be disregarded by foreign courts, so that the contract can be validated. By contrast, the formal rules in Germanic countries make the contract invalid and so are primarily intended to promote the seriousness of contractual intention and to protect contracting parties: the high ceremony of the formality is intended to draw their attention to the momentousness of their act. But the Germanic approach to the transactions which must be formal is very liberal in the commercial context.

Surprisingly, most US States have enthusiastically retained versions of the   **14–27**
English Statute of Frauds 1677 which, amongst other things, requires guarantees, contracts of more than one year and contracts of sale above a certain amount to be evidenced in writing. As Zweigert/Kötz note, a leading US

textbook on contract *Corbin on Contracts* (1950–) devotes more than 800 pages to the subject with a mountain of case law produced by despairing litigants seeking to avoid these unhappy rules. Formalities are retained by the UCC in relation to contracts of sale above a certain amount (s 2–201) and to non-possessory security interests over personal property (s 9–203(1)(a)). Both must be in writing. This is extraordinary for such a commercially-orientated country.

Interpretation

14–28   "Interpretation" is governed by the applicable law: Art 10(1)(a). The US Conflicts Restatement s 204 is to the same effect. This does not necessarily mean that the courts will decide that, say, the use of the word "pounds" in an English contract will mean English pounds. To construe a contract in accordance with its governing law means to apply the rules of construction which form part of that law.

14–29   Hence the applicable law will probably decide:

(a) The principles of construction to be used, e.g. whether the *ejusdem generis* rule applies, whether the French rule that, in cases of doubt, one should construe the contract in favour of the debtor (CC Art 1156) is relevant, whether subjective intention as opposed to expressed intention should prevail, and the extent to which the court can fill in the intentions of the parties if they omitted a point.

(b) Whether trade usages or banking customs or previous correspondence can be taken to fill out the intention of the parties, and whether oral agreements can override the expressed intention.

(c) Whether the parties can be taken to have used terms of art in their technical legal sense. For example, does the term "lien" or "security interest" in a negative pledge bear the narrow meaning given by English law or the wider meaning conferred by American law on the term "lien" or the interpretation given to "security interest" in Art 9 of the US Uniform Commercial Code? Does a security interest include title finance transactions? Does the term "borrowing" in cross-default clauses or borrowing restrictions include deferred purchase considerations and other credit transactions which are not strictly borrowings in English law?

(d) What currency is payable, e.g. if the parties refer to "dollars" (which may be US, Canadian, Australian or Singapore dollars).

Performance

"Performance" is governed by the applicable law: Art 10(1)(b). This covers,   **14–30**
for example, place, time and amount of payment, grace periods, and appro-
priation of payments. Probably this also covers whether the contract has
been discharged, e.g. by frustration, impossibility of performance, moratorium or exchange control legislation. Sections 200 and 205 of the US Conflicts Restatement are to the same effect.

But in "relation to the manner of performance and the steps to be taken
in the event of defective performance, regard should be had to the law of the
country in which performance takes place": Art 10(2). "Manner of performance" is meant to encompass matters of detail, e.g. rules on public holi-
days and (probably) whether payment "in cash" can be made by credit to a
bank account, but not whether a moratorium or exchange control prohibits
payment since this is substantive and not detail. Section 206 of the US Conflicts Restatement also refers the detail of performance to the law of the
place of performance. See also Swiss PILA 1987 Art 125. States may have
different views on whether exact time of performance, currency, and days of
grace are substantive or detail: the US Conflicts Restatement in its comment
on s 206 suggests these are detail.

Consequences of breach

Consequences of breach are governed by the applicable law: "within the   **14–31**
limits of the powers conferred on a court by its procedural law, the consequences of breach, including the assessment of damages in so far as it is governed by rules of law": Art 10(1)(c). The US Conflicts Restatement s 207 is
to the same effect. The applicable law should cover remoteness of damage,
the efficacy of a liquidated damages clause and possibly interest on
damages, but possibly the measure or quantification remains lex fori in England.

If specific performance and final injunctions are applicable law, they may
be qualified by the rule that the remedies are limited by the court's procedural rules so that the English courts may continue to apply the rule that
specific performance will not be awarded if the order would require con-
stant supervision by the court.

Discharge and prescription

Discharge is governed by the applicable law – "the various ways of   **14–32**
extinguishing obligations, and prescription and limitation of actions": Art
10(1)(d). Under both the Rome Convention and the English Foreign Limi-

tation Periods Act 1984, limitation rules appear to be a matter for the governing law, whether they are procedural (in the sense that they only remove the right to sue) or are substantive (in the sense that they cancel the obligation). The effect of Art 16 of the Convention and the 1984 Act is that the English courts may disregard a foreign statute of limitation in a contract claim on grounds of public policy if it would cause undue hardship. The US Conflicts Restatement adopts the previous English rule that foreign statutes which bar the action or remedy but not the right altogether are ignored, but if the statute bars the right, then the governing law decides: ss 142, 143.

Voluntary assignments

14-33   The mutual obligations of assignor and assignee under a voluntary assignment of a right against a debtor are governed by the law applicable to the contract between the assignor and assignee: Art 12(1).

The law governing the right to which the assignment relates determines:

— its assignability;

— the relationship between the assignee and the debtor;

— the conditions under which the assignment can be invoked against the debtor; and

— any question whether the debtor's obligations have been discharged: Art 12(2).

This does not apply to obligations under negotiable instruments (Art 1(2)(c)) or to involuntary assignments, such as bankruptcy, garnishments or expropriations.

For the suggested US position, see the US Conflicts Restatement ss 208–211.

Subrogation

14-34   Article 13(1) provides that where a creditor has a contractual claim against a debtor and a third person has a duty to satisfy the creditor, or has in fact satisfied the creditor in discharge of that duty, the law which governs the third person's duty to satisfy the creditor shall determine whether the third person is entitled to exercise against the debtor the rights which the creditor had against the debtor. Article 13(2) provides that the same rule applies where several persons are subject to the same contractual claim (i.e. joint and several debtors) and one of them has satisfied the creditor. Hence a guarantor's right of subrogation or indemnity against the principal debtor is governed by the applicable law of the guarantee. No doubt this is subject to bankruptcy doctrines, notably the rule against double-proof which may shut out the guarantor's claim for reimbursement against the principal debtor if the guarantor has not paid in full. Further, if the claim paid by the guarantor is secured, in some jurisdictions the guarantor must perfect his right to the security in the relevant land, ship, or aircraft registry.

Summary of issues not covered by applicable law

The main issues in our context *not* covered by the applicable law relate to   **14–35** the following:

–   mandatory statutes and public policy;

–   corporate constitution, powers, and authorities;

–   aspects of security;

–   corporate insolvency;

–   procedure;

–   overriding conventions.

These are reviewed below.

Mandatory statutes and public policy

Mandatory statutes and public policy of the forum override the applicable   **14–36** law: Arts 7(2) and 16. This may in England exclude, for example:

–   Contracts violating laws of a friendly foreign state when entered into, e.g. tax frauds, violation of exchange control or embargoes: see para 14–74 *et seq*. Contrast subsequent introductions of legal restrictions after the contract. In the latter case, the English courts will not enforce a contract which is illegal at the place at which it must be performed if the contract is governed by English law. If it is not governed by English law, then the effect of the subsequent illegality should be a matter for the foreign applicable law under Art 10.

–   A foreign discriminatory law which otherwise applies to the contract but is so oppressive that it should not affect the contract, e.g. a foreign law which imposes exchange controls based on race or creed and which would otherwise modify the contract because it is governed by that foreign law: see *Re Helbert Wagg & Co. Ltd* (1956) Ch 323, 352; *Etler v Kertesz* (1960) 26 DLR (2d) 209 (Ont CA).

- Contracts to pay a bribe to a foreign public official to procure a government contract: see *Lemenda Trading Co Ltd v African Middle East Petroleum Co Ltd* [1988] QB 448.

All of the above are law of the court, i.e. countries apply their own law.

14–37   It is considered that a wagering contract is not contrary to English public policy. Hence the applicable law should decide whether a gaming contract is void or valid under the gaming law of the country of the applicable law. A wagering contract which is valid by its applicable law is valid in England, but, since the English Gaming Act 1845 makes those contracts unenforceable by action and since this is a matter of procedure outside the Convention (Art 1(2)), wagering contracts are unenforceable by court action in England even if valid by the applicable law: Dicey Rule 200.

The contract must conflict with some fundamental moral principle to be void by public policy. This would probably not include contractual penalties unless utterly unconscionable.

14–38   Article 7(1) (which does not have the force of law in the UK) provides that the mandatory rules of the law of a country (other than the country of the applicable law) may have effect if the situation has a close connection with that country. The UK government objected to Art 7(1) on the grounds that it was lacking in certainty and hence derogations are possible. Article 7(1) is evidently intended to establish that foreign public laws, such as exchange contracts and export/import restrictions, should apply even if they do not arise under the applicable law, if the interests of the forum are not unduly violated. The rule is considered unsatisfactory and would destroy the certainty of the insulation of the governing law. A rule similar to the Convention Art 7(1) also appears in the Swiss PILA 1987 although the case must not only be closely connected to the mandatory law of the foreign state, but also the interests of a party must be legitimate and clearly overriding according to Swiss views: perhaps this was influenced by US governmental interest analysis.

Corporate constitution

14–39   Corporate powers, authorities and the like are not governed by the applicable law. Art 1(2): This covers, for example:

(a) Due **incorporation** and continuing existence. English courts have, for centuries, been prepared to recognise foreign corporations. The due incorporation of a foreign corporation and its status as a corporation are determined by the law of the place where it is incorporated, e.g. *Lazard Bros v Midland Bank* [1933] AC 289. Similarly whether it continues in existence or has been dissolved are also determined by the law of the place of incorporation: "The will of the sovereign authority which created it can also destroy it." *Lazard Bros* above at 297; Dicey Rule 155. Problems of due incorporation are extremely rare in this context.

(b) **Authorisations,** including such matters as quorum, board resolutions, power of directors named in the commercial register to bind the company, shareholder consents, etc.

(c) **Powers** The corporate powers of a corporation are generally determined   14–40
by its constitutional documents which are interpreted in accordance with the laws of its place of incorporation: e.g. *Risdon Iron and Locomotive Works v Risdon* [1906] 1 KB 49, CA. Important restrictions in practice are: whether a borrowing or particularly a guarantee is ultra vires; and whether there are any constitutional restrictions on borrowing and guarantee powers. Thus, often the power to issue bonds to the public (as opposed to private offerings) cannot be exercised at all by certain classes of companies, e.g. private proprietary companies.

The ultra vires doctrine is being steadily eroded in many municipal jurisdictions. In Europe, the ultra vires rule for corporations situate in the EC has been modified by statute in many member states pursuant to the Company Law Directives. By 1989 amendments to the British Companies Act 1985, the ultra vires rule has been virtually abolished vis-à–vis outsiders dealing with the company. Members of the company may still obtain an injunction to restrain an ultra vires act (but not if it is to be done in fulfilment of a pre-existing legal obligation of the company), and directors may continue to be liable on the insolvency of the company for misfeasance if they cause the company to act ultra vires.

Most American states have introduced statutes providing that ultra vires shall not be a defence in suits involving either foreign or domestic corporations: see s 3.04 of the United States Revised Model Business Corporation Act which has been enacted or paralleled in most US states, including New York.

(d) **Liability of members,** e.g. whether the shareholders have unlimited liability.

The law of the place of incorporation is dominant in the US Conflicts Restatement on the above issues: see ss 296–313.

For amalgamations, see para 16–2 *et seq*.

Security

14–41   Many aspects of security, e.g. land mortgages and chattel mortgages, are governed by separate rules which are outside the scope of this book but which are discussed in another work in this series. A proprietary transfer is not a contract within the Convention, but contractual aspects should be. But as to voluntary assignments of debts, see Art 12(2).

Corporate insolvency

14–42   Most aspects of corporate insolvency are not covered by the Convention: see Art 1(2). This relates to bankruptcy rules covering, for example, an insolvency moratorium on debts; statutory restrictions on contract cancellations or accelerations on bankruptcy; conversion of foreign currency debts into local currency; provability of debts; preferential creditors; insolvency set-off; publication or registration of security; fraudulent preferences; and director's personal liability.

The private international law of bankruptcy is reviewed in another work in this series.

Procedure

14–43   Procedure is mainly lex fori (Art 1(2)), e.g. whether or not the court has jurisdiction; whether or not the defendant is entitled to sovereign immunity; judgments for foreign currency debts in local currency; certain aspects of remedies, e.g. the availability of injunctions to restrain a breach of covenant or of specific performance to grant a mortgage or to make a loan, but damages appear to be proper law; evidence; right to a jury; proof of foreign law; privileged communications; injunctions to restrain the removal of the assets from the jurisdiction prior to a judgment, e.g. the English Mareva injunction and the French *saisie conservatoire*; and post-judgment attachments and execution.

Overriding conventions

14–44   Certain conventions override (Art 21), e.g. bankruptcy conventions and the IMF Agreement, especially Art VIII 2b: see para 15–26 *et seq.*

Proof of law

The applicable law includes any presumptions of law or burden of proof **14–45** specified by that law: Art 14(1). A contract may be proved by any mode of proof recognised by the law of the forum: Art 14(2). The English courts decide on the basis of expert evidence proferred by witnesses.

States with more than one legal system

Where a state has several territorial units with different systems of law, each **14–46** is considered as a country for the purposes of the Convention: Art 19(1). Thus the Convention applies to a contract involving Scotland and Italy. Article 19(2) covers the case where the situation is connected with several territorial units in a single member state. This is a purely domestic matter for the state concerned.

Choice of law

Express choice of applicable law

Freedom of choice The primary rule is stated in Art 3(1): "a contract shall **14–47** be governed by the law chosen by the parties. The choice must be expressed or demonstrated with reasonable certainty by the terms of the contract or the circumstances of the case. By their choice the parties can select the law applicable to the whole or part only of a contract." Connection with the applicable law is not necessary.

This reflects English common law which allows virtually complete party autonomy in choice of law. Party autonomy is accepted now in most, if not all, developed systems, although in the US there must usually be some connection.

Limitations on the freedom of choice of law in financial markets are a nationalist restrictive practice which should enjoy no approbation. There is no reason why parties should not choose a foreign unconnected system of law if they wish to, e.g. because they trust it or because it is neutral, and indeed vast numbers of financial contracts are subject to unconnected systems e.g. bond issues, syndicated loans and market standard forms for interest swaps and foreign exchange. States which seek to have their own legal views heard, or to ensure that their subjects are ruled by their laws, can impose their policies by mandatory statutes, which will come within the overrider for public policy or mandatory statute in their own courts (but not foreign courts) if indeed they think that these policies are important enough to impose them on their citizenry.

The original English freedom of choice probably grew out of charterparties. In the nineteenth century when Britain owned more than half the world's merchant fleet, owners and charterers located in foreign states were content to refer to a highly developed system of maritime law, as opposed to the law of their own, perhaps undeveloped, state.

14–48   **United States governmental interest analysis** The US Conflicts Restatement attempts in s 6 to set out general principles applying to all conflict of laws issues, whether in contract or in any other area of law, in the grand statement that the factors relevant to the choice of the applicable rule of law include seven factors, namely the needs of the interstate and international systems; the relevant policies of the forum; the relevant policies of other interested states in the relative interests of those states and the determination of the particular issue; the protection of justified expectations; the basic policies underlying the particular field of law; certainty, predictability and uniformity of result; and ease in the determination and application of the law to be applied. Section 10 states that these principles may need to be modified in the case of international conflicts as opposed to interstate conflicts. Clearly these general principles do not get one very far in resolving particular matters.

However s 187 confirms that the law chosen by the parties will be applied unless either (a) the chosen state has no substantial relationship to the parties or the transaction and there is no other reasonable basis for the parties' choice, or (b) the application of the law of the chosen state would be contrary to a fundamental policy of a state which has a materially greater interest than the chosen state and the determination of the particular issue and which, under an objectively ascertained governing law under s 188, would be the state of the applicable law in the absence of an effective choice of law by the parties. The comments make it clear that the old objection that freedom of choice is tantamount to enabling parties to be legislators is now obsolete and further there does not have to be any connection provided there is some reasonable basis for choosing an unrelated system of law, e.g. because the parties wish to refer their contract to some well known and highly elaborated commercial law. Naturally any choice of law must be subject to the public policy of the forum, provided that policy is fundamental.

14–49   The US emphasis upon the interest of states in having their law applied is referred to as the "governmental interest analysis" developed first in a comprehensive manner by Professor Brainerd Currie. There has been much discussion as to whether this approach leads to too much flexibility or too much of a homeward trend or whether courts are equipped to weigh up the policies underlying the rules of law in other countries and whether there is sufficient predictability. Commentators have from time to time observed that there appears to be greater uncertainty in the US rules applicable to contracts, but this could be theoretical and the most careful comparative investigation of the leading cases in the various jurisdictions would be required before one could support that proposition, at least so far as financial contracts (as opposed to torts) are concerned.

Switzerland Article 116 of the Swiss PILA 1987 provides that contracts are   **14–50** governed by the law chosen by the parties if explicit or clearly evident from the agreement or from the circumstances.

Development of freedom of choice Freedom of choice appeared finally in   **14–51** England by 1865: *P&O Navigation Co v Shand* (1865) 3 Moo PC (NS) 272, in Germany in the 1880s, in France in 1910 and finally in Switzerland in 1952. Jurisdictions in the United States have been slow to confer complete freedom of choice and even now the question of whether there must be a reasonable relationship is not clearly established. A leading decision urging freedom was *Siegelman v Cunard White Star Ltd*, 221 F 2d 189 (2d Cir 1959). To set the matter at rest, in 1984 the New York General Obligations Law was amended to enable parties to choose New York law for transactions of more than $250,000, whether or not the contract bears a reasonable relationship to New York: NY General Obligations Law s 5–1401. But still the UCC requires "reasonable relationship" in transactions covered by the code: s 1–105(1).

Terms of express selections An express selection usually states: "This Agree-   **14–52** ment is governed by the law of ...". Language, such as "shall be subject to", "shall be construed in accordance with" should be a sufficient choice. A choice of "British law" should normally be taken as a choice of English law: see *The Laertis* [1982] 1 Lloyds Rep 613.

As to "reasonable certainty by the terms of the contract or the circumstances of the case" the Giuliano-Lagarde Report indicates (emphasis added):

> "... the Convention recognises the possibility that the Court may, in the light of all the facts, find the parties have made a real choice of law although this is not expressly stated in the contract. For example, the contract may be in a **standard form** which is known to be governed by a particular system of law even though there is no express statement to this effect, such as a Lloyd's policy of marine insurance. In other cases a **previous course of dealing** between the parties under contracts containing an express choice of law may leave the court in no doubt that the contract in question is to be governed by the law previously chosen where the choice of law clause has been omitted in circumstances which do not

indicate a deliberate change of policy by the parties. In some cases the choice of a **particular forum** may show in no uncertain manner that the parties intend the contract to be governed by the law of that forum, but this must always be subject to the other terms of the contract and all the circumstances of the case. Similarly **references in a contract to specific Articles** of the French Civil Code may leave the court in no doubt that the parties have deliberately chosen French law, although there is no expressly stated choice of law. Other matters that may impel the court to the conclusion that a real choice of law has been made might include an **express choice of law in related transactions** between the same parties [this might apply to guarantees of loans], or the choice of a place where disputes are to be settled by **arbitration** in circumstances indicating that the arbitrator should apply the law of that place."

14–53   **Variation of governing law** Article 3(2) allows the parties to choose an applicable law either at the time the contract is concluded or at an earlier or later date. This allows the parties to amend a choice of applicable law previously made.

14–54   **No foreign element** Article 3(3) provides that where the parties have chosen a particular foreign law but all the other elements relevant to the situation are connected with another country, the express choice shall not prejudice those rules of that other country which cannot be derogated by contract (i.e. mandatory rules). Article 3(3) is of limited importance because all the elements must be connected with another country. The provision is intended to prevent the use of an artificial applicable law in order to avoid otherwise mandatory rules and is probably redundant.

Evasive choices of law

14–55   Pre-Convention it was said that the English courts will not uphold an express choice of law if the choice is made with a view to evading a mandatory rule of law which would have applied to the contract if an "objectively connected" proper law had been chosen, e.g. validating a loan which would be void or illegal under the legal system which would otherwise have applied. In *Vita Food Products Inc v Unus Shipping Co Ltd* [1939] AC 277, it was said that the choice must be "bona fide and legal".

The Convention endeavours to give certainty to choice of law. The "evasive" rule – which has not been applied in England – is probably covered in any event by the overriding mandatory law/public policy rules in Arts 7(2) and 16.

Applicable law in absence of express choice

Generally Parties to a formal loan agreement or a bond issue usually make an express selection of governing law in the instrument itself. However, there are occasions when no express choice is made, e.g. because the loan is informally documented or because a governmental borrower on grounds of national prestige or some constitutional prohibition is not willing to submit expressly to a foreign law. Interbank deposit contracts will generally not state the applicable law. Financial trading contracts, such as foreign exchange contracts and swap contracts, are generally contracted under a master agreement which applies to all transactions between the parties and which contains an express choice of law.

14–56

Some of the factors which render the discovery of the governing law of some importance to the interests of the parties are noted at para 14–5. Further, the absence of an express choice of law is often, for similar reasons, accompanied by the absence of an express choice of forum. The English courts claim power to exercise a "long-arm" jurisdiction if the contract is expressly or impliedly governed by English law (see para 18–28) so that in such a case the potential availability of the English court could hinge entirely on a favourable determination that English law applies.

Summary of international rules

Municipal rules vary widely in the manner of determining the governing law in the absence of an express choice. Internationally the main theories might be summarised as follows:

14–57

1. Tacit or **implied choice**, e.g. choice of forum.

2. **Centre of gravity** (sometimes called "presumed intention", "substantial connection", "dominant contacts", "most significant relationship"): the flexible English common law position and, prior to the Convention, the principle followed in most Continental European states, except Italy.

3. **Policy interests**, notably those promoted initially by American academic writers, such as "governmental interest analysis" which weighs the interests of the states concerned in having their own law applied: see the US Conflicts Restatement.

4. (In the absence of a tacit choice) **rigid presumptions**, such as common nationality or common residence or the law of place of contracting or performance (mainly French and Spanish-influenced states).

5. Rome Convention – **mixture** of tacit choice, centre of gravity and presumptions, but mainly centre of gravity.

6. **Law of the forum**, i.e. the courts apply their own law (non-commercial jurisdictions, e.g. some Arabian Gulf states).

In many commercial jurisdictions, the courts first see whether there is a tacit choice and, if there is not, they follow one of the other theories, either a flexible view (such as centre of gravity) or an inflexible rule (such as place of contracting).

Convention rules on applicable law in absence of choice

14–58   **Closest connection** Under the Rome Convention, where the parties have not chosen an applicable law "the contract will be governed by the law of the country with which it is most closely connected": Art 4(1).

This is similar to the common law English rule that the contract is governed by the legal system with which it has its closest and most real connection.

14–59   **Presumptions** Apart from a presumption relating to land contracts, the main presumption is the application of the law of the principal place of business of the main performing party, that is, whoever performs the contract's "characteristic" performance, e.g. borrower's payments: Art 4(2). This is not defined, but the Giuliano-Lagarde Report equates this not to the payment of money, but to the performance for which the money is paid, e.g. the delivery of goods by the seller, or the performance of the bailor or the lessor/ bailor of equipment under a hire agreement. It is thought that the characteristic performance of a guarantee is payment by the guarantor, and, of a loan agreement, payment by the borrower. But the Report indicates that the characteristic performance of a banking contract is the law of the country of the banking establishment – this is problematic for syndicated loans and presumably the Report has in mind the ordinary banker-customer relationship. The Report provides at 20–21:

> "Identifying the characteristic performance of a contract obviously presents no difficulty in the case of unilateral contracts. By contrast, in bilateral (reciprocal) contracts whereby the parties undertake mutual reciprocal performance, the counter-performance by one of the parties in a modern economy usually takes the form of money. This is not, of course, the characteristic performance of the contract. It is the performance for which the payment is due, i.e. depending on the type of contract, the delivery of goods, the granting of the right to make use of an item of property, the provision of a service, transport, insurance, banking operations, security, etc., which usually constitutes the centre of gravity and the socio-economic function of the contractual transaction...

> Thus for example, in a banking contract the law of the country of the banking

establishment with which the transaction is made will normally govern the contract. It is usually the case in a commercial contract of sale that the law of the vendor's place of business will govern the contract. To take another example, in an agency contract concluded in France between a Belgian commercial agent and a French company, the characteristic performance being that of the agent, the contract will be governed by Belgian law if the agent has his place of business in Belgium."

Overriding rule of closest connection Article 4(5) provides that all the presumptions are to be disregarded "if it appears from the circumstances as a whole that the contract is more closely connected with another country". This lets in the English flexible approach. **14–60**

But, because of the presumptions, it is important to select the applicable law of a financial contract expressly, especially since the presumptions might result in the borrower's legal system being chosen and hence a loss of insulation. It seems that the presumptions carry greater weight than would be the case under previous English practice.

There are special rules for consumer contracts in Art 5.

Connecting factors Previous English decisions may continue to be relevant to cases governed by the Convention. In the absence of an express choice, under English common law, the enquiry does not involve mere mechanical contact-counting. The links are weighed qualitatively. Merely fortuitous and manipulable contacts may be given little weight, e.g. place of contract. Clear evidences of intention, e.g. the selection of the courts of a particular country to hear disputes, must carry a greater weight. **14–61**

By way of example, some of the factors which have been held in pre-Convention English cases to connote a tacit or objectively connected choice are: **14–62**

- Choice of forum (but less important if the choice is non-exclusive or a choice of arbitral tribunal is in a neutral country).

- Reference to local laws, e.g. contract to be "construed" in accordance with English law.

- Peculiar legal terminology

- Currency: a weak factor

- Language: a weak factor, e.g. English is often used as a commercial lingua franca.

- Contract attraction: e.g. loan governed by English law, so the guarantee is attracted to it.

- Party locations: this is a weak factor where there are many locations, e.g. syndicated loans or bond issues. Under the Convention, the place of business of the party who is to render the "characteristic performance" is the principal presumption for determining the applicable law in the absence of choice: Art 4(2).

- Place of performance, e.g. where payments are to be made. This is a weak factor, e.g. US dollar interbank deposit between London banks, but payable through the New York clearing system.

- Validation rule: the conferring of business efficacy on a contract may be a pointer to choice of law. The courts incline towards applying a system of law under which the contract would be valid because the parties cannot be assumed to have intended to contract under a law by which the agreement would be invalid. But this is no more than a pointer: *Sayers v International Drilling Co NV* [1971] 1 WLR 1176 CA; *Kleinwort, Sons & Co v Ungarische Baumwolle Industrie A/G* [1939] 2 KB 678 CA.

14–63   In the United States, the Conflicts Restatement provides in s 188 that, in the absence of an effective choice by the parties of a governing law, the rights and duties of the parties with respect to an issue in contract are determined by the local law of the state which, with respect to that issue, has the most significant relationship to the transaction and the parties under the principles as stated in s 6: see para 14–48. In the absence of an effective choice of law by the parties, the contacts to be taken into account in applying the s 6 principles include the place of contracting, the place of negotiation of the contract, the place of performance, the location of the subject-matter of the contract and the domicile, residence, nationality, place of incorporation and place of business of the parties. These contacts are to be evaluated according to their relative importance with respect to the particular issue. If the place of negotiation and the place of performance are in the same state, the local law of this state will usually be applied except as otherwise provided in the Restatement. The Restatement then sets out special rules in ss 189 to 197 for contracts for the transfer of interests in land and other land contracts, contracts to sell interests in a chattel, various insurance contracts, suretyship contracts, loan contracts, contracts for the rendition of services and transportation contracts.

Section 194 provides in effect that guarantee contracts are normally governed by the law of principal obligation which is guaranteed unless some other state has a more significant relationship: this is a sensible rule because both the principal debt and the guarantee are governed by the same law.

As to loans, s 195 usually applies the law of the state where repayment has to be made in the absence of an express choice of law which, in the case of a bank loan, will usually be where the bank branch is located through which the loan is made.

In general, the US Restatement rules and the Rome Convention rules on characteristic performance seem to have quite a fair amount in common.

By Art 117 of the Swiss PILA 1987, if no law has been chosen, a contract   **14–64** is governed by the law of the country most closely connected with it. But there are some presumptions which appear to be of stronger force than under the Rome Convention. The closest connection is presumed to exist with the country where the party which must make the characteristic performance has its habitual residence, or, if the contract is based on a business activity, has its business establishment. The characteristic performance of guarantee contracts, is the performance of the guarantor. There are special rules for contracts relating to immovable property, consumer contracts, employment contracts and contracts relating to intellectual property: see Arts 119 to 123.

State contracts

There are no special rules applying to state commercial contracts. It does   **14–65** not follow that the law of the state is applied. "It is an element of weight to be considered, but it is no more than that": *R v International Trustee* [1937] AC 500 at 557. In this case dollar bonds linked to the value of gold were issued in New York by the British Government. Subsequently the American Joint Resolution of 1933 abrogated gold clauses. The English court applied New York law so that the gold clause was unenforceable.

Alternative or optional choices of law

A clause may state that if proceedings are taken in the courts of the bor-   **14–66** rower's jurisdiction, those courts will apply their own law. The principal difficulty is that there must be a governing law of a contract from the outset and this cannot be determined retrospectively by some uncertain event in the future: *The Amar* [1981] 1 All ER 498, [1981] 1 WLR 207. If the governing law is dependent upon an action being brought in a particular court, then the parties will not know what legal system governs their obligations until action is brought: See also *The Iran Vojdan* [1984] 2 Lloyds Rep 380 where the carrier's option to choose forum and governing law in Tehran, Hamburg or London was ineffective as a choice of law.

Probably under the Convention, in such a case the applicable law must be determined in accordance with the rules applying if there is no express choice, until a party exercises his option to choose when this should be a permissible variation and effective choice under Art 3(2) – this provides that the parties may vary the governing law. Parties could therefore validly choose a governing law and provide for a different law to be applied according to the place of enforcement.

Depeçage

14–67 The Rome Convention allows the parties to choose different governing laws for different parts of a contract: Art 3(1). This reflects previous English common law. One can therefore state, for example, that the contract will be governed by English law, but that a waiver of immunity will be construed in accordance with New York law: *Forsikrings A/S Vesta v Butcher* [1989] AC 852, HL. This would be odd.

Incorporation of law

14–68 One should distinguish between the selection of the governing law of a contract and the incorporation of some of the provisions of a foreign law into the contract. Thus if the contract defines a "subsidiary" by reference to the definition in a Companies Act or incorporates certain provisions of the Uniform Commercial Code, then this is merely a shorthand method of setting out the incorporated terms in full and the English courts will construe the contract by reading in the incorporated terms.

A significant distinction between incorporation of foreign law and express choice of governing law is that, in the case of an incorporation of law, the law is incorporated as it stands at the date of the contract notwithstanding a subsequent change in law. Thus a statute is fixed at the time of the contract notwithstanding its subsequent amendment or repeal (unless otherwise provided). However the governing law applies as it exists from time to time. If during the subsistence of the contract the governing law changes, then the contract changes with it. Incorporation is frozen law: governing law is liquid law.

Renvoi

14–69 The governing law is the domestic law of the jurisdiction concerned, not its conflict of laws doctrines. There is no room for renvoi in the law of contract; one could go backwards and forwards like a yo-yo. This is confirmed by Art 15 of the Rome Convention. See also the US Conflicts Restatement s 187(3).

Public international law

Choice of public international law as governing law It may sometimes be the   14–70
case that the parties to a financial contract prefer to choose public international law or one of its off-shoots instead of a municipal system of law as
the governing law of the contract.

The sources of public international law include treaties between the contracting states (if both parties are states), international customs evidenced
by generally accepted state practices, general principles of law recognised by
civilised nations, international judicial decisions and the views of the best
legal scholars: see Art 38(1) of the Statute of the International Court of Justice.

There appears to be no English case where non-governmental parties
chose public international law expressly as the governing law of the contract. It is considered however that, in non-Convention cases, there is no
reason in principle why parties should not choose, say, the general principles of law recognised by civilised nations, at least in a contract to which a
state or governmental institution is a party. It would seem that these general
principles are only one of the sources of public international law. It is uncertain whether they are the lowest common denominator of legal systems or
the highest common denominator or something in between. It seems unclear
whether the Rome Convention allows the choice of public international law
or of any system of law or bundle of principles of law other than that of a
country, e.g. lex mercatoria.

Implied choice There are however numerous cases where the general prin-   14–71
ciples of law have been implied (at least by arbitral tribunals) into agreements to which one of the parties is a government.

> *Lena Goldfields Arbitration* (1920–30) 5 AD, Case No 25; *Petroleum Devel-
> opment (Trucial Coast) Ltd v Sheikh of Abu Dhabi*, 18 ILR (1951) 144; *Saudi
> Arabia v Arabian American Oil Co*, 27 ILR (1963) 117; *Sapphire International
> Petroleum Ltd v NIOC*, 34 ILR (1967) 136; *Texaco Overseas Petroleum Co
> Ltd v Libya*, 53 ILR (1979) 389; *BP v Libya*, 53 ILR (1979) 297; *Deutsche
> Schachtbau-und Tiefbohrgesellschaft mbH v Ras Al Khaimah National Oil Co*
> [1987] 2 All ER 769, [1987] 3 WLR 1023, CA; and see [1988] 2 All ER 833,
> [1988] 3 WLR 230, HL.

In *Petroleum Development (Trucial Coast) Ltd v Sheikh of Abu Dhabi*,
18 ILR (1951) 144, which concerned the interpretation and application of

an oil concession, Lord Asquith as the arbitrator applied the "principles rooted in the good sense and common practice of the generality of civilised nations – a sort of 'modern law of nature'" on the grounds that the objective Islamic municipal law lacked any coherent contractual rules relating to concessions. Similarly in *Sapphire International Petroleum Ltd v NIOC*, 34 ILR (1967) 136, an arbitral tribunal implied a choice of "the principles of law recognised by civilised nations" in a contract between a Canadian concessionaire and Iran which specified that the contract was to be performed "in good faith".

"General principles of law" have been applied in several hundred awards issued by the Iran-United States Claims Tribunal (out of a total of over 3000) established in 1981. These have established an impressive body of jurisprudence on the subject.

14–72   Proof of international law The technical method of proof of international law may differ from proof of foreign municipal law (which is normally proved by expert evidence as a matter of fact) by reason of the fact that England purports to incorporate international law into its own system of law, subject to various exceptions: see, for example, *Trendtex Trading Corpn v Central Bank of Nigeria* [1977] QB 529, CA (a sovereign immunity case).

14–73   Content of international law The objection to a choice of international law or general principles accepted amongst civilised nations is that the content of these systems appears rudimentary and imprecise and therefore incapable of conferring predictability upon international financial transactions. Treaty law seems quite primitive compared to muncipal contract law. A particular difficulty is that some important loans cases tried before international tribunals have never got to the merits but have failed on technical jurisdictional grounds, for example, the *Norwegian Loans Case*, ICJ Rep (1957) 9. Examples of indemnity and loans cases which have been considered internationally are the *Russian Indemnity Case*, Award November 11, 1912 UNRIAA vol I at 421 and the *Serbian and Brazilian Loans Case*, PCIJ (1929) Series A No 20.

A key question is whether a choice of international law achieves the objective of insulating the governing law of the loan contract from legal interference in the borrower's obligations by reason of changes in municipal law. Presumably the application of public international law removes the contract from the realm of municipal law in the same way as does an external choice of domestic law. However this still leaves open the second stage in the investigation, namely whether, for example, public international law or the general principles of law permit constructive or creeping expropriations of a lender's claim where a government determines that national policy requires this.

Contracts contrary to public policy

Public policy overrides

Under Art 16 of the Rome Convention the application of the foreign law **14–74** can only be refused on the ground that it is "manifestly incompatible" with public policy.

The English courts will not enforce a contract governed by foreign law if the application of the foreign law would be opposed to English public policy, i.e. some fundamental moral or legal principle or a foreign law which outrages one's sense of justice or decency. This proposition is universal, e.g. the US Conflicts Restatement s 187(2)(b); Swiss PILA 1987 Art 17.

It should be noted that the contract will fail only if the law offended is some basic notion of public morality or policy. The mere fact that the contract would be void under English law is not enough. Thus, foreign contracts have been enforced by the English courts which would have been void under an English statute if English law had applied, e.g. a money-lending or gaming law. The doctrine of consideration is obviously not fundamental.

Examples of public policy

Examples of contracts invalid on grounds of English public policy are: **14–75**

1. a contract "to raise money to support the subjects of a government in amity with our own, in hostilities against their government": *De Wütz v Hendricks* (1824) 2 Bind 314;

2. a contract whose object is to violate the **import or export** laws of a friendly country, such as the former prohibition legislation of the United States (*Foster v Driscoll* [1929] 1 KB 470, CA) or Indian legislation directed against the shipment of goods from India to South Africa: *Regazzoni v Sethia* [1958] AC 301;

3. a contract to breach foreign tax laws or penal laws: *Re Emery's Investment Trusts* [1959] Ch 410. Whilst English courts do not enforce foreign revenue or penal laws or contracts for the payment of money in satisfaction of a claim for foreign taxes (*United States of America v Harden* (1963) 41 DLR (2d) 721 (Can S Ct)), they acknowledge them in the sense that they will not enforce a contract made with the object of breaking them.

14–76　　The rule applies only if the contract violates the foreign law when the contract is entered into, i.e. it violates an *existing* law. If the law is introduced *subsequently*, the rule has no application.

The rule also has no application if there is no evidence that the object of the contract was to violate the laws of the friendly foreign country; there must be a "wicked intention" and it is not enough that the contract does in fact involve the doing of something which the foreign law prohibits: *British Nylon Spinners Ltd v ICI* [1955] Ch 37 (English company granted another English company exclusive patent licences which infringed US anti-trust laws; licences were not invalidated).

This ground of public policy lets in some unpredictability since it seems difficult to predict in advance when a court will decide that interests of state are involved. Swashbuckling cases on financing rebellions are easily comprehensible, but invalidation on the ground of contravention of foreign economic sanctions or revenue laws invites the proposition that the contractor is exposed to invalidation on the ground of offence against any foreign law which the foreign state takes so seriously as to impinge upon diplomatic relations. One question is whether foreign usury laws, e.g. in Islamic states, would attract the principle.

Exculpation clauses

14–77　　A particular problem concerns rules found in most, if not all, of the developed jurisdictions whereby exculpation clauses and harsh provisions in contracts with parties of little sophistication or weak bargaining power are subjected to close judicial scrutiny and may be nullified. Many of these are now encapsulated in consumer statutes or apply only to contracts involving consumers, but this is not always the case. The contracts particularly under attack are standard terms of business imposed on a party who had neither the bargaining power nor the sophistication to resist their terms. In such a case it could not be said that freedom of contract exists. In many countries, the courts have limited the impact of these clauses by covert means, e.g. that a party is not bound by surprise terms contained by reference in his contract which he could not expect, e.g. an exclusion clause in a laundry ticket or bus ticket, and by rules whereby exclusion clauses are construed strictly against the party relying on them, e.g. by insisting that negligence or liability for a fundamental breach which goes to the root of the contract cannot be excluded except by very clear words, perhaps drawn to the attention of the other party.

14–78　　For example, in Germany the Act for the Control of the Law of General Conditions of Business of April 1, 1977 contains a number of rules applying to standard terms even if they are between merchants so that the Act is not exclusively concerned with consumer protection. The British Unfair Contract Terms Act 1977 is to the same effect and there is a provision in s 27 which limits the ability to contract out in an international setting. In Austria Art 839 of the ABGB renders void any contract prohibited by law or in conflict with good morals, and a new provision (Art 879 para 3) provides that collateral agreements contained in general conditions of business or contractual forms are also void if in view of all of the circumstances of the case, they are "grossly" disadvantageous to one of the parties. There is also a provision striking down unusual surprise clauses: see Art 864A. Both the French and Italian courts, as well as the Swiss courts, have policed exemption clauses and sometimes invalidated them. The same tendencies are to be found in the United States: see ss 203, 206, 211 of the Restatement of Contracts (2nd). See also Art 36 of the Swedish Contract Acts of 1976. For a general review, on which the above paragraph is based, see Zweigert/Kötz, vol 2 chapter 1.

Many financial contracts contain exculpation clauses, e.g. clauses protecting managers of bond issues and syndicate agents, take or pay contracts in project finance, exclusion clauses in finance leases and the like. Also much financial trading is now done on the basis of standard forms or master agreements, such as foreign exchange trading and trading in interest swaps, options and futures. Trading on exchanges is almost invariably on the basis of standard forms. In general terms it is considered somewhat unlikely that these standard forms would be invalidated on the ground of unconscionability on the basis of the public policy exception. Perhaps this might be more likely to happen in relation to bonds which are bought by members of the public – although even here most are purchased by sophisticated investors who are well able to look after themselves.   **14–79**

Contracts illegal at place of performance

The rules relating to contracts which are illegal at the place of performance are relevant primarily to mandatory statutes introduced *after* a contract is entered into and which render performance illegal, for example, an exchange control prohibiting a debtor from paying a foreign currency loan, trading with the enemy embargoes or economic sanctions prohibiting payments to entities in the embargoed countries. These emergency laws raise the question of their extra-territorial scope and their application to foreign contracts.   **14–80**

Under the Convention, validity is determined by the applicable law: Arts 8 and 10. But prior to the Convention, even if the contract was valid by its

governing law, it was in general invalid insofar as the party's performance
was unlawful by the law of the country where it had to be performed by the
contract, e.g. where payments had to be made, even if they could have been
validly performed elsewhere in fact.

> In *Ralli Bros v Cia Naviera Sota y Aznar* [1920] 2 KB 287, CA, a charterer
> agreed to pay the shipowner freight of £50 a ton for jute carried by sea from
> Calcutta to Barcelona. The contract was governed by English law. After the
> date of the contract, but before the arrival of the ship, a Spanish decree made it
> a criminal offence to pay more than £10 a ton freight for jute. The shipowner
> sued the charterer for the excess over £10 in the English courts. *Held*: the char-
> terer was not liable for the excess. It was illegal at the place of performance.
> Note that the illegality arose after the date of the contract so this was not a con-
> tract to break the laws of a friendly foreign country ab initio.

> See also: *Foster v Driscoll* [1929] 1 KB 470 at 520, CA; *Kleinwort Sons & Co v
> Ungarische Baumwolle Industrie A/G* [1939] 2 KB 678, CA; *Lemanda Trading
> Co Ltd v African Middle East Petroleum Co Ltd* [1988] QB 448, *Libyan Arab
> Foreign Bank v Bankers Trust Co* [1988] 1 Lloyd's Rep 259; *Libyan Arab
> Foreign Bank v Manufacturers Hanover Trust Co (No 2)* [1989] 1 Lloyd's Rep
> 608.

Section 202 of the US Conflicts Restatement provides that the effect of
illegality upon a contract is determined by the governing law, but, when performance is illegal at the place of performance, the contract will usually be
denied enforcement.

14–81   The English rule would not appear to be a "mandatory" statute within
the Art 7(2) override. It is not a rule of public policy within the Art 16 override if the illegality was introduced after the date of the contract, but may be
if the illegality was in force at the date of the contract in which event public
policy prevents the enforcement of contracts intended to break the laws of
friendly foreign states.

The better view is that the rule that the English courts will not enforce
contracts illegal at the place of performance applies only to contracts governed by English law and does not apply to contracts governed by a foreign
law (unless of course the foreign law has the same rule). It is thought that if
under a loan contract governed by New York law, payment has to be made
in, say, Holland and involves a breach of Dutch law, it is a matter for the
law of New York to decide the effect of this on the contract, e.g. whether the
illegality is a supervening impossibility which discharges the party from
further performance or whether the place of performance may be switched.
See Dicey p 1245 *et seq*.

The exception does not apply unless the contract *requires* performance in
the place concerned. But a contract will not escape the rule if the contract

could equally well be performed in another jurisdiction where performance was not illegal.

But, in both Convention and non-Convention cases, if the contract is law- **14–82** ful by the applicable law and lawful at the place of performance, then it is immaterial that the party liable to perform would by doing so violate the laws of the foreign country in which he is resident or carries on business or of which he is a national.

> See: *Kleinwort Sons & Co v Ungarische Baumwolle Industrie A/G* [1939] 2 KB 678; *Trinidad Shipping Co v Alston* [1920] AC 888, PC; *Toprak v Finagrain* [1979] 2 Lloyd's Rep 98, CA; *Cargo Motor Corp Ltd v Tofalos Transport Ltd*, 1972 (1) SA 186; *Kahler v Midland Bank Ltd* [1950] AC 24; *Libyan Arab Foreign Bank v Bankers Trust Co* [1988] 1 Lloyd's Rep 259.

The result is that a borrower or lender could be committed to perform a contract even though performance of that contract violated the laws of the country of its incorporation, e.g. an exchange control law or an embargo, provided that there is an external proper law and the illegality does not arise where payments have to be made. Many international loan agreements contain an illegality clause to protect the lender against this eventuality, but not the borrower.

The legal approach seems reasonable. If a state imposes an exchange con- **14–83** trol or moratorium or embargo to protect its economy or to inflict its foreign policy, it is not unreasonable that foreign courts should ignore these local expressions of power if the contractor has not chosen the law of the legislating state. If the debtor had wished to write in an express contractual excuse for non-payment in those events, naturally no international lender would lend to it. The legislating state then has to accept that its subjects will be compelled to do abroad what is criminal at home. But it is understandable that courts will flinch from ordering a party to do something which is illegal where it actually has to do it. Some sympathy at least is shown for the hapless debtor who is often an unwilling participant in this legal warfare.

Discharge

General rule

The discharge of a contract usually depends upon the applicable law of the **14–84** contract: Art 10(1)(b) or (d), reflecting previous English law.

These rules as to discharge are in practice of the greatest importance in financial contracts since a change in law resulting in, say, a moratorium may be recognised if it arises under the applicable law of the contract. The rules have been a strong incentive for the application of an external system of law as the applicable law of an international financial contract so as to exclude ⸙ interference by the laws of the borrower's country.

Examples: moratoriums, exchange controls, annulments, etc

14–85   Examples of the rule are set out below.

Moratorium A moratorium on payments modifies the obligation of a debtor if the moratorium law is enacted in the country of the governing law of the contract. The rule was highlighted by Australian decisions after the passing of the New South Wales Moratorium Act 1931. But this does not apply if the contract law is different from the moratorium law.

> In *National Bank of Greece and Athens v Metliss* [1958] AC 509, the English courts held that a Greek bank was liable to pay the full amount of interest on bearer bonds governed by English law and payable at the holder's option in London or in Athens, notwithstanding that a Greek moratorium law had been passed reducing the interest rate.

> In *Libyan Arab Foreign Bank v Manufacturers Hanover Trust Co (No 2)* [1989] 1 Lloyds Rep 608, the defendant bank argued that a US presidential decree freezing assets of the Libyan government was effective to block payment from the London bank account of LAFB with the bank because the governing law of the bank account was New York law. *Held*: the governing law was English law and the US decree was no defence.

14–86   **Exchange controls** Similar rules have been applied in the case of exchange control regulations. Where a German law provided that a loan governed by German law (although in English pounds payable in England) was to be paid to a local German government office in German currency, it was held that the debtor had validly discharged his obligations by making such payment: *Re Helbert Wagg & Co Ltd* [1956] Ch 323. However the exchange control regime has been affected by the Bretton Woods Agreement of 1944 constituting the International Monetary Fund: see para 15–26 *et seq*.

14–87   **Annulment of claim** Even if the legislation arising under the governing law annuls the claim, this may nevertheless, subject to the exceptions mentioned below, be recognised by the English courts. It was said in *Re Helbert Wagg & Co Ltd* [1956] Ch 323, 340 that "The power of legislation to affect a contract by modifying or annulling some term thereof is a question of dis-

charge of the contract which, in general, is governed by the proper law."
Hence where by Soviet legislation rights under an insurance policy were
annulled, the courts dismissed an action on the policy where the policy was
governed by a Russian law: *Employers' Liability Assurance Corp v Sedg-
wick Collins & Co* [1927] AC 95.

Taxation Whether a debtor can withhold tax from payments at source   **14–88**
depends on whether or not the requirement to deduct the tax arises under
the governing law. Thus where an English resident promised to make maintenance payments to a person in New York under a contract governed by
New York law, the English resident was not permitted to deduct United
Kingdom income tax since New York law did not permit the English resident to do so: *Keiner v Keiner* [1952] 1 All ER 643. Of course, if the payer is
within the taxing jurisdiction, the tax law will override the contract since
parties cannot avoid taxation by choice of law.

Frustration The governing law determines whether a contract has been discharged by an event other than performance, such as impossibility of performance or frustration. This could be significant in the context of events of
default.

Exceptions to control of discharge by governing law

One of the most important exceptions to the above rule that the governing
law exclusively controls discharge is discriminatory or oppressive legislation. An English court will not permit a party's obligations to be wholly or
partly discharged if in the view of the English court the legislation is
"discriminatory", e.g. because it is intended to penalise particular classes of
persons such as British subjects in time of war or members of a particular
race or creed, e.g. *Re Friedrich Krupp A/G* [1917] 2 Ch 188. This should
continue to apply by virtue of the "public policy" exception in Art 16.

CHAPTER 15

GOVERNING LAW: FOREIGN CURRENCY OBLIGATIONS; EXCHANGE CONTROLS; EMBARGOES

Foreign currency obligations

Ambiguity in currency choice

15–1   Where a loan obligation is expressly to be payable in "dollars", "francs", or "pounds", the applicable law decides which currency is referred to: Art 10(1)(a). For example, dollars may refer to the currency of the United States, Canada, Australia or Singapore.

If English law is the applicable law, then the parties are presumed to have referred to the currency of the country with which the contract is most closely connected. There are many decisions: Dicey Rule 207.

Currency of payment

15–2   **Generally** Many commercial jurisdictions permit a debtor to pay in local currency a debt contracted in a foreign currency. These are legal tender rules which must be distinguished from exchange control regulations and from rules of court which require a judgment to be given in a particular currency. The rules give rise to a number of difficulties for lenders:

1. Where a debtor is permitted to repay a loan in currency other than that in which it was advanced, the lender may be involved in a foreign exchange operation in order to purchase the currency of the original advance, e.g. in order to pay back a funding deposit.

2. If the borrower pays late and can convert at a rate of exchange other than that prevailing on the date of payment or if the rate of exchange applied by local law is an official non-commercial rate of exchange different from that prevailing in the lender's market, the lender may receive local currency in an amount inadequate to enable him to pur-

chase the foreign currency in his own market in sufficient amounts to cover the loan.

3.   The lender may not be able to export the local currency and may not be able to convert that currency in an acceptable commercial market.

In practice many loan contracts provide that payment of foreign curren-   **15–3**
cies is to be made in the country of that currency (through the currency's clearing system) so that legal tender rules allowing payment in local currency are irrelevant.

Under the Rome Convention, the currency of payment (and whether the parties can validly contract out of local legal tender rules) are probably matters of detail (and hence governed by the law of the country of performance: Art 10(2), Dicey Rule 208) and not matters of substance governed by the applicable law under Art 10(1).

The rate of exchange used, which determines the amount payable, is clearly substantive and should be determined by the applicable law.

English law As a general rule, if a debt expressed in a foreign currency is   **15–4**
payable in England, it may be paid either in units of the money of account or in sterling converted at the local market rate of exchange (not some official rate): *Marrache v Ashton* [1943] AC 311. But an agreement to pay in foreign currency is valid.

> In *Marrache v Ashton* [1943] AC 311, PC, the debtor covenanted in a mortgage deed to pay to the creditor in Gibraltar a specified number of "pesetas". The market rate for pesetas in Gibraltar was 132 to the pound, as opposed to the official rate of 53 to the pound fixed in Spain for use at the frontier. The debtor claimed that they need only pay the creditor the sterling equivalent of the debt at the rate of 132 pesetas to the pound. *Held*: the debtor succeeded. This was the market rate in Gibraltar. Otherwise the creditor would receive a windfall.

Method of payment

The method of payment, e.g. whether payment must be made in bank notes   **15–5**
or other legal tender or can be made by cheque or by a bank transfer through a clearing system is, unless otherwise stated in the contract, a matter for the law of the place of performance, since generally (but not necessarily) it is a matter of the detail of performance rather than the substance of the obligation: see Art 10(2), Dicey Rule 208. If the parties expressly provide for the manner of payment, e.g. by bank transfer, this should perhaps be tested by the applicable law.

Judgments in foreign currency

15–6   **Generally** Many countries require judgments to be given in the local currency. If a lender in such a case claims a foreign currency in the local courts,
at what date is the conversion made? If the court requires the conversion as
at the original maturity date and if there are fluctuations in rates of
exchange between the due date and the date of payment, then the creditor
may suffer a loss. Alternatively, the creditor may make a gain. Similar losses
or gains could arise where the conversion date is the judgment date or even
the date of the enforcement order. Ideally a creditor should be entitled to
receive whatever amount in the local currency is required, by immediate
conversion in a market reasonably available to the creditor, to retrieve the
foreign currency amount agreed to be payable. This is rarely achieved in the
case of those countries which authorise local currency judgments only.

15–7   **Conflict of laws** The law which determines the currency in which a judgment is given is probably the law of the country in whose courts the action is
brought since it is a matter of procedure which under the Convention is lex
fori: Art 1(2).

15–8   **English law** An English court can give judgment for an amount expressed in
foreign currency: *Miliangos v George Frank (Textiles) Ltd* [1976] AC 443,
HL. For procedural reasons the amount of the judgment must be converted
into sterling before execution can be levied. Generally, the date for conversion will be the last possible moment, i.e. the date upon which the court
authorises enforcement of the judgment.

> In *Halcyon the Great* [1975] 1 WLR 515, it was held that the Admiralty
> Marshal can sell an arrested ship for US dollars and place the proceeds of sale
> in a US dollar deposit account.

15–9   **Other countries** Some English-related countries follow the rule that conversion is at the last possible time – broadly the *Miliangos* rule, e.g. Australia;
New Zealand; and Scotland: *Commerzbank AG v Large*, 1977 SC 375
    It seems that now in Canada conversion can be immediately before pay-
ment: Court of Justice Act RSO 1990 s 121. In South Africa the courts have
a discretion to give judgments in foreign currency: see Dicey p 1583. In New
York, judgments in foreign currency are converted into US dollars at the
rate prevailing on the date of the judgment, not the date of payment: Judiciary Law s 27(b) as amended in 1987.
    Loan agreements may contain topping-up clauses. If a judgment is
expressed in a different currency, the debtor must pay any extra required to

produce the amount of the agreed currency. The efficacy of these clauses appears not to have been tested.

Conversion of currencies on insolvent liquidation

On insolvency proceedings, many bankruptcy laws require that foreign cur-   **15–10**
rency debts are converted into local currency, so that, if the local currency is depreciating, the creditor's claim for a dividend is depreciated. This is so in most developed countries.

As to English corporate insolvencies, IR 1986, r 4.91 states that the date for conversion should be the date of the winding-up order.

This is probably a mandatory rule which cannot be overridden by a topping-up clause. Bankruptcy is outside the Convention. Very few countries provide for revalorisation.

Revalorisation of currencies

In both Rome Convention and non-Convention cases, the governing law of   **15–11**
the contract determines whether and to what extent a debtor is liable in the event of the depreciation of the currency of the debt to make an additional payment to the creditor by way of revalorisation. Dicey Rule 205.

Most commercial nations adopt the nominalistic principle that where a debt is expressed in the currency of a particular country then the obligation of the debtor is to pay the nominal amount of that debt in whatever is legal tender at the time of payment according to the law of the country in whose currency the debt is expressed irrespective of any fluctuations which may have occurred in the value of that currency in terms of any other currency, gold or other asset. In England, this goes back to *Gilbert v Brett* (1604) Davis 18.

However, under some foreign legal systems a debtor is obliged in certain   **15–12**
cases to revalorise a debt expressed in a currency which has depreciated after the debt was incurred and before it becomes payable. This is a matter determined by the governing law. If therefore an insurance company is liable to pay a sum in German Marks under an English policy, it was held prior to the Rome Convention that the English courts will decline to enforce any revalorisation of the German Mark amount although under German law, being the country of the currency, the debtor may be liable to revalorise: *Annerson v Equitable Insurance Society* (1926) 134 LT 557, CA. It was said in that case (at 566) that the law for revalorisation is "a law not affecting the currency, but affecting the particular contracts that come within the

scope of it . . . In other words, it is the debt that is valorised and not the currency". In the result the unfortunate widow received depreciated German Marks notwithstanding that under German law she would have been entitled to a revalorised amount.

Where, however, the debt is governed by a law which provides for revalorisation, the English courts will apply the foreign principles of revalorisation as part of the governing law. The position is presumably the same under the Rome Convention.

> In *Kornatzki v Oppenheimer* [1937] 4 All ER 133, a contract was entered into in 1905 and governed by German law under which the plaintiff was entitled to an annuity in German Marks payable by the defendant, a British subject resident in England. *Held*: the debt should be revalorised in accordance with the German Civil Code.

Maintenance of value and indexation

15–13   **Methods of indexation** Normally lenders take the nominalist risk and preserve the worth of their assets by investing in currencies in which they have confidence and adjusting for the risk of weaker currencies by a higher yield. However, various attempts have been made to maintain the value of the claim, usually in the case of bond issues. Maintenance of value can be achieved in a number of ways.

> **Currency option** A bondholder can be given a currency option so that he may choose the strongest amongst a number of currencies. The conversion rate would be stipulated in the bond at the time of issue. Such an arrangement involves a borrower in a degree of risk since bondholders would be inclined to choose the strongest currency at the time of payment. The borrower would be wise to hedge the risk by purchasing currency options.

> **Indexes** The claim can be indexed according to a commodity such as gold or even minerals or agricultural commodities. Gold clauses were widely used until they were generally outlawed by municipal legislation (but not by England or Switzerland) during the 1930s. The claim can be indexed according to an index, such as a retail price index. The claim can be indexed according to another currency of stable value or a basket of currencies so as to spread the risk. Various bond issues have been floated indexed against European "currency cocktails" and a few issues have been indexed according to the Special Drawing Rights of the International Monetary Fund which comprise a number of leading currencies weighted in accordance with IMF rules. It should be noted

that a claim indexed by reference to, say SDRs is not a claim payable in SDRs but is an amount payable in a domestic currency, such as US dollars, adjusted according to the index. Linking the amount payable to a commodity or index in one of the ways described might make the contract a "contract for differences" within the meaning of the Financial Services Act 1986, with authorisation and conduct of business consequences.

Conflict of laws The numerous cases on gold clauses prior to the Rome Con-   15–14
vention support the proposition that contracts whereby the parties seek to negative the effect of the nominalistic principle, i.e. to protect the creditor against the risk of a depreciation of the currency in which the debt is expressed or to safeguard the debtor against the risk of an appreciation of that currency, are determined by the governing law of the contract. The position is the same under the Rome Convention.

Express indexation clauses will be upheld if the governing law is English. Thus a clause in a mortgage on land in England providing that payment of principal and interest should be index-linked to the Swiss Franc has been upheld: *Multiservice Bookbinding Ltd v Marden* [1979] Ch 84.

Exchange controls

Introduction

Exchange controls appear to be a diminishing feature of international   15–15
monetary relations. They were almost always unattractive. The rationale was that the controls were necessary to protect the currency and Western European controls were based on this proposition. But sometimes they were used to serve the needs of despotic governments whose depredations would cause the citizen to place his assets abroad, or to serve a state restrictive practice (e.g. by insisting that savers invest only in local business), or as a covert method of preventing tax avoidance, or to save a state from its insolvency. One must pardon times of real national emergency, such as war.

Exchange control regulations may render the contract illegal and void in its inception or may imply a condition that the contract is not to be performed except in so far as the consent is granted. They may have retroactive effect.

It will usually be futile for a creditor to endeavour to enforce the contract in the courts of the debtor's country imposing the exchange control since these courts will normally be bound to apply local mandatory regulations irrespective of the governing law of the contract. Thus in *Boissevain v Weil* illegal

[1950] AC 327 a loan to a British subject in Monaco was deemed by an English court to be irrecoverable because it contravened British exchange control regulations. Hence the enquiry is concerned only with the question of whether the foreign exchange control will be recognised by an external court.

It is necessary to examine the position (a) under private international law, including the Rome Convention, and (b) under the Articles of Agreement of the International Monetary Fund signed in 1944 at Bretton Woods ("the IMF Agreement").

Recognition of foreign exchange control regulations

15–16   The English courts may give effect to a foreign exchange control regulation affecting a contract in one of the four cases listed below.

In the absence of one of these grounds for recognition of foreign exchange control regulations, a party to a contract will have no defence to an action on the contract in an English court merely because the exchange control legislation arises under the law of the place where the party resides or carries on business or in the state of which he is a national: *Kleinwort Sons & Co Ltd v Ungarische Baumwolle Industrie* AG [1939] 2 KB 678, CA; *Toprak v Finagrain* [1979] 2 Lloyd's Rep 112, CA.

payment

It follows from this rule that, where none of the exemptions applies, a borrower could be held by an English court to make payments under a loan contract and similarly a lender could be held bound to lend, even though such performance is prohibited by exchange control regulations imposed by the law of the place of incorporation of the borrower or lender.

Exchange controls are often introduced when a state is insolvent. The effect of the international rules is that, one way or another, private contractors can insulate the bare terms of the contract from being modified by exchange controls.

15–17   The main English grounds for recognition of foreign exchange controls are:

1.   **Governing law** The exchange control will be recognised where the legislation is part of the proper law of the contract (unless discriminatory or oppressive): see Art 10.

> In *Re Helbert Wagg & Co Ltd* [1956] Ch 323, a German company carrying on business in Germany borrowed sterling payable in England from an English company under a contract governed by German law. By German exchange control legislation enacted subsequent to the making of the contract, the borrower was required to pay the amounts owing to the lender in German currency to a

German government office and thereby was discharged under German law. *Held*: the liability was validly discharged under the governing law of the contract.

On the other hand in *Kleinwort Sons & Co Ltd v Ungarische Baumwolle Industrie AG* [1939] 2 KB 678, CA, a Hungarian firm declined to pay amounts owing to an English bank under an acceptance credit which were payable in London on the ground that Hungarian exchange control legislation rendered it illegal for the Hungarian firm to remit money abroad. *Held*: this was no defence to the claim of the English bank since English law was the governing law of the contract which was to be performed in London.

Similar results have been reached in the United States.   15–18

In *Mayer v Hungarian Commercial Bank of Pest*, 21 F Supp 144 (EDNY 1937), the Hungarian Government in 1931 enacted legislation blocking the payment of foreign currency bonds abroad. Instead, the foreign bondholders were limited to claiming amounts due on their bonds in Hungary in Hungarian currency. A bondholder's claim in New York on Hungarian municipal bonds failed because the bonds were governed by Hungarian law.

In *French v Banco Nacional de Cuba*, 23 NY 2d 46, 242 NE 2d 704, 295, NYS 2d 433 (1968), a New York court denied recovery on Cuban government certificates of indebtedness governed by Cuban law and therefore subject to a Cuban government decree suspending payment of the certificates.

On the other hand in *Central Hanover Bank & Trust Co v Siemens & Halske AG*, 15 F Supp 927 (SDNY 1936), a trustee for bondholders succeeded in a claim on German municipal bonds whose payment in foreign currency abroad had been blocked by a subsequent German law which required that they be paid only in German scrip. The bonds were governed by New York law and were therefore insulated from the German law. A Russian repudiation was similarly defeated where Russian treasury notes were governed by New York law in the case of *United States v National City Bank of New York*, 90 F Supp 448 (SDNY 1950). See also *Bank Leumi Trust Co v Wulkan*, 735 F Supp 72 (1990).

2. **Place of performance** The exchange control will be recognised (per-   15–19
   haps) where the foreign exchange control regulation is imposed by the
   law of the place in which the contract must be performed and the regulation renders such performance illegal, in any event if the contract is
   governed by English law.

In *Ralli Bros v Cia Naviera Sota y Aznar* [1920] 2 KB 287, CA, an English court declined to enforce an agreement governed by English law for the payment in Spain of chartered freight beyond the maximum permitted by Spanish law.

Hence if payments are *required* to be made under an English contract in a state whose exchange control regulations prohibit such payment, the English courts will refuse to enforce the contract to that extent. See para 14–80 *et seq* for further examples of this principle.

An alternative solution was adopted in the American case of *Pan American Life Insurance Co v Blanco*, 362 F 2d 167 (5th Circ 1966). In this case an insurance policy in favour of Zabaleta, a former Cuban resident, was payable in Cuba. Subsequent exchange control regulations passed by the Cuban Government prohibited payment. *Held*: where performance was prohibited at the place of performance, the place of performance could shift to a country allowing performance, in this case to the head office of the insurance company in the United States. There are numerous US cases on Cuban insurance policies: see Mann, *Money*, p 411.

15–20   3.   **Public policy** The exchange control will be recognised under English law where the real object and intention of the parties necessitates them joining in an endeavour to perform in a foreign and friendly country some act which is illegal by the laws of that country: para 14–75 *et seq*. Hence currency smuggling contracts are invalid and there seems to be widespread international agreement on this: see Mann, *Money*, p 406 *et seq*. Note that this rule does not apply where the exchange control regulations are introduced subsequently to the date of the contract.

   4.   **IMF Agreement** The exchange control will be recognised where the IMF Agreement applies. See below.

International grounds for non-recognition

15–21   Some states, other than England, do not always apply the governing law and have refused to recognise a foreign exchange control affecting the contract in the following main cases, even if the governing law is that of the legislating state:

   1.   **Lex situs external** Where the debt is notionally located outside the jurisdiction of the legislating state, it has been held that the exchange control cannot affect it since a state may not extend its legislation to external assets. It can only do so, subject to exceptions, if the debt is located within its territory. This is the act of state doctrine: para 17–3. The situs of the debt is determined variously, mainly on centre of gravity principles, with the place of payment playing an important role. England applies this doctrine to expropriations transferring the right to the debt, but not to exchange controls which modify the terms of the debt, e.g. the currency or date of payment.

The situs rule appears to be mainly a US doctrine where the place of payment is dominant.

In *Weston Banking v Turkiye Guaranti Bankasi* AS, 57 NY 2d 315, 442 NE 2d 1195, 456 NYS 2d 684 (1982), a Turkish bank owed a debt to a Panamanian bank payable in New York in Swiss francs. The Turkish bank failed to pay on maturity of the note, claiming that it was prevented from doing so by the imposition of Turkish exchange controls. On suit by the Panamanian bank in New York, the debtor raised a defence of the act of state doctrine based upon the governmental action taken by the Turkish Ministry of Finance. *Held*: the act of state doctrine is not applicable to debts located outside the foreign state whose act is being raised as a defence. The debt involved in this case was not located in Turkey because that state did not have the power to enforce or to collect it. Hence the Turkish bank was liable. The English courts would have treated this not as a case of situs but simply as a case to be decided according to the governing law of the contract: see *Re Helbert Wagg & Co Ltd* [1956] Ch 343.

In *Libra Bank Ltd v Banco Nacional de Costa Rica*, 570 F Supp 870 (SDNY 1983), a syndicate had lent US$40 million to a bank wholly-owned by the Costa Rican Government. The Costa Rican Government adopted a resolution limiting repayment of external debts and the loan was not paid. *Held*: the act of state doctrine may only be used as a defence to preclude judicial enquiry where the act of the foreign sovereign occurs within its own territory. The situs of the debt owed by the Costa Rican bank at the time of the resolution passing the exchange controls was in the United States because (i) under the terms of the loan agreement the Costa Rican bank had consented to the jurisdiction of the New York courts, (ii) New York law was the governing law, (iii) payment of interest and principal had to be made in New York through a New York bank and (iv) the Costa Rican bank had assets located in the United States. The English courts would have arrived at the same result but on different reasoning, i.e. that the discharge of a contract is governed by its proper law and, as the proper law was an external system of law, the contract was insulated from Costa Rican exchange control. The English courts would not have required other external contacts.

In *Allied Bank International v Banco Credito Agricola de Cartago*, 757 F 2d 516 (2d Cir 1985), US banks sued nationalised Costa Rican banks on promissory note loans. Costa Rica, being insolvent, had passed exchange controls prohibiting the payment of foreign currency debts. *Held*: the Costa Rican exchange controls did not affect the debts and the Costa Rican banks were liable to pay. This was because the debts were payable in New York and therefore the situs of the debt was outside the territory of Costa Rica.

Illegality

But if the situs of the debt is in the territory of the legislating state, the US courts have refused to interfere by reason of the act of state doctrine: paras 17–21. Thus, when Mexico imposed exchange controls prohibiting the payment of foreign currency debts (because Mexico was   **15–22** insolvent), bank actions in the US to enforce US dollar certificates of deposit were unsuccessful because the CDs were payable in Mexico and were therefore situated within Mexican territory so that the US courts could not question acts of state over local assets.

See *Braka v Multibanco Commermex*, 589 F Supp 802 (SDNY 1984); *Callejo v Bancomer*, 762 F 2d 1101 (5th Cir 1985); *Riedel v Bancam*, 792 F 2d 220 587 (6th Cir 1986); *Grass v Credito Mexicano SA*, 797 F 2d 220 (5th Cir 1986). See also *Citibank v Wells Fargo Asia Ltd*, 110 S Ct 2034 (1990) (an inconclusive case).

15–23 2. **Exchange control not bona fide.** Recognition has been denied where the exchange control regulation is not made with the intention of protecting a state's currency resources but rather for the purposes of waging economic warfare or achieving some other unjustifiable aim. In *Re Helbert Wagg & Co Ltd* (1956) Ch 323, Upjohn J said at 351–52:

"This court is entitled to be satisfied that the foreign law is a genuine foreign exchange law, that is, a law passed with a genuine intention of protecting its economy ... and for that purpose regulating ... the rights of foreign creditors, and is not a law passed ostensibly with that object, but in reality with some object not in accordance with the usage of nations."

A leading Netherlands decision is *Indonesian Corporation PT Escomptobank v NV Assurantie Maatschappij der Nederlanden Van 1845*, 40 ILR (1970) 7:

Indonesian legislation prohibited the transfer of moneys to satisfy debts owing to a Netherlands company. *Held*: the nationalisation measures were politically motivated, that is, to put pressure on the Netherlands to recognise Indonesian claims to Western New Guinea. The court declined to recognise the Indonesian restrictions, regardless of the law governing the claim. For other decisions, see Mann, *Money*, p 401 *et seq*.

Although these decisions as to non-bona fide restrictions set limits on the doctrine that a state has freedom to impose restrictions where the creditor has accepted the law of the debtor state and hence taken the risk of the debtor state's legislation, courts tend to limit the exception to extreme cases, not where a state is running into payments difficulties and the exchange restrictions have been imposed in order to protect the balance of payments position.

15–24 3. **Discrimination** Recognition may be denied where the exchange control restriction is discriminatory in an unjustifiable manner. German courts refused to apply a discriminatory rate of exchange applied by Poland in the inter-war period on the ground that it was specifically intended to injure German subjects: Berlin Court of Appeal, February 25, 1922, 28 October, 1922, November 2, 1928, JW 1922, 398: 1923, 128: 1928, 1462. The Swiss Federal Tribunal refused to recognise a German removal of a gold clause in respect of a contract governed by German law on the ground that the sole purpose was to protect German debtors: "such violent measures, designed to enrich the economy of the legislating States at the expense of foreign States, are irreconcilable with the Swiss sense of justice": Decision of October 8, 1935, BGE, 61 (ii) 242. But the Swiss attitude may have changed as a result of the Swiss Private International Law Act of 1987 Art 13.

4. **Foreign exchange controls never recognised** Some countries have 15–25 refused to recognise foreign exchange controls entirely, on the ground that they are of a public law character and cannot affect private obligations. There are older decisions to this effect in Austria, France, Germany, Norway and Switzerland, but it may be doubtful whether this view is still held. This view is not taken by the Netherlands, Italian or Anglo-American courts: For details see Mann, *Money*, p 398 *et seq.*

Article VIII 2(b) of the IMF Agreement

Summary This Article was designed to encourage comity on exchange con- 15–26 trols. Article VIII 2(b) provides as follows (emphasis added):

> "**Exchange contracts** which involve the currency of any **member** and which are **contrary to the exchange control regulations** of that member maintained or imposed consistently with this Agreement shall be **unenforceable** in the territories of any member."

Article 21 of the Rome Convention provides that the Rome Convention shall not prejudice the application of international conventions to which an EC state is a party. Hence, the IMF Agreement overrides the Convention.

Most states are members of the IMF – more than 150 of them. But Australia, Mexico and Sweden have not introduced this Article into their law.

As to exchange controls maintained "**consistently**" with IMF Agreement, the IMF Agreement has rules restricting exchange controls for current transactions (e.g. trade payments and interest on loans) but allows them for capital transactions.

Note that the sanction is **unenforceability**, not criminal illegality. International case law differs as to whether this means that the contract is alive but cannot be enforced (the German view, it seems) or whether it is invalid – the French view. The English position seems uncertain: Mann, *Money*, p 332 *et seq.*

The Article applies only to contracts, not torts or restitution or judgments, so that a foreign judgement on an exchange contract can be enforced: Mann, *Money*, p 373 *et seq*. But the Article may include transfers and assignments.

15–27   **Subsequent exchange controls** The better view is that the Article applies only if the contract infringes exchange controls at the time the contract is entered into so that the subsequent imposition of exchange controls should not convert a valid contract into an unenforceable exchange contract. But an initially unenforceable exchange contract may become enforceable if the exchange controls are lifted: see Mann, *Money*, p 370 ff.

Where the Article applies, the ordinary rules of private international law are overridden and municipal courts may not ignore the foreign exchange control regulations concerned. The Article may therefore weaken the insulation sought to be achieved by the application to a loan agreement of a system of law external to that of the borrower's country. On the other hand, decisions in some commercial states tend to narrow the scope of Art VIII 2(b), particularly where its application might involve unjust enrichment or where nationals are involved. The Article has not been popular because it aims to sanction the universal validity of virtually whatever capital exchange controls the member thinks proper.

15–28   **"Exchange contracts"** An agreement will not be subject to Art VIII 2(b) if it is not an "exchange contract". There is little international harmony. There are two basic views as to the meaning of this term:

1.   The narrow construction that an "exchange contract" is a contract to exchange the currency of one country into the currency of another and so would not catch a loan agreement or bond issue. This construction enables the courts to side-step the Article which is frequently used by defendants seeking to escape their obligations.

2.   The wide construction that an exchange contract is one which in any way affects a country's exchange resources, and so would catch a loan agreement or bond issue, because the country's exchange resources are affected: the debtor must sell domestic currency to pay for foreign currency in order to pay the debt.

15–29   England adopts the narrow construction.

In *Wilson, Smithett & Cope Ltd v Terruzzi* [1976] QB 703, CA an Italian resident owed sterling to English metal dealers in respect of metal dealing contracts on the London Metal Exchange. Payment was prohibited by Italian exchange controls. *Held*: the IMF Agreement was no defence. A wide definition would run contrary to the second paramount purpose of the IMF Agreement, namely to facilitate and promote international trade, and it would be extremely difficult, if not impossible, for contracting parties carrying out ordinary international contracts concerning goods or service or debts to satisfy themselves that all necessary permissions had been obtained. In the result international trade would be hampered. As it happened, the Italian courts declined to enforce this judgement.

Contrast *United City Merchants (Investments) Ltd v Royal Bank of Canada* [1983] 1 AC 168, HL. A letter of credit was opened by the defendant bank in England on the instructions of a Peruvian bank for the account of a Peruvian company which had agreed to buy goods from the beneficiary of the credit, an English company. In breach of Peruvian exchange control regulations, the price of the goods was inflated and the English company agreed to pay the inflated part of the proceeds of the credit to an account in Miami, presumably as part of a scheme generated by the Peruvian company to siphon money out of Peru. *Held*: letters of credit are not normally "exchange contracts" but this letter of credit was in fact a monetary transaction in disguise, namely an agreement to exchange Peruvian currency into US dollars, contrary to the Peruvian exchange control regulations. The court split the letter of credit, declined to give judgment for the part which related to the exchange contract, but gave judgment for the part which constituted payment for the machinery and freight. The court said that the courts of a country which was a party to the IMF Agreement ought to do their best to promote both international comity and international trade, and that duty could in the circumstances best be carried out by enforcing that part of the contract which did not offend against the law of Peru and refusing to enforce that part of it which was a disguised monetary transaction. See also *Mansouri v Singh* [1986] 1 WLR 1393, CA.

US courts uphold the narrow construction.   15–30

See *Libra Bank Ltd v Banco Nacional de Costa Rica*, 570 F Supp 870 (SDNY 1983) (loan not barred by Costa Rican exchange controls); *Banco do Brasil SA v AC Israel Commodity Co*, 12 NY 2d 371, 190 NE 2d 235, 239 NYS 2d 872 (1st Dep't 1963), cert denied, 376 US 906 (1964); *J Zeevi & Sons Ltd v Grindlays Bank Uganda Ltd*, 37 NY 2d 220, 333 NE 2d 168, 371 NYS 2d 892 (1975) (a letter of credit is not an exchange contract); *Weston Bank Corp v Turkiye Guaranti Bankasi*, 57 NY 2d 315, 442 NE 2d 1195, 456 NYS 2d 684 (1982); *Callejo v Bancomer*, 764 F 2d 1120 (5th Cir 1985).

The Belgian Commercial Tribunal at Courtrai in *Emek v Bossers and Mouthaan*, ILR (1955) 722 also adopted the narrow construction in the case of an international commodities contract.

15–31   Other foreign decisions have preferred the wider interpretation. In some of these cases the courts seem to have taken into account that the stated primary object of the IMF Agreement was "to promote international monetary co-operation" and that this objective could only be achieved by means of the policy of Art VIII (2b) if one interpreted "exchange contracts" to mean any contract which has an effect on the financial situation of the member or in any way affects the currency resources of that country. This interpretation involves ignoring the word "exchange".

The wide interpretation has been adopted by:

– The West German Court of Appeal in *Lessinger v Mirau*, 22 ILR (1955) 725: an action was brought in Germany by former Austrian residents to enforce a loan for a new system of roulette. The loan was in violation of Austrian exchange control regulations. The Austrians lost the money at the tables but Art VIII 2(b) absolved them from repaying the loan. The court said that a loan agreement is an "exchange contract". Other German decisions have treated all contracts as exchange contracts, e.g. guarantees, bills of exchange, sales commissions, and patent licence agreements. See Mann, *Money*, p 381 *et seq*. But in 1988 the Federal Supreme Court held that a sale of goods contract was not an exchange contract: Mann, *Money*, p 381 *et seq*.

– A Luxembourg court in *Societe Filature et Tissage X Jourdan v Epous Heynen Binter*, 22 ILR (1955) 727: a contract of sale of poplin by a French firm to Luxembourg residents was held to be an "exchange" contract.

– The Paris Court of Appeal in *de Boer, Widow Moojen v von Reeichert*, 89 J Droit Int'l 718, Court of Appeal, Paris 1962: a contract of sale of shares of a French company for French francs between a Netherlands resident as seller and a German resident as buyer which contravened Dutch exchange control regulations was held to be "exchange contract" and therefore null and void since the Netherlands had an interest in the repatriation of foreign currency obtained from the sale of the shares. A French decision has also treated a commission agreement as an exchange contract: Court of Cassation, March 7, 1972, Rev Crit 1974, 486.

15–32   **Exchange control regulations** In order to be "exchange control regulations" the regulations must be laws which control the movement of currency, property or services in order to protect the exchange resources of a country. Tariffs, trade restrictions, price controls or trading with the enemy regulations (such as the US embargoes in the 1980s against Iraq and Libya) will not normally be "exchange control regulations". The regulation must conʌtrol financial aspects of the transaction, not the transaction itself, and must be a direct control on payments, not an indirect restriction. ⟋

Legal tender laws (i.e. rules which stipulate that creditors must accept local currency to discharge obligations) are not exchange control regulations. These rules have nothing to do with the conservation of a nation's currency resources.

The distinction may be illustrated by the Karlsruhe Court of Appeal decision in *Loeffler-Behrens v Beermann*, 1964–5 IPRspr No 194:

> While in Brazil a German resident lent another German resident about US$5,500 evidenced by two promissory notes denominated in US dollars. The defendant failed to pay. The plaintiff sued on the notes in Germany. The defendant argued that the notes were void under a Brazilian decree which provided that it was "prohibited ... in contracts to be fulfilled in Brazil, to stipulate payment in a currency that is not the national currency according to its legal value," and thus the notes were void under Art VIII 2(b) of the IMF Agreement. *Held*: the Brazilian decree was not a foreign exchange control regulation and the defendant had no defence.

Overriding public policy A question is whether municipal courts in states   15–33
where the Article applies can ignore the obligations imposed by Art VIII 2(b) if enforcement would conflict with some overriding public policy consideration of the forum, e.g. because the application of the Article results in the effective expropriation of a private claim.

> The defence of public policy was rejected by the American courts in the 1953 decision of *Perutz v Bohemian Discount Bank*, 279 App Div 386, 110 NYS 2d 446 (1952); revised 304 NY 533, 110 NE 2d 6. This case involved an unsuccessful action to recover a pension in the US from a bank with a New York office holding the pension in a blocked account in Prague. The defence was also rejected in *Re Brecher-Wolf Estate*, ILR 22 (1955) 718.

> On the other hand the Netherlands Supreme Court took a different view in the case of *Indonesian Corp PT Escomptobank v NV Assurantie Maatschappij de Netherlanden van 1945*, 40 ILR (1964) 7. The case involved the expropriation by Indonesia without compensation of certain Dutch assets of the plaintiff. *Held:* on grounds of public policy, the Netherlands courts would not allow an expropriating government to use Art VIII 2(b) to give validity to its expropriation.

A forum state refusing recognition on grounds of public policy may argue that the expropriatory regulations were penal and oppressive and could not therefore be said to have been imposed "consistently" with the IMF Agreement.

Market practice in international loans

15–34   Because of the importance of exchange controls (albeit diminishing importance) and the serious risk of loss which faces a creditor who does not comply with local exchange control regulations, attention to exchange control is
an invariable feature of international credit documentation.

1.   **Consents** It will generally be a condition precedent to the drawdown of
loans that all necessary exchange control consents in the country of the
borrower have been obtained for the borrowing and for the repayment
of the loans and other payments under the loan agreement.

2.   **Warranties, covenants and events of default** Loan agreements may contain an express warranty that all necessary exchange control consents
have been obtained for the making and performance of the agreement
by the borrower, breach of which is expressed as an event of default
permitting acceleration of the loan. Loan agreements may also contain
an express provision that the borrower will apply for and maintain all
such exchange control permissions as may be required from time to
time to enable it to perform its obligations and an event of default permitting the lender to accelerate the loan if any exchange control consents should be revoked or materially varied. Events of default may not
be of much assistance if the accelerated amount is itself frozen by the
exchange control.

15–35   3.   **Illegality clause** International loan agreements may include a provision
which permits the lender to call for a mandatory prepayment in the
event that, by reason of any change in law or regulation or any interpretation thereof, the making, maintaining or funding of the loan
becomes illegal. One reason for such provision is that exchange control
restrictions imposed by the country of incorporation of the *lender* preventing it from making the loan may not be recognised by the governing law of the loan agreement. Hence the lender could find himself
committed contractually to perform an obligation which is prohibited
in his country of origin.

Embargoes

15–36   Embargoes are prohibitions directed against enemy countries, or countries
considered to be particularly unfriendly, or countries whose international
conduct is so atrocious that they must be subjected to sanctions in the
eyes of the legislating state. The embargoes, commonly enacted under
trading with the enemy legislation or occasionally, by virtue of UN resolu-

tions, prohibit payments to the entities in the embargoed countries. For example, they will strike at payments of loan proceeds by banks to debtors, payments under letters of credit to embargoed beneficiaries and payments by banks of deposits to embargoed depositors. In the last 30 years the US has imposed embargoes of this type on Cuba, Vietnam, Libya and Iran, amongst others. The UK imposed a limited embargo on Argentina in the Falklands War in the early 1980s. The international community – or some of its members – imposed embargoes on Iraq and Kuwait at the time of the Iraqi invasion of Kuwait in the early 1990s and on warring statelets after the break-up of Yugoslavia in the 1990s.

Conflicts questions have typically arisen where a creditor from an embargoed country, such as a beneficiary under a letter of credit or a depositor at a bank, seeks payments from a bank or a branch of the bank outside the country which is imposing the embargo so that the question is whether the embargo has an extraterritorial effect.

The solution tends to follow the same reasoning as applies to exchange controls, except that Art VIII 2(b) of the IMF Agreement obviously does not apply. Thus the English courts will give effect to a foreign embargo if it arises under the governing law of the contract or if (in the case of a contract governed by English law) it makes payment illegal at the place where payment must be made. If the embargo was in force at the time the contract was entered into, then the English courts may not enforce it on the grounds that they will not enforce contracts conflicting with the mandatory laws of friendly foreign states: para 14–75 *et seq*. Otherwise the embargo will be ignored. **15–37**

> In the English case of *Libyan Arab Foreign Bank v Bankers Trust Co* [1988] 1 Lloyds Rep 259, the Libyan Bank had a US dollar deposit with Bankers Trust in London. The US imposed an embargo on payments to Libyan entities. *Held*: Bankers Trust London Branch must pay. The deposit contract was found to be governed by English law. Although it was customary for US dollars to be paid in New York through the New York clearing system, this was not the compulsory place of performance since Bankers Trust could pay in London and there was no provision absolutely requiring payments in New York. If payments had been required to be made in New York, then the court would not have enforced the contract as being illegal at the place of performance.

The legislating state must then decide whether to exact criminal vengeance on its subject back home for doing abroad what a foreign court compelled the subject to do. Civilised states do not go that far. They seek to resolve the collision by diplomacy.

CHAPTER 16

GOVERNING LAW: ATTACHMENTS; AMALGAMATIONS; INTEREST; TAXATION

Attachments

16–1 Where a foreign court garnishes a debt (which is a form of compulsory assignment), the governing law is irrelevant. The garnishment is recognised only if the English courts recognise the foreign judgment, the debt is located within the jurisdiction of the foreign court, and payment by the garnishee discharges the debt: Dicey p 986.

> In *Martin v Nadel* [1906] 2 KB 26, CA, an English company obtained in England a judgment against a Czech company and garnished an account of the Czech company with an English bank. *Held*: the garnishment was recognised. It would be upheld even if the account was governed by Czech law.
>
> See also *Swiss Bank Corpn v Boehmische Industrial Bank* [1923] 1 KB 673, CA; *Richardson v Richardson* [1927] P 228; *Rossano v Manufacturers' Life Insurance Co* [1963] 2 QB 352; *Power Curber International Ltd v National Bank of Kuwait* [1981] 1 WLR 1233, CA.

The English courts can garnish a debt when the garnishee is in England: Dicey Rule 121. The debt does not have to be situate in England, but, if it is not, then this might affect the court's discretion whether to make an order, e.g. if the order might expose the debtor to having to pay twice, as in *Deutsche Schachtbau v Shell International Petroleum Co Ltd* [1990] 1 AC 295.

Corporate amalgamations

16–2 This topic concerns the amalgamation of corporations by fusion. Contrast takeovers of shares which leave the target company intact. Amalgamation results in a different obligor.

Universal succession

The English courts will only recognise an amalgamation if (a) it is effected under the law of the place of incorporation, and (b) the amalgamation is universal, i.e. the new fused company succeeds to all the assets and liabilities of the two old corporations: *National Bank of Greece and Athens v Metliss* [1958] AC 509. See also *Steel Authority of India v Hind Metals* [1984] 1 Lloyd's Rep 405 at 407. This is not perhaps within the Rome Convention since it is a question governed by the law of companies which is excluded from the Convention by Art 1(2)(e).

It is apparent therefore that a creditor is to some degree exposed to a substitution of debtor by amalgamation by universal succession, and that an external governing law is of limited efficacy in insulating the creditor against this contingency. But an event of default could be triggered on an amalgamation if so provided.

Even if the amalgamation is recognised, the law of the place of incorporation cannot discharge the new debtor of liabilities which vested in it on the amalgamation. Discharge depends upon the governing law: Art 10; *Adams v National Bank of Greece* [1961] AC 255.

No universal succession

If there is not a complete amalgamation by universal succession to assets 16–3
and liabilities by the law of the place of incorporation, then:

1. As regards a transfer of the borrower's **rights**, e.g. the right to borrow a loan under a loan agreement:

    (a) in the case of a voluntary transfer by the borrower to the new entity, assignability depends upon the governing law of that agreement: Art 12(1);

    (b) if the transfer is compulsory, e.g. by virtue of a decree, then it seems that the governing law is irrelevant. The English courts will recognise the transfer only if the state concerned has legislative jurisdiction over the debt: see para 17–17 *et seq*. The Rome Convention evidently does not apply.

2. As regards the transfer of the borrower's **obligations**, e.g. to pay principal and interest, the discharge of the original debtor will be governed by the governing law of the contract so that the borrower is not released if the governing law is external: *Re United Railways of Havana etc. Warehouses* [1960] Ch 52, CA; Rome Convention, Art 10(1)(d) (applicable law governs "the various ways of extinguishing obligations").

Usury and interest

Types of usury laws

16–4   Usury laws are still a significant obstacle to foreign financing notwithstanding substantial tolerance in commercial jurisdictions. Probably the most serious difficulties arise in Islamic fundamentalist countries where the objection to usury has given rise to "Islamic banking".

Internationally, the attitudes of the various jurisdictions to usury generally fall into one of three groups:

1.   Countries which prohibit interest-bearing loans altogether, e.g. some fundamentalist Islamic countries under Sharia law.

2.   Countries which impose a maximum rate of interest which may be charged on a loan. Included in these jurisdictions would be most American states. There are wide exceptions.

3.   Countries which prohibit interest only to the extent that it is unconscionable or grossly extortionate, e.g. Britain. England has not had any usury statutes as such since 1854.

A much larger group of jurisdictions object to capitalised interest and increased or penalty interest on a default.

16–5   The legal sanctions against a usurious contract vary. In some Islamic states, the whole transaction is void and there may be criminal liability. In England, only when the interest is grossly extortionate is the court permitted to substitute a reasonable rate for the rate fixed by the contract: Consumer Credit Act 1974 ss 137–139. Sections 244 and 343 of the Insolvency Act 1986 confer wide powers in insolvency proceedings to set aside or vary extortionate credit bargains. In one case 50 per cent was held not to be extortionate, so the threshold is very high. In those countries which prescribe the maximum level of interest which may be charged, the sanctions may merely deprive the lender of the excess (Delaware) or result in a punitive forfeiture (some US states). One third of the American states impose criminal penalties. Most of these laws are consumerist.

Exemptions from usury laws

16–6   The following are common exemptions:

1.   **Exempt borrowers** Borrowings by corporations and other commercial entities, as well as governments may be exempt. At least twenty Ameri-

can states have a "corporate borrower" exemption. It is not usually evasive to incorporate deliberately.

2. **Exempt lenders** Banks and other financial institutions may be exempt from the usury statutes since they are subject to independent regulatory controls by a monetary authority.

3. **Exempt transactions** Often the usury statute applies only to transactions which are in substance loans and not to other forms of transaction such as sales or leasing. Examples of possible exempt transactions (which are widely used by Islamic banks) are: sales on credit, financial leasing, recourse sale of receivables, sale and repurchase, and sale and lease-back.

A usurious transaction has sometimes been hidden behind a promissory note which expresses the interest as a capital sum. This is somewhat transparent. The interest is sometimes disguised as commission or fees or issuing the loan at a discount. This is also transparent. Less transparent is the issue of preferred shares, but the dividends cannot be mandatory but depend on profits.

Applicable law

General rule Under the Rome Convention the general rule is that the liab-   **16–7**
ility to pay contractual interest, and the rate of such interest payable, are determined by the applicable law of the contract: see Art 10 (1)(b), Dicey Rule 197(1).

It would seem therefore that a foreign usury law would be given effect to by the English courts only in the following cases:

— Where the usury statute is part of the governing law of the contract. This may not be so if the usury statute is oppressive or discriminatory, or does not apply to extraterritorial transactions.

— (Possibly) where the usury statute is imposed by the law of the state in which the contract must be performed and the statute renders such performance illegal, at least in the case of a contract governed by English law. For the cases, see para 14–80 *et seq.*

— Where the real object and intention of the parties necessitates them in joining in an endeavour to perform in a foreign and friendly country some act which is illegal by the laws of that country *when the contract is entered into*: para 14–75 *et seq.* Whether this public policy rule could apply to usury statutes is considered doubtful.

Many US courts have applied a validation rule to validate an otherwise usurious contract by holding that it is governed by the laws of a connected state without the usury bar, e.g. *Gilbert v Fosston Manufacturing Co*, 174 Minn 68, 72, 216 NW 788, 779 (1927), *Crisafuldi v Childs*, 33 App Div 2d 293, 307 NYS 2d 701 (App Div 1970). The US Conflicts Restatement has a tolerant rule in s 203 (contract valid if interest is not greatly in excess of the usury limit of the state whose law governs).

16–8 **Other interest questions determined by the governing law** The governing law should also determine the following questions:

– Whether there is a liability to pay interest, e.g. if the contract makes no provision for interest or the method of calculating the interest proves impracticable (e.g. because the index is abolished or the funding market disappears).

– Whether compound interest is allowed, and interest on interest.

– Whether an increased rate of interest on overdue sums would be a penalty and therefore void. The governing law should not be overridden by the public policy exemption.

– (Probably) whether interest is payable on overdue sums if the contract does not specifically so provide.

However, it seems that whether interest is payable on a judgment debt and the rate of that interest would be governed by the lex fori as a procedural matter within Art 1(2).

Taxation

Withholding taxes

16–9 A withholding tax is a tax collected by deduction at source by the payer of interest. The borrower is obliged to deduct the foreign lender's tax from its interest payments on the loan or the bond and to account for the tax so deducted to the local taxing authorities. Although frequently used as a collection device where both borrower and lender are residents of the same country, withholding at source often offers to a taxing authority the only effective method of collecting tax from non-residents since many courts will not enforce the tax laws of other countries by allowing a foreign state to sue directly or indirectly in the courts for taxes due.

Where a bank lender or a bondholder has an office within the borrower's country, the local tax authorities do not need to rely on withholding at source. They can simply collect the tax from the office within the jurisdiction by deeming that the interest is part of the taxable profit attributable to that office, e.g. because it is "effectively connected" with the local office. This possibility may be the subject of protective clauses in loan agreements, but not in bond issues.

Grossing-up clauses

Common practice for bank loan agreements and bonds is to include a specific protection against withholding taxes and often other taxes as well. Generally these clauses state that all payments by the borrower are to be made free of taxes and that, if any taxes must be deducted, the borrower will pay such additional amounts as may be necessary to ensure that the lender receives a net amount equal to the gross amount provided for. There may also be an express indemnity against taxes. In loans where the interest is fixed as a margin over the cost of funds to the lender from time to time, there may be compensation provisions for taxes which increase funding costs over and above the cost of borrowing matching funds in the relevant market.   16–10

General rule for foreign taxes

The general rule is that English courts have no jurisdiction to entertain an action for the enforcement, either direct or indirect, of a revenue law of a foreign state, e.g. *Government of India v Taylor* [1955] AC 491. The rule is based upon the principle of territorial supremacy which permits courts to decline to enforce claims which in their view are an assertion of a foreign state's sovereign authority.   16–11

Hence a foreign state could not sue in the English courts directly for a foreign tax claim. Indirect enforcement will also not be recognised, e.g. a foreign attachment of a debt for a tax claim (*Rossano v Manufacturers' Life Insurance Co* [1963] 2 QB 352) or a foreign lien on assets for a tax claim: *Brokaw v Seatrain UK Ltd* [1971] 2 QB 476, CA.

Deduction of withholding taxes

Apart from the above rules, the English courts will not, except in the cases specified below, permit a borrower to make a deduction of tax from a payment in respect of the loan where the obligation to make the deduction does not arise under the governing law of the loan contract. This is a matter for validity (Art 8) or performance (Art 10). Thus if the loan agreement is   16–12 governed by English law and the obligation to deduct tax arises under the law of the borrower's country, the borrower will not be permitted by the English courts to deduct the tax, unless one of the exemptions specified below applies.

> In *Indian and General Investment Trust Co Ltd v Borax Consolidated Ltd* [1920] 1 KB 539, a US railway company had in 1905 issued bonds expressed to be governed by English law. In 1919 the United States imposed a withholding tax of three per cent on the interest. *Held*: the issuer was not entitled to deduct the tax.

If, on the other hand, the bonds had been governed by, say, New York law, it would then be a question as to whether the English courts would nevertheless refuse to permit the deduction on the grounds that the courts of this country would not directly or indirectly give effect to foreign tax claims. The matter does not appear to have been decided.

16–13   It is considered that a claim by a lender under a grossing-up clause for compensation in respect of the tax deduction would be allowed by the English courts: such a claim is not an indirect collection of taxes by a foreign state but a claim by a private contractor for ordinary civil loss. See *Re Reid* (1970) 17 DLR (3d) 199 where a personal representative was held entitled to be indemnified out of the estate for a foreign tax claim he had had to meet personally abroad, even though the claim itself would not have been enforceable in England.

Conversely if the loan agreement is governed by a foreign system of law and the obligation to deduct tax arises under English law, the English debtor may be obliged to pay the foreign creditor in full notwithstanding that he also has to account to the Inland Revenue for the amount which should have been deducted: *Keiner v Keiner* [1952] 1 All ER 643 – maintenance payments governed by a US system of law. The courts might, however, treat the obligation to deduct tax as a mandatory rule of law overriding the applicable law.

It is unlikely that the position outlined above is affected by the Rome Convention.

Recognition of foreign revenue laws

16–14   Provided there is no direct or indirect enforcement, a foreign revenue law may nevertheless be recognised by the English courts in the following cases:

(a) **Illegal under governing law** The English courts will not enforce a contract governed by a foreign governing law if the contract is illegal under that law: para 14–30. Thus in *Re Lord Cable* [1977] 1 WLR 7 at 24–25 it was said that a trustee will not be ordered to act in violation of fiscal legislation forming part of the governing law of the trust.

(b) **Illegal at place of performance** Perhaps the English courts will not enforce a contract (at least if it is governed by English law) if such performance would be illegal at the place of performance by virtue of a foreign revenue law: para 14–80 *et seq.*

(c) **Tax frauds** The English courts will not on the grounds of public policy countenance fraudulent tax evasions designed to violate a revenue law of a foreign and friendly state in force when the transaction was entered into: *Re Emery's Investment Trust* [1959] Ch 410. Para 14–75 *et seq.*

Foreign stamp duties

Generally Stamp duties generally affect international financial instruments   16–15
in one of two ways. Either they can be imposed on the financial agreement itself (or on the security for the loan) or else they can be transfer taxes on a transfer of the loan or other agreement. In the United Kingdom, loan agreements, guarantees, and security documents are usually free of stamp duty as are transfers of loans, subject to limited exceptions. Stamp duties are common in many other jurisdictions.

Recognition of foreign stamp duties Before the Rome Convention, the   16–16
attitude of the English courts to foreign stamp duties was that the question depended upon whether non-payment of the foreign stamp duty merely rendered the agreement inadmissible in evidence or whether it made the agreement void. If an agreement would be subject to a stamp duty in a foreign country and the foreign stamp law makes an unstamped contract unenforceable by action or inadmissible in evidence, the English courts would ignore that as procedural, i.e. as a matter governed solely by the law of the courts: *Bristow v Sequeville* (1850) 5 Exch 275. This was so even if the contract was governed by the foreign law.

If on the other hand the foreign stamp law made the agreement void by reason of failure to stamp and the contract was governed by that foreign law, then this was a matter going to validity which the English courts would recognise: *Alves v Hodgson* (1797) 7 Term Rep 24.

The position is probably the same under the Rome Convention. Procedural and evidential matters are outside the scope of the Convention and thus remain a matter for the lex fori: Art 1(2). Where the foreign stamp law makes the agreement void, this may be regarded as a matter of material validity (i.e. going to the existence of the contract) and thus governed by the putative applicable law: Art 8. If on the other hand, a foreign stamp law avoiding the contract is viewed as a matter of formal validity, Art 9 is permissive: if the contract is formally valid by the law of the place of contracting, it matters not that it is formally invalid (i.e. for want of stamping) under the applicable law.

CHAPTER 17

EXPROPRIATIONS

Absolute and creeping expropriations

Expropriations may be absolute or "creeping". An example of an absolute   **17–1**
expropriation is the legislative annulment of a loan contract or the confiscation without compensation of the security for the loan. More usually the
deprivation is creeping, e.g. reduction of the interest rate, imposition of a
withholding tax or a moratorium, cancellation of a maintenance of value
clause, the imposition of exchange controls, the annulment of a provision in
the constitution of a public entity borrower rendering the owning state
liable for all its obligations, or the requisition of certain assets of the borrower. In the area of property and concessions, a creeping expropriation
may be achieved by compulsory liquidation, requisitions, boycotts, the
imposition of taxation, price controls, royalties or monopoly prices, the
removal of construction or trading licences, and forced sales of product.

Historical examples

The law on the subject has been built up on successive waves of the expro-   **17–2**
priation of the claims of foreign investors and is now voluminous. The history goes back into antiquity but for present purposes one could start with
the persistent insolvencies of some Latin American states in the nineteenth
century. In those days different attitudes prevailed. Thus Lord Palmerston:
"The patience and forbearance of HM Government ... have reached their
limits, and that if the sums due to the British Claimants are not paid within
the stipulated time and in money, HM's Admiral commanding on the West
Indian Station will receive orders to take such measures as may be necessary
to obtain Justice from the nation in this matter." Force was used by Great
Britain, Spain and France against Mexico in 1861 to compel the performance of treaty payments. In 1902 Venezuela was subjected to a military
blockade. These measures help to explain the traditional Latin American
resistance to foreign law and courts under the Calvo doctrine.

In 1917 the Soviets repudiated all Czarist and Kerensky issues and expropriated private property. In the 1930s numerous states enacted measures to

relieve their debt burdens including Germany, the State of New South Wales and Victoria. The United States, Norway and others abrogated gold clauses. In 1938 Mexico commenced a programme of nationalisation and after the War communist revolutions in Eastern Europe again led to the cancellation of debts, the introduction of exchange controls and the confiscation of private property. The spate of expropriations continued thereafter: Iran 1951, Indonesia 1958, Cuba 1960, Chile 1971, Libya 1971, Iraq 1972, Iran (again) 1979. In the era of decolonisations, most newly independent countries nationalised their economies.

Act of state doctrine

17–3   The general international rule is that foreign courts will not recognise an expropriation of an asset which is situated outside the territory of the expropriating state. If the asset expropriated is within the territory of the expropriating state, external courts tend to recognise this on the basis that a sovereign state may legislate how it likes for its own territory – this is an act of state.

The classic statement is to be found in the United States Supreme Court case of *Underhill v Hernandez*, 168 US 250 (1897), where Chief Justice Fuller said:

> "Every sovereign state is bound to respect the independence of every other sovereign state, and the courts of one country will not sit in judgment on the acts of a government of another done within its territory. Redress of grievances by reason of such acts must be obtained through the means open to be availed of by sovereign powers between themselves."

17–4   Even if the asset is located within the territory of the expropriating state, foreign courts may refuse to recognise the expropriation in exceptional cases, which vary according to the jurisdiction and which include:

1.   The expropriation is **discriminatory** on grounds of race or creed, e.g. Nazi expropriations of Jews. This is a violation of basic morality.

  In *Frankfurther v W L Exner Ltd* [1947] 1 Ch 629, the court refused to give effect to a Nazi decree effectively expelling the Jewish plaintiff from the operation of its business in Austria (which at that time had been incorporated into Germany) on the grounds that the decree was to be regarded in the same way as a penal law.

2.   The expropriation is **without compensation**. This is said to be in breach of international law. This view is taken by the US, French or Dutch

courts, but not the English or German courts which generally ignore the absence of compensation if the taking is intra-territorial.

The US position is that the courts cannot adjudicate upon intra-territorial expropriations unless the case comes within one of the established exceptions. These are: 17–5

- The "**Bernstein exception**": an act of state can be adjudicated in the United States courts if the government has expressly represented to the court that the "application of the act of state doctrine would not have advanced the interests of American foreign policy".

- The "**Hickenlooper Amendment**": this was an amendment to the Foreign Aid Assistance Act which stated that no United States court shall decline to adjudicate a claim to property based upon an alleged taking by a foreign state in violation of international law. The amendment resulted from the case of *Banco Nacional de Cuba v Sabbatino*, 376 US 398 (1964) involving a seizure of sugar by the Cuban government.

- The "**commercial activity exception**": this applies where the conduct of the foreign state is private and commercial in nature.

- The "**treaty**" exception: this applies where a treaty or other unambiguous agreement sets forth controlling legal principles.

However these exceptions have not all met with judicial approval in the US courts and their status appears to be uncertain.

International law on expropriations

The rules of public international law on the matter are relevant because many states purport to apply international law as part of their municipal laws. A private party who has had his rights interfered with usually regards the interference as a confiscation. It is however a matter of everyday occurrence that private rights are subordinated to some public interest. Domestically, states tax their citizens and impose planning restrictions on how they use their property. Internationally, the right of governments to tax, to impose exchange controls and to take other action in the public interest is widely accepted. The difficulty is distinguishing between a legitimate diminution of a private claim and an abuse of governmental power which offends the minimum standard. There are, or were until recently, two basic views on expropriation in international law. The view of investing countries, mostly western industrialised states, is that an expropriation is lawful only if it satisfies two conditions. The expropriation must be for a public 17–6 purpose (the taking of George Finlay's land by the King of Greece for his garden in 1836 did not qualify) and it must be accompanied by "prompt, adequate and effective compensation": see *Norwegian Shipowners' Claims (United States v Norway)*, UN Rep Vol 1, 307 (1922) and *Arabian-American Oil Co v Saudi Arabia*, ILR 27 (1958) 117, 144, 168 and 205. Hence it is not the expropriation itself which engages international responsibility but the failure to pay for it.

17–7   Communist countries, and to a lesser extent countries of the third world, took a different view. They said that a state may expropriate the means of production, distribution and exchange without compensation.

A series of resolutions of the General Assembly of the United Nations illustrated the manner in which the views of the developing states on compensation tended to prevail: see the 1962 Resolution on "Permanent Sovereignty Over Natural Resources" (Resolution 1803 XVII); Resolution 3171 (XXVIII) (1972) and the "Charter of Economic Rights and Duties of States" adopted on January 15, 1975 by the UN General Assembly.

17–8   In England, notwithstanding occasional cases to the contrary (e.g. *R v Keyn* (1876) Ex D 63), the law of nations is treated as part of the common law of England (see Lord Mansfield in *Heathfield v Chilton* (1767) 4 Burr 2015), subject to contrary municipal precedent, overriding statute and certain sovereign prerogatives. The position in the United States is similar: see Judge Gray in *The Paquete Habana*, 175 US 677 (1898).

In European countries international law may be imported by the constitution, e.g. Art 9 of the Austrian Federal Constitution, Art 10 of the Italian Constitution and Art 25 of the Basic Law of the German Federal Republic. Or it may be a doctrine developed by the courts, as in the Netherlands, Switzerland and France.

In practice municipal courts tend to look at international law from the point of view of the attitudes of their own states. Thus, in the United States, the courts will, if they are permitted by an exception to the act of state doctrine to adjudicate a claim, refuse to acknowledge takings considered to be in breach of international law. A leading case is *First National City Bank v Banco Nacional de Cuba*, 406 US 759 (1972):

> The Cuban bank claimed the return of excess collateral pledged with FNCB after a realisation of collateral for a loan. FNCB alleged that it was entitled to set off, as against the excess, the value of property of FNCB expropriated in Cuba without compensation. *Held*: the act of state doctrine did not bar the FNCB counterclaim because it fell within the Bernstein exception: the executive had stated its approval of the court examining the counterclaim and the court could therefore consider whether there was any basis for the counterclaim under normal legal rules including the rules of international law.

French and Dutch courts have similarly refused to recognise intraterritorial takings without compensation: see below.

Expropriation of goods

Many of the leading decisions on property expropriation are based on very   17–9
similar facts. The plaintiff's assets are expropriated by a foreign country
where they are situate. The expropriating state sells the assets to a third
party who brings them into an external jurisdiction and is sued there by the
original owner on the basis that the expropriatory decree, being contrary to
international law or against public policy, was invalid and therefore ineffec-
tual to transfer title to the property to the third party. The third party may
therefore be deprived of the property. The dispossessed owner does not sue
the state direct, usually because of jurisdictional and immunity problems,
but achieves a similar result indirectly by discouraging third parties from
purchasing the expropriated assets.

English law The leading English case is *Luther v Sagor* [1921] 3 KB 532:   17–10

> Timber belonging to the plaintiff Russian company was seized in Russia by
> Russian officials acting in pursuance of Soviet legislation nationalising the
> property. The timber was sold to the defendant who shipped it to England
> where the plaintiff company brought proceedings to obtain a declaration that it
> was still the owner of the timber. *Held*: the defendant had acquired good title
> because (amongst other things) the validity of the transfer of movables is gov-
> erned by the law of the place where they happen to be and, as this was Russia,
> under Russian law valid title had been granted to the defendant which would
> be recognised by the English courts.

> In *Princess Paley Olga v Weisz* [1929] 1 KB 718, the Princess failed to recover
> pictures which were taken from her palace by a mob of government-encour-
> aged revolutionaries in Russia and which were subsequently sold to a third
> party who brought them to England.

On the other hand a foreign expropriatory decree will not be given extra-
territorial effect and apply to property which is outside the territory of the
expropriating state. In England the court does not enter into an examination
of whether or not compensation was paid. Hence a foreign government
decree removing land or gold situate in England and forming the security for
a loan will be refused recognition, regardless of whether or not the decree is
expropriatory. Thus in the case of *Bank Voor Handel en Scheepvart NV v
Slatford* [1953] 1 QB 248, no recognition was given to a decree of the Netherlands Government temporarily requisitioning gold held in London.
   Where a foreign ship is in an English port a foreign decree requisitioning

the ship will not be recognised: *Government of the Republic of Spain v National Bank of Scotland Ltd*, 1939 SC 413. On the other hand according to dicta in *The Jupiter* [1924] P 236, an expropriatory decree might catch a ship on the high seas if the port of registry is that of the expropriating country.

17–11 **Continental European law** The varying attitudes of countries in Continental Europe may be illustrated by a reference to a series of expropriations in the second half of the twentieth century. In the **Anglo-Iranian oil cases,** in 1951 Iran cancelled an oil concession which it had granted to the British Anglo-Iranian Oil Company with no more than a vague offer to consider the question of compensation. Consignments of oil were sold to third parties. The Anglo-Iranian Oil Company brought actions against these third parties in external jurisdictions wherever the oil could be found.

In the doubtful Aden (English common law) decision of *The Rose Mary* [1953] 1 WLR 246 (expropriated oil in the tanker "Rose Mary" which arrived in Aden), Campbell J held that the Iranian nationalisation decree was contrary to international law because it did not provide for adequate compensation, therefore it was invalid as contrary to English public policy and therefore it was ineffective to pass title to the defendant. However, similar actions failed in Japan (*Anglo-Iranian Oil Co v Idemitsu Kosan Kabushiki Kaisha*, ILR (1953) 305) and in the Italian courts (*Anglo-Iranian Oil Co v SUPOR*, ILR (1955) 19) on the ground that the law of the place where the oil happened to be determined its title and it was not open to the court to investigate whether or not the expropriatory decree was in conformity with international law.

17–12 **The Indonesian tobacco cases** followed the expropriation of tobacco assets by Indonesia and their subsequent sale to third parties in the late 1950s.

> In *NV Verenidge & Deli-Maatschappijen v Deutsch Indonesische Tabak-Handelsgesellschaft*, 28 ILR (1959) 16, an action by the original owners (several Dutch companies) against the German importers in Germany failed. The court said that it could not review the validity of foreign legislation in respect of property within the territory of the foreign state even if in breach of international law. Even if they could, the plaintiffs had not proved that compensation would not be payable, or that the expropriation was discriminatory (since the Dutch were virtually the only property holders in the industry) or that there was such a serious violation of the purpose of German laws and good mores as would upset the fundamentals of the German national and economic life as to require non-recognition of the Indonesian legislation on the grounds of public policy.

However in several Dutch cases on similar facts the courts went out of their way to controvert the German decision on all counts. It was held that while the Dutch courts would not ordinarily review foreign sovereign acts, they would do so when the acts flagrantly violated international law. See O'-Connell, *International Law* (2nd ed 1970) p 809.

In the case of the expropriation of **Chilean copper** in 1971, a French   17–13
lower court in the case of *Braden Copper Company v Groupement D'Importation des Metaux*, 12 ILM 182 (1973) said that it would not give legal effect to an expropriation without proof of an actual indemnity. Unlike England, the French criterion appears to be the justice of the expropriation, not the territoriality of the assets expropriated. The Superior Court of Hamburg decided differently on identical facts. The German court said "even if an expropriation was effected under circumstances of discrimination or was pronounced without indemnification, it remains valid if an item of property which was in the expropriating country at the time of the expropriation has subsequently come into a foreign country": *Sociedad Minera El Teniente SA v Akt Norddeutsche Affinerie*, 12 ILM 251 (1973).

Other cases Decisions in the civilian countries have either followed the terri-   17–14
torial or act of state principle (Italy) or have refused to recognise foreign decrees, either absolutely (Austria) or subject to the discretion of the court if public policy is offended (Switzerland): O'Connell, *International Law* (2nd ed 1970) p 808.
A leading Italian case is *Campione v Peti Nitrogenmuvek and Popular Republic of Hungary*, Riv DI (1974) 101.

> In 1947 an Italian firm Campione contracted with a Hungarian firm Peti to supply sulphur in exchange for turpentine. In 1948 Peti was nationalised. Campione never received the turpentine. The Hungarian government was a guarantor of the obligations of Peti. In 1959 the Hungarian government annulled the guarantee. Campione argued that, since Peti was in economic substance part of the Hungarian government notwithstanding its formal legal separateness, the government was responsible for its obligations. *Held*: nationalisation was an expression of sovereign authority and the court could not review the acts of a foreign government within its own domain.

Expropriation of claims

In the case of claims, such as bank deposits, loans, concessions and other   17–15
contracts, the claim is intangible and so must be given a notional location to test whether it is inside or outside the territory of the expropriating state.
Where a concession is revoked, the attack by the expropriated concessionaire is usually to seek to recover the product, such as oil or minerals,

which was the subject of the concession and which has been sold to third parties who then try to export it: see above.

17–16   **Bank deposits** The rules are important for expropriations of local branch deposits: is head office liable? The expropriation often also expropriates the bank assets out of which the deposit is to be paid. The question then is whether the depositor takes the political risk of the country of the branch at which he places the deposit or whether he retains the ability to recover from the foreign head office of the bank if the local deposit is blocked.

17–17   **English law** The English law position as regards expropriation of intangibles, such as bank deposits and concessions, involves distinguishing between two categories of expropriation.

If the "expropriation" is a decree which changes the substance of the obligation itself, e.g. by imposing a moratorium on payments, by restricting the payment of interest, by imposing an exchange control or by reducing the liability of the debtor, then the matter is governed by the governing law, subject to exceptions.

Thus where Soviet legislation annulled rights under an insurance policy, the English courts dismissed an action on the policy since the policy was governed by Russian law and the policyholder took the risk of changes in that law: *Perry v Equitable Life Assurance Society* (1929) 45 TLR 468.

On the other hand where a Greek law purported to reduce the rate of interest on bonds issued by a Greek bank and governed by English law, the English courts refused to recognise the reduction since it did not arise under the law governing the bonds: *National Bank of Greece and Athens v Metliss* [1958] AC 509.

17–18   But where the "expropriation" does not merely affect the obligation itself but transfers the proprietary right in the loan or the deposit to a third party, the divestment will depend upon the lex situs of the debt. The Rome Convention on the Law Applicable to Contractual Obligations of 1980 would appear to be irrelevant since this is not a contractual matter. If the debt is found to be situate in the expropriating state, then, subject to grossly abusive, penal or discriminatory legislation, the English courts will recognise the transfer. If the debt is found to be located outside the expropriating state, the expropriation will not be recognised by the English courts, even if compensation is paid.

The English courts fix the situs of debts for the purposes of this rule as the place where the debt is properly recoverable or can be enforced. This is usually deemed to be the place where the debtor resides (or, in the case of a company, where it has its centre of operations) for it is only in that place that a creditor can normally enforce payment. Contrast US case law which tends to locate debts at the place of payment which, in a number of cases involving US dollar payments, was in the US and thus enabled the US courts to protect US creditors.

The mere fact that a creditor could sue the debtor in the English courts   **17–19** under the long-arm jurisdiction of the courts does not fix the situs of the debt in England if the debtor is not resident in England: see *Re Banque des Marchand de Moscou* [1954] 1 WLR 1108, 1115–1116.

Where the debtor has two or more places of residence or business and the creditor either expressly or impliedly stipulates for payment in one of them, then the debt will usually be situate there: see *New York Life Insurance Co v Public Trustee* [1924] 2 Ch 101, CA; *Re Russo-Asiatic Bank* [1934] Ch 730; *Bitter v Secretary of State for Canada* [1944] 3 DLR 483, 495–496. Where a debtor has more than one place of residence and there is no express or implied promise to pay at one of them, then the debt is situate at the place of residence where it would be paid in the ordinary course of business: see *Jabbour v Custodian of Israeli Absentee Property* [1955] 1 WLR 139, 146.

In the case of credit balances, under English law the bank's obligation to   **17–20** pay is performable primarily at the branch where the account is kept. In such a case the account would be deemed to be situate at that branch: see *Martin v Nadel* [1906] 2 KB 26, 31 CA; *Clare & Co v Dresdner Bank* [1915] 2 KB 956; *Swiss Bank Corporation v Boehmische Industrial Bank* [1924] 1 KB 673, CA.

> In *Jabbour v Custodian of Israeli Absentee Property* [1954] 1 All ER 145, an English insurance company issued a policy through its agent in Palestine. The Palestinian agent had power to issue policies without reference to the company in London and issued a policy to a Palestinian payable in Palestine. Subsequently, the area of the agent's operations was taken over by the Israelis who vested absentee property in an Israeli custodian. *Held*: the policy money was situated in Israel and therefore within the legislative competence of the Israeli expropriation decree.

> *New York Life Insurance Company v Public Trustee* [1924] 2 Ch 101, CA, a New York insurance company issued a policy through its branch in London and payable in London. As a result of the World War I Treaty of Peace with Germany, legislation was passed in England in 1920 vesting enemy property within His Majesty's Dominions in an English administrator. *Held*: that the policy debt was recoverable in London which is one of the places where the New York insurance company was resident and was therefore caught by the legislation.

> In *Arab Bank Limited v Barclays Bank DCO* [1954] 2 All ER 226, Arab Bank had placed a deposit with the Jerusalem branch of Barclays. War broke out between Israel and Palestine in 1948 and the Israelis subsequently took over the

area where the Jerusalem branch of Barclays was operating and passed legislation vesting absentee property, including the deposit, in an Israeli custodian.
Arab Bank sued Barclays in London for the return of the deposit. *Held*: the
deposit was locally situate within the State of Israel at the time of the passage of
the legislation and therefore Barclays were entitled to pay the deposit to the
Israeli custodian. The Arab Bank could not recover from Barclays London.

17–21 **United States law** Where there is no executive direction to the contrary, the
US courts will generally refuse recognition to foreign decrees expropriating
property outside the jurisdiction of the expropriating state where no compensation is paid, e.g. *Latvian State Cargo & Passenger SS Line v United
States*, 116 F Supp 717 (1953). In the case of debt claims, such as bank
deposits and loans, the crucial question is whether the debt is located inside
or outside the legislative jurisdiction of the expropriating state. But the cases
have tended to show sympathy for the depositor.

> In *Vishipco Line v The Chase Manhattan Bank NA*, 660 F 2d 854 (2d Cir
> 1981), cert denied 459 US 976 (1982), the issue was whether Chase was liable
> in New York to Saigon depositors following the confiscation of the material
> assets of Chase's Saigon branch after the abandonment of the branch. *Held*:
> Chase in New York was liable to the depositors. On closure of the Chase
> branch in Saigon, the situs of the debt changed to a location outside Vietnam so
> that the expropriated asset was outside the jurisdiction of the expropriating
> government. The bank had closed "voluntarily", notwithstanding the advance
> of hostile troops. If the asset had remained within the jurisdiction of the expro-
> priating government, the act of state doctrine would have prevented the court
> from interfering and enquiring whether compensation was paid, despite the
> fact that the taking might be contrary to international law. *Vishipco* used the
> springing situs theory first propounded by Justice Cardozo in the Russian Rev-
> olution *Sokoloff* cases in the 1920s. *Trink v Citibank NA*, 850 F 2d 1164 (6th
> Cir 1988), cert denied 110 S Ct 2602 (1990) is to the same effect.

> In *Garcia v Chase Manhattan Bank*, 725 F 2d 645 2d Cir (1984), *Perez v Chase
> Manhattan Bank*, 61 NY 2d 460, 463 NE 2d 5 (1984) and *Edelmann v Chase
> Manhattan Bank*, 861 2d 1291 (1st Cir 1988), Cuban branches of Chase issued
> certificates of deposit to depositors in return for their deposits. At least in
> *Garcia* and *Perez*, the CDs were payable at any branch of Chase including New
> York. The Cuban branches were nationalised. The depositors claimed from
> Chase in the US. *Held* in *Garcia* and *Edelmann* that the depositors could
> recover (because in *Garcia*, as the CDs were redeemable outside Cuba, the situs
> was not in Cuba), but in *Perez* that the depositor could not recover (because, as
> the CDs could be redeemed in Cuba, the situs was in Cuba and so the act of
> state doctrine prohibited inquiry into the effect of the decree). These cases seem
> somewhat confusing.

As to the US attitude to exchange controls, see para 15–21 *et seq*.

Expropriation of shares

If a shareholder is expropriated, the courts may lift the veil of incorporation   **17–22**
to test whether the assets themselves are within the territory of the expropriating state.

Case law in Switzerland and Germany has established that no distinction
is to be made between direct and indirect nationalisations if the nationalisation has an extraterritorial effect. Thus in the unpublished case of the Swiss
Federal Tribunal, *Rakozi Matyas v Weiss*, May 17, 1956, the court held
that the nationalisation of the shares of a group of Hungarian companies
should be treated as a direct nationalisation and consequently should not
have any effect on corporate assets situate outside the territory of the
nationalising state. The Tribunal pierced the corporate veil and considered
the former shareholders as the actual owners of these assets.

In Germany, courts have also pierced the corporate veil in nationalisation
cases. If a state takes over shareholders' rights, then those rights must
notionally be located wherever the assets of the company are located. The
BGH held in its decision of May 21, 1974 that it would be unacceptable to
circumvent the principle of territoriality through the use of a subterfuge
consisting of a purely artificial legal scheme: BGHZ 62, 340, 1974, WM
969, Doc 23.

There are obviously a number of practical problems in splitting a company or in appointing a local receiver of local assets or substituting the former shareholders of the national entity as the legal shareholders of the
foreign entities.

The English courts will not intervene in the case of the expropriation of   **17–23**
the shares of a local company even if the company concerned has assets in
England: see *Williams & Humbert Ltd v W & H Trade Marks (Jersey) Ltd*
[1986] AC 368.

> In the decision of the Belgian Commercial Court of Namur (October 14, 1986),
> 26 ILM 1251 (1987) in the *Compagnie de Saint-Gobain case*, a French law was
> passed in 1982 nationalising a number of French companies including the
> Compagnie de Saint-Gobain which was a French company. The French com-
> pany held, indirectly through subsidiaries, shares in a Belgian company. The
> French nationalised shareholders in the French company brought an action in
> Belgium claiming ownership of the shares of the Belgian company. *Held*: the
> shareholders were not entitled to an order stripping the French company of its
> Belgian subsidiary. France only seized assets in France – the shares of the
> French parent. The identity of the shareholders of the Belgian subsidiary had
> not changed and there was no justification for piercing the veil of incorporation
> in this case. Belgian public order would be invoked only if there was a spolia-
> tory deprivation without compensation (France had paid market value for the

shares) or if the expropriation was discriminatory in the sense of inequality of treatment of shareholders based on race, religion or political affiliation – which was not the case here. Hence the nationalisation was neither expropriatory nor ethnically discriminatory.

17–24   But if the property is intraterritorial, the act of state doctrine may leave the shareholder remediless.

> In *Ethiopian Spice Extraction Share Company v Kalamazoo Spice Extraction Company*, 543 F Supp 1224 (1982), the Ethiopian Government expropriated a shareholding of Kalamazoo in an Ethiopian company producing spices. The Ethiopian company brought an action against Kalamazoo for the purchase price of spices delivered. Kalamazoo refused to pay on the ground, among other things, that they were owed amounts as a result of the expropriation. *Held*: the act of state doctrine precluded the court's review of the expropriation of Kalamazoo's shares by the Ethiopian Government since the shares were "located" in Ethiopia which was the place of incorporation of the Ethiopian company. Expropriation was thus a taking of property by the Ethiopian Government within its own territory. The Bernstein exception did not apply because there had been no statement from the State Department. The commercial activity exception was inapplicable because expropriation was a public governmental act of a foreign sovereign. The other exception, the Hickenlooper Amendment was also inapplicable since it applied only where the expropriated property was found in the US. For those exceptions, see para 17–5.

Foreign branch bank deposits

17–25   Where a depositor deposits cash with a foreign branch of a parent bank abroad, and the foreign branch is prohibited or prevented from paying the depositor, e.g. because of an exchange control or a local embargo or expropriation, the local depositor may seek to recover the deposit against the parent bank at its head office abroad. This situation will of course only arise where the branch and head office are a single institution, not where the branch is a foreign subsidiary protected by the veil of incorporation in which event the parent shareholder would not in any event be liable for the obligations of its subsidiary in the absence of extraordinary circumstances.

From the point of view of the bank, if the local branch has been expropriated, then the assets out of which the deposit should have been paid are lost. Of course neither depositor nor bank are at fault but since the block is imposed by a government, the courts must decide which of the two innocent parties is to bear the loss.

It has already been seen that the recoverability of the deposit will depend upon a variety of factors, including its situs and its governing law as well as rules concerning contracts illegal at the place of performance. A bank which desires to protect itself against the risk that a head office must pay when the foreign branch has been lost should do so by contract to confer complete predictability, subject only to rules about unfair contracts. Thus, the deposit contract could provide that, in the event of any local provision preventing payment of the deposit locally, the depositor agrees not to claim against the head office.

In the absence of an express restriction, the parties could localise the **17–26** deposit contract so that the depositor takes the local political risk. The deposit contract could provide that the deposit is payable only at the local branch, even though it is payable in foreign currency through a clearing system in the country of the currency (so as to fix the situs for expropriation purposes), that the deposit is governed by local law (so as to absorb any exchange control or moratorium) and that the depositor agrees to the exclusive jurisdiction of the local court.

Clauses on these lines seek to transfer the political risk of the location of the branch where the deposit is kept to the depositor. They do not transfer the risk of insolvency of the bank from the bank as a whole to the foreign branch because, assuming there are no interferences locally, the depositor is entitled to prove as a creditor in any liquidation or bankruptcy of the bank in the normal case in most, if not all, developed jurisdictions.

It is understood that New York and Michigan have introduced statutes which purport to limit the liability of home banks for foreign branch deposits.

Naturally any contracts of this sort might have a discouraging effect on depositors and, for this reason and because of competitive pressures, they are somewhat unusual.

PART III

JUDICIAL JURISDICTION AND FINANCIAL CONTRACTS

CHAPTER 18

JUDICIAL JURISDICTION

Introduction

Generally

This section is concerned with the question of determining the courts which   **18–1**
will have jurisdiction to hear a dispute on a financial contract and to enforce
its terms.

In practice enforcement jurisdiction in this context tends not to be greatly
used since the preferred method of debt recovery is by a consensual debt restructuring agreement. If that fails, the alternative is either a judicial rehabilitation proceeding or liquidation. Attempts by creditors to enforce by suit
and execution are almost invariably met by insolvency proceedings,
initiated either by the debtor or other creditors, which freeze further individual actions so that one creditor does not get ahead of the others. This does
not apply to states since they cannot be judicially bankrupted, and this
explains the greater emphasis placed on jurisdiction clauses in state loan
contracts.

Nevertheless, the availability of court action is a basic sanction. Contracts without sanctions, even if the sanctions are not used in practice, have
no value.

Purposes of forum selection

Most major financial contracts contain a forum selection clause, so that the   **18–2**
general grounds on which courts exercise jurisdiction are of less relevance.
This is also true of master agreements, e.g. for foreign exchange contracts
and interest swaps. But it is not true of inter-bank deposit contracts or
(often) of contracts for international credit transfers. Forum selection
clauses cannot in practice be universal so that the jurisdiction of other
courts to which an obligor has not expressly submitted may be relevant, e.g.
if there are local assets.

18–3   **Additional forum** One purpose of an express forum selection clause is to provide an additional forum outside the borrower's country for enforcement and the adjudication of disputes. The creditor therefore has the option of proceeding locally or, if a local action would be barred or futile for some reason, bringing the suit in the external forum. Because many international borrowers have worldwide assets, the absence of a local judgment is not necessarily fatal. Further, other courts may be prepared to enforce foreign judgments locally. Para 23–20.

18–4   **Insulation** The choice of an external forum in international finance helps to protect the insulation achieved by the choice of an external governing law. It has already been seen that the application of an external governing law can to some degree shield the obligations from adverse legislation introduced by the government of the borrower's country, e.g. exchange control or moratorium legislation, as discussed in chapter 14. This objective might be defeated if the only available forum for enforcement were the courts of the borrower's country since those courts might either ignore the governing law altogether or apply it only to the extent that it is consistent with local laws.

18–5   **Forum and governing law** While it is true that governing law and jurisdiction are theoretically separate in the sense that the courts of commercial countries will not decline to adjudicate on a contract merely because a foreign system of law applies, it is desirable that the forum should follow the governing law in order to confer a greater predictability. At the most basic level, the courts of the country of the governing law, being familiar with their domestic law, are more likely to arrive at the expected result. Further, as a matter of convenience, no delays or expense will be involved in calling expert evidence as to the interpretation of another legal system.

More importantly, a foreign court may not give the governing law the scope that was intended. Courts almost invariably apply their own rules of private international law in matters of contract. The rules of the governing law may be overridden by a local statute which is directly applicable to the issue in question or by considerations of public policy.

18–6   **Standards of the courts** A material consideration in the choice of forum is the standards of the court concerned. The desired characteristics are: (1) a judiciary experienced in international investment disputes, (2) impartiality in the sense that undue preference is not given to local interests and policies in international matters; and (3) commercially-orientated court procedures.

Significant procedural considerations are the accessibility of the court and the length of the queue to get the matter heard, court costs and security for costs, whether summary enforcement procedures are available, the ability to attach assets prior to judgment to prevent them being removed from the jurisdiction thereby frustrating a judgment, the attitude of the courts to sovereign immunity, the absence of technical evidential obstacles in proving the claim, and the availability of effective enforcement procedures.

Immunity. Where the borrower is a state or a state-related institution, then, even if the local courts are prepared to entertain an action against the home government, it is almost universally true that no enforcement proceedings will be permitted. The position may be different if the action is brought externally. Most commercial countries (including the United Kingdom and the United States) are prepared to give effect to express waivers of immunity from enforcement, thereby allowing attachment of assets which come within the jurisdiction. Sovereign immunity is reviewed in another book in this series.

Survey of international rules

Generally

Traditionally, the extent of a court's jurisdiction – at least in common law   **18–7** countries – is associated with the territory over which the government of the country concerned has sovereignty so that if the defendant is within the domain of a court and can be served with due process the court can hear the action. The state has power over the defendant. However states have developed "long-arm" rules whereby their courts can claim jurisdiction merely where one of the parties or the transaction has some connection with the country of the courts. The nexus with the jurisdiction is said to justify the exercise of judicial power. Because the connection can be somewhat tenuous, many countries have developed self-imposed restraints on the exercise of jurisdiction where such exercise would be unjust. The jurisdictional enquiry therefore has two stages; first whether the courts have the *power* to claim jurisdiction and secondly whether they will be prepared to *exercise* this power.

The enquiry here is concerned solely with civil jurisdiction in connection with actions in personam on loan contracts. The jurisdictional rules relating to insolvency, to admiralty actions, to claims in tort (such as actions for negligence or misrepresentation) and those relating to security interests over assets, are different.

The following rules must be read subject to the European Judgments Conventions on Jurisdiction and Judgments in Civil and Commercial Matters, which are in force between most European states.

Universal bases of jurisdiction

18–8 It is thought that all commercial states claim the power to exercise jurisdiction in the following cases:

– The defendant **agreed to submit** to the jurisdiction by advance contract or, of course, actually appeared in the action, otherwise than (sometimes) solely to contest jurisdiction. Submissions to jurisdiction are considered in chapter 21.

– The corporate defendant is **incorporated locally** or has a principal place of business locally.

– The defendant has a **local branch**, although sometimes the action is limited to transactions arising in connection with the branch. In many countries, local branches must register themselves at the local companies or commercial register and designate a person on whom process can be served, see e.g. the British Companies Act 1985 s 695.

Summary of long-arm jurisdiction

18–9 There is substantial disparity between nations as to the exercise of jurisdiction on the basis of more fleeting connections with the forum – often called the long-arm, or extended, or exorbitant or excessive jurisdiction.
The main heads of long-arm jurisdiction are:

1. Transient presence locally of an individual debtor (England, US states), but the presence of a director is not enough to confer jurisdiction over the company.

2. The debtor does business locally, e.g. through an agent.

3. The transaction sued on has local connections, e.g. was made locally (England, but not New York), or the contract is expressly or impliedly governed by local law (England, but not New York – *Hanson v Denkla*, 357 US 235(1958)).

4. Local nationality of plaintiff (France, Luxembourg) (CC Art 14) and Italy (subject to reciprocity – CCP Art 4(4)), but not England, not most US states.

5. Domicile of plaintiff, regardless of nationality: Netherlands (CCP Art 126(3)) and Belgium (subject to reciprocity in the case of Belgium). Not England, not most US states.

6. Local assets of the defendant, however small – the "toothbrush" juris-

diction: Germany (ZPO Art 25), Austria (para 99 (1) of *Jurisdiktions-normen*), Japan, Denmark, South Africa, Sweden.

These may be examined in turn.

Transient presence

In England and some of the Commonwealth countries, jurisdiction is pri-   **18–10**
marily based on the presence of the defendant within the forum state. The
presence may be purely temporary. The court has jurisdiction over an individual if the writ is served on the defendant while he is physically present in
England even though he is merely passing through England, and whatever
his nationality or residence. Thus, in the case of *Maharanee of Baroda v
Wildenstein* [1972] 2 QB 283 (a case involving a painting sold in Paris
alleged to be erroneously attributed to Boucher) the Maharanee secured the
jurisdiction of the English courts by serving the writ on the Parisian Mr
Wildenstein while he was at Ascot Races for the day. Transient presence
was taken to its ultimate conclusion in the United States case of *Grace v
MacArthur*, 170 F Supp 442 (E D Ark 1959) where the writ was served in
an aeroplane while flying over the judicial district.

Doing business locally

The question of whether the courts have jurisdiction is more problematical   **18–11**
where the borrowing corporation is not incorporated locally and does not
have a local branch but has local business contacts.

    In England the courts will have jurisdiction on the grounds of presence if
the foreign corporation carries on business *in* England from a fixed place
there, not merely *with* England. See para 18–26. Occupying a stand at an
exhibition of cars in London for nine days has been held to be sufficient:
Dunlop Pneumatic Tyre Co v AG Cundell & Co [1902] 1 KB 342.

    In the United States each state has its own rules but generally speaking the   **18–12**
degree of local business contact seems to be as slight as that applying in
England:

> In *International Shoe Co v State of Washington*, 326 US 310, 66 S Ct 154, 90 L
> Ed (1945), it was held that the Washington court had jurisdiction over a Mis-
> souri enterprise which had no office in Washington and entered into no con-
> tracts there, but solicited orders through salesmen there and sold products
> there. Those activities constituted "doing business" in Washington. The court
> laid down as a basic principle of judicial jurisdiction that there must be such

"minimum contacts" with the state of the forum as not to offend "traditional notions of fair play and substantial justice" (at 316). The due process clause of the Fourteenth Amendment of the Constitution prohibits the states from acting through their courts when they have no judicial jurisdiction and the due process clause of the Fifth Amendment of the Constitution prohibits the United States from taking similar action.

Bryant v Finnish National Airlines, 15 NY 2d 426 (1965) concerned an accident at Paris Airport. The New York courts took jurisdiction on the basis of the existence of a mailbox representative office of the airline in New York even though the decision on the issue of passages was made in Helsinki. It was held that the airlines were "doing business" in New York.

Frummer v Hilton Hotels International Inc, 227 NE 2d 851 (NYCA, 1967) related to an accident at the Hilton Hotel in London. Jurisdiction was founded on the basis of a reservation office in New York of an associated Hilton company.

But in *Delagi v Volkswagenwerk AG of Wolfsburg*, 328 NYS 2d 653, 29 NY 2d 426 (1972) it was held that the existence of independent distributorships of VW in New York was insufficient to found jurisdiction.

In *Asahi Metal Industry Co v Supreme Court of California Solano County*, 107 S Ct 1026 (1987), it was held that the mere awareness on the part of a foreign defendant that the component it manufactured, sold and delivered outside the United States would reach the forum state in the stream of commerce was insufficient to found jurisdiction.

Lifting veil of incorporation

18–13   Courts have sometimes lifted the veil of incorporation so as to claim jurisdiction over shareholders. The English courts do not do so in the normal case. In the US Supreme Court case of *Cannon Manufacturing Co v Cudahy Packing Co*, 267 US 333 (1925) it was held that a state does not have judicial jurisdiction over a foreign corporation simply by reason of the fact that it has judicial jurisdiction over its wholly-owned subsidiary if the formal separateness between the two entities has been maintained. However the New York courts have been willing to strip away the formal veil of incorporation and to treat a subsidiary as if it were a branch on grounds much more tenuous than those required for piercing the veil in contract and tort cases.

In *Taca International Airlines v Rolls-Royce of England*, 15 NY 2d 97, 204 NE 2d 329 (1965) the parent English company was held to be subject to the jurisdiction of the New York courts because its United States subsidiary, it was said, was a department of the parent company on account of common directorships, common contacts between executives, training of employees and consolidation of accounts. It follows therefore that a local subsidiary can subject a foreign borrower to the jurisdiction of the New York courts.

See also *Public Administrator v Royal Bank of Canada*, 19 NY 2d 378 NE 2d 877 (1967).

Transaction connections

Where the transaction has significant connections with the state concerned **18–14** and the action arises out of that transaction, there is in principle less reason to show a continuous course of doing business within the state than would be the case where the proceedings have nothing to do with the business carried on in the state. The theory is that a person who by his conduct creates a cause of action against himself in a state ought to be subject to action in that state. The transaction derives economic or protective benefit from the local regime and may therefore fairly be subject to its police powers. The essential difference with the "doing business" jurisdiction is that in the case of single transactions the nexus with the forum country is so slight as to justify only an action in respect of that transaction, not some unrelated transaction.

England Thus in England (except where the action falls within the scope of **18–15** the European Judgments Conventions) RSC Ord 11 gives *discretionary* power to the English courts to exercise jurisdiction in relation to a contract which:

(a) was made in England;
(b) was made by or through an agent trading or residing within the jurisdiction;
(c) is expressly or impliedly governed by English law; or
(d) contains a term to the effect that the High Court in England has jurisdiction in respect of an action on the contract.

Thus, where a sovereign state declines to submit to the jurisdiction of the English courts on policy grounds, that jurisdiction may nevertheless be available if the loan agreement is signed in London or is impliedly governed by English law.

However, as will be seen below, these long-arm rules do not confer automatic jurisdiction. The leave of the court is required to serve the writ outside the jurisdiction and in practice, because the jurisdictional base is plainly exorbitant, the English courts exercise their discretion on this matter with great caution and will not claim jurisdiction if another forum would be more appropriate.

18–16 **United States** In the United States there is a great variety in state jurisdictional rules on the matter of transaction connections. The leading case of *Hanson v Denckla*, 357 US 235 (1958) established that the mere fact that the transaction was governed by local law was insufficient to confer jurisdiction without other minimum contacts, a conclusion repeated in *Kulko v Superior Court*, 436 US 84 (1978). In that respect, the English long-arm rules are wider. On the other hand, in the leading Supreme Court case of *McGee v International Life Insurance Co*, 335 US 220 (1957) the minimum contacts were indeed the minimum:

> A foreign insurance company was held subject to the judicial jurisdiction of a state as regards a cause of action arising from a life insurance policy. The only contacts were that the purchase by the domiciliary of the state had been solicited by the company through the mails and that the company had mailed premium notices to the insured in that state.

In New York, a number of cases have given a wide interpretation to the jurisdictional requirements of ss 302(a)(i) of the New York Civil Practice Law and Rules which confers jurisdiction over a defendant who in person or through an agent "transacts any business within the state". While it may not be enough that the only contact is that the loan agreement was actually signed in New York (a contact which is sufficient in England but subject to the court's discretion) the conduct of final negotiations between senior officials coming to New York of their own free will may be sufficient (a contact which is not sufficient in England). Generally and subject to exceptions, American states mostly require more than a coincidental entering into of the contract locally.

Nationality or domicile of plaintiff

18–17 In England, many of the common law Commonwealth jurisdictions, Japan and the United States, the courts will not claim jurisdiction merely on the basis of the nationality, domicile or residence of the plaintiff. An English bank lender could not therefore summon a foreign borrower into the English courts merely on the basis that the lender is incorporated in England.

The position in some Napoleonic countries is different. In **France** the French nationality of the plaintiff is sufficient to give jurisdiction to the French courts even though the defendant may be a foreigner: CC Art 14. A similar rule prevails in **Luxembourg**: CC Art 14.

Generally speaking the nationality of a legal entity such as a corporation is determined by its *siège social* which is usually where its head office is located.

In the **Netherlands,** the Dutch domicile of the plaintiff is enough to confer   **18–18** jurisdiction regardless of nationality (CCP Art 126(3)), while in **Belgium** either domicile or residence will suffice (Judicial Code Art 638). In the case of Belgium, however, the plaintiff's domicile is insufficient if the foreign defendant can show that, if the Belgian domiciliary or resident were sued in the foreigner's courts, those courts would not have jurisdiction. In other words the Belgian rule is a retaliatory measure (directed in particular against France) and would not apply when reciprocity is established.

In **Italy,** nationality of the plaintiff is sufficient to confer jurisdiction only if the Italian national could be sued on the same jurisdictional ground in the courts of the foreign defendant's country: CCP Art 4(4). Again, the Italian rule is retaliatory. For this purpose a corporation is considered to be in Italy if it is incorporated abroad but has the centre of its administration in Italy or it is constituted in Italy, even though its main activities take place abroad: CC Arts 2505, 2509.

On the whole, assignments to a national to secure jurisdiction are disapproved of in these countries.

Local assets

In some countries, the mere presence of assets of the defendant within the   **18–19** forum state is sufficient to ground jurisdiction.

This ground is found in Germany (CCP Art 23), Austria (para 99(1) of *Jurisdiktionsnormen*) Sweden, Denmark and Japan – the "toothbrush" or "umbrella" jurisdiction. Thus the magnificent French skier Jean-Claude Killy was subject to the jurisdiction of the Austrian courts in a patrimony suit on the basis of a pair of boxer shorts which he left behind him in an Austrian hotel. In Japan the courts have tempered the excessiveness of this jurisdictional base by insisting on more than a toothbrush or umbrella. In Germany too there must also be some other sufficient connecting factor: BGH July 2, 1991, Stuttgart, ZR 206/90.

> In *Rosterott v Admiral Sales Co*, 10 Kaminshu 1204 (Tokyo District Court, June 11, 1959), it was held that the procedural provision should not be literally applied to an international case where the assets concerned were a few sample goods and a typewriter and their location in Japan is only coincidental. The court said (at 1213) "justice and fairness require us to rule that the relationship of Japan with the property involved is not sufficient to make the exercise of jurisdiction reasonable".

It is believed that in South Africa the courts will not take jurisdiction if the asset is so trivial as not to be worth the trouble.

The claim is not limited to the value of the property recovered and in

Germany and Austria it is not necessary to attach or garnish the property. On the other hand, in Belgium and the Netherlands seizure of the assets is required.

18–20   Location of assets is not sufficient in either England or France to ground a contractual claim in personam. In the United States, the leading case of *Shaffer v Heitner*, 433 US 186 (1977) establishes that the requirements of *International Shoe Co v State of Washington*, 326 US 310 (1945) apply so that there must be some other "minimum contacts" in addition to the presence of assets so as to satisfy the standards of "traditional notions of fair play and substantial justice".

These "toothbrush" actions in Germany and elsewhere must be distinguished from provisional attachments of local assets by a creditor prior to judgment in order to prevent the debtor from removing the assets from the jurisdiction and thereby frustrating any judgment which may be given, e.g. the Mareva injunction or *saisie conservatoire*. These provisional attachments do not in themselves confer jurisdiction and generally are not available if the seizing creditor would not be able to show jurisdiction for the main action.

The "assets" basis of jurisdiction is insolvency-related. Most countries claim insolvency jurisdiction if the debtor has assets within the jurisdiction. Further, the presence of a mortgaged asset within the jurisdiction is generally sufficient to give jurisdiction to the creditor, e.g. a ship or aircraft, or at least to seize it provisionally, while the main action is heard elsewhere.

Judicial jurisdiction in England

Generally

18–21   This section deals only with actions in personam in the High Court, e.g. actions to pay a debt or for damages for breach of contract, for specific performance or an injunction but not Admiralty actions in rem or motions to set aside arbitral awards or the enforcement of security. The position is different where the European Judgments Conventions apply.

The basic rule in England is that the High Court has jurisdiction in an action in personam whenever a defendant can be and is legally served with a writ, but not otherwise.

Generally speaking, this means that it must be possible to serve the writ either on the defendant himself or some representative or office within the jurisdiction. But under the extended jurisdiction the court can in a limited class of cases permit service abroad in its discretion. Para 18–27.

The only effective method of securing the virtually automatic jurisdiction of the English courts as of right over a foreign obligor which does not carry on business in England is for the obligor to appoint an agent in England for service of the writ in connection with proceedings in the English courts: see below.

Prior agreement to submit

Prior agreement, express or implied, to submit confers jurisdiction on the **18–22** High Court: RSC Ord 10, r 3. But (and this is an important but) the mere agreement of a defendant is insufficient by itself to give the court virtually automatic jurisdiction. The reason is that the defendant must legally be served with the writ within the jurisdiction and, if the submitting defendant is outside the jurisdiction, the leave of the court must be obtained to extra-territorial service under RSC Ord 11, r 1. To avoid the unpredictability of an application for extra-territorial service, it is necessary for the submitting party to nominate an agent resident in England to accept service of process on his behalf. In this case he is deemed to submit to the jurisdiction and service may be affected on the agent in accordance with the contract: *Montgomery, Jones & Co v Lienbenthal & Co* [1898] 1 QB 487, CA.

Presence in England

Presence of individuals Any individual present in England may be served **18–23** with a writ in an action in personam, however short the period for which he is there: *Colt Industries Inc v Sarlie* [1966] 1 WLR 440, CA; *Maharanee of Baroda v Wildenstein* [1972] 2 QB 283, CA. This applies even to foreigners in England for a holiday visit for a day. A writ served on a foreigner at Heathrow Airport is good service, unless possibly he was enticed into the jurisdiction. For an attempt to evade service, see *Barclays Bank of Swaziland v Hahn* [1989] 1 WLR 506, HL. There are special rules for partnerships: RSC Ord 81, r 1.

English incorporated companies In the case of a company registered in Eng- **18–24** land under the Companies Act 1985 or any other Act (notwithstanding that the company's business is carried on abroad) the company is deemed to be present in England by virtue of its incorporation in England and service of the writ can always be effected by leaving it at, or sending it by post to, the registered office of the company in England: Companies Act 1985 s 725(1).

18–25   **Foreign corporations with English branch** The courts have jurisdiction over a foreign corporation which has an English branch, whether or not registered at the Companies Registry. The action is not limited to the activities of the branch. The jurisdiction continues over a previously registered but abandoned branch.

18–26   **Foreign corporations carrying on business in England without registered branch** If a foreign corporation carries on business in England without complying with the requirement to register a person authorised to accept service, the writ may be served at the place of business of the corporation within the jurisdiction, even though the transaction is unrelated to the local business: see the Companies Act 1985 s 695(2).

Jurisdiction is lost if the place of business is abandoned.

Case law shows that the place of business must be a fixed and definite one, and that the activity must have been carried on for a sufficient time for it to constitute a business. The maintenance of a stand at an exhibition in London for nine days has been held sufficient: *Dunlop Pneumatic Tyre Co Ltd v A/G Cudell & Co* [1902] 1 KB 342, CA. Where only an agent of the company is in England, the business must be that of the corporation, not that of the agent who acts for it in England. The business is that of the corporation if the agent has authority to make contracts on behalf of the corporation within the jurisdiction. However the business is not that of the corporation if the agent has no general authority to make contracts on behalf of the corporation but merely has authority to obtain orders and submit them to the foreign corporation for approval. A corporation does not carry on business in England merely because its agent in England sells tickets for a foreign steamship company as part of its own business. The cause of action need not be in respect of a transaction effected through the corporation's place of business in England. It is not necessary that contracts be concluded in England.

> In *South India Shipping Corpn Ltd v Export-Import Bank of Korea* [1985] 2 All ER 219, [1985] 1 WLR 585, CA, a foreign bank was held to have been duly served at a place in England where it conducted external relations with other banks, even although it did not conclude any banking transactions in England.

The mere presence in England of a senior officer of the corporation not carrying on business in England as agent for the corporation is insufficient.

> In *The Theodohos* [1977] 2 Lloyd's Rep 428 a Panamanian shipowning company had no place of business in England notwithstanding that its president resided in London. A writ was issued against the company for damage to cargo and was served on the president. *Held*: the court had no jurisdiction.

English long-arm jurisdiction

Generally If the defendant is not in England and is not served in England   **18–27**
with the writ and does not submit to the jurisdiction, the English courts may
nevertheless exercise a long-arm jurisdiction (called in England the
"extended" jurisdiction) whereby the court has *discretionary* power to permit service of the writ (or notice of the writ) or originating summons on a
defendant who is outside the jurisdiction. The cases in which the court may
do so are primarily set out in RSC Ord 11, rr 1, and RSC Ord 75, r 4. Long-
arm jurisdiction is discretionary, but the presence jurisdiction is not, though
even here the presence jurisdiction is subject to forum non conveniens principles.

Leave is by no means automatic or even probable.

The case law is substantial, but broadly the court takes into account
whether England is the convenient forum. In *The Spiliada* [1987] AC 460,
HL, it was emphasised that the burden of proof is on the plaintiff who must
establish clearly that England is the appropriate forum. Some of the factors
which may be relevant to suitability include: the law governing the matter,
whether there is a foreign court which has jurisdiction, whether the plaintiff
will be deprived of a fair trial in the foreign country for political reasons,
and the convenience of witnesses. If the parties have referred disputes to the
exclusive jurisdiction of foreign courts leave will usually be refused.

The following are the cases set out in RSC Ord 11, r 1 whereby the High   **18–28**
Court may exercise a long-arm jurisdiction.

Contract connected with England The court may assume jurisdiction if the
action begun by the writ is brought against a defendant to enforce, rescind,
dissolve, annul or otherwise affect a contract, or to recover damages or
obtain other relief in respect of the breach of contract, being (in either case)
a contract which:

- — was made in England; or
- — was made by or through an agent trading or resident in England on
  behalf of a principal trading or residing out of England; or
- — is by its terms or by implication governed by English law: RSC Ord
  11, r 1(1)(d).

A contract includes an alleged contract, provided the plaintiff shows a
good arguable case that one exists.

Case law shows that a contract is made (in case of parties physically   **18–29**
present) where the last party signs so as to bring the contract into effect, and
(for postal or telegram contracts) where the letter of acceptance is posted.

If the parties use instantaneous means of communication, such as a telephone, telex or fax, the contract is made where the acceptance is communicated to the offeror, i.e. where the offeror receives the message.

> In *Entores Ltd v Miles Far East Corpn* [1955] 2 QB 327, CA, a party in London sent an offer to buy goods to a party in Amsterdam. The offer was sent by telex as a result of which the message typed on the teleprinter in London was instantaneously recorded in Amsterdam. The Amsterdam party accepted the offer in a similar manner by telex. *Held*: the contract was made in England and the court could assume jurisdiction.

18–30 **Contract breach in England** The court may assume jurisdiction if the action begun by the writ is brought against a defendant, in respect of a breach committed in England, of a contract made in or out of England: RSC Ord 11, r 1(1)(e).

A contract may be broken by express repudiation, by implied repudiation or by failure to perform its terms.

If a party in a foreign country sends a letter of repudiation to a party in England, the breach is not committed in England, because of the English "where posted" rule. *Holland v Bennett* [1902] 1 KB 867, CA. Presumably, on the analogy of the cases at para 18–28, the contrary is the case if an instantaneous method of communication is used, e.g. telex, facsimile. If an agent repudiates the contract in England on the instructions of his foreign principal the breach is committed in England: *Oppenheimer v Rosenthal* [1937] 1 All ER 23, CA.

As to failure to perform in England, it is necessary that some part of the contract was to be performed in England and that there has been a breach of that part, e.g. non-payment of a sum payable in England. It is necessary that the contract was to be performed in England and could not by its terms be performed elsewhere, e.g. payment on a bond issue to a fiscal agent abroad. Financial contracts usually state that payments are to be made in the county of the currency.

18–31 **Tort in England** The court may assume jurisdiction if the action begun by the writ is founded on a tort and the damage was sustained or resulted from an act committed in England: RSC Ord 11, r 1(1)(f). Examples are negligence by an agent bank in the administration of a loan on behalf of a syndicate of lenders, misrepresentation by a borrower or managing bank in inducing participants into a loan, or misrepresentation in a prospectus for a bond issue.

The court may claim jurisdiction if the act causing the damage was committed in the jurisdiction or if damage was suffered in the jurisdiction. It is not necessary that all the damage is sustained there, nor that all the acts complained of were committed in the jurisdiction: *Metall und Rohstoff AG v Donaldson Lufkin & Jenrett Inc* [1989] 3 WLR 563 at 625, [1990] 1 QB 391 at 446, CA (tort of inducing breach of contract was committed in England since the resulting damage occurred there, although the inducement occurred in New York).

Injunction The court may assume jurisdiction if in an action begun by the writ an injunction is sought ordering the defendant to do or refrain from doing anything in England: RSC Ord 11, r 1(1)(b).   18–32

A creditor may wish to obtain an injunction to prevent the creation of a charge over assets in England contrary to a negative pledge, to enjoin a sale of assets in England contrary to a prohibition on disposals or to enjoin a bank from petitioning for the winding-up of an English corporate borrower contrary to a "no-action" clause.

Miscellaneous There are a number of other miscellaneous cases in RSC Ord 11 relating (inter alia) to the following: 18–33

– joining related parties;

– land in England;

– trusts "that ought to be executed according to English law": RSC Ord 11, r 1(1)(j) – this may be relevant to commercial trusts, such as trusts of bond issues and subordination trusts;

– mortgagee actions;

– claims for money had and received or for an account or other relief against a defendant or constructive trustee where the alleged liability arises out of acts in England.

CHAPTER 19

EUROPEAN JUDGMENTS CONVENTIONS

Introduction

19–1   The Brussels and Lugano Conventions of 1968 and 1988 respectively on Jurisdiction and the Enforcement of Judgments in Civil and Commercial Matters (plus the various accession and other protocols) are of great importance for European litigation and have a major impact on both Convention and non-Convention parties. The Conventions were implemented in the United Kingdom by the Civil Jurisdiction and Judgments Acts 1982 and 1991.

19–2   **Countries covered** The Brussels Convention applies to:

Belgium	Italy
Denmark	Luxembourg
France	Netherlands
Germany	Portugal
Greece	Spain
Ireland	United Kingdom

It may be extended to affiliated states, e.g. the Netherlands Antilles, the Faeroes, the Channel Islands and Gibraltar.

The Lugano Convention of 1988 extends the jurisdiction and enforcement rules of the 1968 Convention to European Free Trade Association states:

Austria	Norway
Finland	Sweden
Iceland	Switzerland

The implementation of the Conventions in each state should be checked, namely, whether they have the the force of law locally and whether they have been modified.

The Conventions are in similar, but not identical form. The differences are not likely to be material to international finance.

Basic principles The Conventions effect fundamental changes to normal jur- 19–3
isdiction bases. The first basic tenet of the Convention is that, subject to exceptions, "persons domiciled in a Contracting State shall, whatever their nationality, be sued in the courts of that State": Art 2. It is considered that "persons" includes states. The second tenet is that, generally speaking, a judgment of a court in a Contracting State in accordance with the Convention is to be enforced universally in the entire Community, subject only to a public policy exception: Arts 26, 31.

Non-domiciliaries are subject to the long-arm rules of each Contracting State and judgments on the basis of those rules are enforced in all other states. Although the Contracting State where the action is first brought will generally have exclusive jurisdiction, the position in other Contracting States can be preserved by the wide availability of pre-judgment preservation measures e.g. the Mareva injunction in England or the *saisie conservatoire* in France. The group of 18 Contracting States therefore operates as a monolithic jurisdictional unit with the widest conceivable long-arm jurisdictional rules available to a creditor of a debtor in a non-Convention state, e.g. Japan or the United States..

In the case of a Convention domiciliary, where it is desired to confer jurisdiction on another Contracting State, the creditor should take care to comply with the contracting-out provisions of Art 17. This Article is not without its difficulties. Again the position in other Contracting States can be protected by local preservative measures while the exclusive action continues in the chosen court.

Retroactivity. When brought into force in a state, the Conventions are effec- 19–4
tively retroactive. Generally, they apply to legal proceedings commenced after the coming into force of the relevant provisions of the Convention regardless of the fact that the agreement itself may have been entered into many years beforehand. But the retroactivity was restricted for UK law contracts by a protocol at the time of UK accession. It could effectively apply retrospectively if a debtor moves his domicile (including corporate domicile) into a Contracting State. Hence the need for a clause complying with Art 17 even in the case of non-Convention domiciliaries.

Interpretation The courts are authorised to take into account the official 19–5
reports of Mr P Jenard and Professor Peter Schlosser. Questions can be referred to the European Court of Justice in order to secure uniform interpretation.

Civil and commercial matters: Art 1

19–6   The Conventions apply only to "civil and commercial matters". The most important express exclusions in the financial context are (a) administrative matters, (b) bankruptcy proceedings (intended to be covered by a separate European Bankruptcy Convention presently in draft form, but private restructuring agreements are within the Conventions), (c) arbitration (a possible exit from the Convention rules which is not likely to be used for loan agreements and bond issues on account of the disadvantages of arbitration for loan contracts), and (d) certain other matters, e.g. revenue, the capacity of natural persons, matrimonial property and succession. Certain conventions already in force are overriding, e.g. the 1952 Brussels Arrest Convention (ships): see Art 57.

Mandatory suit at domicile

19–7   The basic principle is mandatory suit at the domicile, subject to exceptions and to contracting-out. The court first seized commences by applying its own domicile tests: see Art 52. In the United Kingdom, a corporation, for example, is domiciled locally if it is incorporated or formed in the United Kingdom and has its registered office there *or* if its central management and control is exercised in the United Kingdom: s 42 of the Civil Jurisdiction and Judgments Act 1982. Other states have different domicile tests.

Subject to exceptions, Scotland and N Ireland are treated as separate jurisdictions and are therefore in a similar position vis-à–vis England to Italy.

Only Convention countries

19–8   It seems that a party can sue a Convention domiciliary in a competent non-Convention court, e.g. New York or Japan. This is important for loans to Convention domiciliaries where it is desired to confer jurisdiction on the courts of a non-Convention state (as is often the case).

> In *Re Harrods (Buenos Aires) Ltd* [1992] Ch 72, CA, it was held that the Convention was intended to regulate jurisdiction only as between Contracting States and the jurisdictional rules did not apply in a case involving a conflict of jurisdiction between the English courts and a non-Contracting State. In that case, it was argued that the defendant, an English company, had to be sued in England in accordance with the basic jurisdictional rule in Art 2, notwithstanding that Argentina might be the more convenient forum. The Court of Appeal held that, as a non-Contracting State was involved, i.e. Argentina, the English

court retained its discretion to decide which jurisdiction was more appropriate and in this case Argentina was more appropriate. Under the Convention, the court could not have applied the forum non conveniens principles.

Alternatives to domicile: Arts 5 and 6

There are a number of cases where a plaintiff can take proceedings other-   **19–9**
wise than at the domicile of a debtor, assuming the courts are competent under their normal jurisdictional rules. In the context of financial trans-actions, the most important additional possibilities are:

Contractual suits: "courts for the place of performance of the obligation in question", e.g. the place where payments have to be made, subject to a Luxembourg exception. The place where the breach occurs is immaterial. The place of performance of the specific obligation upon which the action is founded determines jurisdiction under the Convention. Where the dis-pute is concerned with a number of obligations arising under a contract, the court will look to the principal obligation to determine jurisdiction: *Union Transport Plc v Continental Lines SA* [1992] 1 WLR 15, HL. This jurisdiction does not extend to restitutionary claims where there is no contract e.g. because it is void or a nullity: *Kleinwort Benson Ltd v City of Glasgow District Council, Financial Times* March 4, 1992.

Disputes arising out of the operations of a branch, agency or other estab-   **19–10**
lishment: "courts for the place in which the branch, agency or other establishment is situated". A branch, agency or other establishment denotes a unit under the direction and control of the parent body and having an appearance of permanency. These disputes include those relat-ing to contracts entered into at that place of business (at least where per-formance is in the same Contracting State as that place of business) and actions concerning torts arising from the activities of that place of busi-ness.

Third party actions, e.g. guarantees: "court seized of the original pro-   **19–11**
ceedings, unless these were instituted solely with the object of removing [the third party] from the jurisdiction of the court which would be compe-tent in his case". This head applies where the third party is domiciled in another Contracting State or another part of the United Kingdom. There must be a connection between the actions against the various defendants of such a kind that it is expedient to determine the action together to avoid the risk of irreconcilable judgements resulting from separate pro-ceedings.

19–12 **Tort:** "place where the harmful event occurred". The question arises whether the "place" here is the place where the wrongful act occurred or the place where the damage was suffered. The European Court in *Bier (GJ) BV v Mines de Potasse d'Alsace*, [1978] QB 708, Case 21/76[1976] ECR 1735 held that the "place" was to be determined by a Convention rule, namely that the plaintiff has an option to convene proceedings either at the place where the damage occurs or the place of the event giving rise to it.

> In *Minister Investments Ltd v Hyundai Precision and Industry Co Ltd* [1988] 2 Lloyd's Rep 621, it was held that in the case of a negligent misstatement contained in a certificate sent from Korea to a person in England the "harmful event" occurred in England (i.e. the place where the negligent misstatement was given and acted upon) and accordingly the English court had jurisdiction.

Trusts: where "the trust is domiciled".

19–13 **Actions against more than one defendant:** "place where any one of them is domiciled". There must be a connection between the claims made against each of the defendants, as for example, in the case of joint debtors. The connection must be such that it is desirable to rule on the claims together to avoid inconsistent results. If a defendant domiciled in England has agreed to a foreign court having jurisdiction, the plaintiff cannot use this head to justify bringing an action in England against other defendants domiciled abroad as additional defendants.

Certain counterclaims: "the court in which the original claim is pending".

Actions on a contract related to an action against the same defendant in rem arising out of immovable property: where "the property is situated". This will allow a mortgagee of land to sue for the mortgage debt in the courts of the state where the mortgaged property is situated combined with an action for the enforced sale of the property.

Exclusive jurisdiction: Art 16

19–14 The courts of a Contracting State have exclusive jurisdiction in certain cases, including:

1. *In rem* suits relating to **immovable property**, presumably including mortgage actions, Jurisdiction is fixed where the property is, subject to an exception for in rem suits relating to short-term private lettings.

2.   The validity of the constitution, the nullity or the dissolution of **legal associations** or the decisions of their organs. Jurisdiction is fixed where the seat is. For this purpose the place of the seat of the company is determined by national courts applying their own rules. Thus, s 43 of the UK Civil Jurisdiction and Judgements Act 1982 provides that a corporation or association has its seat in the United Kingdom if, and only if, (i) it was incorporated or formed under the law of a part of the United Kingdom or (ii) its central management and control is exercised in the United Kingdom.

3.   The validity of entries in **public registers**, e.g. land, commercial and ship registers. Jurisdiction is fixed where the register is kept.

Insurance and consumer contracts

There are separate provisions regarding insurance contracts and certain   **19–15** consumer contracts. Broadly speaking, their effect is that the policy holder or consumer must be sued in the courts of his domicile. A bank loan or bond issue would generally be outside the consumer provisions except in the case of credits made to finance the sale of goods: Art 13(2).

Submission

There are provisions conferring jurisdiction over a defendant who submits   **19–16** to the jurisdiction by appearance, except where appearance is entered solely to contest the jurisdiction or the courts of another Contracting State have exclusive jurisdiction: Art 18.

Forum non conveniens

Where a Convention court has jurisdiction, the doctrine of forum non con-   **19–17** veniens does not apply.

Protective measures

Provisional and protective measures, such as Mareva injunctions, *saisie con-*   **19–18** *servatoire* and their equivalent, may be sought in the courts of any Contracting State in accordance with their own rules notwithstanding that the courts of another Contracting State have jurisdiction as to the substance of matter: Art 24. This is a potent provision because it enables scattered Convention assets to be preserved in accordance with local rules while the main action is proceeding elsewhere.

Concurrent and related actions: Arts 21 and 22

19–19 A principle of the Conventions is that only one Contracting State should exercise jurisdiction. Concurrent jurisdictions are possible, e.g. where Contracting States apply different domicile tests or an action is available in an alternative forum under the rules noted in para 3–78 *et seq*. The basic rule is that the court first seized of the matter is to exercise jurisdiction. Related actions can be consolidated in the court first seized. Hence banks seeking a favoured court must act quickly.

Non-Convention defendants: Art 4

19–20 The Conventions are dangerous for obligors who are non-Convention domiciliaries, e.g. borrowers in the United States and Japan. If the defendant is not domiciled in a Contracting State, the jurisdiction of the courts of each Contracting State are, subject to the exclusivity provisions in Art 16 (e.g. proceedings relating to land or regarding corporate authorisations), to be determined by the law of that state. It follows that a non-Convention defendant is subject to the long-arm jurisdictional rules in each Contracting State and judgment obtained against him in one Contracting State will then have full faith and credit in all of the other Convention States. Thus a United States borrower could be sued in a Convention State on the basis of one of the following long-arm rules (these may be subject to forum non conveniens qualifications): (a) contract expressly or impliedly governed by English law (England); (b) the "toothbrush" jurisdiction, i.e. assets of the borrower located in the jurisdiction of the courts (Austria, Germany, Scotland, Denmark, Sweden); (c) nationality of plaintiff (France, Luxembourg); (d) (sometimes) residence of plaintiff (Belgium, the Netherlands, Italy).

Article 59 allows Convention States to agree individually, in reciprocal enforcement conventions with third states, not to recognise exorbitantly-based Community judgments in certain cases. The proposed United Kingdom/United States Convention on this topic is in abeyance. The United Kingdom entered into a convention with Canada on this topic in 1984: SI 1987/468.

Contracting-out: Art 17

19–21 Article 17 is fundamentally important since financial agreements often contract out of the forum of the obligor, e.g. to achieve insulation: para 18–4. The Article is somewhat grudging in permitting derogations – an illiberal view. At that time, the UK was not a member of the EEC and could not influence the drafting. Article 17 provides as follows:

"If the parties, one or more of whom is domiciled in a Contracting State, have agreed that a court or the courts of a Contracting State are to have jurisdiction to settle any disputes which have arisen or which may arise in connection with a particular legal relationship, that court or those courts shall have exclusive jurisdiction. Such an agreement conferring jurisdiction shall be either:–

(a) in writing or evidenced in writing, or
(b) in a form which accords with practices which the parties have established between themselves, or
(c) in international trade or commerce, in a form which accords with a usage of which the parties are or ought to have been aware and which in such trade or commerce is widely known to, and regularly observed by, parties to contracts of the type involved in the particular trade or commerce concerned.

Where such an agreement is concluded by parties, none of whom is domiciled in a Contracting State, the courts of other Contracting States shall have no jurisdiction over their disputes unless the court or courts chosen have declined jurisdiction.

The court or courts of a Contracting State on which a trust instrument has conferred jurisdiction shall have exclusive jurisdiction in any proceedings brought against a settlor, trustee or beneficiary, if relations between these persons or their rights or obligations under the trust are involved.

Agreements or provisions of a trust instrument conferring jurisdiction shall have no legal force if they are contrary to the provisions of arts 12 [insurance] or 15 [consumer contracts], or if the courts whose jurisdiction they purport to exclude have exclusive jurisdiction by virtue of art 16 [e.g. land, corporate constitutions, public registers].

If an agreement conferring jurisdiction was concluded for the benefit of only one of the parties, that party shall retain the right to bring proceedings in any other court which has jurisdiction by virtue of the Convention."

Non-Convention courts It seems that a Convention domiciliary can agree that a non-Convention court can have jurisdiction, e.g. an English company can in a credit agreement agree that the courts of New York or Tokyo shall have jurisdiction. But the French courts have held that a Convention domiciliary cannot confer jurisdiction on the courts of a non-Contracting State: *Bruno v Soc Citibank*, Court of Appeal, Versailles, 1991, 1992 Rev Crit 333.   **19–22**

More than one Convention court It seems that the parties may choose more than one Convention court in which neither party is domiciled, and that a non-exclusive choice of a non-domiciliary Convention court does not prejudice the Art 17 choice of a named court. This is supported by *Meeth v Glacetal Sàrl* [1978] ECR 2133, [1979] 1 CMLR 520.   **19–23**

The contract provided that if the German buyer sued the French seller, the

French courts alone would have jurisdiction. But if the French seller sued the German buyer, the German courts alone would have jurisdiction. The French seller sued the German buyer in Germany. *Held* by the European Court: Art 17 allowed the parties to agree on two or more courts. But note that they were domiciliary courts.

This view that a non-exclusive clause does not forfeit Art 17 has been confirmed in *Kurz v Stella Musical Veranstaltungs GmbH* [1992] 1 All ER 630, in which the court held that a non-exclusive choice of jurisdiction clause did not offend Art 17. Parties are free to choose any number of jurisdictions, subject only to the mandatory provisions in Arts 12, 15 and 16. The Court of Appeal, Paris, reached a similar conclusion in *Hantarex SpA v SA Digital Research* (1993) IL Pr 501.

In *Belle Vue Mauricia Ltd v Canmaga Trade Corp*, Court of Appeal, Paris, 1990 (1991) I L Pr 455, a clause providing for the jurisdiction of the courts of Vaduz or Paris at the plaintiff's option was held valid. In *Soc Lyle & Scott v Soc Lisa Frey*, Court of Appeal, Paris 1989 (1990 Clunet 151), a clause that the vendor could designate jurisdiction of any court, in England or elsewhere, was held ineffective. The matter awaits clarification by the European Court.

19–24   **Assignees** In order to satisfy Art 17, the contracting out must be the result of a consensus between the "parties". Consensus is necessary only as between the original banks parties to the loan agreement or the original parties to the bond issue i.e. assignees and transferees should be bound and a borrower should not be able to object to the clause being invoked by an assignee of one of the banks or a transferee of a bond on the ground that the assignee or transferee was not a party to the Art 17 agreement: see para 19 of the Judgment of the Third Chamber, ECJ in Case 201/82, *Gerling Konzern Speziale Kreditversicherung AG v Amministrazione del Tesoro dello Stato* [1983] ECR 2503; Case 71/83, *The Tilly Russ* [1984] ECR 2417.

19–25   **Disputes** Although Art 17 refers to agreements "to settle any disputes" it is thought that any action for judicial remedies (including summary proceedings), even where there is no contention, should be a dispute within the provision.

19–26   **Benefit of one party** The domicile court can also be retained in certain cases. Thus if the jurisdiction agreement has been concluded for the benefit of only one of the parties, that party retains the right to sue in any other court which has jurisdiction under the Conventions: see Case 22/85, *Anterist v Credit Lyonnais* [1986] ECR 1951, ECJ. It is desirable to state that the clause is for the benefit of the desired party.

If there is more than one lender, e.g. as in a syndicate loan, then strictly the "benefit" provision is not satisfied since Art 17 states that, to permit additional jurisdiction in other Convention courts having jurisdiction under the Conventions, the agreement conferring jurisdiction must be concluded "for the benefit of only one of the parties". There is more than one party benefiting. It is considered that in multilateral loan agreements, "one of the parties" can be construed to mean all of the parties other than the borrower, i.e. one can divide the parties into two sides or teams, or alternatively, "one of the parties" might be capable of meaning all those parties for whose benefit the agreement as to jurisdiction was concluded. The matter has not been decided.

Limits on contracting out Contracting-out is subject to the insurance and   19–27
consumer contract requirements (Arts 12 and 15) and to the exclusive jurisdictions in Art 16.

No discretion Where Art 17 applies, the chosen court has no power to override the jurisdiction agreement.

Agent for service to process An English agent for service of process is strictly not necessary in the case of a Convention defendant, but is often inserted to facilitate process.

Writing The clause must be in writing or evidenced in writing, or in international trade or commerce in a form which accords with usage in that trade etc. Jurisdiction clauses in a bond issue, trust deed or other accompanying bond documentation should be specifically referred to in the bond so as to support consensus on jurisdiction.

Non-Convention domiciliaries If English jurisdiction is required, Art 17 contracting out is advisable even for non-Convention companies, e.g. Japanese and US companies. This is because a company can subsequently move its domicile into a Convention state, e.g. by moving its central management. Although undecided by the European Court, it seems that Art 17 does not require Convention domicile at the time of the jurisdiction agreement.

Luxembourg For Luxembourg obligors it is necessary that there should be   19–28
separate clauses exclusively devoted to jurisdiction whereby the Luxem-
bourg obligors specifically and expressly agree to the jurisdiction clause by signature: see Art 1 of the Annexed Protocols to the Conventions. Signature of bond issue documentation containing the clause is apparently not enough for this purpose: the clause must be signed. See Case 784/79, *Porta-Leasing GmbH v Prestige International SA* [1980] ECR 1517.

19–29   **Non-Convention borrowers** If the borrower is a non-Convention domiciliary, but the trustee of the bonds, or any bondholder or any lending bank are Convention domiciliaries, a jurisdiction clause within Art 17 has the effect of vesting exclusive jurisdiction on the chosen Convention courts vis-à-vis other Contracting States. In other words, even if the issuer is non-Convention domiciled but any other party is Convention-domiciled, Art 17 contracting-out appears to override the provisions of Art 4 which allow each Convention State's exorbitant jurisdictional bases to be relied upon in actions against non-Convention domiciliaries.

It is considered that the effect of an Art 17 prorogation is determined at the time of the agreement and is not affected by subsequent events, e.g. an assignment from a non-Convention domiciliary to a Convention domiciliary.

Mutual recognition and enforcement of judgments

19–30   All "judgments" are enforceable under the Conventions including non-money judgments and interim orders, orders providing for periodical payment, orders freezing assets and injunctions, and no special procedure is required: Arts 25 and 26. A foreign judgment may not be reviewed as to its substance: Art 29.

The courts have no right, except within very confined limits, to investigate the jurisdiction of the court which gave the judgment: Art 28. The jurisdiction of the foreign court may only be investigated if the case falls within s 3 (insurance), s 4 (consumer contracts) or s 5 (exclusive jurisdiction) of Title II to the Conventions: Art 28. Even in these cases the English courts are bound by findings of fact on which the foreign court based its judgment: Art 28.

19–31   There are a limited number of exceptions to the universal recognition principle. The most significant are:

(a) public policy (an escape clause of uncertain scope, but not available for jurisdiction objections): Art 27 (1);

(b) judgments given in default of appearance if the defendant was not properly served in good time: Art 27(2);

(c) where the judgment is irreconcilable with a judgment given in a dispute between the parties in the state in which recognition is sought: Art 27(3);

(d) where the judgment is irreconcilable with an earlier judgment given in a non-Contracting State involving the same cause of action between the same parties and recognisable in the state addressed: Art 27(5). Thus if a bank has obtained a prior New York judgment against a borrower and then obtains a German judgment and seeks to enforce the German judgment in England the English courts must refuse to enforce the German judgment if the New York judgment is enforceable in England.

Enforcement of a judgment in England under the Conventions is by way of registration. The judgment creditor cannot bring an action on the original cause of action. Interest is payable on the registered judgment debt at the rate applicable under the law of the court of origin until satisfaction of the judgment. Judgments are registered in their original currency. Registration is made on ex parte application.

There are detailed rules concerning judgments subject to appeal and appeals from enforcement.

CHAPTER 20

RESTRICTIONS ON JUDICIAL
JURISDICTION

Forum non conveniens

20–1 **General review** Theoretically a debtor could be subject to actions in a multitude of countries at the instance of bank lenders and bondholders. In
practice however long-arm jurisdictional statutes have been tempered by
self-imposed restraints on the exercise of the jurisdiction. The courts in
developed jurisdictions have paid liberal regard to the doctrine known as
forum non conveniens whereby the courts may refuse jurisdiction if they
consider that they are not the most convenient and natural forum for the
hearing of the dispute.

A classic statement of the doctrine is that of Mr Justice Jackson in *Gulf
Oil Co v Gilbert*, 330 US 501 (1947). The judge drew attention to the competing interests: the plaintiff, who should have access to his own courts; the
defendant, who should not be vexed or harassed by an action which has no
connection whatsoever with the state of the forum: the expense and trouble
of defending a foreign action can amount to a denial of justice to a defendant; the action itself such as the availability of witnesses; and the public. As
to the latter he observed at 509:

> "administrative difficulties follow for courts when litigation is piled up in con-
> gested centres instead of being handled at its origin ... there is an appropriate-
> ness, too, in having the trial of a diversity case in the forum that is at home with
> the state law that must govern the case, rather than having a court in some other
> forum untangle problems in conflict of laws and in law foreign to itself".

In *Mizokami Bros of Arizona Inc v Baychem Corpn*, 556 F 2d 975 (9th
Cir 1977) the court said:

> "In an era of increasing international commerce, parties who choose to engage
> in international transactions should know that when their foreign operations
> lead to litigation they cannot expect always to bring their foreign opponents
> into a United States forum whenever reasonable considerations lead to the con-
> clusion that the site of the litigation should be elsewhere."

In practice the doctrine of forum non conveniens is of lesser importance in relation to financial agreements or bond issues for two reasons. First, international borrowers generally have the resources to litigate anywhere in the world and cannot complain of mere inconvenience. Second, where a borrower submits to the jurisdiction of specified courts, he will usually be effectively barred from raising a forum non conveniens defence since it is likely to be presumed that he took into account convenience at the time of the contract.

European Judgments Conventions When the case falls within the scope of   20–2
the European Judgments Conventions, the power to refuse jurisdiction on forum non conveniens principles is curtailed. Thus, where the Conventions confer jurisdiction on UK courts, these courts have no discretion to stay the proceedings in favour of the courts of another Contracting State (or to enjoin proceedings commenced in another Contracting State) except in accordance with the specific rules relating to pending actions in Arts 21 and 23 of the Conventions. These provide that the court must decline jurisdiction if the proceedings involve the same cause of action and are between the same parties and the courts of another Contracting State are first seized of the action.

The English court may stay its proceedings where the courts of another Contracting State have been first seized of a related action which has not been the subject of a judgment: Art 22.

The Conventions apply only where the conflict of jurisdictions is between those of Contracting States. Where the conflict is between a Contracting State and a non-Contracting State, the United Kingdom courts retain jurisdiction to stay proceedings on the ground of forum non conveniens: *Re Harrods (Buenos Aires) Ltd* [1991] 3 WLR 397, CA.

Forum non conveniens in England English courts have an inherent jurisdic-   20–3
tion to stay or strike out an action or to restrain by injunction the institution or continuance of proceedings in a foreign court or the enforcement of foreign judgments, whenever it is necessary to prevent injustice. The principles were restated in *Spiliada Maritime Corpn v Cansulex Ltd, The Spiliada* [1987] AC 460, HL.

The basic principle is that a stay will only be granted on the ground of forum non conveniens where the court is satisfied that there is some other available forum, having competent jurisdiction, which is the appropriate forum for the trial of the action, i.e. in which the case may be tried more suitably for the interests of all the parties and the ends of justice.

The court will look to see what factors there are which point in the direction of another forum with which the action has the most real and substantial connection, e.g. convenience or expense (such as availability of witnesses), the law governing the transaction, and the places where the parties reside or carry on business. There is much case law.

The power to stay actions must be distinguished from the power of the courts to refuse leave to serve a writ outside the jurisdiction where the long-arm jurisdiction of the court is claimed under RSC Ord 11, r 1: see para 18–27 *et seq*.

The underlying principle in forum non conveniens cases is to identify in which forum, having competent jurisdiction, the case could most suitably be tried for the interests of all the parties and for the ends of justice. Similar principles apply in Order 11 cases (see para 18–27 *et seq*) although in those cases the burden lies on the plaintiff from the start. Furthermore the jurisdiction under Order 11 is discretionary and, to some extent, exorbitant. These are factors which must be considered along with all the other circumstances.

20–4   It is thought that it would be virtually impossible for a debtor who has submitted to the jurisdiction of the English courts and appointed an agent for service of process in England on whom process is duly served to claim subsequently that injustice would result from the exercise of that jurisdiction. He will be taken to have agreed in advance that those courts are convenient.

In New York, the General Obligations Law s 5–1402 provides that, if a contract with a foreign party choosing New York law involves at least $1 million, the choice of a New York forum for the adjudication of disputes under the contract must be given effect by the New York courts. This overrides the ability to dismiss on forum non conveniens principles. The statute was applied in *Credit Français International SA v Sociedad Financier de Comercio CA*, 490 NYS 2d 670 (S Ct NY Co 1985).

Multiple actions (lis alibi pendens)

20–5   **Generally** A multiple jurisdiction clause may enable a lender to take simultaneous default proceedings in a number of countries. A lender might wish to do so, for example, because of the availability of assets in several jurisdictions, because it is uncertain which claim can be more speedily pressed to conclusion or because there is a possibility that an action might succeed in one country but not in another.

In England, the court might restrain English proceedings on forum non conveniens grounds: *Castanho v Brown and Root (UK) Ltd* [1981] AC 557. But they are very reluctant to stay foreign proceedings and will not do so merely because England is the more natural forum. It is usually necessary to show vexation, oppression or injustice. It is up to the foreign court to apply convenience rules: *South Carolina Insurance Co v Assurantie Maatschappij "de Zeven provincien" NV* [1987] AC 24, HL.

European Judgments Conventions If the Conventions apply, Arts 21 to 23 20–6
contain specific rules to deal with lis alibi pendens. Where the cause of
action is the same, any court other than the first court seized of the matter
must decline jurisdiction in favour of the first court seized. Where the cause
of action is not the same, any court other than the first court seized may,
while actions are pending at first instance, stay its proceedings.

CHAPTER 21

JURISDICTION CLAUSES

Typical clauses

21–1 **Terms of clause** A full English jurisdiction clause in a financial contract may provide as follows:

> "**Submission** For the benefit of the Bank, the Borrower agrees that the courts of England have jurisdiction to settle any disputes in connection with this Agreement and accordingly submits to the jurisdiction of the English courts.
>
> **Service of process** Without prejudice to any other mode of service, the Borrower:–
>
> (a) irrevocably appoints [   ] as its agent for service of process relating to any proceedings before the English courts in connection with this Agreement;
>
> (b) agrees that failure by a process agent to notify the Borrower of the process will not invalidate the proceedings concerned; and
>
> (c) consents to the service of process relating to any such proceedings by prepaid posting of a copy of the process to it at [address].
>
> **Forum convenience and enforcement abroad** The Borrower:–
>
> (a) waives objection to the English courts on grounds of inconvenient forum or otherwise as regards proceedings in connection with this Agreement; and
>
> (b) agrees that a judgment or order of an English court in connection with this Agreement is conclusive and binding on it and may be enforced against it in the courts of any other jurisdiction.
>
> **Non-exclusivity** Nothing in this Clause limits the right of the Bank to bring proceedings against the Borrower in connection with this Agreement:
>
> (a) in any other court of competent jurisdiction; or

(b) concurrently in more than one jurisdiction."

A short-form clause may provide:

"For the benefit of the Bank, the Borrower agrees that the English courts shall have jurisdiction in connection with this Agreement, and appoints [   ] as its agent in England for service of process for this purpose. The jurisdiction of the English courts does not exclude any other court of competent jurisdiction."

Principal objectives The principal objective of the jurisdiction clause is to   **21–2** confer an effective jurisdiction upon the desired courts by fulfilling all the procedural requirements, thereby minimising the risk that the forum might decline jurisdiction.
    Other points are:

1. The advantages listed at para 18–2 *et seq.*

2. An express submission greatly enhances the eligibility of a judgment of those courts for recognition and enforcement in foreign countries which might not be prepared to enforce judgments based on a more tenuous jurisdiction.

3. In international loan transactions the ability of a borrower to complain that the specified court should not exercise jurisdiction on the grounds of the forum non conveniens doctrine is reduced almost to vanishing point where the borrower has expressly consented in advance to the jurisdiction of the stated court; he must be regarded as having taken into account questions of convenience at the time of the contract: see, e.g. *Scherk v Alberto-Culver Company*, 94 S Ct 2449 (1974), 417 US 506 (1976).

4. Where the borrower is located in a country which has ratified a European Judgments Convention a written agreement to confer jurisdiction on external courts is essential to contract out of the general rule that, subject to exceptions, the courts of the borrower's domicile are to have sole jurisdiction: para 19–54 *et seq.*

Multiple jurisdiction The named courts are stated to be non-exclusive.   **21–3** Without such an express statement, those courts may be construed as the exclusive forum. A non-exclusivity provision should not prejudice an Art 17 contracting-out: para 19–56.

Appointment of agent The appointment of an agent for service of process   **21–4** serves two functions in common law jurisdictions.
    In countries such as England the appointment of an agent within England

to receive the writ is essential for the English courts to accept their virtually compulsory jurisdiction: para 18–22. If the borrower were merely to submit and the writ could not be served on the borrower in England, then it would be necessary to apply to the court for leave to serve the writ outside the jurisdiction. While the grant of leave would be probable in the normal case where there is a submission, this is not a foregone conclusion. The second function of the appointment of an agent is to comply with due process requirements. An agent for service of process is not necessary for Convention cases, but remains desirable to strengthen the availability of the judgment for enforcement in non-Convention countries.

In England the agent can be anybody. The preferred practice is to appoint an independent institution which performs these services. In state loans, it is desirable not to appoint the state's ambassador because of possible diplomatic immunity.

The clause includes a requirement that the borrower maintains an agent within the jurisdiction at all times in case the appointed agent should disappear. If the borrower should fail to do so, one imagines that the English courts would show readiness to allow service of the writ outside the jurisdiction.

It is generally expressed to be a condition precedent to the draw-down of loans that the agent bank for lenders receives a copy of the acceptance by the process agent of its appointment. While it seems to be open whether an effective agency contract between the borrower and the agent is strictly necessary in England, foreign enforcing courts might be less inclined to approve the jurisdictional basis of the judgment in the absence of the agent's acceptance of his agency.

21–5 **Mailing of process** A provision for the simultaneous mailing of service of process is intended, from the creditor's side, to place due process beyond peradventure and, from the debtor's side, to protect him against delays or loss. While it is usually expressly stated that the mailing of process is optional and that failure by the borrower to receive notice of process is no defence, lenders would be prudent to ensure that the proceedings are actually brought to the attention of the borrower so that it can not be said that he did not have an opportunity to be heard.

21–6 **Venue** A distinction must be drawn between jurisdiction and venue. Jurisdiction refers to the powers of the courts of a country generally to hear an action. Venue denotes the particular court in that country which will be seized of the dispute. Venue depends upon such matters as the location of the defendant, the amount of the claim and, in federal systems, the division of functions between the federal and state courts. In England it is not necessary to specify the particular court which will be the venue for the dispute since venue is exclusively decided by procedural rules. In New York it is useful to specify courts which have greater experience in investment disputes.

Sovereign immunity Where the borrower may be entitled to sovereign immunity, specific waivers would also be included. These are discussed in another book in this series.

Civilian practice Civilian jurisdiction clauses normally cover (a) an express 21–7 submission to the non-exclusive jurisdiction of named courts, (b) the designation of a court of venue, e.g. the court of Frankfurt am Main and (c) the appointment of an agent (or election of domicile) for service of process within the jurisdiction.

French cases have held that the mere election by the borrower of a domicile within the jurisdiction may be construed not as a choice of forum but rather as an address for service of process: see *Enterprise Generale Transshipping v Etablissements Billiard*, Cass June 18, 1958, Rev Crit Dr Int Pr 1958 754 and *Cie Luxembourgeoise d'Assurances Le Foyer v Dulac*, Cass November 13, 1957, Rev Crit Dr Int Pr 1958, 735.

Exclusive and multiple jurisdiction clauses

Generally An occasionally controversial issue between lenders and bor- 21–8 rowers is whether the rights of the lender or the bondholders to bring an enforcement action should be limited exclusively to the courts of a particular country. The view of lenders may be that default remedies should on no account be limited in any way. On the other hand a borrower may argue that he has a legitimate interest in the identity of the courts. Unless the forum is exclusive he could be exposed to litigation in a possibly hostile country. There could be language problems. In bond issues and large syndications, he may be exposed to a multiplicity of actions in a great many countries and to "forum shopping" whereby the investor seeks a jurisdiction most favourable to his case and disadvantageous to the borrower and it is therefore unreasonable to limit the possibilities of enforcement. In practice the lender's view generally prevails for the simple reason that in most financial contracts there is no dispute or complex factual or legal issue, but merely a non-payment.

But if an exclusive clause is agreed, then in **England, France, Belgium and Germany** the courts are, as a general rule, liberal in upholding derogations from their jurisdiction in favour of foreign courts.

In **England** the courts will stay the English proceedings unless the plaintiff 21–9 proves that it is just and proper to allow them to continue. But there can be exceptional circumstances:

In *Carvalho v Hull Blyth (Angola) Ltd* [1979] 1 WLR 1228, CA, the court held that owing to a revolution in the foreign country the foreign court to which the parties exclusively submitted was a different court from that contemplated in the contract and therefore had no application.

The onus is on the plaintiff to show that there should be no stay. This is because the ground on which the court grants a stay is that the court makes people abide by their contracts.

The plaintiff must show a strong case, more than a balance of convenience. There is a heavier burden on the plaintiff who applies to serve a foreign defendant out of the jurisdiction than on a plaintiff who institutes proceedings in England against a defendant present in England.

Case law shows that, in exercising its discretion whether or not to grant a stay, the court takes into account all the circumstances of the case, and in particular (i) in which country the evidence is available, and the effect of that on the relative convenience and expense of the trial in England or abroad; (ii) whether the contract is governed by the law of the foreign country in question, and if so, whether it differs from English law in any material respect; (iii) with what country either party is connected, and how closely; (iv) whether the defendants genuinely desire trial in a foreign country, or are only seeking procedural advantages; (v) whether the plaintiffs would be prejudiced by having to sue in the foreign court because they would be deprived of security for their claim, or be unable to enforce the judgment in their favour, or be faced with a time-bar not applicable in England, or for political, racial, religious or other reasons be unlikely to get a fair trial.

21–10   Courts in the *United States* have generally tended to uphold exclusivity clauses.

In the leading United States Supreme Court case of *The Bremen v Zapata Offshore Corpn*, 407 US 1 (1972) 92 S Ct (1907 32 L Ed 2d 513) it was held that the courts, in determining the effectiveness of an exclusivity clause, should give effect to freely negotiated private international agreements unaffected by undue influence or overweening bargaining power. The court said (per Burger CJ at 9):

"The expansion of American business and industry will hardly be encouraged if, notwithstanding solemn contracts, we insist on a parochial concept that all disputes must be resolved under our laws and in our courts ... We cannot have trade and commerce in world markets and international waters exclusively on our terms, governed by our laws and resolved in our courts."

The court further held that the old doctrine whereby a choice of forum clause intended to oust a court of jurisdiction was void was "hardly more than a vestigial legal fiction". See also *Scherk v Alberto-Culver Co*, 94 S Ct 2449, 417 US 506 (1974).

In **Italy** on the other hand under CCP Art 2 the validity of a derogation **21–11** clause is limited to obligations between aliens or between an alien and an Italian citizen who neither resides in, nor is a domiciliary of, Italy.

Where an issuer succeeds in obtaining an exclusive forum selection, it does not necessarily follow that bondholders will be bound by the exclusivity provisions. The reason is that derogation clauses are less likely to be upheld in "contracts of adhesion" where one party had no real opportunity to negotiate the terms of the clause. In a number of foreign jurisdictions forum selection clauses must be expressly agreed to in writing. In the Japanese case of *Tokyo Marine and Fire Insurance KK v Royal Interocean Lines* (13 Kaminshu 1477, Kobe District Court, July 18, 1963) the Supreme Court held that the comparable Japanese requirement of acceptance in writing should be relaxed in international litigation. In a judgment of the Japanese Supreme Court (29 Minshu 1554, Supreme Court, November 28, 1975) it was held that an exclusive submission to a foreign court will be valid under Japanese law if (i) the parties are not subject to an exclusive jurisdiction of a Japanese court in relation to the dispute concerned, and (ii) the designated court had jurisdiction in accordance with the laws of the country of the designated court.

Article 17 of the European Judgments Conventions (which deals with exclusive jurisdiction clauses) removes the discretion in the cases to which it applies: see para 19–60. Thus, where the Conventions apply, unless the defendant submits to the jurisdiction, the court has no jurisdiction to determine the dispute if the parties have agreed in accordance with Art 17 that the courts of a Contracting State other than the domicile are to have jurisdiction.

Governing law of jurisdiction clauses

A number of issues arise on the law applicable to issues regarding jurisdic- **21–12** tion clauses.

Interpretation Interpretation of the clause is determined by the governing law of the contract. Thus the governing law of the contract determines whether a foreign jurisdiction clause provides for the exclusive jurisdiction of the foreign court or merely that the parties will not object to the exercise of jurisdiction by that court: *Evans Marshall & Co Ltd v Bertola SA* [1973] 1 WLR 349, CA. Article 1(2)(d) of the Rome Convention on applicable laws excludes "agreements on the choice of court" from the scope of the Convention, so that states apply their own conflicts rules on this.

21–13   **Void "container" contract** If a contract is void, there is a question whether the jurisdiction clause goes with it. It seems that an exclusive jurisdiction clause will fail if the "container" contract is void. The whole contract lapses: *Trendtex Trading Corpn v Credit Suisse* [1980] QB 629, CA; affirmed [1982] AC 679, HL. On the other hand it may survive if the contract (e.g. of insurance) is merely voidable for non-disclosure of a material fact: *Mackender v Feldia AG* [1967] 2 QB 590 at 598, CA.

21–14   **Ouster of jurisdiction** The lex fori should determine whether or not an exclusive jurisdiction clause or arbitration clause is effective to oust the jurisdiction of the court in which the action is brought. Even if the governing law determines this question, the ouster may nevertheless be void on grounds of the public policy of the forum.

21–15   **Constitutional prohibitions** It is thought that the governing law of the contract (as opposed to the law of the sovereign debtor) determines whether a state's constitutional prohibition on submission to the jurisdiction of foreign courts (e.g. as is the case with Colombia and Venezuela in certain cases) is effective. Thus, in the case of Venezuela, if the governing law is Venezuelan, the submission is ineffective. If the governing law is English, the Venezuelan law is excluded. The matter should not be decided by the state's constitution because, if it were, a state could exclude all its contracts from foreign jurisdiction, merely on the basis that it lacked capacity.

CHAPTER 22

ARBITRATION

Suitability of arbitration for financial contracts

Arbitration as a method of settling disputes is not generally favoured by   22–1
commercial financiers and this section does no more than indicate why this
should be so. However, arbitration is sometimes (though very rarely)
resorted to in the case of governmental loans where the state borrower is
constitutionally prohibited or is unwilling to submit to the jurisdiction of
foreign courts, e.g. Brazil. Arbitration is sometimes employed by international development banks which have a different attitude to enforcement
sanctions.

One may now review aspects of arbitration in the context of international
loans.

Finality A general feature of arbitration laws is to exclude appeal from the   22–2
arbitrator's award except on very limited grounds such as absence of jurisdiction or fraud. This principle is espoused by arbitration statutes in the
United States, many Continental European countries, Japan and in England
but at the option of the parties: Arbitration Act 1979 s 3.

Finality can be important in, say, construction contracts where it is desirable that a decision be handed down one way or the other so that the work
can proceed. Such considerations do not generally apply to financial contracts.

Is expert adjudication required? Where a contract involves complicated   22–3
technical or factual matters, it may be an advantage for disputes to be heard
by experts who do not have to be educated in the field concerned. However
disputes on financial agreements do not generally involve technical questions of fact and the proceedings are commonly brought to enforce payment
or to decide the law rather than to resolve factual matters. Further, the
commercial courts of internationally orientated jurisdictions are well
equipped to settle complex investment contests.

Privacy The privacy and confidentiality of arbitration may be inimical to the
interests of lenders since arbitration weakens the sanction of adverse publicity which a defaulting borrower might wish to avoid.

22–4   **Condition precedent** Arbitration of the dispute is generally a condition precedent to enforcement through the courts. Parties who agree to submit disputes solely to arbitration will generally be bound by their agreement: *Scott v Avery* (1855) 5 HL Cas 811; Arbitration Act 1979 s 1. In view of the time which it can take to set up the arbitral tribunal, the inability of a lender to proceed to summary judgment in municipal courts where there is nothing seriously in dispute can be a significant disadvantage. It follows that the arbitral tribunal is the exclusive forum unless otherwise agreed.

   Procedure Generally speaking the rules of evidence and procedure established by arbitration tribunals are (often intentionally) less developed than court procedures. The result is that the course of the arbitration can be unpredictable and rapid resolution blocked if one of the parties is not prepared to cooperate. The absence of formal procedures confers a useful flexibility in construction disputes but not generally in financial contracts.

22–5   **Enforcement** Arbitration is often held in some neutral country where neither party is situate or has assets. It will almost invariably be necessary to implement the arbitration award by further proceedings for enforcement in other jurisdictions. The court may be slower to recognise a foreign arbitral award and more inclined to investigate its validity than in the case of a judgment of a foreign court. The position has however been improved by the New York Convention on the Recognition and Enforcement of Foreign Arbitral Awards of 1958 which has been ratified by a great many countries including some European countries (including Austria and the United Kingdom), Finland, Greece, Japan, Mexico, Nigeria, Norway, Philippines, Poland, Sweden, Switzerland and the United States.

   Public contracts In some countries the arbitrability of state or public contracts may be subject to restrictions which might avoid the arbitration clause altogether or prevent effect being given to an arbitration award when enforcement is sought in the prohibiting country. An example is a Venezuelan Law of July 1967.

22–6   **Jurisdictional disputes** Unless the arbitration clause is carefully drafted, there can be an initial dispute as to its validity and interpretation and as to whether the tribunal has jurisdiction at all. Jurisdiction clauses, which do not have to develop the methods of choosing the arbitral tribunal or the matters which may be subject to proceedings, are inherently less susceptible to this difficulty.

   Expense and delay It is not necessarily the case that arbitration is speedier and less expensive than process through commercially orientated courts.

Unlike judges, arbitrators have to be paid. A venue has to be arranged and paid for.

Decision ex aequo et bono It is possible that arbitrators are more inclined to make compromise awards or to apply general equitable principles than to determine the matter in accordance with strict principles of municipal law. This is not necessarily a disadvantage in, say, construction contracts where compromise solutions may not be unacceptable but in financial contracts predictability is vital. Much of course depends upon the constitution of the arbitral tribunal, the law under which the arbitration is to be conducted, and the expertise of the arbitrators.

International Centre for Settlement of Investment Disputes ("ICSID")

ICSID was established under the auspices of the World Bank specifically for the purpose of resolving investment disputes between contracting states and nationals of other contracting states. There are currently more than 80 signatories to the Convention.   **22–7**

Jurisdiction Article 25(1) of the Convention provides:

> "The jurisdiction of the Centre shall extend to any legal dispute arising directly out of an investment between a Contracting State (or any constituent subdivision or agency of a Contracting State designated to the Centre by the State) and a national of another Contracting State, which the parties to the dispute consent in writing to submit to the Centre. When the parties have given their consent, no party may withdraw its consent unilaterally."

It will be noted that ICSID is not available for intergovernmental disputes or for disputes between two nationals. Consider whether a loan is an "investment".

Under Art 26 consent of the parties to arbitration under the Convention is deemed to be consent to arbitration to the exclusion of any other remedy unless otherwise stated. It is therefore possible for a lender expressly to reserve the option to proceed municipally if so agreed and also, if so agreed, to pursue provisional measures, such as obtaining a Mareva injunction, to prevent the removal of assets from the jurisdiction.

It is also provided in the Convention that "a Contracting State may require the exhaustion of local administrative or judicial remedies as a condition of its consent to arbitration under this Convention": Art 26. Many private parties would consider such a limitation to be significantly adverse.

22–8   **Applicable law** Article 42(1) provides:

> "The Tribunal shall decide a dispute in accordance with such rules of law as
> may be agreed by the parties. In the absence of such agreement, the Tribunal
> shall apply the laws of the Contracting State party to the dispute (including its
> rules on the conflict of laws) and such rules of international law as may be appli-
> cable."

Hence the parties can agree on a choice of law.

22–9   **Enforcement** Article 54 provides that each Contracting State must recognise
an award rendered pursuant to the Convention as binding and enforce the
pecuniary obligations imposed by that award within its territories as if it
were a final judgment of a court of that state. Execution of the award is to
be governed by the laws concerning the execution of judgments in force in
the state in whose territories such execution is sought.

A particular feature of this provision is that the courts of a Contracting
State are not permitted to raise the objection of public policy, a defence
which is available under the 1958 New York Arbitration Convention and is
available, it is thought, in numerous jurisdictions. The enforcement arrangements are therefore strong. On the other hand, the Convention does not
remove a borrower's sovereign immunity from execution if the rules of the
recognising state forbid execution on these grounds. This howsoever does
not prevent the parties from agreeing that the sovereign borrower will not
claim immunity from execution.

The grounds of appeal are very limited: Art 52. Awards are confidential
unless otherwise agreed Art 48(5).

CHAPTER 23

ENFORCEMENT OF FOREIGN JUDGMENTS

Introduction

This section surveys in broad terms the enforceability in local jurisdictions   **23–1**
of judgments for contract debts obtained in foreign countries. Where a
lender obtains a judgment in an external court the question arises as to
whether that judgment has any value in other countries. If it is enforceable
in other jurisdictions, then the holder of the judgment could follow assets of
the borrower into those jurisdictions and perhaps into the country of the
borrower. Only judgments for contract claims in personam are considered
here, not e.g. admiralty actions in rem or actions in respect of security interests or immovable property or torts or injunctions and the like.

Some of the international detail in this section is based on Charles Platto
(ed) *Enforcement of Foreign Judgments Worldwide* (1989), which contains
country and regional reports prepared by members of the International Bar
Association (the "IBA Survey").

It is considered to be universally true that a lender cannot enforce a judgment directly in a foreign country: enforcement almost invariably requires
the fiat of the local court, e.g. the civilian *exequatur*. However legal develop-
ments have greatly facilitated the free movement of judgments and it is now
possible for a lender to leap-frog on a money-judgment from one jurisdiction to another with relative ease, provided – and this is an important proviso – that the original court had proper jurisdiction: proper jurisdiction
will almost invariably be constituted by an express submission clause in the
financial agreement.

Generally speaking there are three possibilities: **23–2**

1. The lender may be able to commence a new action: this is limited in
    many jurisdictions because there must be an end to litigation.

2. The lender may be able to sue on the foreign judgment locally as a debt
    due.

3. The lender may be able to enforce his foreign judgment on the basis of a
    reciprocal enforcement convention or statute.

As remarked earlier, the enforcement of foreign judgments for contract debts in international finance is commonly frozen by the institution of insolvency proceedings so that the topic is less crucial than might appear. But the legal ability to enforce internationally is an important sanction: contracts without effective sanctions, even if the remedies are not used, are futile.

Most developed jurisdictions are prepared to recognise and enforce foreign judgments by permitting the lender to sue on the foreign judgment locally as a debt due or by the equivalent civilian procedure of *exequatur*. It will be seen however that the enforcement of foreign judgments in this way is subject to conditions.

There is, parenthetically, a difference between recognition and enforcement. Enforcement involves positive relief, such as an order for attachment or an injunction. Recognition does not require affirmative action but the judgment is regarded as affecting interests e.g. it is treated as having decided the matter (res judicata) thereby preventing further litigation. An example is the judicial sale of a ship.

Reciprocal enforcement conventions generally

23–3   **Advantages** A number of jurisdictions, particularly those enjoying close cultural or political ties, have entered into treaties providing for reciprocal enforcement of each other's judgments if the conditions specified in the applicable statutes are satisfied. Although conventions vary greatly, the advantages of reciprocal enforcement conventions may include some or all of the following:

> **Jurisdiction** It is generally not necessary for the enforcing court to have jurisdiction over the defendant under the normal court rules. All that may be required is that the judgment be registered in the enforcing court and notice sent to the defendant in accordance with the statute. In the absence of a reciprocal enforcement statute, it is usually the case that the court called upon to enforce a foreign judgment must have jurisdiction over the defendant in accordance with its usual jurisdictional rules. But in the US, the attachment of US assets (including local bank accounts) is enough to confer jurisdiction for this purpose to the extent of those assets – an exception to the usual rule that there must also be other minimum contracts: *Shaffer v Heitner*, 433 US 186 (1977).

23–4   **Procedure** The procedural aspects of enforcement are generally simpler and more expeditious. The reciprocal enforcement statute may provide for a simple registration process as opposed to obtaining a judgment of the enforcing court or the equivalent procedure of *exequatur*.

Review of merits Reciprocal enforcement statutes often limit the ability of the courts to review the foreign judgment on its merits. Indeed the purpose of a convention is precisely to avoid retrial by setting out agreed circumstances in which the courts of the contracting states will honour each other's judgments.

Defences Reciprocal enforcement statutes may exclude other defences available to a defendant, e.g. that there was no fair trial. Contracting states tend to respect each other's judicial processes.

Reciprocity Reciprocal enforcement statutes avoid the need for the court to consider whether reciprocity would exist. This is because the convention is entered into on the basis of reciprocity of treatment.

Judgments on judgments But it is often not possible to leap-frog into a jurisdiction and then to leap-frog into other countries on the basis of that jurisdiction's treaties, e.g. enforce a Japanese judgment in England and then use the UK's treaties to enforce in the UK's treaty partners. The UK Foreign Judgments (Reciprocal Enforcement) Act 1933 does not allow this, nor does Canada's Reciprocal Enforcement of Judgments (UK) Act 1984.

Federal and domestic reciprocal enforcement states

Internal treaties in federal or quasi-federal countries may be distinguished **23-5** from truly international treaties. Examples of domestic statutes include the following:

United Kingdom Pt II of the Civil Jurisdiction and Judgments Act 1982 applies as between England, Scotland and Northern Ireland. A certified judgment to which it applies obtained in one part of the United Kingdom is registrable under the Act as of right in another part and thereupon acquires the force and effect of a local judgment.

Canada The Reciprocal Enforcement of Judgments Act 1958 has been adopted by all Canadian provinces and territories other than Quebec.

United States The full faith and credit clause of the Constitution (Art IV, **23-6** para 1) requires that judicial proceedings "shall have the same full faith and credit in every court within the United States and its Territories and Possessions as they have by law or usage in the courts of such State, Territory or Possession from which they are taken". The due process clauses of the Fifth and Fourteenth Amendments invalidate, even in the state of rendition, judgments that have been rendered without judicial jurisdiction or without compliance with the constitutional requirements of notice and of opportunity to be heard. However the United States full faith and credit clause does not apply to judgments rendered in foreign countries and it follows that there is greater room for individual rules on the part of the states with respect to the recognition and enforcement of external judgments: see the Restatement on the Conflict of Laws (1971), introductory note to chapter 5. However, the rules of the several states are very similar.

The US has not entered into any international judgments conventions as such apart from the 1958 New York Arbitration Convention.

23–7   The United States Uniform Foreign Money-Judgments Recognition Act is an internal treaty which mainly codifies rules that have long been applied by the majority of courts in the United States, principally to increase the likelihood that United States judgments would be recognised abroad in civilian countries with reciprocity requirements. At least 16 states have enacted versions closely following the uniform text including Alaska, California, Georgia, Illinois, Maryland, Massachusetts, Michigan, New York, Oklahoma, Texas and Washington although the latest position should be checked. According to s 3 of this Act a foreign country judgment "is enforceable in the same manner as the judgment of a sister state which is entitled to full faith and credit". New York however requires that the foreign country judgment be enforceable by an action on the judgment but there is an expedited procedure comparable to the English Order 14 summary process.

Some states have in addition adopted the US Uniform Enforcement of Foreign Judgments Act of 1948 (either in its 1948 version or in its revised 1964 version) which applies only to sister state judgements but allows for a simplified registration process. States which have accepted both Acts include Alaska, Illinois, New York, Oklahoma and Washington. Again, the latest position should be checked. The effect of the combination is that foreign judgments are directly enforceable in these states and do not have to be reduced to a local judgment first.

23–8   **United Kingdom international reciprocal enforcement statutes** Apart from the European Judgments Conventions, there are three main United Kingdom statutes providing for the reciprocal enforcement of foreign judgments.

Administration of Justice Act 1920 This Act has been extended to almost the whole of the British Commonwealth, including Nigeria, Bermuda, Hong Kong, Malaysia, Singapore, Australia and New Zealand, as well as numerous other states in Africa and elsewhere and a multitude of island states. There are detailed modifications in the case of New

Zealand, Newfoundland and some of the Australian states (Queensland, Victoria, Western Australia and New South Wales).

The Act provides for the reciprocal enforcement of the judgments of superior courts of the countries concerned. Registration is discretionary, but tends to follow the usual common law grounds. Registration is not permitted if the original court acted without jurisdiction or if the defendant establishes one of a limited number of defences: see s 9(2). These defences are very similar to those available at common law. A duly registered judgement is to have the same force and effect as a judgment of the registering court: s 9(3).

Foreign Judgments (Reciprocal Enforcement) Act 1933 The Act provides   23–9
for the replacement of the system set up by the Administration of Justice Act 1920 and has been extended to India, Pakistan, the Australian Capital Territory, Canada, Guernsey, Jersey, the Isle of Man, Tonga, Israel and Surinam. Most of the other countries have been overtaken by the European Judgments Conventions. Registration is available as of right provided that the judgment sought to be registered has not been wholly satisfied and is enforceable by execution in the country of the original court: s 2(1). The Act contains rules determining whether the foreign court had jurisdiction: s 4(2) – these rules are similar to those prevailing at common law and are discussed below. The grounds upon which registration must be set aside are similar to those upon which a foreign judgment is impeachable at common law. A registered judgment will have the same force and effect as if the judgment had been a judgment originally given in the High Court and entered on the date of registration: s 2(2).

State Immunity Act 1978 Part II of the State Immunity Act 1978 provides for the recognition of certain judgments rendered against the United Kingdom in countries which are parties to the European Convention on State Immunity.

Other treaty networks

Apart from numerous European and Nordic bilateral treaties, which have   23–10
usually been overtaken by the European Judgments Conventions, the following are examples of treaty networks (this is based mainly on the IBA Survey):

Australia Reciprocal treaties with numerous British Commonwealth States; also Germany, France, Israel, Italy, Japan, Korea, but not the US, and not Latin American states. See the Foreign Judgments (Reciprocal Enforcement) Act 1973.

Belgium Treaties affecting Hong Kong and New Zealand.

Canada Only one treaty, with the UK: Reciprocal Enforcement of Judgments (UK) Act 1984.

China Apparently has treaties with Belgium, France and Poland, but this should be checked.

Germany Israel (1978).

23–11   **India** Has reciprocal arrangements with the UK, Hong Kong, Singapore, Trinidad and Tobago, New Zealand, Cook Islands, Western Samoa, Papua New Guinea and Bangladesh.

New Zealand Treaties with some British Commonwealth states, and also Belgium and France: see Reciprocal Enforcement of Judgments Act 1934.

Singapore Reciprocal treaties with, for example, Australia, Brunei Darussalam, Sri Lanka, Hong Kong, most of India, Malaysia, New Zealand, Pakistan, Papua New Guinea and the Windward Islands.

Spain Treaties with the former Czechoslovakia (1927) and Colombia (1908).

Switzerland Treaties with the former Czechoslovakia (1926) and with Liechtenstein (1968).

23–12   Note also in **Latin America**:

-   the Montevideo International Procedural Law Treaties of 1889 and 1940: Argentina, Paraguay, Bolivia, Peru, Brazil, Colombia;

-   the Pan-American Code of Private International Law of 1928 (the Bustamente Code) Arts 423–437;

-   the Montevideo Interamerican Convention on the Extraterritorial Validity of Foreign Judgments and Arbitral Awards of 1979 Arts 2 to 6;

-   the La Paz Convention on Jurisdiction in the International Sphere for the Extraterritorial Validity of Foreign Judgments of 1984.

Japan, Korea, Thailand and the **United States** are examples of countries which do not have any reciprocal enforcement treaties.

Usual conditions of enforcement: summary

The conditions upon which jurisdictions are prepared to recognise and 23–13 enforce a foreign judgment vary but the principal rules may be summed up as follows:

1. The foreign court had substantial jurisdiction – long-arm jurisdiction is usually insufficient. An express submission usually is enough: this underlines the desirability of an express submission to jurisdiction.

2. Reciprocity, i.e. the foreign court would recognise in similar circumstances in reverse. There is some international division on this issue.

3. Due notice, fair trial, no fraud, e.g. adequate notice of proceedings and observance of the basic rules of justice. This is a universal requirement.

4. The judgment does not conflict with local public policy. This is a universal requirement, but there are differing views of public policy.

5. The judgment is for a liquidated money sum, not e.g. for an injunction. Practice differs.

6. The judgment is not for foreign taxes, fines or penalties. This is universal.

7. (Often) the judgment is final and conclusive, i.e. not subject to appeal, or (if appealable) is enforceable locally. This is a universal requirement, but there are detailed differences.

8. The judgment does not conflict with a local judgment on the same cause of action. This is a universal requirement.

   In substance, the two main dividing principles are:

- reciprocity (the tit-for-tat);

- review of the merits of the original judgment (i.e. a retrial on some issues – effectively not a recognition).

Country summary

According to the IBA Survey and other sources, the following are a sample 23–14 list of countries which do recognise and enforce foreign money judgments on contracts on the basis of all, or some only, of the conditions of enforcement listed above:

Europe   –   Belgium: Judicial Code Art 570 subject to limited review of merits

- England (and probably most English-influenced states)
- Germany: ZPO s 328, as extensively amended by the Act to Reform Private International Law of 1986
- Italy: CCP Art 797
- Netherlands: by case law, in practice, although the Netherlands formal position is that a treaty is required
- Spain: CCP Arts 951–58
- Switzerland: Private International Law Act of 1987 (mainly federal, but cantons have limited procedural provisions)

North America
- Canada (similar to English principles)
- United States (state law exhibits liberal attitude to foreign judgments; practice does not vary widely)

23–15 **Far East**
- Australia (English-based)
- China: Law of Civil Procedure Art 204. Principles unsettled
- Hong Kong (English-based)
- India: CCP 1908 s 2
- Japan: Civil Procedure Law Art 200 (based on the German ZPO of 1877 and since amended) – about 30 cases by 1988.
- New Zealand (English-based)
- Pakistan: CCP 1908 s 2
- Philippines

Latin America
- Argentina: provincial codes and Federal District Code of Civil and Commercial Procedure Arts 517–519.
- Brazil: Law of Introduction to the Civil Code; CCP
- Chile: CCP Arts 242–51
- Colombia: CCP Art 623
- Guatemala
- Mexico: National CPC Art 571, Federal District PC Arts 605–6
- Peru: CC Arts 2102–11
- Puerto Rico: mainly case law
- Uruguay
- Venezuela: CCP Arts 850–858

Africa   —   It is suggested that many African states are likely to
                            have adopted the rules of former metropolitan
                            states, e.g. Britain and France.

The following four states do not recognise and enforce foreign judg-   **23–16**
ments, in the absence of a treaty.

Indonesia: *Reglement op de Rechtsvordering* Art 436

Netherlands, unless there is a treaty, but foreign judgments have strong
evidentiary force and in practice they are enforced, without reopening, on
the basis of the usual conditions.

Sweden (and perhaps other Nordic countries) – Sweden requires a treaty,
but it is believed that foreign money judgments have strong evidential
force and are not reopened.

> In the *Vakis* case, NJA 1973, p 628, Vakis sued a Swedish charterer for money
> in Greece and obtained judgment. It had been agreed that the Greek courts had
> exclusive jurisdiction. The charterer did not appear in the Greek court. Vakis
> sued on the judgment in Sweden. *Held* by the Swedish Supreme Ct: the Greek
> judgment would be upheld. Only the Greek courts had jurisdiction. Enforce-
> ment was not contrary to Swedish public policy.

Thailand: The position is uncertain since foreign judgments are not
mentioned in the codes. But see Supreme Court Judgment no 585/2461
(1918), decided pre-codes, where a Saigon judgment for the delivery of 15
rickshaws and two bicycles was not enforced on the ground that the
Saigon judgment was made without the defendant's presence at the trial.

Re-examination of the merits

If the various conditions are satisfied, but the court will nevertheless re-   **23–17**
examine a foreign judgment on its merits, then effectively the foreign judgment is not recognised. The argument for not reopening is that there must
be an end to litigation and no-one should be sued twice on the same action,
even if the foreign court got it wrong. The argument against rubber-stamp-
ing has partly been an attempt to control forum shopping, partly distrust of
foreign states, partly a desire to protect local citizens.

The Belgian courts will re-examine the merits (Art 570 of the Judicial
Code) although the review is limited and is not a new trial. The Italian
courts will do so if the foreign judgment was a default judgment or there is
an error of fact on the record: CCP Art 798.

In 1964 the French courts abandoned the *revision à fond* of a foreign judgment and now do not generally review the merits except where the foreign court applied the wrong conflicts rule in French eyes: *Munzer Case*, Clunet 1964, 302; JCP 64, II, 13590, Court of Cassation. Bolivia re-examines, as does the Philippines if there is a clear mistake of fact or law.

Jurisdiction of court of origin

23–18   The most important condition often applied is that the court of origin must have been a court of competent jurisdiction. This may be a double test, i.e. first the original court must have had domestic jurisdiction in accordance with its own rules and second the original court's exercise of jurisdiction must have been consistent with the enforcing court's ideas of international jurisdiction. Many courts do not for the latter purpose recognise a foreign court as having jurisdiction if the foreign court claims jurisdiction on some long-arm rule, e.g. location of assets or nationality of plaintiff. The stringent rules forestall the device of using the exorbitant jurisdiction of one country and then enforcing it everywhere.

Thus, in **England** the courts are not willing to recognise a foreign court as having jurisdiction even though that foreign court claimed jurisdiction on the basis of a long-arm rule corresponding to the English long-arm rules under RSC Ord 11 whereby, for example, English courts can claim jurisdiction over a contract which is made or broken within England or is expressly or impliedly governed by English law. Location of assets and the claimant's nationality are not enough.

23–19   In the **United States** usually the foreign court must have had jurisdiction in accordance with its own rules and in accordance with rules of international jurisdiction. The Uniform Foreign-Money Judgments Recognition Act, which also on this issue reflects the practice in most non-adopting states, provides in s 5(a) that a foreign judgment will not be refused recognition for lack of personal jurisdiction if (amongst other things) the defendant corporation was incorporated or had its principal place of business in the relevant state, or had a business office in that state and the claim arose out of business done through that office.

France requires a "characteristic link" with the judgment country: *Simitch Case*, February 6, 1985 (RCDIP, p 369, p 243, Court of Cassation). **Belgium** will not recognise foreign jurisdiction based on the claimant's nationality: Judicial Code Art 570. Nor will **Germany** recognise jurisdiction based on the claimant's nationality (France) or the English fleeting presence jurisdiction, but will recognise the "toothbrush" assets jurisdiction since this reflects the German rule. The Swiss rules for jurisdiction of foreign judgments are contained in the Private International Law Act of 1987 and (apart from the defendant's domicile residence) include foreign judgments relating to performance of a contract if the judgment was rendered in the country of that performance, and relating to claims arising from the operation of a business if rendered at the place of business: Art 149(2).

But universally it seems that a valid advance agreement to submit disputes on a contract to the courts of the rendering country is sufficient, e.g. Switzerland (Art 26 of the above Act of 1987, Germany (if between businessmen – ZPO s 38 (1), England (at common law and under the 1920 and 1933 Acts referred to at para 23–8), and the United States: Uniform Foreign-Money Judgments Recognition Act, s 5(a). **23–20**

A foreign court will not be regarded as having jurisdiction if the enforcing court regards itself as having exclusive competence and will ignore a foreign judgment trespassing on this domain. Typically this applies to disputes concerning local land or where the parties have agreed to the exclusive jurisdiction of the local court. In France the courts have exclusive jurisdiction if the defendant is a French national and he has not either expressly or impliedly waived his right to have the case tried in France (CC Arts 14 and 15) and also where the defendant is permanently resident in France and has not accepted the jurisdiction of the foreign courts (CCP Art 59). Italy is another country which has discriminatory rules for local jurisdiction where Italian nationals are concerned. The principle of the exclusive competence of local courts has been espoused in certain matters by the European Judgments Conventions: para 19–14. **23–21**

Where the parties themselves have validly agreed that a court other than the court of origin will have exclusive competence, it will not usually be possible to enforce a foreign judgment obtained contrary to that agreement: see, e.g. s 32 of the Civil Jurisdiction and Judgments Act 1982.

In most developed countries, a principal place of business of the debtor locally is enough; but jurisdiction on the basis of a local branch or local performance, where there is no principal place of business locally, is commonly limited to claims arising out of that branch or relating to that performance.

Sovereign immunity

It is considered to be universally true that a court addressed will not enforce a foreign judgment if the court addressed accords immunity to the judgment debtor or its assets. A creditor could not therefore in this way outflank the immunity accorded by the court addressed. **23–22**

By s 31 of the UK Civil Jurisdiction and Judgments Act 1982, a judgment given by a court of an overseas country against a state other than the United Kingdom or the state to which that court belongs will be recognised and enforced in the United Kingdom if, and only if, it would be so recognised and enforced if it had not been given against a state and the court would have had jurisdiction in the matter if it applied rules corresponding to those applicable to such matters in the United Kingdom in accordance with ss 2–11 of the State Immunity Act 1978. "State" includes constituent territories of a federal state. This section applies to separate entities (being those which are distinct from the executive organs of a state) only where the proceedings relate to anything done by the separate entity in the exercise of the sovereign authority of the state. Sections 12, 13 and 14(3) and (4) of the State Immunity Act 1978 (service of process, procedural privileges and enforcement) apply to proceedings for the recognition or enforcement in the United Kingdom of a judgment given by a court of an overseas country as they apply to the proceedings. These sections confer various immunities and privileges on sovereign states.

Reciprocity

23–23   Under the doctrine of reciprocity the enforcing court will recognise the foreign judgment only if the original court would recognise a corresponding judgment of the enforcing courts in similar circumstances. The doctrine has little to commend it. Commonly reciprocity tends to be limited to reciprocation of jurisdictional rules: thus a German court has refused to recognise a South African judgment on the grounds that South Africa would not reciprocate a German judgment based upon the "toothbrush" jurisdiction: Judgment of September 30, 1964, 42 BGHZ 194. But the German reciprocity, required by ZPO s 238 para 1, no 5, has been reduced almost to vanishing point, e.g. only if the foreign court would re-open on the merits or would never enforce a German judgment or there are substantial impediments.

The English courts do not require proof of reciprocity at common law. Notwithstanding the United States Supreme Court's decision of *Hilton v Guyot*, 159 US 113 (1895), which required reciprocity, the New York courts and other state courts have also rejected the doctrine: see *Johnston v Companie Generale Transatlantique*, 242 NY 381, 152 NE 121 (1926). According to the IBA Survey reciprocity is also not required in Belgium, France, Italy or Switzerland.

23–24   Japan and some Latin American states (e.g. Bolivia, Colombia, Chile, Paraguay and Venezuela but only two out of 22 Argentine provinces) require reciprocity, although insistence upon literal correspondence is less marked in some states than in others. In a leading decision of the Japanese Great Court of Cassation *Z Witkosky & Co* (Shimbun (No 3670) 16 Gr Ct Cass, December 5, 1933), the court held that the requirement was satisfied if substantial reciprocity could be shown: it did not have to be identical. A subsequent decision (37 Minshu 611, Supreme Court, June 7, 1983 (*The Yong Chung v Barroughs*)) relaxed the reciprocity requirement further. Because many states recognise judgments on a similar basis to Japan's Art 200 of the Civil Procedure Law, reciprocity will often be satisfied. The Japanese courts have recognised judgements of California, Hawaii, Nevada, Switzerland, Washington and Texas but not those of Belgium.

Possibly reciprocity is also required in: 23–25

— China: Law of Civil Procedure 1982 Art 204

— Spain: CCP Arts 952–3, but see Art 954

— Korea

Fair trial without fraud

It is invariably a requirement that the requirements of a fair trial were satis-   23–26
fied, e.g. the defendant was given adequate notice of the proceedings, had an opportunity to be heard and that the basic rules of natural justice were observed.

The Fifth and Fourteenth Amendments of the United States Constitution insist upon due process. The requirements of a fair trial were elaborated upon in the leading United States Supreme Court decision of *Hilton v Guyot*, 159 US 113, 202 (1895) as follows:

> "there has been opportunity for a full and fair trial abroad before a court of competent jurisdiction, conducting the trial upon regular proceedings, after due citation or voluntary appearance of the defendant, and under a system of jurisdiction likely to secure an impartial administration of justice between the citizens of its own country and those of other countries, and there is nothing to show either prejudice in the court or in the system of laws under which it was sitting or fraud in procuring the judgment".

The fact that the foreign judgment has been obtained by fraud will generally be a bar to enforcement. Many international conventions do not specifically provide for the impeachment of judgments on the ground of fraud since this falls within the general exception of judgments objectionable on grounds of public policy.

But in the US the absence in the foreign court of a jury trial, or testimony under oath or cross-examination do not usually connote unfair trial.

Technical distinctions may be made between "extrinsic" and "intrinsic" fraud. Intrinsic fraud is one which occurred during the course of the trial, e.g. perjury. Extrinsic fraud exists when "the unsuccessful party has been prevented from exhibiting fully his case": *US v Throckmorton*, 98 US 61 (1878). Examples are bribing a witness or fabricating evidence.

Due notice of proceedings

23–27   Failure to serve process on the defendant or to give him time to prepare a defence are commonly grounds to refuse enforcement, e.g. in Belgium, England, Germany and the United States. Many countries permit service of process by substituted methods, e.g. notice upon a statutory official or by publication. When it comes to enforce a foreign judgment based on such notice, the enforcement may fail because the fact of the proceedings must actually have been drawn to the attention of the defendant. The leading case on the subject in the United States is *Mullane v Central Hanover Bank and Trust Co*, 339 US 306 (1950) where the requirements of due notice are authoritatively reviewed.

23–28   Standards have been set by the Hague Convention on the Service Abroad of Judicial and Extra-Judicial Documents in Civil or Commercial Matters of November 15, 1965.

Default judgments – rendered in default of appearance by a defendant who was duly served – are usually eligible, but not in Spain unless the non-appearance was "tactical".

> In *Adams v Cape Industries plc* [1990] Ch 433, CA, it was held that the judgment of a United States Federal Court for asbestosis tort damages was impeachable on the ground that it offended English views of substantial justice. The judgment was contrary to natural justice because the defendants were entitled under US law to a judicial assessment, and they did not have one; the award of damages was arbitrary and not based on evidence. The judgment was, in addition, not enforceable against those defendants who had not been given notice of the claims, because justice required that notice of the claims be given to a defendant.

If a defendant agreed in advance to submit to the jurisdiction of the foreign court, he cannot complain if he received insufficient notice. His agreement to submit to the jurisdiction is deemed to include an agreement to submit to its rules of procedure. Cases in England, Australia and Canada have so held.

No violation of public policy

It is an invariable requirement that the judgment does not conflict with local   **23–29**
ideas of public policy.

The English courts limit the scope of the public policy defence. Examples
of contracts fouled on grounds of public policy are given in para 14–75 *et
seq*. The main rules in this context are contracts involving trading with the
enemy and contracts which oppose British interests of state, such as financing foreign rebellions, or contracts intended to offend the export/import,
revenue or penal laws of friendly countries, and foreign anti-trust actions
controlled by the Protection of Trading Interests Act 1980.

At common law, there appear to be very few English cases in which   **23–30**
foreign judgments on business contracts have been denied enforcement or
recognition for reasons of public policy. Most of the cases relate to family
matters.

> In *Israel Discount Bank of New York v Hadjipateras* [1983] 3 All ER 129,
> [1984] 1 WLR 137, CA, a bank obtained judgment in default in New York on
> a guarantee. In an action in England by the bank seeking Order 14 summary
> judgment, one of the defendants pleaded that the guarantee had been obtained
> by undue influence. The English court *held* (1) that the English courts could
> refuse to enforce on public policy grounds a judgment obtained by undue
> influence, but (2) that, since the defendant had not raised the undue influence
> defence in New York, he could not do so in England.

German courts have refused recognition on public policy grounds where
the debt was a gambling debt and where a German defendant ran up huge
losses in New York on commodity futures contracts which he could not
enter into in Germany under the Stock Exchange Law: BGH, June 4,1975.

The US courts sharply limit the public policy defence to the most basic
notions of morality and justice.

It seems that many foreign courts will not enforce US judgments for punitive damages or treble damages on public policy grounds: para 23–33.

Money judgments only

Enforcement is generally available only for money judgments and not, for   **23–31**
example, for an injunction or specific performance. This is not usually an
obstacle for financial contracts, but it could be, e.g. where it is desired to
obtain an injunction to stop a contravention of clauses prohibiting charges,
disposals of substantial assets or mergers.

Judgment is not for taxes, fines or penalties

23–32   It is a rule of general application that the courts of one country will not help another country to collect its taxes and will therefore not enforce judgments which are for foreign tax claims: para 16–11.

This excludes the possibility of a foreign lender becoming subject to foreign enforcement of local judgments for taxes exacted by the borrower's jurisdiction. On the other hand it is thought that a claim by a lender for, say, an indemnity in respect of a withholding tax deducted from an interest payment would not be a tax claim within the scope of this limitation: the claim is a private claim in respect of compensation for taxes and not a claim by the foreign authorities to collect their taxes.

23–33   Nor will courts enforce a foreign penalty. A penalty in this sense normally means a sum payable to the state and not to a private plaintiff so that an award of punitive or exemplary damages may not be penal in England. However s 5 of the Protection of Trading Interests Act 1980 prohibits the enforcement in the UK courts of foreign judgments for multiple damages and other foreign judgments specified by statutory instrument as concerned with restrictive trade practices. The section was primarily intended as a retaliation against United States anti-trust actions. There has been similar legislation in Australia and Canada. The IBA Survey doubts that US treble damages would be enforceable in Germany or France.

Article 200(3) of the Japanese Code of Civil Procedure requires compliance of the foreign judgment with the public policy of Japan and US judgments for punitive damages offend this policy.

> In *Northcon I v Mansei Kogyo Kabushiki Kaisha*, 1376 Hanrei Jiho 79, Tokyo District Court, February 18, 1991, the plaintiff obtained a judgment in California requiring the defendant to pay damages including punitive damages. The plaintiff sought approval to enforce the judgment of the California court. *Held*: the enforcement of the California judgment to the extent of punitive damages conflicted with the public policy of Japan. This decision was upheld by the Tokyo High Court, *Hanrei Times* 823–126, June 28, 1993. See also the *Kansai-Tekko Case* (361) Hanta 127.

Judgment is final and conclusive

23–34   It is a common requirement that the judgment was final and conclusive but jurisdictions differ in their attitude where the foreign judgment is appealable. In England (usually) and the United States the possibility of an appeal does not at common law prevent enforcement but the court has a discretion to stay enforcement until the appeal has been heard: *Hearst v Hearst*, 150

NYS 2d 746 (1955) (S Ct) and ss 2 and 6 of the Uniform Foreign Money-Judgments Recognition Act. In France it is enough if the foreign judgment is provisionally enforceable notwithstanding that an appeal may be in the offing and Belgium agrees. In Germany on the other hand it appears that the possibility of an appeal precludes enforcement: Code of Civil Procedure (ZPO) Art 723(2). This also is true of Japan.

No conflict with local judgment

Special rules apply where a foreign judgment conflicts with another judgment. A plaintiff who is pursuing (and is allowed to pursue – see para 20–5) several concurrent suits in different jurisdictions for the same debt may end up with different results, i.e. lose in one country and win in another because of, say, conflicting attitudes to the rules of private international law on the issue in dispute. The enforcing court may not permit him to choose the favourable judgment for enforcement. The position is too detailed to summarise.

23–35

Currency of enforced judgment

Where a foreign judgment is given by the court of origin in a foreign currency, the enforcing court may nevertheless convert the judgment into local currency under its normal rules. If the conversion date is before the date of payment and the local currency is depreciating, the creditor suffers a loss. The English courts can now give judgments in foreign currency at common law and foreign judgments are registered in foreign currencies under both the 1920 Act and the 1933 Act, referred to at para 23–8 *et seq*. According to the IBA Survey, countries which either order payment in foreign currency or require the plaintiff to be paid in sufficient local currency to buy the foreign currency of the judgment at the date of payment appear to include Belgium, France, Germany, Italy, the Netherlands, Ontario (see Courts of Justice Act s 131), Japan and Korea. Switzerland appears to convert at the date of the order for payment: LDEB Art 67(1) no 3. Whether the rule that conversion at the date of the original judgment still applies in Australia (see *MAN v Altikar Pty Ltd* (1984) 3 NSWLR 152), New Zealand and Singapore should be checked.

23–36

In the United States, the usual rule (modified in New York) is that judgments are rendered only in US dollars converted at the date of the judgment granting enforcement: e.g. *Competex SA v LaBow*, 783 F 2d 333 (2d Cir 1986).

Even if foreign currency is ordered, payment may be restricted by exchange controls.

CHAPTER 24

PRE-JUDGMENT ATTACHMENTS

Generally

24–1   All the developed jurisdictions provide methods for the enforcement of judgments by execution over the property of the judgment debtor. There is considerable convergence in principle, although divergence in matters of detail.

But final execution over the assets of a major debtor in the international markets is extremely unusual, either because a consensual private restructuring of the debt is agreed amongst the banks or, if this is hopeless, because the debtor is put in liquidation. Few creditors will tolerate a situation where some creditors steal a march on the others by seizing assets and the inevitable result of this type of creditor activity is a petition to impose the hierarchy of the bankruptcy distribution. The most common example however of seizures of assets has occurred in relation to sovereign states which, by reason of revolutions or the like, have repudiated their international debts and which of course cannot seek refuge in a bankruptcy freeze since the bankruptcy laws cannot apply to them.

On the other hand, prejudgment or provisional attachments of the assets of a debtor to prevent assets being swept out of the jurisdiction in advance of judgment or restructuring agreement or liquidation are much more common. The reason for this is that creditors are often understandably concerned that assets will be dissipated by being moved to jurisdictions where they either cannot be followed or where the creditors will have no jurisdiction over the debtors. The objective of preservative or protective orders is to stop this happening and is intended to preserve the status quo. It is therefore worth outlining briefly the international attitudes to these provisional attachments.

Availability of provisional attachments

24–2   It would appear that all of the leading jurisdictions contemplate an application to the court by a creditor prior to the commencement of proceedings for an order prohibiting a debtor from removing assets from the jurisdiction. Claims can be made even where the amount of the debt is not certain. Examples are:

— England and many of the English-based states have the Mareva injunction after a maritime case of that name. The Mareva injunction is available in such countries as Canada, Australia, Ireland and New Zealand, as well as (probably) the numerous English-based states or colonies such as Hong Kong, Singapore, Bermuda, the Cayman Islands, India and Malaysia. The English courts have extended the ambit of the Mareva injunction to include assets situated in foreign jurisdictions (world-wide Mareva injunctions) although the cases in which it will do so are limited. See below.

— The *saisie conservatoire* or *saisie arrêt* available in France and, no doubt, many of the French-based jurisdictions, as well as the central Francophone states such as Belgium and Luxembourg. This procedure is mandated by Arts 48–56 of the French Code of Civil Procedure of 1806 and Arts 557–579 of the New Code of Civil Procedure 1972. See also Belgium, CCP Arts 1413–1428 and 1445–1460; Luxembourg, CCP Arts 806–811 and 557–567.

— The German *Arrest* which is mandated by ZPO ss 916–927. It appears   **24–3** that this is also found in Austria and Switzerland.

— The Dutch *Conservatoir beslag*: CCP Arts 700–767

— Italy – *sequestro conservativo*: CCP Arts 669–700

— Greece – *asfalisika metra*: CC Arts 682–721

— Japan – *kari-sashiosae*

— Denmark – the *arrest* under the Administration of Justice Act (*Retsplejeloven*) 1916, ss 627–640

— China (it is believed)

— Spain: *embargo preventivo*: Civil Procedure Act (*Ley de Enjuiciamiento Civil*) Arts 1397–1428

— Portugal: *arresto*: Procedural Code Arts 407–07

— United States: a prejudgment attachment which is mandated by the procedural rules of most of the US states

Conditions of availability

Generally the application for the restraining order has to be made by the   **24–4** creditor by way of ambush without the debtor knowing because, if the debtor were to be aware of the proceedings, it is obvious that the debtor would simply whisk his assets out of the jurisdiction before the creditor could obtain his restraining order. Hence there cannot be any sort of hearing in which the debtor's position can be heard. As a consequence courts routinely impose reasonably high standards of disclosure and proof upon creditors who are generally obliged to show that there are some grounds for believing the debtor has assets within the jurisdiction (and should try to identify where and what they are) and that there are serious grounds for believing that circumstances are such that if an injunction was not granted, the defendant is likely to remove his assets from the jurisdiction or dissipate them within it. A creditor must show that he has a good prima facie claim and the grounds for making an urgent application, and, in many jurisdictions, the creditor will be under an obligation to disclose all material facts to the court as the application is heard in the debtor's absence.

In some jurisdictions, such as Spain and Japan, arrests will only be granted when the creditor has exhausted any security already pledged to him by the debtor: this might result in fatal delays.

Subject to this, it would seem that in the leading developed nations, these applications can be made and granted within a matter of hours. This is certainly so in the English Commercial Court and in the French Tribunals in Paris.

Security for costs and damages

24–5   It is invariably the case that the creditor is liable in damages to the debtor if an order is made and it turns out that the order is unjustified because the creditor's claim is groundless. A freeze on the debtor's ability to use its bank account, for example, could have cataclysmic effects on its business and therefore the damages for a wrongful application could be very considerable. Often the main difference between jurisdictions is the punishment they inflict upon creditor action and how expansive they are in awarding damages. In Germany damages for loss of profits are available. In Denmark damages for loss of reputation and loss of credit facilities can be recovered: Administration of Justice Act 1916 s 639.

Further, especially if the creditor seeking the order is foreign and has no significant assets within the court's jurisdiction, the court may require the creditor to deposit cash security or to obtain a bank bond or guarantee as security for any damages which the debtor may suffer. As examples of the amounts involved, Nova Scotia in Canada requires an amount equal to $1\frac{1}{4}$ times the value of the property sought to be attached with two sufficient sureties or other sufficient security. The Geneva courts generally impose a security requirement of 10 per cent of the claim. On occasions, security may be ordered to obtain a release of the attachment at the debtor's request, as in

Switzerland and Thailand. Security is routinely required of applicants, whether local or foreign, in Chile, Taiwan, Mexico, Philippines and Argentina. Most courts have jurisdiction to order the provision of security should circumstances require it.

If the creditor's evidence is insufficient to justify the grant of an injunction, in many countries the court may still sanction the order if the applicant provides security: Germany (ZPO Art 921) Japan, Chile, Taiwan, Italy. 24–6

The creditor may also be required to pay the expenses of any banks or other persons on whom the order is served in implementing it. This is the position, for example, in England, and in many of the English-based systems like Hong Kong and New Zealand.

In many jurisdictions the court will fix an amount which the debtor may deposit by way of security to obtain the lifting of the arrest. This is the case in Germany, Switzerland, France, Belgium, Argentina and the Philippines.

Jurisdiction

It is usually the case that the court must be satisfied that the court will have jurisdiction over the debtor in the case of a main action. The main heads of jurisdiction have been briefly summarised above, e.g. submission to jurisdiction, carrying on business locally, nationality of plaintiff in the Francophone countries, toothbrush or umbrella jurisdiction in the Germanic and Scandinavian countries, as well as Japan, and the various versions of long-arm jurisdictional rules in the Anglo-American countries, such as fleeting presence and "contract breach within the jurisdiction". Whether or not the excessive or long-arm jurisdictional bases are available often involves the application of forum non conveniens doctrines. 24–7

It is obvious therefore that those countries which adopt the toothbrush or umbrella jurisdiction based upon the presence of local assets are more favourable to the availability of these prejudgment attachments because the very availability of local assets – on which the application is inevitably grounded – is sufficient to give jurisdiction without hunting around for some other basis of jurisdiction.

However there is an important exception to the above. As has been seen, under the European Judgments Conventions the normal rule is that defendants must be sued at their domicile, subject to exceptions, including contracting-out under Art 17. However under Art 24 of the Conventions preservative measures against a debtor are not affected by this rule and it is possible for these preservative measures to be taken throughout the contracting states in support of an order made by a state with primary jurisdiction over the creditor's claim. When the judgment is obtained in the main forum prescribed by the Convention, the creditor can avail himself of the assets which have been blocked in all of the other countries. The result is that compulsory jurisdiction in a single state does not prejudice interim measures elsewhere.

Assets available

24–8   The assets available for protection are usually limited to those which could be removed from the jurisdiction. The debtor cannot move land or a building, although he could sell the land; but many jurisdictions allow the attachment of immovable property by registration – a slower process.

Orders are usually available in respect of bank deposits (by far the most important blocked asset), securities and the like. In Nova Scotia any share, bond, debenture or other interest of a defendant in a body corporate may be attached. In New Zealand, a creditor may attach any shares held by a debtor in any New Zealand company or overseas company having an office in New Zealand in which transfers of shares may be registered. However in Greece bank deposits are virtually unattachable as third parties are required to acknowledge formally that they hold the debtor's assets in order to render the order effective and Greek bank secrecy laws render any such disclosure of a customer's affairs a criminal offence. In some jurisdictions, assets in third party hands can only be attached if they can be clearly identified by the creditor, for example, in Denmark, Liechtenstein, Netherlands and Switzerland.

24–9   In some jurisdictions the arrest is limited to assets held by third parties at the time when the order is served. For example, in France a bank can open a new account for the debtor without risk if the entries on the account do not pre-date the *saisie arrêt*.

However, apart from the usual list of assets which are not attachable and which relate mainly to individuals, e.g. earnings and pensions, most of the leading jurisdictions restrict a party from attaching sums payable under letters of credit, first demand bank guarantees and surety bonds. The objective of this is to maintain the liquidity and certainty of these instruments as payment obligations essential to confidence in international trade. The subject is discussed in another volume in this series.

Generally the assets remain in the hands of the debtor or third party. Exceptions include Brazil, Taiwan, Greece, Austria, Portugal where the assets are held by a court-appointed custodian.

The granting of an arrest rarely grants the applicant priority over other creditors in the event of the debtor's insolvency: for this, the creditor must obtain a final judgment and order of execution before the opening of the proceedings and must also usually have completed the execution. However, in Uruguay, Liechtenstein and Portugal an arrest does give priority.

Set-off

If a deposit owed by a bank to its customer is attached by a creditor of the   24–10
customer, the question arises as to whether the bank can set off a loan, say,
owed by its customer as against the attaching creditor. If the bank is unable
to set off, then it is surprised and the security function of set-off rendered
futile. The international position is complex and is reviewed in another
volume in this series. One question is whether in the Franco-Latin countries
a contract of set-off can beat the attaching creditor: normally the set-off is
not available in these countries against the attaching creditor unless the set-
off had actually accrued by both debts becoming due and payable before
notice of the attachment. This is of course impossible to know in advance.

Discovery

In England, a Mareva injunction may be granted together with an order that   24–11
that defendant disclose the full value and whereabouts of his assets wherever they are situated. Such an order is ancillary to the Mareva injunction
itself. This principle appears also to apply equally to world-wide Mareva
injunctions. The court has the power to order a bank not party to the proceedings to disclose the state of the account of a customer and documents
relating to the account, where the plaintiff's claim against the customer is a
tracing claim.

In Germany, if the assets frozen are insufficient to satisfy the creditor's
claim the debtor may be required to identify his assets on oath.

A problem for large or international banks is their duty to inform all of
their branches of the presence of the order and the degree of diligence which
they must exercise.

Freezing of world-wide assets

A number of recent English cases have shown that the courts will be pre-   24–12
pared to freeze the assets of a debtor wherever they are situated. It is, however, rare for the court to make a world-wide Mareva injunction and the
three English cases that extended the jurisdiction of a Mareva to foreign jurisdictions all concerned claims for £10 million or more. The court must have
jurisdiction over the debtor himself either because being an individual he is

present within the jurisdiction or is a company doing business through a branch locally or incorporated locally. A proviso is inserted into the order (the Babanaft proviso – after *Babanaft International Co SA v Bassatne* [1990] Ch 13) which provides that, where the order purports to have extra-territorial effect, no person shall be affected by it until it is declared enforceable by a foreign court and then it shall only affect to the extent of such declaration or enforcement unless the affected person is : (a) the defendant or other party to the proceedings in which the order is granted, or (b) persons who are subject to the jurisdiction of the English court, have been give notice of the order and are able to prevent breaches of the order outside England and Wales.

In *Derby v Weldon* [1990] Ch 48, CA the first two defendants were formerly directors of two of the plaintiff companies. The plaintiffs, all companies in a large group of associated companies, sought substantial damages, inter alia, for breach of contract, alleging that the defendants, contrary to their obligations to the plaintiffs, had dealt in commodities on their own behalf on a large scale world-wide, and had allowed the plaintiff to suffer huge trading losses. The plaintiffs sought Mareva injunctions freezing and ordering disclosure to the defendants of assets up to the value of $25 million both inside and outside the jurisdiction. *Held*: in view of the very large sum involved, the insufficiency of English assets, the existence of foreign assets and the finding that there was a real risk that they would be dissipated before trial, it was appropriate as a matter of justice to the plaintiffs to make a pre-judgment world-wide Mareva injunction, but that such an order would only be made in an exceptional case.

In *Republic of Haiti v Duvalier* [1991] QB 202, CA, the plaintiffs started proceedings in France (where the defendants were resident) to recover US$120 million alleged to be the Republic's money embezzled by the defendants, former rulers of Haiti. The plaintiffs also issued a writ in England claiming orders restraining the defendants from disposing of certain of their assets. *Held*: there is jurisdiction to grant a Mareva injunction, pending trial, over assets world-wide, although the cases where it would be appropriate to grant such an injunction would be rare.

24–13   The attitude of foreign jurisdictions will depend upon their view about foreign judgments. The reciprocal enforcement of final foreign judgments is examined at para 23–1 *et seq*, but it will be seen from that analysis that a judgment must usually be final and non-appealable for it to receive recognition in foreign states. There appears to be no instance of recognition being given to the prejudgment attachment orders of one state other than under the European Judgments Conventions and (curiously) in Paraguay where legislation provides that the court must enforce preventative orders of foreign courts if those measures are consistent with the laws of Paraguay and the applicant gives security. Also in Uruguay recognition will be given if reciprocal recognition will be given by the foreign court.

The way in which courts ensure that their orders are enforced is, so far as England is concerned, by contempt of court penalties upon the debtor personally if he does not ensure that the assets remain frozen, for what this is worth. In Belgium and Luxembourg criminal sanctions for breach are not available although the defendant can be fined. Both fines and imprisonment can be ordered in Italy, Portugal, Denmark and Germany.

PART IV

INTERNATIONAL PAYMENT SYSTEMS

CHAPTER 25

PAYMENT SYSTEMS: INTRODUCTION

Generally

This section deals with international transfers of money, mainly large-value **25–1** credit transfers. It is not proposed to consider retail payments, credit cards, or the law relating to cheques or bills of exchange, nor is it proposed to describe the detail of particular national payment systems or giros beyond the principles.

The amounts involved in credit transfers are huge and annually are a many times multiple of the total GNP of the entire world. Cashless payments are thought to be 180 times GNP in Switzerland, but only 10 times GNP in Italy. Foreign exchange transactions probably account for about 85 per cent of total net market turnover between banks. The average turnover in foreign exchange markets in April 1992 was estimated by the BIS at US$880 billion per day. The actual number of transfers is also gigantic. The average cheque amount is small but there are billions of them. The average commercial transfer is in millions, but there are less of them. The amount of actual cash transferred in terms of value is probably less than one per cent of the total in the major industrialised countries – a negligible amount.

This brief review would seem to indicate that the law in developed countries on payment systems is highly refined, with many issues having been presented to the courts. This is not to say that the solutions are what people want. It would also seem that many questions can be answered by applying elementary principles of the law of contract and agency, modified by the less elementary principles of insolvency law and conflicts of law. But much further work needs to be done to assemble and compare the various approaches.

Bank money

In international financial markets debtors pay their creditors by "bank **25–2** money". In other words, a debtor arranges for the beneficiary's bank account to be credited with the amount due. Debtors do not pay by legal tender, e.g. handing over a sackful of notes, or by employing a Wells Fargo coach and horses.

Where payment to a beneficiary's bank account is permitted, payment is the conferring of an unconditional claim in favour of the creditor against a bank acceptable to the creditor in the amount of the agreed payment. Payment is not made in full if the creditor could not withdraw the funds immediately without having to pay interest so that the creditor does not receive the full amount: *The Chikuma* [1981] 1 All ER 652, HL.

The claim of a creditor against his bank constitutes a debtor-creditor relationship. The bank is the debtor which owes the amount of the deposit to its customer as the creditor. Any money which was paid into the account by the creditor can be used by the bank as its own: the bank does not have to set that money aside in kind nor hold it as custodian for the creditor. This proposition is universally accepted; see for example, *Joachinsom v Swiss Bank Corpn* [1921] 3 KB 110, CA (England); *Gullas v The Philippines National Bank*, 62 Phil 519 (1935) (Philippines); *Royal Trust Co v Molsons Bank* (1912) 27 OLR 441(Ontario).

Payment in cash

25–3   Whether or not a debtor who agrees to pay in cash can pay by arranging for the beneficiary's bank account to be credited instead of handing over legal tender in the form of notes and coins is a matter of construction of the agreement.

The general principle accepted by most developed jurisdictions is that a creditor is entitled to be paid in cash, i.e. notes and coins, unless the right to cash has been waived or varied by the contract. This is the position in England: see for example *Libyan Arab Foreign Bank v Bankers Trust Co* [1989] 3 WLR 314, 347. In general in England the courts are very ready to treat an agreement to pay "cash" as meaning bank money, i.e. payment by credit to the beneficiary's bank account in an appropriate case: see, for example, *The Brimnes* [1972] 2 Lloyd's Rep 465, 476.

25–4   If the creditor has not agreed to this means of payment he takes the solvency risk of a bank instead of receiving real money in the form of notes and coins. The notes represent a claim against the central bank. But if the creditor nevertheless expressly or impliedly accepts the bank money, then the debt is discharged. For example Art 118(2) of the Italian Civil Code provides that payment to a party not authorised to receive the payment discharges the debt if the creditor subsequently approves the payment or derives a benefit from it. Withdrawal of the bank credit or possibly failure to object for a sufficiently long period would normally be an acceptance of the bank credit. In Switzerland bank money is not payment of a money debt but a creditor may expressly or impliedly consent to payment by means of bank money. This will especially be the case where it would be unreasonable to require the debtor to pay in cash as in the case of an international transfer. A creditor will impliedly accept payment by cash where he provides the name of his bank and account number or if he accepts a payment of bank money without objection within a reasonable time.

Payment in foreign currency

The consensus of developed systems appears to be that, where a debt is   25–5
expressed in foreign currency, the debtor may pay in the foreign currency concerned or in the domestic currency converted at the local market rate of exchange. However an express or implied agreement to pay in the foreign currency is valid and is not against public policy. This is the position in England for example: see para 15–4.

In Germany s 244(1) of the BGB states:

> "If a money debt expressed in a foreign currency is payable within the country, payment may be made in the currency of such country unless payment in the foreign currency is expressly stipulated."

In Japan, CC Art 403 provides that a debtor can pay in Japanese currency at the exchange rate at the place of performance unless otherwise agreed. It was held in a Japanese Supreme court decision of July 15, 1975 that a creditor can demand a foreign currency claim either in the foreign currency or in yen.

In Switzerland CO Art 84 provides that foreign obligations must be paid   25–6
in national currency but if the contract provides for a currency which is not legal tender at the place of payment, the debt may be paid in national currency, according to its value at the date of maturity, unless, through the use of the term "effective" or another similar addition, literal performance of the contract has been agreed upon.

In Italy, CC Art 1278 provides that a debtor may choose to pay foreign currency in legal tender in the State but Art 1279 excludes this option if the foreign currency is indicated by an "effective" clause or other equivalent clause, unless it is not possible to acquire such currency at the maturity of the obligation.

The general rule in the Netherlands appears to be that a debtor may elect to pay local currency if the debt is payable in the Netherlands, unless there is an agreement to the contrary.

Place of payment

25–7   In the absence of agreement, jurisdictions are divided as to whether the place of payment is the residence of the creditor or the residence of the debtor. In the context of banks, payment at the residence of the debtor would mean that the bank pays deposits at the branch at which the deposit- or's account is kept.

There is much discussion in the academic literature as to which solution is the most reasonable. But, however interesting this discussion, it is not of much relevance in international finance when usually it is perfectly clear that the payment is to be made to a particular bank. The residence of the debtor or creditor are irrelevant. The point only tends to become of signifi- cance in deciding the lex situs of the debt, especially bank deposits, for the purposes of attachments, expropriations and assignability and for the pur- poses of determining illegality at the place of performance.

Codes governing international bank transfers

25–8   One country at least has codified the law relating to funds transfers. This is the United States which sets out rules for high volume non-consumer pay- ments in Art 4A of the Uniform Commercial Code. This is a companion to the Electric Funds Transfer Act of 1978 (15 USC s 1693 *et seq*) which con- tains elaborate consumer protections. Article 4A applies to high volume commercial payments and does not apply to consumer related transfers which are covered by EFTA.

The United Nations Commission on International Trade Law (UNCI- TRAL) adopted a Model Law on International Credit Transfers in May 1992, but for various reasons many states consider this model law to be defective. Its future remains to be seen.

Towards the end of 1990 the International Chamber of Commerce in Paris recommended its Guidelines on International Interbank Funds Transfers and Compensation (ICC Publication No 457). The ICC guidelines are not greatly favoured in industrialised countries.

The result therefore is that payment systems are governed either by the contracts between the parties concerned or, in the absence of contract, by ordinary principles of law, which in both cases are overridden by the man- datory provisions of bankruptcy law.

Definition of parties to a credit transfer

25–9   Following international usage, one may refer to the parties to a credit transfer as follows:

Originator The person who proposes to make a payment, e.g. typically a debtor such as a borrower, buyer or lessee.

Originator's bank This is the originator's bank which transmits the first payment order for a transfer of funds.

Beneficiary This is the person receiving the payment, usually the creditor.

Beneficiary's bank This is the bank of the creditor or beneficiary of the debt which is to be paid.

Intermediary bank This is a bank between the originator's bank and the beneficiary's bank through which a payment order passes.

Sender This is a bank which sends a payment order. It may be the originator's bank or an intermediary bank.

Receiving bank This is a bank which receives a payment order. It may be an intermediary bank or the beneficiary's bank.

Payment order This is a message or instruction to make a payment.

Payment This is the conferring of an unconditional claim against a bank in favour of the creditor. Payment is sometimes referred to as "settlement" or "cover".

The terms "originator" and "beneficiary" are employed in international   **25–10** usage instead of debtor and creditor in order to cover gifts, salary remittances by foreign workers and other non-contractual payments.

To put these terms into context, if a creditor wishes to pay his debtor by bank money, then the creditor as originator instructs his bank – the originator's bank – by a payment order to pay the creditor as beneficiary. The originator's bank may instruct its correspondent bank – the intermediary bank – to make the payment and the intermediary bank in turn instructs the beneficiary's bank to credit the account of the creditor beneficiary. Each instruction is by means of a payment order and the bank which sends a payment order is the sender and the bank which receives a payment order is a receiving bank.

The payment itself in each case is made when the receiving bank becomes entitled to a claim against another bank acceptable to it in the full amount of the payment order.

Payment orders

25–11   As mentioned, a payment order is the instruction to make a funds transfer. This can be in any form, e.g. letter, telephone, computer message from the originator's terminal linked to the bank's computer, the handing over of tapes containing computer-readable messages (often used for salaries) or alternatively some form of paper such as a cheque, direct debit order, bankers draft or bill of exchange. Each payment order is initially directed to the originator's bank. However a distinction may be made between credit transfers and debit transfers. In the case of a credit transfer the originator gives the order direct to the originator's bank. In the case of a debit transfer the originator typically gives the order to the beneficiary who then arranges, usually via his bank, for this order to be presented to the originator's bank. For example, an originator debtor may hand his creditor beneficiary a cheque for the amount due which the creditor then sends through his bank for collection at the originator's bank. We are concerned here only with credit transfers which form by far the greatest bulk in terms of amount of funds transfers.

25–12   Note that some payment orders are paperless while others are in the form of paper. The paperless payment order is an electronic message sent between two computers. Payment orders between banks may be transmitted via the banks' computers themselves or more commonly via a private telecommunications system known as S.W.I.F.T. S.W.I.F.T. stands for the Society for Worldwide Interbank Financial Telecommunications and is a bank-owned organisation which has a secure means of sending bank messages electronically. The greatest value of payment orders are sent electronically, but paper-based systems still predominate in many countries.

In practice payment orders must be certain, unconditional and very simple. Banks cannot accept conditional payment orders (e.g. "pay against receipt of the global bond") in the absence of a special arrangement. The result is that payment orders share the policies of bills of exchange which must also be certain, unconditional and simple.

Payment order and payment

25–13   A payment order, when accepted, is a contract to make a payment. Payment itself is the performance of that contract. If a person enters into a contract to pay money, then in English-based jurisdictions failure to perform that contract results in a liability for damages as opposed to specific performance. On normal principles of contract law, the damages are those which naturally flow from the breach of contract plus any special damages which may specifically have been contemplated. If therefore one bank enters into a contract with another bank to make a payment to the other bank and the first bank fails to do so then it may well be that the damages are zero. But if the other bank, in reliance on that contract has credited its customer's account, then the liability of the first bank for failure to make payment would be the full amount. These rules have been well established in English law in relation to contracts to make a loan which the proposed lender fails to carry out.

As already explained, the payment itself is not the handing over of a sackful of notes but rather the establishment of a credit in favour of the beneficiary at a bank acceptable to the beneficiary.

Payment procedures generally

A funds transfer is not an assignment or sale of a claim. The originator does **25–14** not assign the benefit of his deposit at the originator's bank to the beneficiary. A cheque is not an assignment of the customer's credit balance to the holder of the cheque: *Schroeder v Central Bank* (1876) 34 LT 735; Bills of Exchange Act 1882 s 53(1). The "transfer" terminology is pure commercial vernacular. In essence, a funds transfer from originator to beneficiary is a reduction in the credit balance owed by the originator's bank to the originator and an increase in the credit balance owed by the beneficiary's bank to the beneficiary. If both accounts are overdrawn, then the funds transfer is an increase in the debit balance owed by the originator to the originator's bank and a decrease in the debit balance owed by the beneficiary to the beneficiary's bank.

Payment procedure: same branch or same bank

If the originator and beneficiary both have accounts at the same branch of **25–15** the same bank, then the credit transfer is simply effected by that bank branch debiting the account of the originator and crediting the account of the beneficiary.

If the originator and beneficiary both bank at the same bank but at different branches, then the originator's branch debits the account of the originator and the beneficiary's branch credits the account of the beneficiary. The originator's branch simply sends a message to its other branch and no other banks are involved. Intrabank transfers form a high percentage in countries with concentrations of a few banks, e.g. 30 per cent of credit transfers in France.

Payment procedures: international transfers

25–16   Let us say that an originator in London wishes to pay 100 to a beneficiary in Paris by credit transfer. One may ignore the foreign currency element for the moment.

A typical chain of banks could be the originator's bank in London which has a US dollar account with a correspondent intermediary bank in New York which banks with a money centre settlement bank in New York which has an account with the Federal Reserve and is a member of a settlement system known as the Clearing House Interbank Payment System. The settlement bank is the second intermediary bank on the originator's side.

On the beneficiary's side, there is first the beneficiary's bank in Paris which has a US dollar account with a correspondent intermediary bank in New York which in turn has an account with a money centre settlement bank in New York, which has an account with the Federal Reserve.

Hence the chain on the originator's side is three banks: originator's bank, correspondent intermediary bank and correspondent intermediary settlement bank. The chain on the beneficiary side is also three banks: beneficiary's bank, correspondent intermediary bank and correspondent intermediary settlement bank.

At the apex of the triangle is the central bank which has accounts for the two settlement banks.

Sending of payment orders

25–17   The originator sends its payment order to the originator's bank which sends a corresponding payment order to the first intermediary bank which sends a payment order to the second intermediary settlement bank on the beneficiary's side, which sends a payment order to the first intermediary correspondent bank on that side which sends a payment order to the beneficiary's bank. The inter-bank payment orders are usually sent via S.W.I.F.T.

In practice, the payment orders may not follow this strict sequence up one side of the triangle and down the other. For example, the originator's bank may send a payment order direct to the beneficiary's bank and follow up with other payment orders through the chain. But one can ignore this for the present.

Acceptance of payment orders

These payment orders are at this point revocable instructions to pay or, in   **25–18**
contract parlance, offers capable of acceptance. It is immaterial whether one
characterises them as instructions, mandates or directions to an agent, or
authorities – they still result in contracts. As a matter of contract law they
become irrevocable contracts that the sender will pay the receiving bank if
any master interbank contract so provides (or if the banking contract
between the originator and the originator's bank so provides – which is
usually the case by implication if there is enough money in the account) or if
a receiving bank accepts by a return message or acts on the order, e.g. by
debiting the sender's account or crediting the beneficiary's account or by
entering into an irrevocable commitment to another party to pay the
amount of the order.

Again, as a matter of contract law, unless otherwise agreed, each receiving bank could refuse to accept the payment order of the sender, e.g. if the
sender has insufficient funds in its account with the receiving bank to cover
the amount of the payment. The receiving bank accepts the payment order,
either by a message back or by acting on the payment order by sending a
further order down the chain, or by debiting the sender's account, or by
crediting the beneficiary's account, or by some other step required under
contract law to conclude the contract.

Article 4A of the UCC has detailed rules for the action connoting accept-   **25–19**
ance. For example, if a receiving bank does nothing, the payment order is
deemed non-accepted after five days automatically if the sender does not
have money on deposit to cover the order: s 4A–211(d). If the sender does
have sufficient money on deposit and the receiving bank neither accepts nor
rejects, the receiving bank must pay interest on the money until the sender
learns of the non-action or the five days expire. If the receiving bank accepts,
the only way it can do this is by sending on the payment order down the line
to the beneficiary's bank: s 4A–209(a). The objective of these inertia rules is
to reduce the paperwork and hence the cost. The beneficiary's bank is at the
end of the line and so it does not accept by sending. The Article sets out a
number of acts and communications which suffice for an acceptance by the
beneficiary's bank, e.g. the receipt of full payment by the beneficiary's bank
or informing the beneficiary of the receipt of funds for its benefit:
s 4A–209(b).

Thus, at this point, there are a series of payment orders down the line;
some may be revocable offers, while others may have been converted into
irrevocable contracts to pay. Some could be conditional contracts, e.g. conditional on payment being made. It is all a matter of contract law and the
terms of the individual contracts.

Payments by debit and credit

25–20   The next step is payment, which, as stated, is the conferring of an unconditional claim against a bank acceptable to the receiving bank or beneficiary in the full amount of the payment.

Under the classical scheme, the originator's bank debits the account of the originator, the first intermediary bank debits the account of the originator's bank, the second intermediary bank on this side debits the account of the first intermediary bank, the central bank debits the account of the second intermediary bank and credits the account of the second intermediary bank on the beneficiary's side, the second intermediary bank credits the account of the first intermediary bank on this side and the first intermediary bank credits the account of the beneficiary's bank which in turn credits the account of the beneficiary.

If an account is overdrawn, a debit increases the overdrawn balance and a credit decreases the overdrawn balance.

Payment by set-off

25–21   The payment may be made by way of set-off. For example, if the originator's bank owes 100 to the intermediary bank by reason of a payment order and the intermediary bank owes the originator's bank 100, they may set off the reciprocal amounts on the payment date. Set-off is common between settlement banks who accumulate large reciprocal commitments between each other as a result of payment orders. This is discussed further below.

Conditional payment

25–22   Payment may be conditional. For example, the beneficiary's bank may credit the beneficiary's account as soon as it receives a message from the originator's bank of the intended payment, but before the beneficiary's bank has received a claim against a bank acceptable to it, such as a claim against the central bank or its correspondent bank by a credit to its account. If the condition is not fulfilled, the beneficiary's bank debits the account of the beneficiary with the failed payment. If the beneficiary has in the meantime withdrawn the money the debit further depletes the account, so that, if the account becomes overdrawn, the beneficiary's bank runs the risk that the beneficiary may become insolvent.

Payment solely between correspondent banks

25–23   The above summary describes a series of payments which include a debit and credit at accounts maintained at the central bank. Payment need not involve the central bank. For example, both the originator's bank and the beneficiary's bank may have dollar accounts with the same New York correspondent bank. When the payment of 100 is to be made, the common New York correspondent bank may simply debit the account of the originator's bank and credit the beneficiary's bank. The correspondent bank may allow the originator's bank's account to become overdrawn and not require that the originator's bank arrange for a credit in its favour with the Federal Reserve or another New York money centre bank.

In short, therefore payment may be made by debits and credits by correspondent banks or by a credit in favour of the payee by a third party bank – either the central bank or a commercial bank.

Foreign currency payments

Where the originator wishes to make a foreign currency payment abroad, **25–24** then the originator must acquire the foreign currency.

If, say, an originator in London wishes to pay US$100 to a beneficiary in Paris, the originator's bank will purchase the US$100 with sterling and debit the sterling cost to the originator's account. The originator's bank may acquire the US$100 from another bank in the market in which event that other bank will arrange for the US$100 to be credited to an account with a bank in New York acceptable to the originator's bank.

Alternatively, if the originator's bank has a US dollar account with a correspondent bank in New York, the originator's bank will instruct the correspondent bank to debit the account of the originator's bank in the amount of US$100 and in turn the originator's bank will debit the originator's account in the amount of the sterling equivalent.

The payment to the beneficiary in Paris in US dollars will usually be to the beneficiary's bank in New York. If the beneficiary requires French Francs, it must use the US dollar deposit with the beneficiary's bank to buy French Francs and arrange for that to be credited to its account at a bank in France.

Alternatively, the beneficiary's bank in France may be prepared to open a US dollar account in France. In that event the French beneficiary bank will require a claim against a US bank in the dollar amount.

Nostro and loro accounts

Where a foreign bank has an account with a domestic bank in the foreign **25–25** bank's currency, this is called a nostro account from the perspective of the domestic bank and a loro account from the perspective of the foreign bank.

CHAPTER 26

INSOLVENCY RISKS IN PAYMENT SYSTEMS

Summary of main insolvency risks

26–1 The main issues which tend to arise on insolvency of an originator, beneficiary or bank involved in the payment process are:

1. Whether payment orders given to banks as agents or sub-agents are automatically cancelled on the insolvency of the sender or his principal. It seems to be almost universally the case that final liquidation proceedings do cancel mandates to pay if revocable and not already performed.

2. Whether payment has already been made when the guillotine comes down. The time of payment is discussed at para 28–1 *et seq*.

3. Whether the proceedings revoke all payments made after the actual time of the insolvency order or at the beginning of the day on which the order is made and whether the bank is protected if it does not know of the order. Back-dating to zero hour is relatively common and protections to banks by no means universal. Thus in Italy, by BA 1942 Art 78, bankruptcy proceedings against the originator terminate the contract between bank and customer and the bank must stop uncompleted transfers. The bank is deemed to know of the opening of the proceedings even if in fact it is not actually aware of them. In English insolvencies, all dispositions of the insolvent company's property after the commencement of the winding-up are void: IA 1986 s 127. The commencement is usually the time that the petition is presented and there is no back-dating to zero hour on that day. Debits to an account after that time are void: *Re Hone* [1950] 2 All ER 716. Apart from special protections to paying bankers in the case of the insolvency of individuals in IA 1986, s 284, the court has power to validate transactions by banks who paid after petition but before they were aware of the petition but it does not automatically follow that the court will do so: see *Re Gray's Inn Construction Co Ltd* [1980] 1 All ER 814, CA.

4. Whether a bank is liable to return a payment which was a fraudulent

preference by the originator. The law as to preferential transfers is reviewed in another book in this series.

Payment prior to reimbursement

In an ideal world all payments in the chain of banks would be simultaneous,   26–2
that is, each receiving bank on the originator's side would debit the sender simultaneously and each receiving bank on the beneficiary's side would credit the next bank simultaneously, and all the debits and credits would be simultaneous. In that way, no party would be exposed to the risk that it has credited an account but has not been paid.

In practice however, payments tend to take place at periodic intervals in batches, e.g. each night or every few days, depending on the practices and degree of automation of the banks concerned. However the beneficiary may require the money immediately, e.g. because the payment is required for securities or goods sold and the beneficiary will not deliver to its buyer unless its bank account is credited with the price. The money may be required intra-day for margin collateral to be deposited with an exchange or the sale of foreign exchange or to pay for services.

In the result, the beneficiary's bank may credit the beneficiary's account   26–3
immediately before having been paid by a credit to its account with an acceptable bank. In the meantime the beneficiary's bank runs the risk that the sender may become insolvent before it has arranged for the beneficiary's bank to be paid by an acceptable solvent bank. The period of risk of the beneficiary's bank runs from the time at which it credits the beneficiary's account to the time at which an account at a bank acceptable to it is credited – this may be a few hours or days or even longer in paper-based systems or in centres not using telex or other electronic means of communication.

As mentioned, the beneficiary's bank may reserve the right to debit the beneficiary's account by a reversing entry if the beneficiary's bank is not paid, but if in the meantime the beneficiary has withdrawn the money and the debit would cause the beneficiary's account to become overdrawn, the beneficiary's bank has an insolvency exposure to the beneficiary who may be unable to pay back. ✔

Reciprocal payments of foreign exchange: time zones

An insolvency risk arises where two banks agree to exchange currencies   26–4
under a foreign exchange agreement, say, yen for US dollars. The bank delivering the yen may arrange for the yen to be credited to the account of

the counterparty bank at the counterparty's bank in Tokyo at GMT plus eight hours, and the counterparty may become insolvent before it has arranged for an account of the first bank at its New York correspondent bank to be credited with the US dollars in New York at GMT minus eight hours. The gap between yen and US dollar payments exchange is between seven and 16 hours, depending on the system used.

This is sometimes known as the "Herstatt risk", a term derived from the spectacular collapse of a private German bank in the mid–1970s. Herstatt closed its doors after it had received payments German time but before it was due to make payments later in the day New York time.

Insolvency of originator's bank

26–5   If a receiving bank fails after debiting the account of the sender, but before its own account has been debited by the next bank in the chain, the question arises as to whether the sender loses. For example, the originator's bank may debit the originator's account, fail to pay on a payment order to the intermediary bank so that its account with the intermediary bank has not been debited before the originator's bank fails. The originator still has to pay the beneficiary and has lost the money from its account – and so pays twice. The estate of the originator's bank has a windfall because it still has the extra money in its account with the intermediary bank which has not been debited or it has not committed to pay the beneficiary's bank.

26–6   The English courts have on occasion used the constructive trust to assist the originator. There is a substantial body of case law on the topic.

Where the credit is made by an intermediary bank, it has been held that the intermediary bank may hold this credit on trust back to the originator if the originator's bank fails.

> In *Farley v Turner* (1857) 26 LJ Ch 710, an originator deposited money in the originator's bank and instructed it to pay a bill of exchange which would become due within a week at the office of a correspondent beneficiary bank. The originator's bank debited the originator's account and forwarded various bills to an intermediary bank which discounted the bills and paid the proceeds to the correspondent beneficiary bank with instructions to pay the originator's bill of exchange. Before anything further happened the originator's bank failed. *Held*: the originator was entitled to payment in full from the correspondent beneficiary bank and was not compelled to prove with the general creditors of the originator's bank. The reason given was that the money paid into the originator's bank was to be applied in a particular way. It is suggested that the proper explanation is that, although the originator's bank at the outset was

under a merely personal contract liability to the originator, when it sent money to its correspondent beneficiary bank with instructions to pay the originator's debt, it acquired a claim against its correspondent beneficiary bank which was not merely a part of its general assets but was specifically earmarked as held for the benefit of the originator. In other words, the originator's bank had ceased to be under a mere contract liability and had become trustee of its claim against its beneficiary bank. It is true that the beneficiary bank did not become trustee of the money forwarded to it, since it was entitled to use the money as its own; but the beneficiary bank was under a contract duty to the originator's bank, and the rights under the contract were held by the originator's bank in trust for the originator. If the correspondent beneficiary bank had failed, the loss would have fallen upon the originator.

But more usually, the courts have found a debtor-creditor relationship.

In *Johnson v Robarts* (1875) LR 10 Ch App 505, customer D deposited bank notes and bills of exchange with deposit bank D1 with instructions to remit the deposit to a correspondent bank D2 to pay acceptances of the customer D payable at the correspondent bank D2. The deposit bank D1 sent some bank notes to the correspondent bank D2 plus the bills with instructions. The deposit bank D1 debited customer D with the bills and notes and credited the correspondent bank D2 with another sum. Deposit bank D1 failed, owing a large sum to the correspondent bank D2. *Held*: customer D had no right to the bills and notes because the correspondent bank was not a trustee of these for D. As between the two banks, the correspondent bank D2 did not know that these bills and the notes were specifically appropriated to meet the acceptances and hence they could claim a lien over them to cover the debt owing to them by deposit bank D1. The case is to be explained either on the ground that deposit bank D1 did not hold any claim on the correspondent bank D2 in trust for its customer D or, if it did, that the trust claim was defeated by the correspondent bank's lien against deposit bank D1. See also *Bolton v Puller* (1796) 1 Bros & P 539; *Re Watson & Co, ex p Lloyd* (1904) 91 LT 665; *Calley v Short* (1815) Coop G 148, affirmed (1821) Jac 631; *Re Broad, ex p Neck* (1884) 13QBD 740; *Re Mills, Bawtree & Co, ex p Stannard* (1893) 10 Morr 193; *Re Barned's Banking Co* (1870) 39 LJ Ch 635.

Some of the old cases on money transmissions are particularly instructive **26–7** and arrived at correct results which are just as relevant now as they were when decided. In one case it was held that where Bank 1, on the instructions of its customer to pay a creditor, pays an agent Bank 2 who pays a sub-agent Bank 3 which uses the payment to discharge a debt owed to it by the agent Bank 2 and then the agent Bank 2 becomes insolvent, the instructing Bank 1 does not have a direct claim against sub-agent Bank 3 unless the payment was impressed with a trust in favour of the ultimate creditor, agreed to by the sub-agent Bank 3, resulting back to Bank 1 on the failure of the transfer – a highly complex analysis.

> In *Grant v Austen* (1816) 3 Price 59, debtor D sent a cheque for £70 to Bank 1 drawn on Bank 2 directing Bank 1 to pay creditor Bank C. Bank 1 sent the cheque to Bank 2. Bank 2 made remittances to its correspondent Bank 3 (as Bank 2's agent) in cash, notes and short bills with directions to make various payments for the account of Bank 2. It was unclear what happened to the cheque. The remittances fell short of those payments and the shortfall was to be debited to Bank 2's account with Bank 3. One of the directed payments was debtor D's £70 requested payment to creditor Bank C. Bank 2 credited its account with Bank 3 with the amount of the remittances. Bank 3 used the remittances to discharge debts owing by Bank 2 and demanded notes payable by Bank 2 which as a result became bankrupt greatly indebted to Bank 3. Bank 1 insisted that Bank 3 refund the £70. *Held*: Bank 3 was not liable to return the money. The reason was that Bank 2, in sending the remittance to Bank 3 had not specifically appropriated the £70 out of the remittances to pay creditor Bank C and, even if they had, Bank 3 had not assented to any appropriation. Wood B said at 67:

> "In order to constitute an appropriation of this sum, there must have been a consent. This is not the case of a specific sum sent for this particular purpose – there is a general sum remitted, with directions to pay various particular sums, but not expressing that those payments should be made out of the sums sent. No notice was given to the persons to whom the money was so directed to be paid"

> In modern terms, the explanation of this decision is that the £70 was not impressed with a trust as a segregated fund which Bank 3 could not use as its own and that, when Bank 2 became bankrupt, Bank 3 had already used the remittances to pay themselves. As a result, Bank 3 owed nothing to Bank 2 and, even if Bank 2 by reason of its insolvency had become a trustee for the benefit of Bank 1 of its claim against Bank 3, there was no property (e.g. in the form of a credit balance) on which the trust could fix. As a result, Bank 3 was not a debtor to Bank 1 for the £70. Further the ultimate payees would have had no claim against Bank 3 since Bank 3 had not committed to pay them.

26–8   A number of decisions have held that if a payment is for a special purpose which cannot be fulfilled because of an insolvency, then the payee holds the money on a resulting trust for the payor. This generally requires that the money must be identifiable or traceable.

In a remarkable Australian case it was held that, as soon as a bank instructed to make a credit transfer for a special purpose debits the customer's account and then becomes insolvent, the bank holds the proceeds on trust for the customer. The case is a manifestation of the "special purpose" trusts of money developed by the courts in common law countries in order to protect creditors by giving them a super-priority bankruptcy claim.

> In *Re City of Melbourne Bank Ltd, ex p The Melbourne & Metropolitan Board of Works* (1895) 21 VLR 563 (Victoria S Ct), the customer had a credit of about £7,600 at its bank and deposited a cheque for that amount (plus an amount for costs) with the bank requesting the bank to transmit the money to England to pay interest on debentures issued by the customer. The bank debited the customer's account and then went into liquidation without paying the interest. *Held*: the bank held the money as property of the customer who could recover it in full. Holroyd J said at 570:

> "It has been admitted in argument that if the Board had brought to the Bank the amount of the cheque in cash, and given the instructions contained in the letter of the 17th of May, and the Bank had undertaken to act in accordance with those instructions, the fiduciary relation of agent and principal would have been established between the Bank and the Board on the Bank receiving the cash. What happened was that the Board was debited with the amount of the cheque at the time when the Bank undertook to act according to the instructions in the letter. The meaning of that debiting could only be one thing – that the Bank had honoured the cheque. In honouring the cheque it did not, of course, take so much cash out of one of its hands, so to speak, and put it into the other, but it virtually appropriated a particular sum of money to the specific purpose to which the Board had required it to be appropriated and to the extent of that cheque it diminished the fund on which the Board could operate. If the Bank had been paying interest for the use of the Board's money it would also have diminished the amount of the interest which the Bank would have had to pay from the very day on which the Board was debited with the amount of the cheque. We fail to appreciate the distinction which has been drawn between handing over so much cash and doing that which was done in this case and it is the exact equivalent of it."

But the real reason for the decision was probably that the bank had debited the customer's account without matching this with a corresponding liability to pay so that the creditors of the insolvent bank would receive a windfall. It is not the case that all special purposes payments impress the money with a trust or create a proprietary claim, since otherwise all payments would create a proprietary claim on the insolvency of the bank since all payments are for a special purpose.

A few English cases have held that, where a payment is made for a special   26–9
purpose and the originator's bank fails still holding the paper, the paper and its proceeds may be held on trust for the beneficiary, but this is most unusual. See, for example, *Re Harrison, ex p Carrick* (1858) 2 De G&J 208; contrast *Hill v Royds* (1869) LR 8 Eq 290; *WP Greenhalgh & Sons v Union*

Bank of Manchester [1924] 2 KB 153 (on the facts the originator had assigned the benefit of his deposit account at the bank to his creditor).

Insolvency of beneficiary's bank

26–10   If the beneficiary's bank, as agent of the beneficiary, or an intermediary sub-agent bank of the beneficiary becomes insolvent, the English courts have been readier to find a trust relationship, notably in cases involving collections. For example, if the beneficiary's bank becomes insolvent before its account has been credited by the intermediary bank, any subsequent credit to its account by the intermediary bank may be held by the beneficiary's bank on trust for the beneficiary who thereby has a direct claim against the intermediary bank. But if the intermediary bank has credited the beneficiary's bank and then the beneficiary's bank becomes insolvent, the beneficiary bank does not hold its claim against the intermediary bank on trust for the beneficiary and the beneficiary cannot leap-frog over his insolvent bank.

> In *Re Farrow's Bank Ltd* [1923] 1 Ch 41, CA, a customer P deposited a cheque drawn on bank D with deposit bank A for collection. Bank A credited customer P with the proceeds of the cheque but this was not a purchase of a cheque and they reserved the right not to permit a drawing against the cheque until it had been cleared. Bank A used sub-agent bank SA as its clearing agent. Bank SA credited the amount of the cheque to bank A subject to the cheque being met by bank D, i.e. this was also a conditional credit and the deposit bank A could not use the cash as its own. It was not a question of the deposit bank A being subject to a duty to pay back if the cheque was not met but being in the meantime in the position to use the money as its own. The cheque was sorted in the clearing house, presented to bank D's branch and bank D's branch advised bank D's head office that the cheque would be met. This was on a Saturday. At 8.30 a.m. on the next Monday – the crucial date – deposit bank A stopped payment. On the same day bank D – which was a clearing bank – then settled with sub-agent bank SA through the clearing, i.e. bank SA's account with the Bank of England was credited with the cheque and bank D's account debited and bank SA advised the deposit bank A that the cheque was cleared. This was done at 12.30 p.m. At 2.20 p.m. a petition to wind up the deposit bank A was presented and a winding up order was made some time later. If deposit bank A had been paid before the insolvency, then deposit bank A would be a debtor to customer P; if after the insolvency, deposit bank A would hold the proceeds on trust for customer P who would then have a proprietary claim. *Held*: customer P had a proprietary claim because deposit bank A stopped payment prior to clearance of the cheque and could no longer deal with any further proceeds of collection as its own. The liquidator of deposit Bank A was ordered to pay out of the assets the full amount of the cheque. The notice of intention to stop payment was the critical point, not the petition to wind up. The sub-agent bank SA had not been paid at 8.30 a.m. but only at 12.30 p.m. when the transfer took place at the

Bank of England. The fact that the sub-agent bank SA credited deposit bank A prior to the clearing and prior to the stoppage was not a payment to the deposit bank A by the sub-agent bank SA because the deposit bank A was not entitled to draw upon the credit and deal with the money as they pleased. The position would have been different if deposit bank A had purchased the cheque because the customer P would merely have had a money claim on deposit bank A. The case is vague in its analysis of the identification of the trust property. The proper solution is that the trust property was the benefit of deposit bank A's claim against bank SA.

Other cases have held that if a customer deposits negotiable paper for col-   **26–11**
lection (such as a promissory note, a bond, a draft or a cheque) with his bank, presumptively the beneficial interest in the paper is retained by the customer until collection and the deposit bank holds the paper as bailee or trustee for the depositor. If prior to collection, the deposit bank becomes insolvent, the customer should be entitled to the return of the paper as a property claim subject to any lien of the deposit bank, because the insolvency terminates the ability of the bank to treat the money as its own and hence become a debtor to the customer. But if the bank has collected and credited the customer's account before the bank's insolvency, the bank is presumptively entitled to treat the money as its own and so to become a debtor to the customer who is thereby a mere creditor of the bank and does not have a proprietary claim ranking ahead of the general creditors of the insolvent bank.

In *Giles v Perkins* (1807) 9 East 11, a customer deposited bills with bankers for   **26–12**
collection. The bankers credited him with the amount of the bills and charged him interest. But the bankers did not purchase the bills. The bankers became bankrupt and thereafter they received payment of the bills. At the time of the bankruptcy the bankers owed a credit balance to the customers excluding the amount of the bills. *Held*: the bills and hence the proceeds were the property of the customer. The bankers did not have a lien on the bills because the customers did not owe the bankers any money and the bankers had not advanced money on the security of the bills. If on the other hand the account had been overdrawn then the bankers would have had a lien by custom on the bills.

In *Thompson v Giles* (1824) 3 B&C 422, a customer deposited term bills with his bankers for collection. The bankers credited the proceeds to the customer's account and charged interest. The bankers became bankrupt. *Held*: the bills and the proceeds belonged to the customer. The bankers had not purchased the bills. See also *Re Dilworth, ex p Benson* (1852) 1 D & Ch 435; *Re Gothenburg Commercial Co* (1881) 44 LT 166; *Re Forster* (1840) 1 Mont D & De G 10; *Re Wise, ex p Edwards* (1842) 3 Mont D & De G 103; *Re Harrison* (1858) 2 De G & J 194.

In *Tennant v Strachan* (1829) 4 Car & P 30, a customer delivered bills to a banking firm for collection and for credit of the proceeds to the customer's account. The firm became insolvent. Some proceeds were received after the commission but before the insolvency representatives were appointed. Other proceeds were received after such appointment. *Held*: the customer could not maintain a proprietary claim for the pre-appointment bills: the customer was only a creditor. But the customer could maintain a proprietary claim for proceeds received after the appointment of the insolvency representatives. See also *Re West of England and South Wales District Bank, ex p Dale* (1879) 11 ChD 772.

In *Re Agra & Masterman's Bank* [1866] WN 399; LJ Ch 151, a firm paid a cheque into a branch bank in India to their current account after the stoppage of the parent bank in England, but before the branch had notice of that stoppage. Afterwards, on the same day, the branch received notice of the stoppage of the bank in England, and stopped itself. *Held*: an application by the firm to be repaid the amount of the cheque in full would be refused if the cheque was cashed before the branch had received notice of the stoppage, but would be allowed if the cheque had not been cashed until after the branch had received notice of the stoppage of the bank in England. Wood V-C said that after a bank had ceased all functions it could not receive anything in specie for a special purpose if the special purpose had become impossible. In other words the bank could not then treat the proceeds received as its own and would hold them on trust.

CHAPTER 27

PAYMENT CLEARING HOUSES AND CENTRAL BANK PAYMENTS

Clearing systems

In some countries, credit transfers go through clearing banks in the country 27–1
of the currency. Clearing banks are leading banks of undoubted credit status
which, for a variety of historical, commercial and legal reasons, are permitted to have an account with the central bank in the currency concerned, e.g.
the Bank of England. All other banks have to go through a clearing bank (or
a settlement bank as they are called in the United States). A tiered system,
whereby a small core of banks have settlement accounts with the central
bank and act as correspondents for other participants, exists in Belgium
(CEC), Canada (IIPS), Japan (Zengin System), the United Kingdom
(CHAPS) and the United States (CHIPS). Ecus are settled via a system using
accounts at the Bank for International Settlements.

The payments clearing system may be owned and operated by an associ-
ation of banks, as in the United Kingdom, or by the central bank itself, as in
France. The Federal Reserve plays an active part in interbank funds transfer
services, mainly via Fedwire, which is a message system from the Federal
Reserve which guarantees that the account at the Fed will be credited. The
Bank of Japan operates a system – BOJ-NET: the Bank of Japan Financial
Network System. In Italy there is the BISS (the Banca d'Italia continuous
settlement system) and SIPS, the Interbank Payment System operated by the
Interbank Society for Automation.

Other examples are the New York Clearing House Interbank Payment
Systems (CHIPS) (which is the world's largest payment system), the Clear-
ing House Automated Payment System (CHAPS) in London, and SAGIT-
TAIRE in France.

Let us say that an originator wishes to pay US$100 to a beneficiary. The 27–2
originator's bank has an account at a New York settlement bank which one
may call the "originator's clearing bank". Similarly the beneficiary's bank
has an account at its opposite number in New York which is also a settlement bank – the "beneficiary's clearing bank". Both are intermediary
banks.

The originator's bank instructs the originator's clearing bank in New York to pay the beneficiary's clearing bank for ultimate account of the beneficiary.

Accordingly the originator's clearing bank debits the originator's bank 100 and undertakes to pay this to the beneficiary's clearing bank. The beneficiary's clearing bank may at that point credit the beneficiary's bank so that the beneficiary's bank has now, so far as it is concerned, been paid, i.e. it has received a claim against a bank acceptable to it.

The only outstanding amount which has not yet been "paid" is the commitment of the originator's clearing bank to the beneficiary's clearing bank.

This is paid, usually at the end of each day, by the central bank debiting the account which the originator's clearing bank has with the central bank for 100 and crediting the account of the beneficiary's clearing bank for 100.

27–3   The effect of this is that the beneficiary's clearing bank now has a claim against a bank acceptable to it, that bank being the central bank. A claim against a central bank in its own currency is the most acceptable credit available in that country. This is because the central bank can, if it wants to, create as much money as it needs, albeit at the risk of devaluing its currency.

It follows also that the claim of the beneficiary against his bank is ultimately reflected in the country of the currency by a claim by a bank in that currency against the central bank.

Interbank daylight overdrafts

27–4   The transfer at the central bank from the account of the originator's clearing bank to the account of the beneficiary's clearing bank may take place at the end of each day some time during the night. The reason for this is that all the commitments to pay criss-crossing between the clearers can then be totalled up and only net balances transferred: this netting out of payments vastly reduces the number of actual gross transfers funnelled through to the narrow channel of the clearers which would otherwise have to be made. The gross amount of the transfers would otherwise run into billions or trillions of units of the currency concerned and there is no point in laboriously transferring each transfer separately in the central bank's accounts if they can all be netted out and only net balances transferred between the banks concerned.

However it will often be the case that the ultimate beneficiary will want the money immediately during the day – *before* the clearing. As explained, the reason that the beneficiary may want his account to be credited at once may be, for example, that the money owed to him by the originator is the price for securities or commodities sold by the beneficiary to the originator and the beneficiary may be unwilling to deliver the assets to the originator until he has been paid for the assets. Or the money paid by the originator to the beneficiary may be loan proceeds paid by a bank to a borrower which the borrower requires to use immediately.

Because of these commercial pressures, the beneficiary's bank may there- **27-5** fore agree to credit the beneficiary's account immediately it receives notification from the originator's bank of the credit transfer even though at that point the beneficiary's bank is merely relying on a commitment from the originator's bank. The credit of the originator's bank may not be sufficient in the eyes of the beneficiary's bank and the beneficiary's bank will require a claim against the beneficiary's clearing bank in New York in US dollars.

For similar commercial reasons, the beneficiary's clearing bank may agree to commit in advance to pay the beneficiary's bank so that the beneficiary's bank can immediately credit the account of the creditor. Hence the beneficiary's clearing bank will have an exposure to the originator's clearing bank which is committed to ensure that at the end of the day the beneficiary clearing bank is paid, i.e. by the originator's clearing bank arranging for the central bank to confer a claim for 100 in favour of the beneficiary's clearing bank.

The fact that all of these banks may become committed before the final **27-6** payments by settlement through the central bank in the evening means that banks have an exposure to each other during the day. This is often called the "daylight overdraft" and can run into gigantic amounts. The participants may operate a system of caps which results in either delaying excess payment orders (resulting in queuing bottlenecks and delaying payments, potentially leading to customer claims) or collateralising them. There may be loss-sharing provisions if a bank defaults.

Multilateral clearings

As mentioned, settlement of the claims of the clearing banks against each **27-7** other is sometimes made at the end of each day by transfer on accounts of the clearers with the central bank.

The procedure is two-fold: (1) the reciprocal amounts owing between each pair of clearers is netted out so as to produce a single bilateral balance, and (2) the bilateral balances are netted out multilaterally between the clearers.

Thus, A owes 100 net to B who owes 100 net to C who owes 60 net to A. A is deemed to owe his 100 to C (instead of B) so that A owes C 100. C owes 60 to A. These are set-off, so that A owes C 40. Hence A transfers 40 to C at their respective accounts at the central bank. The result is that only one transfer is required, instead of three.

27–8   As regards the bilateral set-off between pairs of banks, the bankruptcy laws must permit insolvency set-off. Insolvency set-off is permitted in most common law, Germanic and Scandinavian jurisdictions, but not most Franco-Latin jurisdictions. Secondly the set-off must not be capable of being destroyed by an intervener – an assignee, chargee, attaching creditor, undisclosed principal or undisclosed beneficiary. The principles are complicated internationally and are reviewed in another book in this series on international finance. Generally in England a contract to set-off will take priority over an intervener as regards reciprocal debts incurred before notice of the intervener. The greatest risk in practice stems from the fact that each bank may be taken to know that the other is an agent which holds claims owing to it on trust for and as the property of its principal, namely the beneficiary's bank or an intermediary beneficiary bank, so that there is no mutuality between the reciprocal claims. If the agent sets off, as against its liability to another bank, the claim which is owed to it by that other bank and which it holds for the benefit of its principal, then the principal's property has been used to pay the agent's debt. The principal is expropriated. This risk can presumably be overcome by contracts binding on all the banks involved and on ultimate beneficiaries that agent banks do not hold on trust for their respective principals. A mere authorisation by the principal to the agent to use the principal's claim for set-off collapses on the insolvency of either of them and hence the principal must in advance have renounced its proprietary claim against the agent: for the law on the subject see Wood, *English and International Set-Off* (1989) para 1981 *et seq*. Normally clearing-house rules are not binding on ultimate beneficiaries unless they have assented to them: *Barclays Bank plc v Bank of England* [1985] All ER 385. In the US, the rules of a funds transfer system, such as CHIPS, can bind parties outside the association: UCC s 4A–501(b).

27–9   But even if bilateral set-off is permitted, the multilateral set-off is universally void after the commencement of insolvency proceedings against a clearer. This is because the multilateral set-off is non-mutual and involves an asset of the insolvent being used to pay the debt of another: see *British Eagle International Airlines Ltd v Air France* [1975] 2 All ER 390, HL (IATA multilateral settlement of airline charges). Thus, in the example given, if B becomes insolvent before the evening clearing, the effect of the multilateral set-off is to deprive B of the asset of 100 owed to B by A. The assets of an insolvent are frozen on the opening of insolvency proceedings and are henceforward available only for creditors. Hence the clearers would suddenly find themselves with large unexpected exposures which could have a domino or cascade or knock-on effect and thus threaten the system. In the example, C would find himself with an exposure of 100 to B, when C expected the exposure to be zero.

Special legislation applying to CHIPS in the United States validates the multilateral netting. Some systems provide for an unwinding of the multilateral netting if a participant fails – the participant is deleted so that the risk falls on those banks dealing with that participant.

Real time gross settlement

As an alternative to periodic clearings, all credit transfers could be debited   **27–10** and credited with all the banks (including the central bank) simultaneously. In other words, when a payment is made, the account of the originator's clearing bank at the central bank is debited immediately during the day and the account of the beneficiary's clearing bank at the central bank is simultaneously credited.

The result is that the beneficiary's bank account can be credited at once. The insolvency risk with regard to end-of-day multilateral settlements is obviated.

The disadvantages are that each payment must be processed individually (a disadvantage substantially reduced by automation) and that the clearing banks must either maintain large balances at the central bank to cope with sudden large payments or must be able to deposit liquid collateral with the central bank to cover any overdraft allowed by the central bank or must have borrowing facilities with other banks. If the central bank allows unsecured overdrafts, then the central bank is exposed to the originator's clearing bank and the exposure might effectively be passed on to the public purse if the originator's clearing bank fails. During the course of 1995, the London clearing system for sterling through the Bank of England was converting to real time gross settlement.

CHAPTER 28

TIME OF PAYMENT

Relevance of time of payment

28–1   The time at which payment is finally made affects the following questions, amongst others:

- whether the debtor has paid his creditor on time;

- the time from which interest ceases or starts to run on credit balances;

- the ability of the originator to revoke a payment order;

- insolvency of the originator or beneficiary or a bank in the chain;

- attachments of bank accounts by creditors;

- freeze orders or embargoes on making payments;

- expropriation orders seizing bank accounts;

- set-off against bank deposits.

In each case the question tends to turn on whether a payment has been made and to whom. It is worth noting that a payment may have been made, but the payment is not final because it is revocable. For example, payment may be revoked if the contract so provides or if bankruptcy proceedings are commenced against the sender and the payment is made after their commencement – which may be back-dated to zero hour on the date the insolvency order is made.

Revocation by originator

28–2   An originator may wish to revoke a payment order for a variety of reasons. For example the originator may be a buyer whose seller has become insolvent and is therefore unable to deliver so that the buyer wishes to cancel payment of the purchase price, e.g. for foreign exchange, securities or goods. Or alternatively a borrower may become insolvent and a lending bank may wish to cancel the payment over of the loan proceeds. If the bene-

ficiary's bank becomes insolvent the beneficiary will wish to change the
bank which receives the payment.

Electronic transfers are made at enormous speed once they have been set
in motion and so the ability to revoke an order once action has been taken
to process it is very limited.

Under s 4A–211 of the UCC a stop order or an order amending a prior   28–3
order must be received in time to give "the receiving bank a reasonable time
to act on the communication before the bank accepts the payment order".
There are more restrictive rules for stopping or amending an order which is
in the hands of the beneficiary's bank.

Under English law, subject to any agreement to the contrary, if the originator revokes the bank's mandate to pay, the bank must comply with the
customer's instructions and stop the process if this is practicable. The stop
order must be clear and given to the branch of the bank where the account is
kept: see the cases on cheques such as *Burnett v Westminster Bank Ltd*
[1966] 1 QB 742. A countermand can be given up to the time when the
funds have been transferred or credit given to the beneficiary: *Gibson v
Minet* (1824) 130 ER 206. The originator who has given a payment order to
his bank cannot revoke from the time that the bank incurs a commitment to
the third party: see *The Zographia M* [1976] 2 Lloyds LR 382.

If the originator's bank stops payment or becomes subject to insolvency
proceedings, its mandate is automatically terminated: *Re Farrow's Bank*
[1923] 1 Ch 41, CA; *Re Gothenburg Commercial Co* (1881) 44 LT 166.

In France, according to a decision of the Court of Cassation of January   28–4
26, 1983, a transfer is completed with respect to the originator at the time
when his account is debited. As a result the originator loses the right to
revoke the payment order from this time regardless of whether the amount
has been credited to the beneficiary's account.

In Switzerland an originator can revoke the order to the originator's bank
so long as the originator's bank has not indicated its acceptance of the order
to the receiving bank, i.e. so long as no credit has been made: see CO Art
472.

Conditional or unavailable funds

A number of cases on when payment is made may now be referred to.   28–5
The distinction between revocable payment orders, irrevocable payment
orders, conditional payments and unconditional payments needs to be kept
in mind.

No payment has been made when the originator's bank has merely requested the beneficiary's bank to credit the beneficiary's account because at that point the beneficiary does not have the free use of the funds in his account: *The Effy* [1972] 1 Lloyds Rep 18; *The Brimnes* [1975] QB 929. The same applies if the credit to the account is conditional, e.g. if the beneficiary's bank reserves the right to cancel the payment if the payment is not cleared: *Re Farrow's Bank* [1923] 1 Ch 41.

In *The Brimnes* [1973] 1 WLR 386, 402, approved on appeal [1957] 1 QB 929, the court said:

"when payment of a debt is effected by a transfer of funds within a bank from the account of customer A to that of customer B pursuant to an order given to the bank by customer A, the time of the payment must, in principle, be the time when the order to transfer is executed and not the time when it is given or received. According to the evidence on the bank's practice given before me, the effective time of execution of the order, from the point of view of availability of the funds to customer B, is the time of the decision to debit the one account and credit the other. That is, accordingly, in my view, the time of transfer or payment."

In *Gaden v Newfoundland Savings Bank* [1899] AC 281, PC, a customer drew a cheque on her bank payable to herself drawing out her entire deposit, went to another bank, opened an account there and deposited her cheque. The new bank entered in her passbook the amount of the deposit and then presented the cheque to the old bank for payment. The old bank failed before payment. *Held*: the new bank had not purchased the cheque. The new bank merely held it as the customer's property for collection. The result was that the customer was still a creditor of the insolvent old bank and the new bank was not her debtor.

Time of payment at same bank

28–6   If both originator and beneficiary have an account at the same branch of the same bank, payment is complete when the entries are made in the bank's books debiting the originator and crediting the beneficiary, or at the time when entries are made in the computer for debiting or crediting. The beneficiary need not have received notification of the transfer: *Eyles v Ellis* (1827) 130 ER 710; *Momm v Barclays Bank International Ltd* [1977] 1 QB 790.

In *Momm v Barclays Bank International Ltd* [1977] 1 QB 790, a German bank, which on June 25 agreed to transfer pounds sterling to another German bank, instructed an English bank, where both German banks had accounts, to make the transfer "value June 26". On June 25 the English bank credited the transferee's account, debited the transferor's account, and prepared appropriate entries for overnight processing by the computer. On June 25 the transferor bank was insolvent and ceased trading. On June 27, the English bank cancelled the entries, so that it would not have to claim against the transferor bank in the insolvency since its account after the transfer was in overall debit. *Held*: the transfer had been complete on June 26 and accordingly the English bank was not entitled to reverse the entries, even though the original transfer had not been notified to the transferee.

Contrast *Rekstin v Severo Sibirsko* [1933] 1 KB 47. A customer instructed his bank to transfer the total balance standing to his credit to an account maintained with the same branch by another customer to escape a creditor's judgment. After the bank had effected the transfer by making the required ledger entries but before notification was given to the payee, a judgment creditor served a garnishee order nisi attaching the transferor's balance. *Held*: at the time the order nisi was served, the amount transferred was still accruing to the transferor. The transferor did not owe any debt to the transferee, and there was nothing to indicate that the transferee had anticipated payment. As there was no evidence to establish the transferee's assent to the transfer of the amount involved, the bank could not be regarded as having the authority to hold the amount involved as a debt accrued to him. This decision holds that payment is incomplete until the transferee manifests his consent to the transfer of the funds and should be limited to its special facts. Normally the beneficiary's bank has authority to credit the payee's account by virtue of the bank-customer contract: see *Momm v Barclays Bank International Ltd* [1977] QB 790.

Time of payment at different banks

As regards transfers between different banks, payment is complete when the   28–7
beneficiary's bank is notified that funds are made available for the credit of the beneficiary's account. Consequently, the originator has no claim against his bank for not effecting the transfer if the beneficiary's bank becomes insolvent after such notification, since the transfer is complete at that point: *Royal Products v Midland Bank* [1981] 2 Lloyd's Rep LR 194. The originator will have to pay the transferee again if it has not been paid by the beneficiary's bank.

Once the beneficiary's bank has credited the beneficiary's account uncon-   28–8
ditionally, it cannot revoke the transfer.

In *Libyan Arab Foreign Bank v Manufacturers Hanover Trust Co (No 2)* [1989] 1 Lloyd's LR 608, Manufacturers Hanover Trust (MHT) in New York sent a tested telex at 5.44 p.m. on January 7 to MHT London: "We are crediting you [$62 million] for the account of Libyan Arab Foreign Bank Tripoli". MHT London acted on this telex on the morning of January 8, credited LAFB, debited MHT New York on the same sum in their nostro account, and notified LAFB of the transfer. At 6 p.m. on January 7, however, MHT New York purported to cancel the transfer, and it was never posted in MHT New York's computerised books of account either to LAFB's account with MHT New York or to MHT London's nostro account at MHT New York. Eventually, MHT London purported to cancel the transfer as well. *Held*: the cancellation was ineffective. The actions by MHT London constituted completion of the payment of the $62m, and were not affected by the absence of similar entries at MHT New York.

In *Delbrueck & Co v Manufacturers Hanover Trust Co*, 609 F 2d 1047 (1979), affirming 464 F Supp, 989 (1979), a German bank, which maintained an account with the defendant bank in the United States, entered into exchange contracts with another German bank, Herstatt. An amount of US$12.5 million was payable by the plaintiffs to Herstatt under these contracts on June 26. On June 25 the plaintiffs sent a telex message to the defendant bank requesting it to credit Herstatt's account with the Chase Manhattan Bank with the amount involved. At 10.30 a.m. on June 26 (at Eastern Standard Time in New York), Herstatt was closed down by the German banking authorities. At approximately 11.40 a.m. the defendant bank transferred to Chase the amount of $12.5 million through CHIPS. Within the next thirty minutes the plaintiffs called the defendant bank in order to stop this payment, and immediately thereafter confirmed the countermand by telex. At 9.00 p.m. on the same day, Herstatt's account with Chase was formally credited with the amount involved. *Held*: a transfer executed through the CHIPS automated network reached the recipient bank almost as soon as it was released or executed by the computer terminal of the transferring bank. It was the understanding of all the banks participating in the system that funds transferred by means of CHIPS could be drawn upon by the payee as soon as the electronic message was received by the recipient bank. Accordingly, the transfer of funds to the credit of Herstatt's account was complete as soon as it was effected by the defendant bank. The fact that the credit was not entered in Herstatt's account until 9.00 p.m. on June 26 was merely a matter of bookkeeping and hence irrelevant. The defendant bank had not acted negligently when it failed to revoke the transfer of the funds to Chase.

28–9   In *Royal Products Ltd v Midland Bank Ltd* [1981] 2 Lloyd's Rep 194, the plaintiffs, Maltese merchants, wished to transfer £13,000 from their account in the United Kingdom with the Midland Bank to Malta. In Malta they had two current accounts: one with the B Bank, and the other with the N Bank. The plaintiffs were deterred from ordering a direct transfer by the high banking charges of the N Bank and therefore ordered Midland to remit the amount involved to the credit of their account with the B Bank, intending to complete the cycle by eventually remitting the amount involved from the B Bank to the N Bank.

The plaintiffs issued their instruction to Midland on November 23, 1972. On the same day, Midland sent a telex message instructing its correspondent in Malta, which by coincidence happened to be the N Bank, to credit the amount in question to the plaintiffs' account with the B Bank. The N Bank received the telex on November 24. Usually the N Bank would have completed the transfer by delivering a bankers' payment to the B Bank. But as there were rumours on the morning of the day in question that the B Bank was facing liquidity problems, the N Bank departed from this procedure and credited the amount involved to a suspense account opened by it in the B Bank's name. The N Bank, which recognised that the plaintiffs were its own customers and was aware that the ultimate destination of the funds was the plaintiffs' account with the N Bank itself, contacted the plaintiffs and suggested that the funds be diverted directly to the credit of this account. However, as the N Bank did not disclose its reasons for making this suggestion, the plaintiffs mistook that bank's motives, and insisted that the amount be transferred as instructed. On the evening of November 24 it was thought that the B Bank had overcome its financial crisis. On the same evening, or possibly on the morning of November 25, the N Bank notified the B Bank, by means of a credit note, that it had passed a remittance for the amount involved to the credit of the plaintiff's account.

On the morning of November 25, the B Bank was forced to suspend operations and, in due course, was put into liquidation. As general creditors, the plaintiffs were unable to recover any part of the amount involved and attempted to recover their loss from Midland. *Held*: Midland was entitled to use the services of a correspondent to effect the transfer ordered by the plaintiffs. Midland owed the plaintiffs a duty of care and skill in choosing the correspondent involved, and Midland was vicariously liable for any negligence committed by the correspondent. The sub-agent bank – the N Bank – had no privity of contract in respect of the transaction with the plaintiffs. The N Bank had not been in breach of a duty of care in carrying out the instruction to transfer the amount involved to the credit of the plaintiffs' account with the B Bank. The N Bank was precluded, by a duty of secrecy owed to the B Bank, from disclosing to the plaintiffs the disturbing information received by it. Hence Midland was not liable.

The payment was complete. The B Bank was entitled to draw on the funds made available for transmission to the plaintiffs' account when it obtained the payment order on the evening of November 24 (or early on the morning of November 25). The B Bank had been informed that the funds were to be made available to the plaintiffs. The transfer was complete even before the payees, the plaintiffs, were notified that the funds had been credited to their account.

In the United States, UCC s 4A – 406(a) provides that the originator is **28–10** generally deemed to make payment to the beneficiary when the beneficiary's bank accepts the payment order directed to it.

In France, the originator loses his right to revoke when his account is debited: Court of Cassation decision of January 26, 1983. Further the credit balance cannot be attached from that time and, if the originator becomes insolvent, the amount debited cannot be recovered by the insolvent estate – even if the beneficiary's account has not yet been credited. But the time of payment to the beneficiary is when his account is credited at the beneficiary's bank: Court of Cassation decision of February 7, 1944 (II *Jur-isclasseur Périodique* at 2.604 1944) and see Cass civ soc of May 3, 1984, in 1985 Rev TD Com 341.

Time of payment to agents

28–11   Where a debtor pays an agent of the creditor, the initial question is whether the agent has actual or ostensible authority to accept the payment on behalf of the principal. If he does and has authority to accept or reject tender, then payment to the agent is payment to the principal.

> In *Central Estates (Belgravia) Ltd v Woolgar (No 2)* [1972] 1 WLR 1048, managing agents of property accepted a payment of rent from a tenant and had ostensible authority to do so even though the owner had instructed them not to accept payment. *Held*: by accepting rent through his agent the landlord was deemed to have waived a breach of the tenancy agreement. See also *Delbrueck & Co v Manufacturers Hanover Trust Co*, 609 F 2d 1047 (1979).

But if the agent has actual or ostensible authority merely to receive payment pending instructions from his principal but not to accept or reject a tender, a payment to the agent is not payment to the principal if the principal declines to accept the payment after it is made, e.g. because it was overdue.

> In *The Laconia* (1977) AC 850, a charterer made a late payment of hire to the owner's bank account. The owner subsequently rejected the payment. *Held*: the owner was entitled to withdraw the vessel. The bank had no actual or ostensible authority to waive a late payment.

28–12   Where a debtor pays a correspondent bank of the creditor's bank, payment to the correspondent bank as sub-agent may be deemed to be payment to the creditor as ultimate principal: see *Mackersey v Ramsays, Bonar & Co* (1843) 9 Cl & F 818.

> In *Williams v Deacon* (1849) 4 Exch 397, a depositor paid money to the London agents of a country bank for credit to his account with the country bank. The country bank stopped payment the next day. After receiving notice of this, the London agents advised the country bank of the payment. *Held*: the payment to the London bank as agent was payment to the country bank and the depositor could not recover from the London agents.
>
> In *Re Home Bank of Canada, Bank of Montreal Set-off Claims* (1924) 5 CBR 176 (Ontario S Ct), a customer lodged a draft with a deposit bank for collection. The deposit bank forwarded the draft to a correspondent bank which in due course notified the deposit bank that it had collected the proceeds. The

deposit bank advised its customer of this receipt and credited the amount of the proceeds to the customer's account, although at this point the deposit bank had not been paid. The deposit bank forwarded a ticket to the clearing-house in order to be paid by the correspondent bank. The correspondent bank became insolvent. The clearing house returned the ticket so that the deposit bank was not paid either by credit in the books of the correspondent bank or by credit at the central bank to the account of the deposit bank. *Held*: payment to the correspondent bank was payment to the deposit bank (following *Mackersey v Ramsays, Bonar & Co* (1843) 9 Cl & F 818). But as it happened the deposit bank was entitled by contract with the customer to reverse the credit to the customer's account.

CHAPTER 29

LIABILITY FOR INCORRECT PAYMENTS AND CONFLICT OF LAWS

Liability for incorrect payments

Main heads of liability: summary

29–1   A great many things can go wrong in the payment process. On the originator's side an employee may act fraudulently by changing the payee or changing the amount or forging the whole order. The directors may be acting in
breach of duty in wrongfully paying away the company's money, e.g.
because of a conflict of interest or breach of company law known to the
bank so that the bank is liable as a participant or, in the quaint English
phrase, as a constructive trustee. There is much case law involving actions
against banks to recover corporate money wrongfully paid away on the
basis that the bank was involved in the wrong-doing.

29–2   In the case of the bank, there may be fraud on the part of an employee, or
an external interloper may break into the computer system, or there may be
a mistake whereby money is paid from the wrong account, or a wrongful
refusal to debit, e.g. if there is in fact enough money in the account, or there
is delay in making a payment order, or there is a failure to act on revocation
of the order, or wrong instructions are given, e.g. wrong payee, wrong
amount, wrong currency, wrong bank. Communication systems may break
down or a machine may not have enough paper in it. A receiving bank may
deduct charges in making the payment with the result that the full amount
does not get through to the beneficiary's bank so that the originator is in
default for non-payment.

Errors not only cause potential losses to participants, but can also
threaten the banking system if large enough. Breakdown of systems could
cause acute liquidity problems if banks fail to settle because their machinery
is not in operation.

Illustrative case law on liability for errors

There is much case law on incorrect payments and a few examples may be   29-3
given.

In France the courts have held the originator's bank liable for damages if
an exchange rate loss occurs due to devaluation of the franc and this devaluation takes place between the issuing of the payment order and the late
execution.

> In a decision of November 10, 1962 of the Paris court (II *Semaine Juridique*
> 13.016 (1963)), a bank did not carry out an order until more than a week after
> it was issued and the equivalent sum in Italian currency dropped due to a
> devaluation of the Franc which took place in the meantime. *Held*: the bank
> which did not carry out the order with proper speed must compensate the origi-
> nator for damages suffered in the delayed transfer. See also a decision by the
> Paris court of September 22, 1988.

> In a decision of the Court of Cassation of June 7 1983, a French bank issued
> cheques for US$13,000 payable in Mexico drawn on its correspondent bank
> Banamex in Mexico. To cover the cheques it initiated a transfer of $10,000 for
> the benefit of the Mexican bank. The customer needed the $10,000 in Mexico
> by December 19, 1976 in order to exercise a purchase option for which he had
> already advanced $5000. If the $10,000 was not paid in time, the customer
> would lose the $5000 already paid and also pay a penalty of $10,000. When
> the customer arrived at Banamex in Mexico on December 17, 1976 (two days
> prior to the date on which he had to exercise the option and pay the $10,000),
> he was not able to obtain payment of the three cheques. The $10,000 had not
> been paid to the Banamex on time. *Held*: the French bank was liable for the
> customer's losses in the amount of $16,782, consisting of the $5000 which he
> had advanced for the option, the $10,000 which he had to pay as a contract
> penalty, and $782 for his travel costs to Mexico. The $10,000 which the cus-
> tomer had originally provided to the French bank had already been reimbursed.

Two Tokyo District Court decisions have held an originator's bank liable   29-4
for an originator's foreseeable consequential damages that were caused by
the bank's delay in executing an electronic credit transfer: *Fuji Bank*, 660
Kinyûhômujijô 26 (Tokyo District Court, June 29, 1972); *Sanwa Bank*
case, 794 Kinyûhômujijô 30 (Tokyo District Court, January 26, 1976).

> In the *Sanwa Bank* case, which involved an international credit transfer, a ship-
> ping company (the originator) instructed Sanwa Bank, Tokyo (the originator's
> bank) to credit a New York account of an agent of the originator (the benefici-
> ary). Because the originator's bank misidentified the originator in its message to
> the beneficiary's bank, the agent was unable to comply with the payment terms
> of charter money to a New York shipowner, which cancelled the originator's

ship charter. *Held*: the originator's bank should have foreseen the originator's consequential damages. The Tokyo District Court allowed the originator's damages claim for approximately three million dollars.

Extent of liability for errors

29–5   The amount of liability may be as follows:

- The amount of principal lost, e.g. if there was fraud or a mistake.

- The amount of interest lost, e.g. if there was delay in the payment.

- The amount of currency losses if there were fluctuations in the rates of exchange and there was a delay in payment.

- Consequential loss, e.g. if the payment is made late and as a result the beneficiary who is the owner of a vessel withdraws the vessel for non-payment of charterhire, or if the result is a default under a loan agreement and the lender calls in the loan thereby sparking off cross-default clauses in other agreements, or if the creditor cancels a licence or a lease or sales contract or an insurance policy, or if the payment was margin collateral which is not duly posted in time in market dealings and as a result the exchange closes out the originator's bargains on the exchange.

29–6   The ordinary English principles of damages are that damages are calculated as those which would naturally flow from the breach of contract together with such other damages as were specifically contemplated when the contract was made.

In *Evra Corp v Swiss Bank Corp*, 673 F2d 951 (7th Cir) cert denied 459 US 103 1982, the originator of an electronic funds transfer was initially awarded $2.1m in a consequential damages claim as a result of the lost value of his ship charter. A bank negligently lost the payment order that was intended to pay the ship charterhire to the owner, possibly because there was no paper in a telex machine at the bank which received the message. Subsequently this damages award was set aside and lost interest awarded instead.

29–7   The policy followed by Art 4A of the UCC is that, because of the low cost of the transfers and the huge potential liabilities for consequential damages, banks should not be responsible beyond a liability for interest. For example, if a receiver has made an error and as a result the payment goes to the intended beneficiary late, then under Art 4A–305a the error-making receiver is liable for the payment of interest only. If a receiver mishandles a transfer and the funds do not reach the beneficiary at all, then under the same section, the damages are also interest plus expenses of the originator and incidental expenses. Art 4A–305 specifically states that additional damages are not recoverable. If a particular funds transfer is time-sensitive and the originator wishes to ensure that it will arrive in time, then the originator must monitor the payment manually and pay whatever extra price is needed for this extra precaution. However a bank can agree with a customer to assume greater risk by an express written agreement pursuant to s 4A–305c. If the beneficiary's bank does not accept a payment order, the originator need pay nothing and if the originator has already made payment, it will be returned – the "money back" guarantee. See s 4A–402.

Exclusion of liability

A bank may exclude liability for errors or negligence in his contract with the   29–8
sender. In some countries the major banks employ standard contracts with their customers which are in the same form for all the banks and which contain exclusion clauses, e.g. Austria, Germany, Japan, the Netherlands and Switzerland. These clauses must be judged in accordance with the normal contract rules governing exculpation clauses. For a brief summary, see para 14–26.

Liability of originator's bank for intermediary banks: network liability

If a mistake is made, the originator may have an action against his own   29–9
bank or a direct action against an intermediary bank. An important question in practice is the liability of the originator's bank for errors by intermediary banks.

In general one would expect the originator's bank to be the agent of the originator, any intermediary bank to be the agent of the originator's bank (a sub-agent) and the beneficiary's bank to be the agent of the beneficiary. If other banks are interposed after the initial intermediary bank instructed by the originator's bank, then the second intermediary bank may be a sub-agent of the beneficiary's bank or alternatively a sub sub-agent of the originator's bank.

It is also perfectly possible that one or other of the parties is an indepen-   29–10
dent contractor. For example S.W.I.F.T. (which transmits payment instructions) should be treated as an independent contractor and not as an agent of anybody.

Whether a party is an independent contractor or an agent perhaps does not make a great deal of difference to liability since in both cases the agent or the independent contractor must carry out the contract with reasonable care and skill in accordance with its terms. But the agency relationship can make a great deal of difference in deciding whether a party holds a claim on trust for another and also when payment is made to the beneficiary because payment to the beneficiary's agent may be deemed to be payment to the beneficiary itself: see para 28–11 *et seq*.

The sub-agent may not be a sub-agent at all but rather a direct agent of the principal. It will always be a matter of construction as to whether the principal authorised the agent to appoint an agent in substitution for himself or in addition for himself or whether the authority was to appoint a sub-agent not in privity with the principal.

Policy approaches

29–11   There are two broad policy approaches to liability. The first is that the originator's bank should not be responsible for intermediaries provided the intermediary was properly chosen. Therefore if, for example, an intermediary bank makes a mistake by putting the wrong account in its payment order to the beneficiary's bank with the result that the money goes to the wrong person who then takes it out and disappears, the originator's bank has no responsibility for this default by the intermediary bank on the basis that the originator's bank had only a duty of reasonable care in the selection of the intermediary bank but not responsibility for the actions of the intermediary bank which it could not control.

The other view is that, as far as originators and beneficiaries are concerned, it is the job of the banking system to deliver the payment and therefore, if something goes wrong as a result of the fault of anybody in the system, the originator should be entitled to his money back. This is the solution which, in general, is followed by Art 4A of the UCC which establishes what is known as "network liability". In practice such a system would have to be statutory and would adopt the policy that confidence in the banking system overrides the attribution of particular fault to a particular participant.

Network liability in the United States

29–12   In the United States, the basic policies adopted by Art 4A of the UCC are that consumer protection concepts are not relevant to high volume commercial payments, that high speed and accuracy are more important than checking and monitoring and that the systems must be extremely low cost in order to reduce the costs to the user. Typically a transfer costs between $10 and $20 and hence, for such a small charge, the banks should in principle accept only minimal risks. Risks running potentially into billions of dollars are simply not paid for and, if realised, could threaten the banking system. Customers can agree different arrangements with their banks if they wish.

As regards unauthorised or fraudulent payment orders, Art 4A has   **29–13** detailed rules about security procedures. The procedure is defined to be one for the purposes of verifying that the order is that of the customer or that it is free of error. Section 4A–202 provides that if the security procedure has been agreed upon by sender and receiver, it may be relied upon by the receiver as the sender's order if (a) the procedure is commercially reasonable and (b) the receiving bank complied with the procedure and any accompanying order or instruction of the sender. There are various rules covering situations where there is, for example, improper interference in the system not caused by the sender, a payment order is not enforceable or if a payment order is erroneously transmitted because a security system was not properly used. Further detailed rules cover the situation where there are inconsistencies between names and numbers – the most frequent cause of errors in payment systems.

Network liability in England

In England it seems that the originator's bank may in some circumstances be   **29–14** vicariously liable for the negligence or default of its correspondent: see *Equitable Trust Co of New York v Dawson Partners Ltd* (1927) 27 Lloyds LR 49, where a bank issuing a letter of credit was held responsible for a correspondent. The principle is applicable also to the engagement of a correspondent by a bank mandated by its customer to collect a bill of exchange drawn on a merchant overseas: *Mackersey v Ramsays, Bonars & Co* (1843) 9 Cl & F 818. But it is considered doubtful that this liability is absolute.

As the intermediary is engaged by the originator's bank, there is no privity of contract between the intermediary bank and the originator.

> In *Calico Printers' Association v Barclays Bank Ltd* (1931) 36 Comm Cas 71; affirmed 36 Comm Cas 197, (1931) 145 LT 51, the plaintiffs engaged Barclays as their agent for the presentment of a bill of exchange, accompanied by commercial paper for goods, to the buyers. Barclays, in turn, engaged its correspondent, the AP Bank. As the bill was dishonoured, the plaintiffs ordered Barclays to arrange for the storing and insurance of the goods. This instruction was transmitted by Barclays to the AP Bank, which stored the goods but failed to insure them. When the goods were destroyed by fire, the plaintiffs sued the two banks for breach of contract and in negligence for their failure to adhere to

their mandate. *Held*: Barclays was not liable, as an exemption clause included in the contract between it and the plaintiffs exonerated it from liability for the negligence of its correspondents. The AP Bank was held not to be liable to the plaintiffs as there was no privity of contract between a principal and his agent's sub-agent.

29–15   This rule was followed in *Royal Products Ltd v Midland Bank Ltd* [1981] 2 Lloyd's Rep 194 in relation to a credit transfer: see para 28–9.

Although generally the immediate agent is liable to the principal for the defaults of the sub-agent in the course of his employment, the principal may have a direct action in tort against a sub-agent on the usual basis of the leap-frog by a victim through to the tortfeasor, as in the product liability case of *Donaghue v Stevenson* [1932] AC 562, HL.

Network liability in France

29–16   French courts have imposed network liability.

In a decision of the French Court of Cassation of November 13, 1983, a customer of the Finindus Bank who had purchased land in Brazil instructed the bank to pay the price. Finindus instructed another French bank which instructed its agent in Sao Paulo. The money was transferred to the wrong person. It was unclear who made the mistake. *Held*: the originator's bank Finindus was liable to reimburse the originator for the full amount.

In a decision of the Paris court of September 22, 1988, a French company instructed its bank to transfer FF2m to its branch in the US. The bank sent a payment order to Société Generale which transmitted the order to an American bank. The order was to be carried out in French Francs because the originator in the US wished to have French Francs available. The American bank converted the FF2m into US dollars. The dollar exchange rate then fell. The French company refused to accept the dollars. The dollars were exchanged back into Francs. There was an exchange rate loss and as a result only FF 1.6m remained from the original FF2m. *Held*: the originator's bank was liable for damages. A bank is responsible to the originator for the agent which it employs.

Network liability in Switzerland

29–17   In Switzerland the responsibility of the originator's bank is not absolute. A bank has a duty to its customer to diligently select, instruct and monitor a foreign correspondent bank through which a foreign transaction is to be carried out: see CO Art 399. If the originator's bank has carried out this duty, it is not liable for damages resulting from the insolvency of the correspondent bank. A bank's duty is limited to due care in the selection of the foreign bank but not for a default by a foreign bank. But liability, if not based on contract, may nevertheless be found in tort if, e.g. the sub-agents or other independent contractors owed a duty of care to the originator.

Network liability in Italy

In Italy, the bank must comply with the duties of care of an agent, for which   **29–18** the law stipulates strict requirements: Art 1710(1) CC; Art 1856 CC. Banks have been held liable, e.g. for not making sure that the transfer order was carried out by the correspondent bank. See *Trib Torino*, May 16 1949, *Rivista bancaria*, 1949, p 366; *Trib. Foggia*, July 14, 1987, *Giurisprudenza di merito*, 1989, p 65. The bank must inform the customer promptly of any circumstances which occur after the transfer order is submitted and which could influence the execution of the transfer agreement, such as the closing of the beneficiary's account or the bankruptcy of the beneficiary: Art 1710(2) CC; Cass, February 20, 1988, No 1764 *Banca, borsa, titoli di credito*, 1989, II, p 440. The bank cannot simply rely on the instructions which it is given but must stop the execution of the transfer, if possible, if circumstances arise which are unknown to the originator or cannot be reported to him in time and which are plainly of substantial significance for him.

Network liability in Germany

The German courts have imposed a direct liability on an intermediary bank   **29–19** to the originator.

> In the German decision of a Düsseldorf court, OLG Düsseldorf, DB 1982, 749, on December 28 the plaintiff instructed his bank to transfer DM 30,000 to the beneficiary's bank, stating that, if the transfer was not made by December 31, the originator would lose tax reliefs on the payment. The originator's bank transmitted the order to a central giro institution on the same day and, on that day, the giro transmitted the funds to the beneficiary's bank. But the giro omitted the name and account number of the beneficiary and accordingly the payment was late. The plaintiff lost tax savings of DM 19,604 and claimed damages direct from the giro institution. *Held:* the giro was liable. Although there was no direct contract, the giro owed the originator a direct duty of care on the basis of a fictional third party beneficiary theory. The originator's bank was not liable because its only responsibility was to select a responsible and properly qualified intermediary bank.

Network liability in Japan

29–20 Japanese decisions have refused to impose liability on the originator's bank for errors by intermediaries where the originator designated the intermediary: see CC Art 105.

In *Sato v Joyo Bank* 698 Shûkan Kinyû Shôji Hanrei 16 (Tokyo High Court, February 14, 1984) an originator had instructed the originator's bank Joyo Bank to credit a beneficiary's account at Banker's Trust Company and to notify the beneficiary, who was a US citizen, that the credit could be withdrawn. Banker's Trust Company failed to notify the beneficiary and the originator incurred a loss that included consequential damages. *Held*: the originator's bank was not liable. This was because the originator had chosen the sub-agent.

In *Imasa Corp v Tokiwa Mutual Bank* 1260 Hanreijihô 15 (Tokyo High Court, October 28, 1987), an originator had instructed the originator's bank to credit a beneficiary's account with an agricultural society with the assistance of two intermediary financial institutions, both of which had been designated by the originator. Because of an error by one of the designated intermediary institutions, the wrong account was credited. *Held*: because the originator had selected the intermediary financial institutions as well as the beneficiary's financial institution, the originator's bank's duty was limited to transmitting the payment order to the designated intermediary financial institution and providing cover. The originator's damages claim against the originator's bank was rejected.

But in *Yamaguchi v Iyo Bank*, 839 Kinyû Shôji Hanrei 3 (Takamatsu High Court, October 18, 1989) an originator instructed the originator's bank to credit the beneficiary's account at the beneficiary's bank. The beneficiary's bank, however, mistakenly credited the wrong account. The money was withdrawn from the account and the originator incurred a loss. *Held*: the court allowed the originator's damages claim against the originator's bank, ruling that the bank was liable to the originator for a loss caused by an error of the beneficiary's bank, which was a sub-agent of the originator's bank.

Conflict of laws

29–21 International credit transfers are governed by the ordinary rules of private international law as with any other contract, and special rules are unusual. Of course the actual rules will depend on the topic, e.g. contract, tort, expropriation, attachment or insolvency law. It would be impracticable to subject all of the potential issues to a single unitary system of law.

In the United States, s 4A–507 of the UCC deals with choice of law for credit transfers within Art 4A. The parties may agree upon the law of any jurisdiction that they choose, whether or not it has any relationship to the transaction. Funds transfer systems may also select a governing law. Whether the selected law binds third parties is largely based upon the third party's advance notice that the system will be used and of its choice of law rules.

Apart from this, the conflict rules are:

— in an issue between a sender and a receiving bank, the receiving bank's law applies;

— issues between the beneficiary's bank and the beneficiary are governed by the law of the beneficiary's bank;

— the issue of when payment is made from the originator to the beneficiary is governed by the law of the beneficiary's bank.

As to Europe, under the Rome Convention of 1980 on the Law Applicable to Contractual Obligations, the parties may expressly choose the applicable law. This need have no relationship to the transaction. Standard banking conditions in Germany, Italy, the Netherlands and other countries contain a choice of law clause. However if the parties do not make an express choice of law, then various presumptions apply, including the residence of the party owing the characteristic performance, whatever that may be. It is suggested that, as between the originator and his bank, the law of the bank applies. As between sending and receiving bank, the law of the receiving bank applies. As between the beneficiary's bank and the beneficiary, the law of his bank applies. But there is an override for the law of the most substantial connection. There are special rules for agency. See generally chapter 14.   **29–22**

One possibility in determining the law of the most substantial connection is to use the accessory principle, namely, that where there is one main contract, the law of all of the others may be attracted to it so that there is a single law for the sake of consistency and certainty in the same way that the governing law of a guarantee may be attracted to the law of the loan agreement. But this is considered to be only a pointer.

PART V

MATERIALS

Appendix A

MAIN ARTICLES OF THE ROME CONVENTION ON THE LAW APPLICABLE TO CONTRACTUAL OBLIGATIONS OF 1980

After recitals, the Convention provides:

TITLE I

SCOPE OF THE CONVENTION

Article 1
Scope of the Convention

1. The rules of this Convention shall apply to contractual obligations in any situation involving a choice between the laws of different countries.

2. They shall not apply to:

    (a) questions involving the status or legal capacity of natural persons, without prejudice to Article 11;
    (b) contractual obligations relating to:
        - wills and succession,
        - rights in property arising out of a matrimonial relationship,
        - rights and duties arising out of a family relationship, parentage, marriage or affinity, including maintenance obligations in respect of children who are not legitimate;
    (c) obligations arising under bills of exchange, cheques and promissory notes and other negotiable instruments to the extent that the obligations under such other negotiable instruments arise out of their negotiable character;
    (d) arbitration agreements and agreements on the choice of court;
    (e) questions governed by the law of companies and other bodies corporate or unincorporate such as the creation, by registration or otherwise, legal capacity, internal organisation or winding up of

companies and other bodies corporate or unincorporate and the personal liability of officers and members as such for the obligations of the company or body;

(f) the question whether an agent is able to bind a principal, or an organ to bind a company or body corporate or unincorporate, to a third party;

(g) the constitution of trusts and the relationship between settlors, trustees and beneficiaries;

(h) evidence and procedure, without prejudice to Article 14.

3. The rules of this Convention do not apply to contracts of insurance which cover risks situated in the territories of the Member States of the European Economic Community. In order to determine whether a risk is situated in these territories the court shall apply its internal law.

4. The preceding paragraph does not apply to contracts of re-insurance.

Article 2
Application of law of non-contracting States

Any law specified by this Convention shall be applied whether or not it is the law of a Contracting State.

TITLE II

UNIFORM RULES

Article 3
Freedom of choice

1. A contract shall be governed by the law chosen by the parties. The choice must be express or demonstrated with reasonable certainty by the terms of the contract or the circumstances of the case. By their choice the parties can select the law applicable to the whole or a part only of the contract.

2. The parties may at any time agree to subject the contract to a law other than that which previously governed it, whether as a result of an earlier choice under this Article or of other provisions of this Convention. Any variation by the parties of the law to be applied made after the conclusion of the contract shall not prejudice its formal validity under Article 9 or adversely affect the rights of third parties.

3. The fact that the parties have chosen a foreign law, whether or not accompanied by the choice of a foreign tribunal, shall not, where all the other elements relevant to the situation at the time of the choice are connected with one country only, prejudice the application of rules of the law of that country which cannot be derogated from by contract, hereinafter called "mandatory rules".

4. The existence and validity of the consent of the parties as to the choice of the applicable law shall be determined in accordance with the provisions of Articles 8, 9 and 11.

Article 4
Applicable law in the absence of choice

1. To the extent that the law applicable to the contract has not been chosen in accordance with Article 3, the contract shall be governed by the law of the country with which it is most closely connected. Nevertheless, a severable part of the contract which has a closer connection with another country may by way of exception be governed by the law of that other country.

2. Subject to the provisions of paragraph 5 of this Article, it shall be presumed that the contract is most closely connected with the country where the party who is to effect the performance which is characteristic of the contract has, at the time of conclusion of the contract, his habitual residence, or, in the case of a body corporate or unincorporate, its central administration. However, if the contract is entered into in the course of that party's trade or profession, that country shall be the country in which the principal place of business is situated or, where under the terms of the contract the performance is to be effected through a place of business other than the principal place of business, the country in which that other place of business is situated.

3. Notwithstanding the provisions of paragraph 2 of this Article, to the extent that the subject matter of the contract is a right in immovable property or a right to use immovable property it shall be presumed that the contract is most closely connected with the country where the immovable property is situated.

4. A contract for the carriage of goods shall not be subject to the presumption in paragraph 2. In such a contract if the country in which, at the time the contract is concluded, the carrier has his principal place of business is also the country in which the place of loading or the place of discharge or the principal place of business of the consignor is situated,

it shall be presumed that the contract is most closely connected with that country. In applying this paragraph single voyage charter-parties and other contracts the main purpose of which is the carriage of goods shall be treated as contracts for the carriage of goods.

5. Paragraph 2 shall not apply if the characteristic performance cannot be determined, and the presumptions in paragraphs 2, 3 and 4 shall be disregarded if it appears from the circumstances as a whole that the contract is more closely connected with another country.

Article 5
Certain consumer contracts

1. This Article applies to a contract the object of which is the supply of goods or services to a person ("the consumer") for a purpose which can be regarded as being outside his trade or profession, or a contract for the provision of credit for that object.

2. Notwithstanding the provisions of Article 3, a choice of law made by the parties shall not have the result of depriving the consumer of the protection afforded to him by the mandatory rules of the law of the country in which he has his habitual residence:

    – if in that country the conclusion of the contract was preceded by a specific invitation addressed to him or by advertising, and he had taken in that country all the steps necessary on his part for the conclusion of the contract, or
    – if the other party or his agent received the consumer's order in that country, or
    – if the contract is for the sale of goods and the consumer travelled from that country to another country and there gave his order, provided that the consumer's journey was arranged by the seller for the purpose of inducing the consumer to buy.

3. Notwithstanding the provisions of Article 4, a contract to which this Article applies shall, in the absence of choice in accordance with Article 3, be governed by the law of the country in which the consumer has his habitual residence if it is entered into in the circumstances described in paragraph 2 of this Article.

4. This Article shall not apply to:

    (a) a contract of carriage;
    (b) a contract for the supply of services where the services are to be supplied to the consumer exclusively in a country other than that in which he has his habitual residence.

5. Notwithstanding the provisions of paragraph 4, this Article shall apply to a contract which, for an inclusive price, provides for a combination of travel and accommodation.

Article 6
Individual employment contracts

1. Notwithstanding the provisions of Article 3, in a contract of employment a choice of law made by the parties shall not have the result of depriving the employee of the protection afforded to him by the mandatory rules of the law which would be applicable under paragraph 2 in the absence of choice.

2. Notwithstanding the provisions of Article 4, a contract of employment shall, in the absence of choice in accordance with Article 3, be governed:

   (a) by the law of the country in which the employee habitually carries out his work in performance of the contract, even if he is temporarily employed in another country; or
   (b) if the employee does not habitually carry out his work in any one country, by the law of the country in which the place of business through which he was engaged is situated;

   unless it appears from the circumstances as a whole that the contract is more closely connected with another country, in which case the contract shall be governed by the law of that country.

Article 7
Mandatory rules

1. When applying under this Convention the law of a country, effect may be given to the mandatory rules of the law of another country with which the situation has a close connection, if and in so far as, under the law of the latter country, those rules must be applied whatever the law applicable to the contract. In considering whether to give effect to these mandatory rules, regard shall be had to their nature and purpose and to the consequences of their application or non-application. [Art 7(1) does not apply in the UK.]

2. Nothing in this Convention shall restrict the application of the rules of the law of the forum in a situation where they are mandatory irrespective of the law otherwise applicable to the contract.

Article 8
Material validity

1. The existence and validity of a contract, or of any term of a contract, shall be determined by the law which would govern it under this Convention if the contract or term were valid.

2. Nevertheless a party may rely upon the law of the country in which he has his habitual residence to establish that he did not consent if it appears from the circumstances that it would not be reasonable to determine the effect of his conduct in accordance with the law specified in the preceding paragraph.

Article 9
Formal validity

1. A contract concluded between persons who are in the same country is formally valid if it satisfies the formal requirements of the law which governs it under this Convention or of the law of the country where it is concluded.

2. A contract concluded between persons who are in different countries is formally valid if it satisfies the formal requirements of the law which governs it under this Convention or of the law of one of those countries.

3. Where a contract is concluded by an agent, the country in which the agent acts is the relevant country for the purposes of paragraphs 1 and 2.

4. An act intended to have legal effect relating to an existing or contemplated contract is formally valid if it satisfies the formal requirements of the law which under this Convention governs or would govern the contract or of the law of the country where the act was done.

5. The provisions of the preceding paragraphs shall not apply to a contract to which Article 5 applies, concluded in the circumstances described in paragraph 2 of Article 5. The formal validity of such a contract is governed by the law of the country in which the consumer has his habitual residence.

6. Notwithstanding paragraphs 1 to 4 of this Article, a contract the subject matter of which is a right in immovable property or a right to use immovable property shall be subject to the mandatory requirements of form of the law of the country where the property is situated if by that

law those requirements are imposed irrespective of the country where the contract is concluded and irrespective of the law governing the contract.

Article 10
Scope of the applicable law

1. The law applicable to a contract by virtue of Articles 3 to 6 and 12 of this Convention shall govern in particular:

   (a) interpretation;
   (b) performance;
   (c) within the limits of the powers conferred on the court by its procedural law, the consequences of breach, including the assessment of damages in so far as it is governed by rules of law;
   (d) the various ways of extinguishing obligations, and prescription and limitation of actions;
   (e) the consequences of nullity of the contract. [This para (e) does not apply in the UK.]

2. In relation to the manner of performance and the steps to be taken in the event of defective performance regard shall be had to the law of the country in which performance takes place.

Article 11
Incapacity

In a contract concluded between persons who are in the same country, a natural person who would have capacity under the law of that country may invoke his incapacity resulting from another law only if the other party to the contract was aware of this incapacity at the time of the conclusion of the contract or was not aware thereof as a result of negligence.

Article 12
Voluntary assignment

1. The mutual obligations of assignor and assignee under a voluntary assignment of a right against another person ("the debtor") shall be governed by the law which under this Convention applies to the contract between the assignor and assignee.

2. The law governing the right to which the assignment relates shall

determine its assignability, the relationship between the assignee and the debtor, the conditions under which the assignment can be invoked against the debtor and any question whether the debtor's obligations have been discharged.

Article 13
Subrogation

1. Where a person ("the creditor") has a contractual claim upon another ("the debtor"), and a third person has a duty to satisfy the creditor, or has in fact satisfied the creditor in discharge of that duty, the law which governs the third person's duty to satisfy the creditor shall determine whether the third person is entitled to exercise against the debtor the rights which the creditor had against the debtor under the law governing their relationship and, if so, whether he may do so in full or only to a limited extent.

2. The same rule applies where several persons are subject to the same contractual claim and one of them has satisfied the creditor.

Article 14
Burden of proof, etc.

1. The law governing the contract under this Convention applies to the extent that it contains, in the law of contract, rules which raise presumptions of law or determine the burden of proof.

2. A contract or an act intended to have legal effect may be proved by any mode of proof recognised by the law of the forum or by any of the laws referred to in Article 9 under which that contract or act is formally valid, provided that such mode of proof can be administered by the forum.

Article 15
Exclusion of renvoi

The application of the law of any country specified by this Convention means the application of the rules of law in force in that country other than its rules of private international law.

Article 16
"Ordre public"

The application of a rule of the law of any country specified by this Convention may be refused only if such application is manifestly incompatible with the public policy ("ordre public") of the forum.

Article 17
No retrospective effect

This Convention shall apply in a Contracting State to contracts made after the date on which this Convention has entered into force with respect to that State.

Article 18
Uniform interpretation

In the interpretation and application of the preceding uniform rules, regard shall be had to their international character and to the desirability of achieving uniformity in their interpretation and application.

Article 19
States with more than one legal system

1. Where a State comprises several territorial units each of which has its own rules of law in respect of contractual obligations, each territorial unit shall be considered as a country for the purposes of identifying the law applicable under this Convention.

2. A State within which different territorial units have their own rules of law in respect of contractual obligations shall not be bound to apply this Convention to conflicts solely between the laws of such units. [The UK did not disapply Art. 19(1).]

Article 20
Precedence of Community law

This Convention shall not affect the application of provisions which, in relation to particular matters, lay down choice of law rules relating to contractual obligations and which are or will be contained in acts of the institutions of the European Communities or in national laws harmonised in implementation of such acts.

Article 21
Relationship with other conventions

This Convention shall not prejudice the application of international conventions to which a Contracting State is, or becomes, a party.

Article 22
Reservations

1. Any Contracting State may, at the time of signature, ratification, acceptance or approval, reserve the right not to apply:

    (a)   the provisions of Article 7(1);
    (b)   the provisions of Article 10(1)(e).

2. Any Contracting State may also, when notifying an extension of the Convention in accordance with Article 27(2), make one or more of these reservations, with its effect limited to all or some of the territories mentioned in the extension.

3. Any Contracting State may at any time withdraw a reservation which it has made; the reservation shall cease to have effect on the first day of the third calendar month after notification of the withdrawal.

[Title III, Arts 23 to 33 contain final provisions regarding, e.g. amendments, new multilateral conventions, application to overseas territories, ratification and other matters. The Brussels Protocol of December 19, 1988 provides that the EC Court of Justice has jurisdiction to give rulings on the interpretation of the Convention.]

Appendix B

BRUSSELS CONVENTION OF 1968 ON JURISDICTION AND THE ENFORCEMENT OF JUDGMENTS IN CIVIL AND COMMERCIAL MATTERS AS AMENDED BY THE SAN SEBASTIÁN CONVENTION

This text given is that of the original Brussels Convention as amended by the **B–1** San Sebastián Convention of 1989.

ARRANGEMENT OF PROVISIONS

TITLE I

SCOPE (Article 1)

TITLE II

JURISDICTION

TITLE III

RECOGNITION AND ENFORCEMENT

Definition of judgment (Article 25)

Section 1.   Recognition (Articles 26–30)
Section 2.   Enforcement (Articles 31–45)
Section 3.   Common provisions (Articles 46–49)

TITLE IV

AUTHENTIC INSTRUMENTS AND COURT SETTLEMENTS
(Articles 50 and 51)

TITLE V

GENERAL PROVISIONS (Articles 52 and 53)

TITLE VI

TRANSITIONAL PROVISIONS (Articles 54 and 54A)

TITLE VII

RELATIONSHIP TO OTHER CONVENTIONS (Articles 55–59)

TITLE VIII

FINAL PROVISIONS (Articles 60–68)

CONVENTION
on jurisdiction and the enforcement of judgments
in civil and commercial matters

PREAMBLE

THE HIGH CONTRACTING PARTIES TO THE TREATY
ESTABLISHING THE EUROPEAN ECONOMIC COMMUNITY,

Desiring to implement the provisions of Article 220 of that Treaty by virtue of which they undertook to secure the simplification of formalities governing the reciprocal recognition and enforcement of judgments of courts or tribunals;

Anxious to strengthen in the Community the legal protection of persons therein established;

Considering that it is necessary for this purpose to determine the international jurisdiction of their courts, to facilitate recognition and to introduce an expeditious procedure for securing the enforcement of judgments, authentic instruments and court settlements;

Have decided to conclude this Convention and to this end have designated as their Plenipotentiaries;

(Designations of Plenipotentiaries of the original six Contracting States)

WHO, meeting within the Council, having exchanged their Full Powers, found in good and due form,

HAVE AGREED AS FOLLOWS:

TITLE I

SCOPE

Article 1

This Convention shall apply in civil and commercial matters whatever the nature of the court or tribunal. It shall not extend, in particular, to revenue, customs or administrative matters.

The Convention shall not apply to:

1. The status or legal capacity of natural persons, rights in property arising out of a matrimonial relationship, wills and succession.

2. Bankruptcy, proceedings relating to the winding-up of insolvent companies or other legal persons, judicial arrangements, compositions and analogous proceedings.

3. Social security

4. Arbitration

TITLE II

JURISDICTION

Section 1
General provisions

Article 2

Subject to the provisions of this Convention, persons domiciled in a Contracting State shall, whatever their nationality, be sued in the courts of that State.

Persons who are not nationals of the State in which they are domiciled shall be governed by the rules of jurisdiction applicable to nationals of that State.

Article 3

Persons domiciled in a Contracting State may be sued in the courts of another Contracting State only by virtue of the rules set out in Sections 2 to 6 of this Title.

In particular the following provisions shall not be applicable as against them:

- in Belgium: Article 15 of the civil code (Code civil – Burgerlijk Wetboek) and Article 638 of the judicial code (Code judiciaire – Gerechtelijk Wetboek);
- in Denmark: Article 246(2) and (3) of the law on civil procedure (Lov om rettens pleje);
- in the Federal Republic of Germany: Article 23 of the code of civil procedure (Zivilprozeßordnung);
- in Greece, Article 40 of the code of civil procedure (Κώδικαζ Πολιτικήζ Δικονομίαζ);
- in France: Articles 14 and 15 of the civil code (Code civil);
- in Ireland: the rules which enable jurisdiction to be founded on the document instituting the proceedings having been served on the defendant during his temporary presence in Ireland;
- in Italy: Articles 2 and 4, nos 1 and 2 of the code of civil procedure (Codice di procedura civile);
- in Luxembourg: Articles 14 and 15 of the civil code (Code civil);

- in the Netherlands: Articles 126(3) and 127 of the code of civil procedure (Wetboek van Burgerlijke Rechtsvordering);

- in Portugal: Article 65(1)(c), Article 65(2) and Article 65A(c) of the code of civil procedure (Código de Processo Civil) and Article 11 of the code of labour procedure (Código de Processo de Trabalho);

- in the United Kingdom: the rules which enable jurisdiction to be founded on:

  (a) the document instituting the proceedings having been served on the defendant during his temporary presence in the United Kingdom; or
  (b) the presence within the United Kingdom of property belonging to the defendant; or
  (c) the seizure by the plaintiff of property situated in the United Kingdom.

Article 4

If the defendant is not domiciled in a Contracting State, the jurisdiction of the courts of each Contracting State shall, subject to the provisions of Article 16, be determined by the law of that State.

As against such a defendant, any person domiciled in a Contracting State may, whatever his nationality, avail himself in that State of the rules of jurisdiction there in force, and in particular those specified in the second paragraph of Article 3, in the same way as the nationals of that State.

Section 2
Special jurisdiction

Article 5

A person domiciled in a Contracting State may, in another Contracting State, be sued:

1. In matters relating to a contract, in the courts for the place of performance of the obligation in question; in matters relating to individual contracts of employment, this place is that where the employee habitually carries out his work, or if the employee does not habitually carry out his work in any one country, the employer may also be sued in the courts for the place where the business which engaged the employee was or is now situated.

2. In matters relating to maintenance, in the courts for the place where the maintenance creditor is domiciled or habitually resident or, if the matter is ancillary to proceedings concerning the status of a person, in the court which, according to its own law, has jurisdiction to entertain those proceedings, unless that jurisdiction is based solely on the nationality of one of the parties.

3. In matters relating to tort, delict or quasi-delict, in the courts for the place where the harmful event occurred.

4. As regards a civil claim for damages or restitution which is based on an act giving rise to criminal proceedings, in the court seised of those proceedings, to the extent that that court has jurisdiction under its own law to entertain civil proceedings.

5. As regards a dispute arising out of the operations of a branch, agency or other establishment, in the courts for the place in which the branch, agency or other establishment is situated.

6. As settlor, trustee or beneficiary of a trust created by the operation of a statute, or by a written instrument, or created orally and evidenced in writing, in the courts of the Contracting State in which the trust is domiciled.

7. As regards a dispute concerning the payment of remuneration claimed in respect of the salvage of a cargo or freight, in the court under the authority of which the cargo or freight in question:

    (a) has been arrested to secure such payment, or
    (b) could have been so arrested, but bail or other security has been given;

    provided that this provision shall apply only if it is claimed that the defendant has an interest in the cargo or freight or had such an interest at the time of salvage.

Article 6

A person domiciled in a Contracting State may also be sued:

1. Where he is one of a number of defendants, in the courts for the place where any one of them is domiciled.

2. As a third party in an action on a warranty or guarantee or in any other third party proceedings, in the court seised of the original proceedings, unless these were instituted solely with the object of removing him from the jurisdiction of the court which would be competent in his case.

3. On a counter-claim arising from the same contract or facts on which the original claim was based, in the court in which the original claim is pending.

4. In matters relating to a contract, if the action may be combined with an action against the same defendant in matters relating to rights in rem in immovable property, in the court of the Contracting State in which the property is situated.

Article 6a

Where by virtue of this Convention a court of a Contracting State has jurisdiction in actions relating to liability from the use orf operation of a ship, that court, or any other court substituted for this purpose by the internal law of that State, shall also have jurisdiction over claims for limitation of such liability.

Section 3
Jurisdiction in matters relating to insurance

Article 7

In matters relating to insurance, jurisdiction shall be determined by this Section, without prejudice to the provisions of Articles 4 and 5 point 5.

Article 8

An insurer domiciled in a Contracting State may be sued:

1. in the courts of the State where he is domiciled, or

2. in another Contracting State, in the courts for the place where the policy-holder is domiciled, or

3. if he is a co-insurer, in the courts of a Contracting State in which proceedings are brought against the leading insurer.

An insurer who is not domiciled in a Contracting State but has a branch, agency or other establishment in one of the Contracting States shall, in disputes arising out of the operations of the branch, agency or establishment, be deemed to be domiciled in that State.

Article 9

In respect of liability insurance or insurance of immovable property, the insurer may in addition be sued in the courts for the place where the harmful event occurred. The same applies if movable and immovable property are covered by the same insurance policy and both are adversely affected by the same contingency.

Article 10

In respect of liability insurance, the insurer may also, if the law of the court permits it, be joined in proceedings which the injured party had brought against the insured.

The provisions of Articles 7, 8 and 9 shall apply to actions brought by the injured party directly against the insurer, where such direct actions are permitted.

If the law governing such direct actions provides that the policy-holder or the insured may be joined as a party to the action, the same court shall have jurisdiction over them.

Article 11

Without prejudice to the provisions of the third paragraph of Article 10, an insurer may bring proceedings only in the courts of the Contracting State in which the defendant is domiciled, irrespective of whether he is the policy-holder, the insured or a beneficiary.

The provisions of this Section shall not affect the right to bring a counter-claim in the court in which, in accordance with this Section, the original claim is pending.

Article 12

The provisions of this Section may be departed from only by an agreement on jurisdiction:

1. which is entered into after the dispute has arisen, or

2. which allows the policy-holder, the insured or a beneficiary to bring proceedings in courts other than those indicated in this Section, or

3. which is concluded between a policy-holder and an insurer, both of whom are domiciled in the same Contracting State, and which has the

effect of conferring jurisdiction on the courts of that State even if the harmful event were to occur abroad, provided that such an agreement is not contrary to the law of that State, or

4. which is concluded with a policy-holder who is not domiciled in a Contracting State, except in so far as the insurance is compulsory or relates to immovable property in a Contracting State, or

5. which relates to a contract of insurance in so far as it covers one or more of the risks set out in Article 12a.

Article 12a

The following are the risks referred to in point 5 of Article 12:

1. Any loss of or damage to:

    (a) sea-going ships, installations situated offshore or on the high seas, or aircraft, arising from perils which relate to their use for commercial purposes;

    (b) goods in transit other than passengers' baggage where the transit consists of or includes carriage by such ships or aircraft.

2. Any liability, other than for bodily injury to passengers or loss of or damage to their baggage:

    (a) arising out of the use or operation of ships, installations or aircraft as referred to in point 1(a) above in so far as the law of the Contracting State in which such aircraft are registered does not prohibit agreements on jurisdiction regarding insurance of such risks;

    (b) for loss or damage caused by goods in transit as described in point 1(b) above.

3. Any financial loss connected with the use or operation of ships, installations or aircrafts as referred to in point 1(a) above, in particular loss of freight or charter-hire.

4. Any risk or interest connected with any of those referred to in points 1 to 3 above.

Section 4
Jurisdiction over consumer contracts

Article 13

In proceedings concerning a contract concluded by a person for a purpose which can be regarded as being outside his trade or profession, hereinafter called "the consumer", jurisdiction shall be determined by this Section, without prejudice to the provisions of Article 4 and point 5 of Article 5, if it is:

1.   a contract for the sale of goods on instalment credit terms, or

2.   a contract for a loan repayable by instalments, or for any other form of credit, made to finance the sale of goods, or

3.   any other contract for the supply of goods or a contract for the supply of services, and

     (a)   in the State of the consumer's domicile the conclusion of the contract was preceded by a specific invitation addressed to him or by advertising; and

     (b)   the consumer took in that State the steps necessary for the conclusion of the contract.

Where a consumer enters into a contract with a party who is not domiciled in a Contracting State but has a branch, agency or other establishment in one of the Contracting States, that party shall, in disputes arising out of the operations of the branch, agency or establishment, be deemed to be domiciled in that State.

This Section shall not apply to contracts of transport.

Article 14

A consumer may bring proceedings against the other party to a contract either in the courts of the Contracting State in which that party is domiciled or in the courts of the Contracting State in which he is himself domiciled.

Proceedings may be brought against a consumer by the other party to the contract only in the courts of the Contracting State in which the consumer is domiciled.

These provisions shall not affect the right to bring a counter-claim in the court in which, in accordance with this Section, the original claim is pending.

Article 15

The provisions of this Section may be departed from only by an agreement:

1.   which is entered into after the dispute has arisen, or

2.   which allows the consumer to bring proceedings in courts other than those indicated in this Section, or

3. which is entered into by the consumer and the other party to the contract, both of whom are at the time of conclusion of the contract domiciled or habitually resident in the same Contracting State, and which confers jurisdiction on the courts of that State, provided that such an agreement is not contrary to the law of that State.

Section 5
Exclusive jurisdiction

Article 16

The following courts shall have exclusive jurisdiction, regardless of domicile:

1. (a) in proceedings which have as their object rights in rem in immovable property or tenancies of immovable property, the courts of the Contracting State in which the property is situated;
   (b) however, in proceedings which have as their object tenancies of immovable property concluded for temporary private use for a maximum period of six consecutive months, the courts of the Contracting State in which the defendant is domiciled shall also have jurisdiction, provided that the landlord and the tenant are natural persons and are domiciled in the same Contracting State.

2. In proceedings which have as their object the validity of the constitution, the nullity or the dissolution of companies or other legal persons or associations of natural or legal persons, or the decisions of their organs, the courts of the Contracting State in which the company, legal person or association has its seat.

3. In proceedings which have as their object the validity of entries in public registers, the courts of the Contracting State in which the register is kept.

4. In proceedings concerned with the registration or validity of patents, trade marks, designs, or other similar rights required to be deposited or registered, the courts of the Contracting State in which the deposit or registration has been applied for, has taken place or is under the terms of an international convention deemed to have taken place.

5. In proceedings concerned with the enforcement of judgments, the courts of the Contracting State in which the judgment has been or is to be enforced.

Section 6
Prorogation of jurisdiction

Article 17

If the parties, one or more of whom is domiciled in a Contracting State, have agreed that a court or the courts of a Contracting State are to have jurisdiction to settle any disputes which have arisen or which may arise in connection with a particular legal relationship, that court or those courts shall have exclusive jurisdiction. Such an agreement conferring jurisdiction shall be either:

(a) in writing or evidenced in writing, or

(b) in a form which accords with practices which the parties have established between themselves, or

(c) in international trade or commerce, in a form which accords with a usage of which the parties are or ought to have been aware and which in such trade or commerce is widely known to, and regularly observed by, parties to contracts of the type involved in the particular trade or commerce concerned.

Where such an agreement is concluded by parties, none of whom is domiciled in a Contracting State, the courts of other Contracting States shall have no jurisdiction over their disputes unless the court or courts chosen have declined jurisdiction.

The court or courts of a Contracting State on which a trust instrument has conferred jurisdiction shall have exclusive jurisdiction in any proceedings brought against a settlor, trustee or beneficiary, if relations between these persons or their rights or obligations under the trust are involved.

Agreements or provisions of a trust instrument conferring jurisdiction shall have no legal force if they are contrary to the provisions of Articles 12 or 15, or if the courts whose jurisdiction they purport to exclude have exclusive jurisdiction by virtue of Article 16.

If an agreement conferring jurisdiction was concluded for the benefit of only one of the parties, that party shall retain the right to bring proceedings in any other court which has jurisdiction by virtue of this Convention.

In matters relating to individual contracts of employment an agreement conferring jurisdiction shall have legal force only if it is entered into after the dispute has arisen or if the employee invokes it to seise courts other than those for the defendant's domicile or those specified in Article 5(1).

Article 18

Apart from jurisdiction derived from other provisions of this Convention, a court of a Contracting State before whom a defendant enters an appearance shall have jurisdiction. This rule shall not apply where appearance was entered solely to contest the jurisdiction, or where another court has exclusive jurisdiction by virtue of Article 16.

Section 7
Examination as to jurisdiction and admissibility

Article 19

Where a court of a Contracting State is seised of a claim which is principally concerned with a matter over which the courts of another Contracting State have exclusive jurisdiction by virtue of Article 16, it shall declare of its own motion that it has no jurisdiction.

Article 20

Where a defendant domiciled in one Contracting State is sued in a court of another Contracting State and does not enter an appearance, the court shall declare of its own motion that it has no jurisdiction unless its jurisdiction is derived from the provisions of the Convention.

The court shall stay the proceedings so long as it is not shown that the defendant has been able to receive the document instituting the proceedings or an equivalent document in sufficient time to enable him to arrange for his defence, or that all necessary steps have been taken to this end.

The provisions of the foregoing paragraph shall be replaced by those of Article 15 of the Hague Convention of 15th November, 1965 on the service abroad of judicial and extrajudicial documents in civil or commercial matters, if the document instituting the proceedings or notice thereof had to be transmitted abroad in accordance with the Convention.

Section 8
Lis pendens-related actions

Article 21

Where proceedings involving the same cause of action and between the same parties are brought in the courts of different Contracting States, any court other than the court first seised shall of its own motion stay its proceedings until such time as the jurisdiction of the court first seised is established.

Where the jurisdiction of the court first seised is established, any court other than the court first seised shall decline jurisdiction in favour of that court.

Article 22

Where related actions are brought in the courts of different Contracting States, any court other than the court first seised may, while the actions are pending at first instance, stay its proceedings.

A court other than the court first seised may also, on the application of one of the parties, decline jurisdiction if the law of that court permits the consolidation of related actions and the court first seised has jurisdiction over both actions.

For the purposes of this Article, actions are deemed to be related where they are so closely connected that it is expedient to hear and determine them together to avoid the risk of irreconcilable judgments resulting from separate proceedings.

Article 23

Where actions come within the exclusive jurisdiction of several courts, any court other than the court first seised shall decline jurisdiction in favour of that court.

Section 9
Provisional, including protective, measures

Article 24

Application may be made to the courts of a Contracting State for such provisional, including protective, measures as may be available under the law of that State, even if, under this Convention, the courts of another Contracting State have jurisdiction as to the substance of the matter.

TITLE III

RECOGNITION AND ENFORCEMENT

Article 25

For the purposes of this Convention, "judgment" means any judgment given by a court or tribunal of a Contracting State, whatever the judgment may be called, including a decree, order, decision or writ of execution, as well as the determination of costs or expenses by an officer of the court.

Section 1
Recognition

Article 26

A judgment given in a Contracting State shall be recognised in the other Contracting States without any special procedure being required.

Any interested party who raises the recognition of a judgment as the principal issue in a dispute may, in accordance with the procedures provided for in Sections 2 and 3 of this Title, apply for a decision that the judgment be recognised.

If the outcome of proceedings in a court of a Contracting State depends on the determination of an incidental question of recognition that court shall have jurisdiction over that question.

Article 27

A judgment shall not be recognised:

1.   If such recognition is contrary to public policy in the State in which recognition is sought.

2.   Where it was given in default of appearance, if the defendant was not duly served with the document which instituted the proceedings or with an equivalent document in sufficient time to enable him to arrange for his defence.

3.   If the judgment is irreconcilable with a judgment given in a dispute between the same parties in the State in which recognition is sought.

4.   If the court of the State of origin, in order to arrive at its judgment, has decided a preliminary question concerning the status or legal capacity of natural persons, rights in property arising out of a matrimonial relationship, wills or succession in a way that conflicts with a rule of the private international law of the State in which the recognition is sought, unless the same result would have been reached by the application of the rules of private international law of that State.

5.   If the judgment is irreconcilable with an earlier judgment given in a non-contracting State involving the same cause of action and between the same parties, provided that this latter judgment fulfils the conditions necessary for its recognition in the state addressed.

Article 28

Moreover, a judgment shall not be recognised if it conflicts with the provisions of Sections 3, 4 or 5 of Title II, or in a case provided for in Article 59.

In its examination of the grounds of jurisdiction referred to in the foregoing paragraph, the court or authority applied to shall be bound by the findings of fact on which the court of the State of origin based its jurisdiction.

Subject to the provisions of the first paragraph, the jurisdiction of the court of the State of origin may not be reviewed; the test of public policy referred to in point 1 of Article 27 may not be applied to the rules relating to jurisdiction.

Article 29

Under no circumstances may a foreign judgment be reviewed as to its substance.

Article 30

A court of a Contracting State in which recognition is sought of a judgment given in another Contracting State may stay the proceedings if an ordinary appeal against the judgment has been lodged.

A court of a Contracting State in which recognition is sought of a judgment given in Ireland or the United Kingdom may stay the proceedings if enforcement is suspended in the State of origin, by reason of an appeal.

Section 2
Enforcement

Article 31

A judgment given in a Contracting State and enforceable in that State shall be enforced in another Contracting State when, on the application of any interested party, it has been declared enforceable there.

However, in the United Kingdom, such a judgment shall be enforced in England and Wales, in Scotland, or in Northern Ireland when, on the application of any interested party, it has been registered for enforcement in that part of the United Kingdom.

Article 32

1. The application shall be submitted:

   - in Belgium, to the tribunal de première instance or rechtbank van eerste aanleg;
   - in Denmark, to the byret;
   - in the Federal Republic of Germany, to the presiding judge of a chamber of the Landgericht;
   - in Greece, to the Μονομελές Πρωτοδικείο;
   - in Spain, to the Juzgado de Primera Instancia;
   - in France, to the presiding judge of the tribunal de grande instance;
   - in Ireland, to the High Court;
   - in Italy, to the corte d'appello;
   - in Luxembourg, to the presiding judge of the tribunal d'arrondissement;
   - in the Netherlands, to the presiding judge of the arrondissementsrechtbank;
   - in Portugal, to the Tribunal Judicial de Círculo;
   - in the United Kingdom:
     (a) in England and Wales, to the High Court of Justice, or in the case of a maintenance judgement to the Magistrates' Court on transmission by the Secretary of State;
     (b) in Scotland, to the Court of Session, or in the case of a maintenance judgement to the Sheriff Court on transmission by the Secretary of State;
     (c) in Northern Ireland, to the High Court of Justice, or in the case of a maintenance judgment to the Magistrates' Court on transmission by the Secretary of State.

2. The jurisdiction of local courts shall be determined by reference to the place of domicile of the party against whom enforcement is sought. If he is not domiciled in the State in which enforcement is sought, it shall be determined by reference to the place of enforcement.

Article 33

The procedure for making the application shall be governed by the law of the State in which enforcement is sought.

The applicant must give an address for service of process within the area of jurisdiction of the court applied to. However, if the law of the State in which enforcement is sought does not provide for the furnishing of such an address, the applicant shall appoint a representative *ad litem*.

The documents referred to in Articles 46 and 47 shall be attached to the application.

Article 34

The court applied to shall give its decision without delay; the party against whom enforcement is sought shall not at this stage of the proceedings be entitled to make any submissions on the application.

The application may be refused only for one of the reasons specified in Articles 27 and 28.

Under no circumstances may the foreign judgment be reviewed as to its substance.

Article 35

The appropriate officer of the court shall without delay bring the decision given on the application to the notice of the applicant in accordance with the procedure laid down by the law of the State in which enforcement is sought.

Article 36

If enforcement is authorised, the party against whom enforcement is sought may appeal against the decision within one month of service thereof.

If that party is domiciled in a Contracting State other than that in which the decision authorising enforcement was given, the time for appealing shall be two months and shall run from the date of service, either on him in person or at his residence. No extension of time may be granted on account of distance.

Article 37

1. An appeal against the decision authorising enforcement shall be lodged in accordance with the rules governing procedure in contentious matters:

   - in Belgium, with the tribunal de première instance or rechtbank van eerste aanleg;
   - in Denmark, with the landsret;
   - in the Federal Republic of Germany, with the Oberlandesgericht;
   - in Greece, with the Εφετείο;
   - in Spain, with the Audiencia Provincial;
   - in France, with the cour d'appel;
   - in Ireland, with the High Court;
   - in Italy, with the corte d'appello;
   - in Luxembourg, with the Cour supérieure de justice sitting as a court of civil appeal;
   - in the Netherlands, with the arrondissementsrechtbank;
   - in Portugal, with the Tribunal de Relação;
   - in the United Kingdom:
     (a) in England and Wales, with the High Court of Justice, or in the case of a maintenance judgment with the Magistrates' Court;
     (b) in Scotland, with the Court of Session, or in the case of a maintenance judgment with the Sheriff Court;
     (c) in Northern Ireland, with the High Court of Justice, or in the case of a maintenance judgment with the Magistrates' Court.

2. The judgment given on the appeal may be contested only:

   - in Belgium, Greece, Spain, France, Italy, Luxembourg and in the Netherlands, by an appeal in cassation;
   - in Denmark, by an appeal to the højesteret, with the leave of the Minister of Justice;
   - in the Federal Republic of Germany, by a Rechtsbeschwerde;
   - in Ireland, by an appeal on a point of law to the Supreme Court;
   - in Portugal, by an appeal on a point of law;
   - in the United Kingdom, by a single further appeal on a point of law.

Article 38

The court with which the appeal under Article 37(1) is lodged may, on the application of the appellant, stay the proceedings if an ordinary appeal has been lodged against the judgment in the State of origin or if the time for such an appeal has not yet expired; in the latter case, the court may specify the time within which such an appeal is to be lodged.

Where the judgment was given in Ireland or the United Kingdom, any form of appeal available in the State of origin shall be treated as an ordinary appeal for the purposes of the first paragraph.

The court may also make enforcement conditional on the provision of such security as it shall determine.

Article 39

During the time specified for an appeal pursuant to Article 36 and until any such appeal has been determined, no measures of enforcement may be taken other than protective measures taken against the property of the party against whom enforcement is sought.

The decision authorising enforcement shall carry with it the power to proceed to any such protective measures.

Article 40

1. If the application for enforcement is refused, the applicant may appeal:
    - in Belgium, to the cour d'appel or hof van beroep;
    - in Denmark, to the landsret;
    - in the Federal Republic of Germany, to the Oberlandesgericht;
    - in Greece, to the Εψετείο;
    - in Spain, to the Audiencia Provincial;
    - in France, to the cour d'appel;
    - in Ireland, to the High Court;
    - in Italy, to the corte d'appello;
    - in Luxembourg, to the Cour Supérieure de justice sitting as a court of civil appeal;
    - in the Netherlands, to the gerechtshof;
    - in Portugal, to the Tribunal da Relaçào;
    - in the United Kingdom:
      (a) in England and Wales, to the High Court of Justice, or in the case of a maintenance judgment to the Magistrates' Court;

(b) in Scotland, to the Court of Session, or in the case of a maintenance judgment to the Sheriff Court;

(c) in Northern Ireland, to the High Court of Justice, or in the case
of a maintenance judgment to the Magistrates' Court.

2. The party against whom enforcement is sought shall be summoned to
appear before the appellate court. If he fails to appear, the provisions of
the second and third paragraphs of Article 20 shall apply even where he
is not domiciled in any of the Contracting States.

Article 41

A judgment given on appeal provided for in Article 40 may be contested
only:

- in Belgium, Greece, Spain, France, Italy, Luxembourg and in the
Netherlands, by an appeal in cassation;
- in Denmark, by an appeal to the højesteret, with the leave of the
Minister of Justice;
- in the Federal Republic of Germany, by a Rechtsbeschwerde;
- in Ireland, by an appeal on a point of law to the Supreme Court;
- in Portugal, by an appeal on a point of law;
- in the United Kingdom, by a single further appeal on a point of law.

Article 42

Where a foreign judgment has been given in respect of several matters and
enforcement cannot be authorised for all of them, the court shall authorise
enforcement for one or more of them.

An applicant may request partial enforcement of a judgment.

Article 43

A foreign judgment which orders a periodic payment by way of a penalty
shall be enforceable in the State in which enforcement is sought only if the
amount of the payment has been finally determined by the courts of the
State of origin.

Article 44

An applicant who, in the State of origin has benefited from complete or partial legal aid or exemption from costs or expenses, shall be entitled, in the

procedures provided for in Articles 32 to 35, to benefit from the most favourable legal aid or the most extensive exemption from costs or expenses provided for by the law of the State addressed.

However, an applicant who requests the enforcement of a decision given by an administrative authority in Denmark in respect of a maintenance order may, in the State addressed, claim the benefits referred to in the first paragraph if he presents a statement from the Danish Ministry of Justice to the effect that he fulfils the economic requirements to qualify for the grant of complete or partial legal aid or exemption from costs or expenses.

Article 45

No security, bond or deposit, however described, shall be required of a party who in one Contracting State applies for enforcement of a judgment given in another Contracting State on the ground that he is a foreign national or that he is not domiciled or resident in the State in which enforcement is sought.

Section 3
Common provisions

Article 46

A party seeking recognition or applying for enforcement of a judgment shall produce:

1. a copy of the judgment which satisfies the conditions necessary to establish its authenticity;

2. in the case of a judgment given in default, the original or a certified true copy of the document which establishes that the party in default was served with the document instituting the proceedings or with an equivalent document.

Article 47

A party applying for enforcement shall also produce:

1. documents which establish that, according to the law of the State of origin the judgment is enforceable and has been served;

2. where appropriate, a document showing that the applicant is in receipt of legal aid in the State of origin.

Article 48

If the documents specified in point 2 of Articles 46 and 47 are not produced, the court may specify a time for their production, accept equivalent documents or, if it considers that it has sufficient information before it, dispense with their production.

If the court so requires, a translation of the documents shall be produced; the translation shall be certified by a person qualified to do so in one of the Contracting States.

Article 49

No legalislation or other similar formality shall be required in respect of the documents referred to in Articles 46 or 47 or the second paragraph of Article 48, or in respect of a document appointing a representative *ad litem*.

TITLE IV

AUTHENTIC INSTRUMENTS AND COURT SETTLEMENTS

Article 50

A document which has been formally drawn up or registered as an authentic instrument and is enforceable in one Contracting State shall, in another Contracting State, be declared enforceable there, on application made in accordance with the procedures provided for in Article 31 *et seq*. The application may be refused only if enforcement of the instrument is contrary to public policy in the State addressed.

The instrument produced must satisfy the conditions necessary to establish its authenticity in the State of origin.

The provisions of Section 3 of Title III shall apply as appropriate.

Article 51

A settlement which has been approved by a court in the course of proceedings and is enforceable in the State in which it was concluded shall be enforceable in the State addressed under the same conditions as authentic instruments.

TITLE V

GENERAL PROVISIONS

Article 52

In order to determine whether a party is domiciled in the Contracting State whose courts are seised of a matter, the court shall apply its internal law.

If a party is not domiciled in the State whose courts are seised of the matter, then, in order to determine whether the party is domiciled in another Contracting State, the court shall apply the law of that State.

Article 53

For the purposes of this Convention, the seat of a company or other legal person or association of natural or legal persons shall be treated as its domicile. However, in order to determine that seat, the court shall apply its rules of private international law.

In order to determine whether a trust is domiciled in the Contracting State whose courts are seised of the matter, the court shall apply its rules of private international law.

TITLE VI

TRANSITIONAL PROVISIONS

Article 54

The provisions of the Convention shall apply only to legal proceedings instituted and to documents formally drawn up or registered as authentic instruments after its entry into force in the State of origin and, where recognition or enforcement of a judgment or authentic instruments is sought, in the State addressed.

However, judgments given after the date of entry into force of this Convention between the State of origin and the State addressed in proceedings instituted before that date shall be recognised and enforced in accordance with the provisions of Title III if jurisdiction was founded upon rules which accorded with those provided for either in Title II of this Convention or in a convention concluded between the State of origin and the State addressed which was in force when the proceedings were instituted.

If the parties to a dispute concerning a contract had agreed in writing before 1st June 1988 for Ireland or before 1st January 1987 for the United Kingdom that the contract was to be governed by the law of Ireland or of a part of the United Kingdom, the courts of Ireland or of that part of the United Kingdom shall retain the right to exercise jurisdiction in the dispute.

Article 54a

For a period of three years from 1st November 1986 for Denmark and from 1st June 1988 for Ireland, jurisdiction in maritime matters shall be determined in these States not only in accordance with the provisions of Title II, but also in accordance with the provisions of paragraphs 1 to 6 following. However, upon the entry into force of the International Convention relating to the arrest of sea-going ships, signed at Brussels on 10th May 1952, for one of these States, these provisions shall cease to have effect for that State.

1. A person who is domiciled in a Contracting State may be sued in the Courts of one of the States mentioned above in respect of a maritime claim if the ship to which the claim relates or any other ship owned by him has been arrested by judicial process within the territory of the latter State to secure the claim, or could have been so arrested there but bail or other security has been given, and either:

   (a) the claimant is domiciled in the latter State, or
   (b) the claim arose in the latter State, or
   (c) the claim concerns the voyage during which the arrest was made or could have been made, or
   (d) the claim arises out of a collision or out of damage caused by a ship to another ship or to goods or persons on board either ship, either by the execution or non-execution of a manoeuvre or by the non-observance of regulations, or
   (e) the claim is for salvage, or
   (f) the claim is in respect of a mortgage or hypothecation of the ship arrested.

2. A claimant may arrest either the particular ship to which the maritime claim relates, or any other ship which is owned by the person who was, at the time when the maritime claim arose, the owner of the particular ship. However, only the particular ship to which the maritime claim relates may be arrested in respect of the maritime claims set out in (5)(o), (p) or (q) of this Article.

3. Ships shall be deemed to be in the same ownership when all the shares therein are owned by the same person or persons.

4. When in the case of a charter by demise of a ship the charterer alone is liable in respect of a maritime claim relating to that ship, the claimant may arrest that ship or any other ship owned by the charterer, but no other ship owned by the owner may be arrested in respect of such claim. The same shall apply to any case in which a person other than the owner of a ship is liable in respect of a maritime claim relating to that ship.

5. The expression "maritime claim" means a claim arising out of one or more of the following:

   (a) damage caused by any ship either in collision or otherwise;
   (b) loss of life or personal injury caused by any ship or occurring in connection with the operation on any ship;
   (c) salvage;
   (d) agreement relating to the use of hire of any ship whether by charterparty or otherwise;
   (e) agreement relating to the carriage of goods in any ship whether by charterparty or otherwise;
   (f) loss of or damage to goods including baggage carried in any ship;
   (g) general average;
   (h) bottomry;
   (i) towage;
   (j) pilotage;
   (k) goods or materials wherever supplied to a ship for her operation or maintenance;
   (l) construction, repair or equipment of any ship or dock charges and dues;
   (m) wages of master, officers or crew;
   (n) master's disbursements, including disbursements made by shippers, charterers or agents on behalf of a ship or her owner;
   (o) dispute as to the title to or ownership of any ship;
   (p) disputes between co-owners of any ship as to the ownership, possession, employment or earnings of that ship;
   (q) the mortgage or hypothecation of any ship.

6. In Denmark, the expression "arrest" shall be deemed as regards the maritime claims referred to in 5(o) and (p) of this Article, to include a "*forbud*", where that is the only procedure allowed in respect of such a claim under Articles 646 to 653 of the law on civil procedure (*lov om rettens pleje*).

TITLE VII

RELATIONSHIP TO OTHER CONVENTIONS

Article 55

Subject to the provisions of the second subparagraph of Article 54, and of Article 56, this Convention shall, for the States which are parties to it, supersede the following conventions concluded between two or more of them:

– the Convention between Belgium and France on jurisdiction and the validity and enforcement of judgments, arbitration awards and authentic instruments, signed at Paris on 8th July 1899;

– the Convention between Belgium and the Netherlands on jurisdiction, bankruptcy, and the validity and enforcement of judgments, arbitration awards and authentic instruments, signed at Brussels on 28th March 1925;

– the Convention between France and Italy on the enforcement of judgments in civil and commercial matters, signed at Rome on 3rd June 1930;

– the Convention between the United Kingdom and the French Republic providing for the reciprocal enforcement of judgments in civil and commercial matters, with Protocol, signed at Paris on 18th January 1934;

– the Convention between the United Kingdom and the Kingdom of Belgium providing for the reciprocal enforcement of judgments in civil and commercial matters, with Protocol, signed at Brussels on 2nd May 1934;

– the Convention between Germany and Italy on the recognition and enforcement of judgments in civil and commercial matters, signed at Rome on 9th March 1936;

– the Convention between the Federal Republic of Germany and the Kingdom of Belgium on the mutual recognition and enforcement of judgments, arbitration awards and authentic instruments in civil and commercial matters, signed at Bonn on 30th June 1958;

– the Convention between the Kingdom of the Netherlands and the Italian Republic on the recognition and enforcement of judgments in civil and commercial matters, signed at Rome on 17th April 1959;

- the Convention between the United Kingdom and the Federal Republic of Germany for the reciprocal recognition and enforcement of judgments in civil and commercial matters, signed at Bonn on 14th July 1960;

- the Convention between the Kingdom of Greece and the Federal Republic of Germany for the reciprocal recognition and enforcement of judgments, settlements and authentic instruments in civil and commercial matters, signed in Athens on 4th November 1961;

- the Convention between the Kingdom of Belgium and the Italian Republic on the recognition and enforcement of judgments and other enforceable instruments in civil and commercial matters, signed at Rome on 6th April 1962;

- the Convention between the Kingdom of the Netherlands and the Federal Republic of Germany on the mutual recognition and enforcement of judgments and other enforceable instruments in civil and commercial matters, signed at The Hague on 30th August 1962;

- the Convention between the United Kingdom and the Republic of Italy for the reciprocal recognition and enforcement of judgments in civil and commercial matters, signed at Rome on 7th February 1964, with amending Protocol signed at Rome on 14th July 1970;

- the Convention between the United Kingdom and the Kingdom of the Netherlands providing for the reciprocal recognition and enforcement of judgments in civil matters, signed at The Hague on 17th November 1967;

- the Convention between Spain and France on the recognition and enforcement of judgment arbitration awards in civil and commercial matters, signed at Paris on 28th May 1969;

- the Convention between Spain and Italy regarding legal aid and the recognition and enforcement of judgments in civil and commercial matters, signed at Madrid on 22nd May 1973;

- the Convention between Spain and the Federal Republic of Germany on the recognition and enforcement of judgments, settlements and enforceable authentic instruments in civil and commercial matters, signed at Bonn on 14th November 1983;

and, in so far as it is in force:

- the Treaty between Belgium, the Netherlands and Luxembourg on jurisdiction, bankruptcy, and the validity and enforcement of judgments, arbitration awards and authentic instruments, signed at Brussels on 24th November 1961.

Article 56

The Treaty and the conventions referred to in Article 55 shall continue to have effect in relation to matters to which this Convention does not apply.

They shall continue to have effect in respect of judgments given and documents formally drawn up or registered as authentic instruments before the entry into force of this Convention.

Article 57

1. This Convention shall not affect any conventions to which the Contracting States are or will be parties and which in relation to particular matters, govern jurisdiction or the recognition or enforcement of judgments.

2. With a view to its uniform interpretation, paragraph 1 shall be applied in the following manner:

   (a) this Convention shall not prevent a court of a Contracting State which is a party to a convention on a particular matter from assuming jurisdiction in accordance with that Convention, even where the defendant is domiciled in another Contracting State which is not a party to that Convention. The court hearing the action shall, in any event, apply Article 20 of this Convention;

   (b) judgments given in a Contracting State by a court in the exercise of jurisdiction provided for in a convention on a particular matter shall be recognised and enforced in the other Contracting State in accordance with this Convention. Where a convention on a particular matter to which both the State of origin and the State addressed are parties lays down conditions for the recognition or enforcement of judgments, those conditions shall apply. In any event, the provisions of this Convention which concern the procedure for recognition and enforcement of judgments may be applied.

3. This Convention shall not affect the application of provisions which, in relation to particular matters, govern jurisdiction or the recognition or enforcement of judgments and which are or will be contained in acts of the institutions of the European Communities or in national laws harmonised in implementation of such acts.

Article 58

Until such time as the Convention on jurisdiction and the enforcement of judgments in civil and commercial matters, signed at Lugano on 16th September 1988, takes effect with regard to France and the Swiss Confederation, this Convention shall not affect the rights granted to Swiss nationals by the Convention between France and the Swiss Confederation on jurisdiction and enforcement of judgments in civil matters, signed at Paris on 15th June 1869.

Article 59

This Convention shall not prevent a Contracting State from assuming, in a convention on the recognition and enforcement of judgments, an obligation towards a third State not to recognise judgments given in other Contracting States against defendants domiciled or habitually resident in the third State where, in cases provided for in Article 4, the judgment could only be founded on a ground of jurisdiction specified in the second paragraph of Article 3.

However, a Contracting State may not assume an obligation towards a third State not to recognise a judgment given in another Contracting State by a court basing its jurisdiction on the presence within that State of property belonging to the defendant, or the seizure by the plaintiff of property situated there:

1. if the action is brought to assert or declare proprietary or possessory rights in that property, seeks to obtain authority to dispose of it, or arises from another issue relating to such property, or

2. if the property constitutes the security for a debt which is the subject-matter of the action.

TITLE VIII

FINAL PROVISIONS

Article 60

[Deleted]

Article 61

This Convention shall be ratified by the signatory States. The instruments of ratification shall be deposited with the Secretary-General of the Council of the European Communities.

Article 62

This Convention shall enter into force on the first day of the third month following the deposit of the instrument of ratification by the last signatory State to take this step.

Article 63

The Contracting States recognise that any State which becomes a member of the European Economic Community shall be required to accept this Convention as a basis for the negotiations between the Contracting States and that State necessary to ensure the implementation of the last paragraph of Article 220 of the Treaty establishing the European Economic Community.

The necessary adjustments may be the subject of a special convention between the Contracting States of the one part and the new Member States of the other part.

Article 64

The Secretary-General of the Council of the European Communities shall notify the signatory States of:

(a)   the deposit of each instrument of ratification;

(b)   the date of entry into force of this Convention;

(c)   [Deleted];

(d)   any declaration received pursuant to Article IV of the Protocol;

(e)   any communication made pursuant to Article VI of the Protocol.

Article 65

The Protocol annexed to this Convention by common accord of the Contracting State shall form an integral part thereof.

Article 66

This Convention is concluded for an unlimited period.

Article 67

Any Contracting State may request the revision of this Convention. In this event, a revision conference shall be convened by the President of the Council of the European Communities.

Article 68

This Convention, drawn up in a single original in the Dutch, French, German and Italian languages, all four texts being equally authentic, shall be deposited in the archives of the Secretariat of the Council of the European Communities. The Secretary-General shall transmit a certified copy to the Government of each signatory State.

(Signatures of Plenipotentiaries of the original six Contracting States)

ANNEXED PROTOCOL

The High Contracting Parties have agreed upon the following provisions, which shall be annexed to the Convention.

Article I

Any person domiciled in Luxembourg who is sued in a court of another Contracting State pursuant to Article 5(1) may refuse to submit to the jurisdiction of that court. If the defendant does not enter an appearance the court shall declare of its own motion that it has no jurisdiction.

Any agreement conferring jurisdiction, within the meaning of Article 17, shall be valid with respect to a person domiciled in Luxembourg only if that person has expressly and specifically so agreed.

Article II

Without prejudice to any more favourable provisions of national laws, persons domiciled in a Contracting State who are being prosecuted in the criminal courts of another Contracting State of which they are not nationals for an offence which was not intentionally committed may be defended by persons qualified to do so, even if they do not appear in person.

However, the court seised of the matter may order appearance in person; in the case of failure to appear, a judgment given in the civil action without the person concerned having had the opportunity to arrange for his defence need not be recognised or enforced in the other Contracting States.

Article III

In proceedings for the issue of an order for enforcement, no charge, duty or fee calculated by reference to the value of the matter in issue may be levied in the State in which enforcement is sought.

Article IV

Judicial and extrajudicial documents drawn up in one Contracting State which have to be served on persons in another Contracting State shall be transmitted in accordance with the procedures laid down in the conventions and agreements concluded between the Contracting States.

Unless the State in which service is to take place objects by declaration to the Secretary-General of the Council of the European Communities, such documents may also be sent by the appropriate public officers of the State in which the document has been drawn up directly to the appropriate public officers of the State in which the addressee is to be found. In this case the officer of the State of origin shall send a copy of the document to the officer of the State applied to who is competent to forward it to the addressee. The document shall be forwarded in the manner specified by the law of the State applied to. The forwarding shall be recorded by a certificate sent directly to the officer of the State of origin.

Article V

The jurisdiction specified in Articles 6(2) and 10 in actions on a warranty or guarantee or in any other third party proceedings may not be resorted to in the Federal Republic of Germany. In that State, any person domiciled in another Contracting State may be sued in the courts in pursuance of Articles 68, 72, 73 and 74 of the code of civil procedure (*Zivilprozeßordnung*) concerning third-party notices.

Judgments given in the other Contracting States by virtue of point 2 of Article 6 or Article 10 shall be recognised and enforced in the Federal Republic of Germany in accordance with Title III. Any effects which judgments given in that State may have on third parties by application of Articles 68, 72, 73 and 74 of the code of civil procedure (*Zivilprozeßordnung*) shall also be recognised in the other Contracting States.

Article Va

In matters relating to maintenance, the expression "court" includes the Danish administrative authorities.

Article Vb

In proceedings involving a dispute between the master and a member of the crew of a sea-going ship registered in Denmark, in Greece, in Ireland or in Portugal, concerning remuneration or other conditions of service, a court in a Contracting State shall establish whether the diplomatic or consular officer responsible for the ship has been notified of the dispute. It shall stay the proceedings so long as he has not been notified. It shall of its own motion decline jurisdiction if the officer, having been duly notified, has exercised the powers accorded to him in the matter by a consular convention, or in the absence of such a convention has, within the time allowed, raised any objection to the exercise of such jurisdiction.

Article Vc

Articles 52 and 53 of this Convention shall, when applied by Article 69(5) of the Convention for the European patent for the common market, signed at Luxembourg on 15th December 1975, to the provisions relating to "residence" in the English text of that Convention, operate as if "residence" in that text were the same as "domicile" in Articles 52 and 53.

Article Vd

Without prejudice to the jurisdiction of the European Patent Office under the Convention on the grant of European patents, signed at Munich on 5th October 1973, the courts of each Contracting State shall have exclusive jurisdiction, regardless of domicile, in proceedings concerned with the registration or validity of any European patent granted for that State which is not a Community patent by virtue of the provisions of Article 86 of the Convention for the European patent for the common market, signed at Luxembourg on 15th December 1975.

Article VI

The Contracting States shall communicate to the Secretary-General of the Council of the European Communities the text of any provisions of their laws which amend either those articles of their laws mentioned in the Convention or the lists of courts specified in Section 2 of Title III of the Convention.

(Signatures of Plenipotentiaries of the original six Contracting States)

TEXT OF 1971 PROTOCOL, AS AMENDED

Article 1

The Court of Justice of the European Communities shall have jurisdiction to give rulings on the interpretation of the Convention on jurisdiction and the enforcement of judgments in civil and commercial matters and of the Protocol annexed to that Convention, signed at Brussels on 27th September 1968, and also on the interpretation of the present Protocol.

The Court of Justice of the European Communities shall also have jurisdiction to give rulings on the interpretation of the Convention on the accession of the Kingdom of Denmark, Ireland and the United Kingdom of Great Britain and Northern Ireland to the Convention of 27th September 1968 and to this Protocol.

The Court of Justice of the European Communities shall also have jurisdiction to give rulings on the interpretation of the Convention on the accession of the Hellenic Republic to the Convention of 27th September 1968 and to this Protocol, as adjusted by the 1978 Convention.

The Court of Justice of the European Communities shall also have jurisdiction to give rulings on the interpretation of the Convention on the accession of the Kingdom of Spain and the Portuguese Republic to the Convention of 27th September 1968 and to this Protocol, as adjusted by the 1978 Convention and the 1982 Convention.

Article 2

The following courts may request the Court of Justice to give preliminary rulings on questions of interpretation:

1. – in Belgium: la Cour de Cassation – het Hof van Cassatie and le Conseil d'État – de Raad van State;

- in Denmark: højesteret;
- in the Federal Republic of Germany: die obersten Gerichtshöfe des Bundes;
- in Greece: the ανώτατα διδαατήζια;
- in Spain: el Tribunal Supremo;
- in France: la Cour de Cassation and le Conseil d'État;
- in Ireland: the Supreme Court;
- in Italy: la Corte Suprema di Cassazione;
- in Luxembourg: la Cour supérieure de Justice when sitting as Cour de Cassation;
- in the Netherlands: de Hoge Raad;
- in Portugal: o Supremo Tribunal de Justiça and o Supremo Tribunal Administrativo;
- in the United Kingdom: the House of Lords and courts to which application has been made under the second paragraph of Article 37 or under Article 41 of the Convention.

2. The courts of the Contracting States when they are sitting in an appellate capacity.

3. In the cases provided for in Article 37 of the Convention, the courts referred to in that Article.

Article 3

1. Where a question of interpretation of the Convention or of one of the other instruments referred to in Article 1 is raised in a case pending before one of the courts listed in point 1 of Article 2, that court shall, if it considers that a decision on the question is necessary to enable it to give judgment, request the Court of Justice to give a ruling thereon.

2. Where such a question is raised before any court referred to in point 2 or 3 of Article 2, that court may, under the conditions laid down in paragraph 1, request the Court of Justice to give a ruling thereon.

Article 4

1. The competent authority of a Contracting State may request the Court of Justice to give a ruling on a question of interpretation of the Convention or of one of the other instruments referred to in Article 1 if judgments given by courts of that State conflict with the interpretation given either by the Court of Justice or in a judgment of one of the courts of another Contracting State referred to in point 1 or 2 of Article 2. The

provisions of this paragraph shall apply only to judgments which have become *res judicata*.

2. The interpretation given by the Court of Justice in response to such a request shall not affect the judgments which gave rise to the request for interpretation.

3. The Procurators-General of the Courts of Cassation of the Contracting States, or any other authority designated by a Contracting State, shall be entitled to request the Court of Justice for a ruling on interpretation in accordance with paragraph 1.

4. The Registrar of the Court of Justice shall give notice of the request to the Contracting States, to the Commission and to the Council of the European Communities; they shall then be entitled within two months of the notification to submit statements of case or written observations to the Court.

5. No fees shall be levied or any costs or expenses awarded in respect of the proceedings provided for in this Article.

Article 5

1. Except where this Protocol otherwise provides, the provisions of the Treaty establishing the European Economic Community and those of the Protocol on the Statute of the Court of Justice annexed thereto, which are applicable when the Court is requested to give a preliminary ruling, shall also apply to any proceedings for the interpretation of the Convention and the other instruments referred to in Article 1.

2. The Rules of Procedure of the Court of Justice shall, if necessary, be adjusted and supplemented in accordance with Article 188 of the Treaty establishing the European Economic Community.

Article 6

[Deleted]

Article 7

This Protocol shall be ratified by the signatory States. The instruments of ratification shall be deposited with the Secretary-General of the Council of the European Communities.

Article 8

This Protocol shall enter into force on the first day of the third month following the deposit of the instrument of ratification by the last signatory State to take this step; provided that it shall at the earliest enter into force at the same time as the Convention of 27th September 1968 on jurisdiction and the enforcement of judgments in civil and commercial matters.

Article 9

The Contracting States recognise that any State which becomes a member of the European Economic Community, and to which Article 63 of the Convention on jurisdiction and the enforcement of judgments in civil and commercial matters applies, must accept the provisions of this Protocol, subject to such adjustments as may be required.

Article 10

The Secretary-General of the Council of the European Communities shall notify the signatory States of:

(a)   the deposit of each instrument of ratification;

(b)   the date of entry into force of this Protocol;

(c)   any designation received pursuant to Article 4(3);

(d)   [Deleted].

Article 11

The Contracting States shall communicate to the Secretary-General of the Council of the European Communities the texts of any provisions of their laws which necessitate an amendment to the list of courts in point 1 of Article 2.

Article 12

This Protocol is concluded for an unlimited period.

Article 13

Any Contracting State may request the revision of this Protocol. In this event, a revision conference shall be convened by the President of the Council of the European Communities.

Article 14

This Protocol, drawn up in a single original in the Dutch, French, German and Italian languages, all four texts being equally authentic, shall be deposited in the archives of the Secretariat of the Council of the European Communities. The Secretary-General shall transmit a certified copy to the Government of each signatory State.

SELECT BIBLIOGRAPHY
ON INTERNATIONAL FINANCIAL LAW

This bibliography covers all the works in this series of books on international financial law. Articles from the journals are not listed. The main English journals on international finance include *International Financial Law Review* (Euromoney), *Journal of International Banking Law* (ESC Publishing Ltd/Sweet & Maxwell), and *Butterworths Journal of International Banking and Financial Law*. Bibliographies referring to the article literature may be found in many of the works listed below. In the main, this list only includes works which contain comparative or international law and not standard works on the domestic law of a jurisdiction and is not intended to be a comprehensive bibliography.

1. General works

The following works contain discussions of term loans and bond issues and related topics together with conflicts of laws so far as it relates to international finance.

Cresswell, Blair, Hill, Wood	*Encyclopaedia of Banking Law* (1982–) Butterworths
Penn, Shea and Arora	*The Law and Practice of International Banking* (1987) Sweet & Maxwell
Ravi Tennekoon	*The Law and Regulation of International Finance* (1991) Butterworths
Frank Graaf	*Euromarket Finance: Issues of Euromarket Securities and Syndicated Eurocurrency Loans* (1991) Kluwer. Contains useful lists of legal articles

A classic work is by Georges H Delaume, *Legal Aspects of International Lending and Economic Development Financing* (1967) Oceana. See also:

Norbert Horn (ed)	*The Law of International Trade Finance* (1989) Kluwer

Kheng Koh (ed)	*Current Developments in International Banking and Corporate Financial Operations* (1989) Butterworths/National University of Singapore
Joseph J Norton	*International Finance in the 1990s: challenges and opportunities* (1993) Blackwells
David Pierce et al (eds)	*Current Issues of International Financial Law* (1985) National University of Singapore
RS Rendell (ed)	*International Financial Law: lending, capital transfers and institutions* (2nd ed 1983) Euromoney

2. Comparative law

For general comparative law surveys, one may mention K Zweigert and H Kötz, *An Introduction to Comparative Law* translated by Tony Weir (2nd ed 1987) Clarendon Press, Oxford; René David and John Brierley, *Major Legal Systems in the World Today* (3rd ed 1985) Stevens; and the *International Encyclopaedia of Comparative Law* under the auspices of the International Association of Legal Science, which contains some excellent essays, although many are now 25 years old. Country reports abound, including: the *Digest of Commercial Laws of the World* (1966) Dobbs Ferry; *Commercial Business and Trade Laws* Dobbs Ferry, a collection of primary sources; a series on *Legal Aspects of Doing Business in ...* (D Campbell ed) and *Modern Legal Systems Cyclopaedia* under the general editorship of K F Redden. There are numerous others. Digests include the indefatigable *Martindale-Hubbell Law Digest* and the indispensable, Thomas H Reynolds and Arturo A Floras (eds), *Foreign Law: Current Sources of Codes and Legislation in Jurisdictions of the World* (American Association of Law Librarians Service No 33). This is intended as a librarian's guide, but goes far beyond that. Another work sponsored by the American Association of Law Libraries and containing useful bibliographies is Richard A Danner and Marie–Louise H Bernal, *Introduction to Foreign Legal Systems* (1994) Oceana. See also Robert Drake and James Rider, *European Financing Laws* (1994) Chancery Law Publishing.

3. Conflict of laws

The literature is vast. Apart from classic works such as *Dicey and Morris on the Conflict of Laws* (12th ed 1993) Sweet & Maxwell, under the general editorship of Lawrence Collins, leading comparative studies include Ernst

Rabel, *The Conflicts of Laws: A Comparative Study* (1958–1964) and Ole Lando "Private International Law: Contracts" (1977) in *International Encyclopaedia of Comparative Law*, vol III chapter 24. There are many others. See also Georges H Delaume *Transactional Contracts: applicable law and settlement of disputes* (1983) Oceana; Norbert Horn & Clive Schmitthoff (eds), *The Transnational Law of International Commercial Transactions* (1982) Kluwer; Ross Cranston (ed), *Legal Issues of Cross-Border Banking* (1989) The Chartered Institute of Bankers, Centre for Commercial Law Studies, Queen Mary College, University of London; Adrian Briggs and Peter Rees, *Norton Rose on Civil Jurisdiction and Judgments* (1993) Lloyds of London Press; Peter Kaye, *Civil Jurisdiction and Enforcement of Foreign Judgments Worldwide* (1987) Professional Books. For the reciprocal enforcement of judgments, see Charles Platto (ed), *Enforcement of Foreign Judgments Worldwide* (1989) Graham & Trotman; P R Weems, *Enforcement of Money Judgments Abroad* (1988) Matthew Bender.

4.   Term loans and syndicated loans

See the works listed under **General works** above. See also:

Peter Gabriel	*Legal Aspects of Syndicated Loans* (1986) Butterworths
Stanley Hurn	*Syndicated loans: a handbook for banker and borrower* (1990) Woodhead-Faulkner
R P McDonald	*International Syndicated Loans* (1982) Euromoney
Tony Rhodes	*Syndicated Lending: practice and documentation* (1993) Euromoney

5.   International bond issues

See the works listed under **General works** above. The following may also be consulted: FG Fisher III, *Eurobonds* (1988) Euromoney; Roger McCormick & Harriet Creamer, *Hybrid Corporate Securities: International Legal Aspects* (1987) Sweet & Maxwell; Terence Prime, *International Bonds and Certificates of Deposit* (1990) Butterworths; G Ugeux, *Floating Rate Notes* (2nd ed 1985) Euromoney.

6. Securities regulation

The literature on securities regulation in the form of domestic books and articles in the legal periodicals is substantial. There are a few compilations of country reports which, by reason of the volatile nature of securities regulation, quickly become out of date. Note especially:

Harold Bloomenthal (ed)	*International Capital Markets and Securities Regulation* (1982), 5 vols, up-dated (Clark Boardman Callaghan). Reports cover more than a dozen countries and include some general surveys
Roy M Goode (ed)	*Conflicts of Interest in the Changing Financial World* (1986) Institute of Bankers
Euromoney	*International Securities Law* (1992). Reports cover 22 countries
Euromoney	*Issuing Securities*, IFLRev Supplement, March 1993. Brief country reports
Francis W Neate (ed)	*Developing Global Securities Market* (1987) Graham & Trotman/IBA
Robert C Rosen	*International Securities Regulation* (1986–) Oceana

7. Banking regulation

Marc Dassesse	*EC Banking Law* (2nd ed 1994) Lloyds of London Press

8. Insolvency

There is a very substantial and excellent literature on the domestic insolvency laws of the leading countries. This list comprises mainly comparative works.

Allen & Overy	*Butterworths International Insolvency Law* (1995) Butterworths (contains translations of the insolvency laws of nine leading jurisdictions)
David Botwinik and	*European Bankruptcy Laws* (2nd ed 1986)

Kenneth Weinrib (ed)	American Bar Association
Dennis Campbell (ed)	*International Corporate Insolvency law* (1992) Butterworths (country reports)
Dennis Campbell and Anthony Collins (ed)	*Corporate Insolvency and Rescues: the International Dimension* (1993) Kluwer
J H Dalhuisen	*International Insolvency and Bankruptcy* (1982) Matthew Bender
Ian Fletcher (ed)	*Cross-Border Insolvency: Comparative Dimensions* (1990) United Kingdom Comparative Law Series Vol 12
Richard A Gitlin and Rhona R Mears (ed)	*International Loan Workouts and Bankruptcies* (1989–)
Harry Rajak (ed)	*A Practitioner's Guide to European Corporate Insolvency Law* (1992/3) Westminster Management Consultants Ltd (country reports)
Jacob S Ziegel (ed)	*Current Developments in International and Comparative Corporate Insolvency Law* (1994) Clarendon Press Oxford

In addition, accountant's firms have published international guides, such as the *Touche Ross Guide to International Insolvency* (1989) Probus Publishing; Deloitte Touche Tohmatsu International, *Guide to Insolvency in Europe* (1993) CCH; Klynveld Peat Marwick Goerdeler, *International Insolvency Procedures* (1988).

See also:

Campell/Meroni (eds)	*Bankers' Liability: Risks & Remedies* (1993) Kluwer
Donald L Rome	*Business Workouts Manual* (2nd ed 1992) Warren, Gorham & Lamont, Inc. Cumulative supplements
Weil, Gotshal & Manges	*Restructurings* (1993) Euromoney

The English literature on insolvency is substantial. Without being comprehensive, one may mention Ian F Fletcher, *The Law of Insolvency* (1990) Sweet & Maxwell; Roy M Goode, *Principles of Corporate Insolvency Law* (1990) Sweet & Maxwell; James R Lingard *Corporate Rescues & Insolvencies* (2nd ed 1990) Butterworths; Robert R Pennington, *Pennington's Corporate Insolvency Law* (1991) Butterworths; Harry Rajak, *Insolvency Law:*

Theory and Practice (1993) Sweet & Maxwell; Philip St J Smart, *Cross-Border Insolvency* (1991) Butterworths; Gordon Stewart, *Administrative Receivers and Administrators* (1987) CCH Editions; Peter Totty and Michael Jordan, *Insolvency* (1986) Longmans. There are many other first-class works. A standard work on personal bankruptcy is Muir Hunter and David Graham, *Williams & Muir Hunter on Bankruptcy* (19th ed 1979) Stevens, since supplemented by *Muir Hunter on Personal Insolvency* (1987 –) Stevens. In the United States, the literature is also substantial. See, for example, *Collier's Bankruptcy Manual* (loose-leaf) Matthew Bender; Richard F Broude, *Reorganisations under Chapter 11 of the Bankruptcy Code* (1986 –) Law Journal Seminars – Press; Thomas H Jackson, *The Logic and Limits of Bankruptcy Law*; Robert D Albergotti *Understanding Bankruptcy in the US* (1992) Blackwells.

9. Security and title finance

See the 11–volume series by David Allen, Mary Hiscock and Derek Roebuck *Credit and Security* (1970s), University of Queensland Press/Crane, Russak & Company, Inc covering Pacific rim and Asian countries. Also useful is Michael G Dickson, Wolfgang Rosener, Paul M Storm (eds), *Security on Movable Property and Receivables in Europe* (1988) ESC Publishing Ltd. See also:

Tom Clark	*Leasing Finance* (2nd ed) Euromoney
Norton, Gillespie, Rice (ed)	*Corporate Finance Guide* (1990–) Matthew Bender
Judith Mabry	*International Securities Lending* (1992) Macmillan
Howard Rosen (ed)	*Leasing Law in the European Union* (Euromoney) 1994

10. Securitisations

David Bonsall (ed)	*Securitisation* (1990) Butterworths
Eilis Ferran	*Mortgage Securitisation: Legal Aspects* (1992) Butterworths
Tamar Frankel	*Securitisation – Structured Financing, Financial Asset Pools and Asset-Backed Securities* (1991) 2 vols, Little Brown & Co 1991

Henderson & Scott	*Securitisation* (1988) Woodhead-Faulkner
Helena Morrissey	*International Securitisation* (1992) IFR Publishing
Norton & Spellman (eds)	*Asset Securitisation – International Financial and Legal Perspectives* (1991) Blackwell
Schwarcz S	*Structured Finance – A Guide to the Fundamentals of Asset Securitisation* (1990) PLI
Stone, Zissu, Lederman (eds)	*Asset Securitisation: Theory and Practice in Europe* (1991) Euromoney

Securitisation: An International Guide, IFLRev Supplement, August 1993 (Canada, Germany, Japan, UK, US)

Securitisation, Corporate Finance Supplement, September 1992, Euromoney Publications (essays by bankers, legal overviews and articles on US, Japan and Spain).

11. Ship and aircraft finance

The Greek Code of Private Maritime Law, translation by Theodoros Karatzas and Nigel Ready (1982) Nijhoff

JD Buchan	*Mortgages of Ships: Marine Security in Canada* (1986) Butterworths
John Cahillane	*Cross-Border Aircraft Leasing: an industry report* (1992) Lloyds of London Press
Constant	*The Law Relating to the Mortgage of Ships* (1920)
Lennart Hagberg (ed)	*Maritime Law*, Kluwer/IBA, several volumes published in the 1970s and 1980s
Simon Hall (ed)	*Aircraft Financing* (2nd ed 1993) Euromoney
Richard Hames and Graham S McBain	*Aircraft Finance: registration, security and enforcement* (1988) Longman
David C Jackson	*Enforcement of Maritime Claims* (1985) Lloyds of London Press
David C Jackson	*Civil Jurisdiction and Judgments – Maritime Claims* (1987) Lloyds of London Press
Nigel Meeson	*Ship and Aircraft Mortgages* (1989) Lloyds of London Press

Stephenson Harwood · *Shipping Finance* (1991) Euromoney

W Tetley · *Maritime Liens and Claims* (1985) Business Law Communications

D Rhidian Thomas · *Maritime Liens* (1980) Stevens

Numerous articles on aircraft finance are to be found in the legal journals, e.g. the *Journal of Air Law & Commerce*.

12.   Set-off and netting

Rory Derham · *Set-off* (1987) Oxford

Sheelagh McCracken · *The Banker's Remedy of Set-off* (1993) Butterworths

Francis Neate (ed) · *Using Set-off as Security* (1990) Graham & Trotman

Philip Wood · *English & International Set-off* (1989) Sweet & Maxwell

13.   International payments

Anu Arora · *Electronic Banking and the Law* (1988) IBC Financial

Charles del Busto · *Funds Transfer in International Banking* (1992) International Chamber of Commerce

Carl Felsenfeld · *Legal Aspects of Electronic Funds Transfer* (1988) Butterworths

W Hadding and U H Schneider (eds) · *Legal Issues in International Credit Transfers* (1993) Duncker & Humblot (contains an extensive international bibliography).

UNCITRAL · *Legal Guide on Electronic Funds Transfers*, UN 1987 (A/CN 9/SER B/1)
Transformation of the Banking System, OECD 1993

Bank for International Settlements · *Central Bank Payment and Settlement Services with respect to Cross-Border and Multi-currency Transactions*, Basle, September 1993

Benjamin Geva	*The Law of Electronic Funds Transfers* (1992) Matthew Bender
R M Goode	*Payment Obligations in Commercial and Financial Transactions* (1983) Sweet & Maxwell
R M Goode (ed)	*Electronic Banking – The Legal Implications* (1985) Institute of Bankers
D I Baker/R E Brandel	*The Law of Electronic Fund Transfer Systems* (2nd ed 1988) Warren Gorham & Lamont

Reference should also be made to the standard works on banking. There is a substantial literature in the legal periodicals.

14. Project finance

Peter K Nevitt	*Project Financing* (5th ed) Euromoney
Graham D Vinter	*Project Finance: A Legal Guide* (1995) Sweet & Maxwell

15. Swaps and derivatives

Paul Goris	*The Legal Aspect of Swaps* (1994) Graham & Trotman
Price and Henderson	*Currency and Interest Rate Swaps* (2nd ed 1988) Butterworths

16. Subordination

Philip Wood	*The Law of Subordinated Debt* (1990) Sweet & Maxwell. This work contains a bibliography

17. State loans

Kalderen, Siddiqui, Chronnell, Watson (ed)	*Sovereign Borrowers: Guidelines on Legal Negotiations with Commercial Lenders* (1984) Butterworths
Padazis Karamanolis	*The Legal Implications of Sovereign Syndicated Lending* (1992) Oceana

The standard works on public international law contain treatments of sovereign immunity, state succession, state recognition and international organisations. See also Charles Lewis, *State and Diplomatic Immunity* (3rd ed 1990) Lloyds of London Press.

For state insolvency, see Borchard & Wynne, *State Insolvency & Foreign Bondholders* (1951) 2 Vols, Yale; Feis, *Europe, The World's Banker 1870–1914* (1930) Yale; reprinted AM Kelley, Clifton, 1974. The article literature on state insolvency is immense.

18. Legal opinions

Gruson, Hutter, Kutschera	*Legal Opinions on International Transactions* (2nd ed 1989) Graham & Trotman
Wilfred M Estey	*Legal Opinions in Commercial Transactions* (1990) Butterworths

Both works contain extensive bibliographies, lists of articles and bar association guidelines.

LIST OF RESEARCH TOPICS

This list contains a selection of topics which could be considered for a research thesis or a shorter article. The topics relate to the areas covered by this book. Research topics in relation to the areas covered by other books in this series on international financial law will be found in the volumes concerned.

The selection is based on relative originality and usefulness. Topics which have already been extensively covered by the legal literature are not included. For example, there is already a huge literature on choice of law for contracts so that this subject is not appropriate for the researcher contemplating an advanced thesis on a new area. In many cases there is an existing literature on the listed topics, but further work is considered worthwhile to develop what has already been achieved or to explore a new approach. It is possible that some of the listed topics may not be at all original and the author is simply unaware of the work which has already been done. If the chosen titles do not appeal, it is hoped that they will be suggestive of those which do. Some of the titles are no more than pointers which would have to be developed into a proper topic.

The author would be very glad to receive a copy of an essays which may be written and which are derived from this list.

Chapters 1 to 3: Comparative financial law

Classification of jurisdictions

— Criteria for classification of comparative financial legal regimes

— Criteria for classification of comparative insolvency law

Comparative financial law: general

— Legal theory of financial law

— Financial law and jurisprudence

— Natural financial law: generally accepted principles

— Legal compromises between competing policies in financial law

- Utility, morality and ideology in financial law
- Stability and change in financial law
- Financial law and politics
- Economic influences on financial law
- History of financial and commercial law from Justinian to the nineteenth century
- Financial law and economic development
- Comparative codification of financial law
- Comparative attitudes to predictability in financial law
- Comparative attitudes to commercial liberalism in financial law
- Comparative criminalisation of financial law
- Comparative law of big pocket liability
- Comparative role of hard and soft law in financial legal regimes
- Comparative role of hard and soft law in securities and banking regulation
- Financial law and fraud: comparative survey
- Comparative law attitudes to the doctrine of specificity
- Comparative law attitudes to the doctrine of false wealth
- Nationalism in comparative financial law

Comparative financial law: particular topics

- English and Roman commercial and financial law
- English and American financial law
- Comparative financial law in English-based states
- Why is the financial law of France and England so different?
- Financial law in collision jurisdictions: Belgium, Italy, Quebec
- Financial law in Group 2 countries (Mixed Roman/common law)
- Financial law in Group 3 countries (Germanic and Scandinavian)
- Financial law in Group 4 countries (Mixed Franco-Latin/Germanic)
- Financial law in Group 5 countries (Traditional Franco-Latin)

- Financial law in Group 6 countries (Emerging jurisdictions)
- Essentials of financial law infrastructure for emerging jurisdictions
- Financial law in Group 7 countries (Islamic jurisdictions)
- Which group should the Group 6 emerging jurisdictions join?
- Reception and use of the trust in commercial and financial law
- Comparison of the law of tangible and intangible movables (e.g. sale, hire, security and custody)
- Simplicity and complexity in financial law
- Transactional flexibility of financial law: comparative survey

Legal harmonisation

- Harmonisation of financial law
- Do different societies need a different financial law regime?
- Harmonisation of laws or harmonisation of conflicts rules? Two approaches to international order in financial law
- Harmonisation of financial law in federal countries: Australia, Canada and the United States
- Harmonisation of financial law in federal countries compared to the European Union
- Pro-debtor and consumerist influences on international commercial law conventions (negotiable instruments, aircraft, ships, leasing, funds transfers, judgments, sales, etc.)
- Priorities for harmonisation in financial law

Chapters 14 to 24: Governing law and judicial jurisdiction

There is a vast existing literature on choice of law, contractual conflicts and jurisdiction over contracts. Some additional subjects worth considering are:

- Governing law of bank deposits and financial trading contracts
- Taxation in the conflict of laws
- Subrogation in the conflict of laws

- Voluntary assignments and the conflict of laws

- Comparative long-arm jurisdiction rules

- Comparative jurisdiction rules based on local business operations

- Comparative review of forum non conveniens

- Corporate amalgamations and universal successions: conflict of laws

- Foreign prejudgment attachments and preservation orders: conflict of laws

- Foreign post-judgment judicial attachments and enforcement orders: conflict of laws

- Public policy ground for non-recognition of foreign judgments for contract claims

- Dirigism and freedom of choice in forum selection

- Enforcement of non-consumer credit obligations: judicial attachments, insolvency proceedings and consensual rescheduling

Chapters 25 to 29: International payment systems

- Insolvency risks and payment systems: comparative law

- Payment clearing systems: comparative law

- Comparative law of network liability in payment systems

- Harmonisation of the law of payment systems

- Payment systems and the conflict of laws

INDEX OF JURISDICTIONS BY GROUP

This table lists the world's jurisdictions in alphabetical order, showing the group to which they are allocated in chapters 5 to 13.

Afghanistan	Group 7
Albania	Group 6
Alderney & Sark	Group 2
Algeria	Group 5
American Samoa	Group 1B
Andorra	Group 5
Angola	Group 5
Anguilla	Group 1A
Antigua and Barbuda	Group 1A
Argentina	Group 5
Armenia	Group 6
Aruba	Group 3
Australia	Group 1A
Austria	Group 4
Azerbaijan	Group 7
Bahamas	Group 1A
Bahrain	Group 7
Bangladesh	Group 1A
Barbados	Group 1A
Belgium	Group 5
Belize	Group 1A
Belarus	Group 6
Benin	Group 5
Bermuda	Group 1A
Bhutan	Group 8
Bolivia	Group 5
Bosnia	Group 6
Botswana	Group 2
Brazil	Group 5
British Indian Ocean Territory	Group 1A
Brunei Darussalam	Group 1A
Bulgaria	Group 6
Burkina Faso	Group 5

Burma	Group 1A
Burundi	Group 5
Cambodia	Group 8
Cameroon	Group 5
Canada (except Quebec)	Group 1A
Cape Verde	Group 5
Cayman Islands	Group 1A
Central African Republic	Group 5
Chad	Group 5
Chile	Group 5
China	Group 6
Christmas Island	Group 1A
Cocos (Keeling) Islands	Group 1A
Colombia	Group 5
Comoros	Group 5
Congo	Group 5
Cook Islands	Group 1A
Costa Rica	Group 5
Croatia	Group 6
Cuba	Group 5
Cyprus	Group 1A
Czech Republic	Group 4
Denmark	Group 4
Djibouti	Group 5
Dominica	Group 1A
Dominican Republic	Group 5
Ecuador	Group 5
Egypt	Group 5
El Salvador	Group 5
England	Group 1A
Equatorial Guinea	Group 5
Eritrea	Group 8
Estonia	Group 6
Ethiopia	Group 8
Faeroe Islands	Group 4
Falkland Islands	Group 1A
Fiji	Group 1A
Finland	Group 3
France	Group 5
French Guiana	Group 5
French Polynesia	Group 5
Gabon	Group 5
Gambia	Group 1A

Germany	Group 3
Ghana	Group 1A
Gibraltar	Group 1A
Georgia	Group 6
Greece	Group 5
Greenland	Group 4
Grenada	Group 1A
Guadeloupe	Group 5
Guam	Group 1B
Guatemala	Group 5
Guernsey	Group 2
Guinea	Group 5
Guinea-Bissau	Group 5
Guyana	Group 1A
Haiti	Group 5
Honduras	Group 5
Hong Kong	Group 1A
Hungary	Group 4
Iceland	Group 3
India	Group 1A
Indonesia	Group 3
Iran	Group 5
Iraq	Group 5
Ireland (N)	Group 1A
Ireland (Republic)	Group 1A
Isle of Man	Group 1A
Israel	Group 1A
Italy	Group 4
Ivory Coast	Group 5
Jamaica	Group 1A
Japan	Group 2
Jersey	Group 2
Johnston and Sand Islands	Group 1B
Jordan	Group 5
Kazakhstan	Group 7
Kenya	Group 1A
Kirghizstan	Group 7
Kiribati	Group 1A
Korea, North	Group 8
Korea, South	Group 2
Kuwait	Group 7
Laos	Group 8
Latvia	Group 6

Lebanon	Group 5
Lesotho	Group 2
Liberia	Group 1B
Libya	Group 5
Liechtenstein	Group 2
Lithuania	Group 6
Louisiana	Group 4
Luxembourg	Group 5
Macao	Group 5
Madagascar	Group 5
Malawi	Group 1A
Malaysia	Group 1A
Maldives	Group 8
Mali	Group 5
Malta	Group 5
Marshall Islands	Group 1B
Martinique	Group 5
Mauritania	Group 5
Mauritius	Group 2
Mayotte	Group 5
Mexico	Group 5
Micronesia	Group 1B
Midway Islands	Group 1B
Moldova	Group 6
Monaco	Group 5
Mongolia	Group 6
Montserrat	Group 1A
Morocco	Group 5
Mozambique	Group 5
Namibia	Group 2
Nauru	Group 1B
Nepal	Group 8
Netherlands	Group 3
Netherlands Antilles	Group 3
New Caledonia	Group 5
New Zealand	Group 1A
Nicaragua	Group 5
Niue	Group 1A
Niger	Group 5
Nigeria	Group 1A
Norfolk Island	Group 1A
Northern Ireland – see Ireland (N)	
Northern Marianas	Group 1B

Norway	Group 3
Oman	Group 7
Pakistan	Group 1A
Palau (Belau)	Group 1B
Panama	Group 4
Papua New Guinea	Group 1A
Paraguay	Group 5
Peru	Group 5
Philippines	Group 4
Pitcairn Island	Group 1A
Poland	Group 3
Portugal	Group 5
Puerto Rico	Group 5
Qatar	Group 7
Quebec	Group 2
Reunion	Group 5
Romania	Group 5
Russia	Group 6
Rwanda	Group 5
St Helena	Group 1A
St Kitts and Nevis	Group 1A
St Lucia	Group 1A
St Pierre and Miquelon	Group 5
St Vincent and the Grenadines	Group 1A
San Marino	Group 8
Saō Tomé e Principe	Group 5
Saudi Arabia	Group 7
Scotland	Group 2
Senegal	Group 5
Serbia	Group 6
Seychelles	Group 1A
Sierra Leone	Group 1A
Singapore	Group 1A
Slovak Republic	Group 4
Slovenia	Group 6
Solomon Islands	Group 1A
Somalia	Group 8
South Africa	Group 2
Spain	Group 5
Sri Lanka	Group 2
Sudan	Group 1A
Surinam	Group 3
Swaziland	Group 2

Sweden	Group 3
Switzerland	Group 3
Syria	Group 5
Tajikistan	Group 7
Taiwan	Group 3
Tanzania	Group 1A
Thailand	Group 4
Togo	Group 5
Tokelau	Group 1A
Tonga	Group 1A
Trinidad and Tobago	Group 1A
Tunisia	Group 5
Turkey	Group 4
Turkmenistan	Group 7
Turks and Caicos Islands	Group 1A
Tuvalu	Group 1A
Uganda	Group 1A
Ukraine	Group 6
United Arab Emirates	Group 7
United Kingdom – see Alderney & Sark, England, Guernsey, Ireland (N), Isle of Man, Jersey, Scotland	
United States of America (except Louisiana)	Group 1B
Uruguay	Group 5
Uzbekistan	Group 7
Vanuatu	Group 1A
Vatican	Group 8
Venezuela	Group 5
Vietnam	Group 6
Virgin Islands (British)	Group 1A
Virgin Islands (US)	Group 1B
Wake Island	Group 1B
Wallis and Futuna Islands	Group 5
Western Sahara	Group 8
Western Samoa	Group 1A
Yemen	Group 7
Zaire	Group 5
Zambia	Group 1A
Zimbabwe	Group 2

INDEX

All references are to paragraph